INFORMATION
SECURITY
FOR
MANAGERS

INFORMATION SECURITY FOR MANAGERS

William Caelli
Dennis Longley
Michael Shain

stockton
press

© Macmillan Publishers Ltd, 1989
Softcover reprint of the hardcover 1st edition 1989

Published in the United States and Canada by
STOCKTON PRESS 1989
15 East 26th Street, New York, N.Y. 10010.

Library of Congress Cataloging-in-Publication Data

Caelli, William.
  Information security for managers/by William Caelli,
  Dennis Longley, and Michel Shain.
  p. cm.
  Includes index.
  ISBN 978-0-935859-73-7 : $100.00
  1. Electronic data processing departments — Security
  measures.
2. Computers — Access control. I. Longley, Dennis. II.
Shain, Michael. III. Title.
HF5548.37.C34 1989
658.4'78 — dc20

                                        89-4614
                                        CIP

Published in the United Kingdom by
MACMILLAN PUBLISHERS LTD (Journals Division), 1989

Distributed by Globe Book Services Ltd
Brunel Road, Houndmills
Basingstoke, Hants RG21 2XS

British Library Cataloguing in Publication Data

Caelli, Bill
  Information security for managers.
  1. Computer systems. Security measures. Management aspects
  I. Title II. Longley, Denis III. Shain, Michael
  658.4'78

  ISBN 978-1-349-10139-9   ISBN 978-1-349-10137-5 (eBook)
  DOI 10.1007/978-1-349-10137-5

Introduction

How seriously should management take information security? Until recently only a few managers fully appreciated how their day-to-day business administration was dependent on the availability and integrity of their data processing services. Several things are changing this, including the growing recognition of information as an asset, and the continuing development of information technology and its application in a business context. But at the same time the existence of information technology is providing new weapons for those intent on causing damage or criminal gain.

Automation of clerical processes makes information systems more vulnerable, because they no longer require the prudent manual checks and balances which were once an unspoken part of the job. When combined with the pressures of cost of implementation and timescale, this has meant that few, if any, security controls have been built into systems from the outset. It may be realised only when it is too late that protective controls have been sacrificed; security vulnerabilities are invisible until an incident occurs.

Thus, as information systems have become more valuable to their users they have also become more vulnerable to attack. They have consequently become more attractive targets for criminal and terrorist groups, holding the possibility of high rewards for minimal effort, and with little chance of detection until it is too late. A single, compromised password can lead to fraud involving electronic funds transfer (EFT), or to the exposure of corporate secrets through industrial espionage.

All managers have to deal with risk as a natural part of business life. No one can absolutely guarantee that a mishap will not occur in his or her department. However, the wise manager can strive to be fully acquainted with the nature of the risk, develop an organisational structure, and invest time and money to minimise the chance of an unwanted incident and reduce the effect of any damage.

The purpose of this book is to enable the manager to become aware of the information security risk and the methods of counter-attack. In this way and through the development of a management structure and a set of counter-measures to deter attack and initiate recovery procedures, he or she can take a more aggressive, pro active stance in the face of deliberate threats. As we shall see many times in this book, good information security depends first and foremost upon good management. In many cases substantial increases in security can be achieved by improved management practices; on the other hand the effectiveness of sophisticated gadgetry, software, and crytographic systems can easily be nullified by bad management.

'Computers don't steal, people do', is a wise maxim. Security is a "people" issue and effective security has to be pervasive. To reach such an objective demands a corporate policy that calls for commitment from staff and management, and needs to be integrated into both management and system structures. Once implemented it has to be constantly maintained and monitored for effectiveness.

This book is designed as a work of reference. The first chapter provides the foundation upon which subsequent sections are built, but the authors do not expect the work to be read in sequence, from cover to cover, as a novel. Hence the question and answer format has been chosen — the reader can examine the list of questions at the beginning of the book and select the ones that seem most relevant. Often asking the right question is half way to finding the right answer, and through extensive use of cross-referencing, the reader is able to place the question in its relevant context.

Acknowledgement
The authors would like to thank the following: Chris Reed of Queen Mary College, London University, for advice on copyright, Robin Moses, formerly of CCTA, now of BIS Applied Systems for help on risk analysis, Stuart Dresner for advice on privacy legislation and John Foster of GE Information Services for help with insurance issues.

Contents

Contents

1 Data Security

D. Longley

1.1 Overview

1.1.1 Data security awareness among management
Data security is defined as:

- the protection of data from accidental or malicious modification, destruction, or disclosure (FIPS);
- the science and study of methods of protecting data in computer and communications systems against unauthorized disclosure, transfer, delay, modifications, or destruction, whether accidental or intentional.

To put it rather more concisely, data security means providing the users of your data with the data that you intend them to have, and with that data only, at the time that you mean them to have it.

Managerial interest in data security has often been triggered by media reports of hacker exploits, massive frauds in banking networks, warnings on the spread of computer viruses, proposed changes in legislation affecting the use and misuse of computers, etc. It can be extremely difficult for management to judge the implications of data and computer security in the context of their own organizations. In some cases the warnings about failures in data and computer security emanate from bodies with a vested interest in selling equipment or providing services geared to security. On the other hand, there will be reassurances from data processing managers that security has always been taken very seriously, and that there is no danger to the organization's computing systems. Comfort is also drawn from the Twenty Year Rule: 'Anything that has not happened in the last twenty years is unlikely to occur in the future'.

1

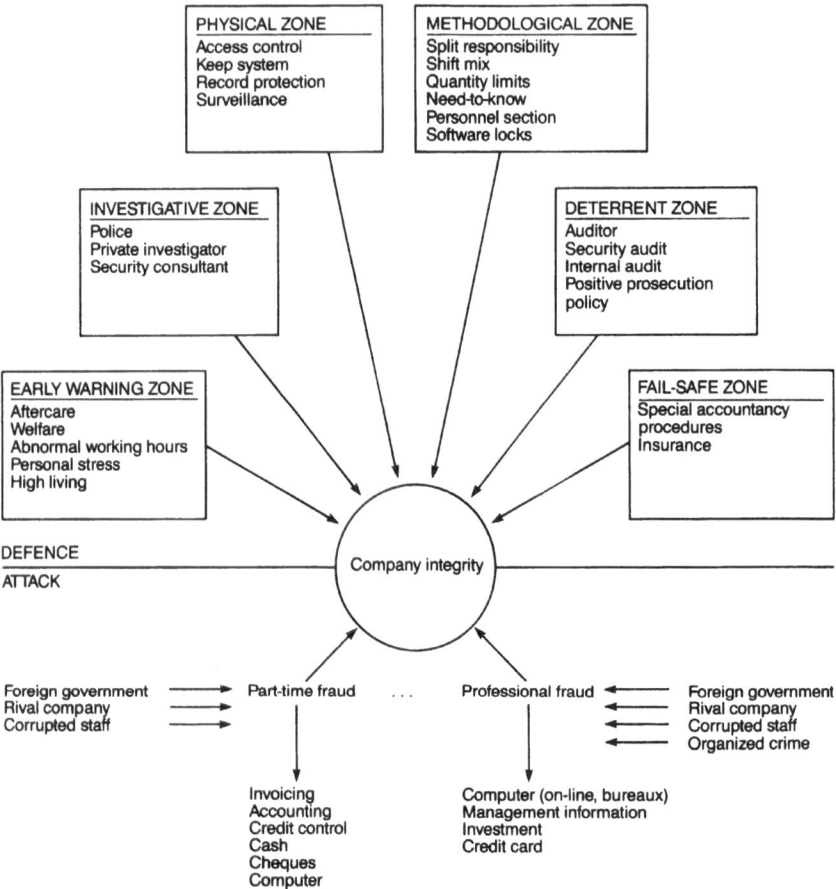

Fig. 1-1   A schematic view of computer security (*source*: *Handbook of Security*, Kluwer)

How seriously should management take data security? Well, it is clear that every organization, no matter how security conscious, is at risk: there is no guaranteed defence against every conceivable accidental or malicious act affecting an organization's information asset. On the other hand, management deals with, and lives with, risk as a natural part of life. No manager can ever give an absolute guarantee that some mishap will not occur in his or her department. However, the wise manager is fully acquainted with the nature of the risk, develops an organizational structure, and invests time and money, both to minimize the probability of an incident and to reduce the damage accruing from the unavoidable event. The purpose of this chapter is to enable the manager to develop an awareness of the data security risk, and some of the methods to counteract it.

At the outset one might ask why data security has apparently become so important recently. After all, many companies installed their first computers over twenty years ago; during the intervening period considerable computing expertise has been employed within the organization and, to date, no catastrophes have occurred. The factors that have caused data security to become of critical importance in recent times are:

- the continual development of information technology systems over the past twenty years;
- the enhanced importance of the information asset to organizations;
- electronic funds transfer;
- the legal responsibilities placed upon users of information processing systems;
- the relationship between employers and information processing staff;
- public image.

Consider first the developments of information technology that have taken place over the last two to three decades:

- replacement of paper-based processing by mainframe computers;
- integration of organizational files into databases;
- interconnection of data processing centres by data communication links;
- distribution of processing power to end-users with personal computers;
- integration of office systems: local area networks, desktop publishing systems, and central processing facilities;
- development of complex, real-time information processing systems with highly volatile and valuable data.

Each of these developments tended to remove inherent safeguards of the previous systems.

- Manual information processing had a high level of redundancy and associated safeguards; clerks handling invoices would be aware of normal suppliers and be likely to recognize suspect documents or significant variations from usual patterns.
- Databases can readily provide unauthorized users with access to

3

- integrated data that would be difficult to obtain from a variety of computer files held by different departments.
- Data communications provide external access to data processing facilities and open the door to hackers.
- The widespread use of end-user computing removes the close control on data previously exercised by the data processing manager.
- Data entered into personal workstations can be channelled into central databases with insufficient checks on its integrity. Floppy diskettes containing corporate data downloaded from a central database can be stolen or copied. The security advantage of limited access to data stored on the hard disk of a manager's personal computer can be lost when that computer is linked into an integrated office system with local area networks.
- In the current financial world, with round-the-clock international trading, programmed buying and selling, etc., the speed of response in communication/processing systems has a direct and critical impact on the well-being of the whole institution. Delays or errors that could be tolerated or corrected in previous systems would be disastrous in the current environment. Thus such systems are extremely vulnerable to design faults, system failures, accidents, and malicious attacks.

The implication of these developments is that increased information processing for managers also provides vastly increased opportunities for unauthorized access. Thirty years ago industrial espionage involved individuals breaking into company offices and opening safes; today it can be performed in the comfort of a hacker's lounge with a few hundred pounds' worth of electronics and some technical expertise.

It is also clear from the above that computerization was not a big bang that occurred twenty years ago; rather it has been a continuous development, each stage introducing new vulnerabilities. Moreover, the greatest vulnerabilities have been introduced within the last few years. The comfort of the Twenty Year Rule tends to evaporate when it is realized that many of the current dangers did not exist for nineteen of the twenty years.

Another important factor, concerning the degree of risk that organizations now face, is that the advent of computers changed the nature of the organization. If the initial computer systems had proved to be failures, then administration could have easily reverted to its previous manual data processing. However, as information technology provided massive improvements in processing power, storage capabilities, and communication facilities, and simultaneously hardware costs were slashed, then organizations underwent fundamental changes in their *modus operandi*. The increasing productivity of information processing has encouraged organizations to develop their information assets so as to provide managers with access to more, and better, information. Organizations have thus become dependent upon that enhanced level of available information. Loss, unauthorized modification, or disclosure of that information can now have extremely serious consequences to the normal operations of a company. The information asset developed by a company can also have a corresponding value to a competitor; the sole possession of the information by the acquirer, in such cases, can therefore represent a significant competitive advantage. In many industrial and commercial sectors, assets either directly consist of intellectual property (e.g. computer software, marketing intelligence) or their realization could be dramatically affected by poor information security (e.g. disclosure of marketing plans).

In the financial world, money and information can be almost synonymous; the exchange of financial assets is achieved, not by the physical transfer of bullion or paper currency, but by the exchange of messages over data communication links. Financial organizations soon appreciated the necessity for stringent information security. If commercial or government bodies intend to streamline their handling of money by using direct communication links into banking networks, they will need to ensure that their in-house computer/communication systems meet the stringent security requirements of such networks (see chapter 5).

The development of information processing systems also impacted upon the relationship between organizations and the general public. Concern was expressed as early as the mid-1960s on the use of personal data in computers; in the 1970s there was a ground swell of opinion that individuals should be granted legal rights when organizations stored and processed data concerning them. Data protection legislation (see chapter 7) has now been introduced in many European countries and is spreading throughout the world. Such legislation places restraints on the information processing within organizations, and also places a requirement on management to ensure the security of personal data. There is now a legal requirement for many managers to ensure an appropriate level of data security. The legal implications of data security also extend beyond processing of personal data. Computer software, contents of large databases, etc. are now subject to copyright protection; managers must therefore be concerned that they do not infringe the copyright of others, and also protect the copyright of their own intellectual assets (see chapter 7).

The development of computing also introduced a new class of employee, the computer professional. When computers first moved from the university research laboratory into commercial organizations, they introduced a major change in the employment pattern of companies. For the first time technical staff were employed in commercial head offices; the 'backroom boys' in the data processing department introduced a new, and still somewhat ill-defined category of employee. Highly computerized organizations are now heavily dependent upon the skill, dedication, and integrity of their computing staff. In some cases there can be an excessive dependence upon a few key personnel, and such a situation can be a cause for serious concern.

Finally, management may suddenly find itself under unwelcome public scrutiny owing to media interest in hackers and computer crime. It is widely believed that many organizations do not report computer crime because they fear that it would adversely affect public, or stockholder, confidence. A television programme featuring an anonymous hacker, who demonstrates an apparent ability to access a company's computer, can be extremely damaging to client relationships and confidence in the organization. The fact that the security system actually foiled the hacker's attempts to log on would be of no avail. Management need to have a sufficient level of security awareness to cope with such incidents and maintain confidence in their organizations.

To summarize: data security is the flip side of information technology. It has become an important issue because it provides the attacker with those very powerful organizational information processing facilities designed for the legitimate user. Not only have information systems become more valuable to their users and more vulnerable to attack, they have also become more attractive targets for criminal and terrorist groups. The liability of organizations with respect to the information they control has also increased in recent years. In addition to data protection legislation there is the danger of litigation from clients, or the general public, if information trusted to an organization is compromised. The increased importance of data security to organizations has also created a situation in which the relation between employers and employees, particularly, but not exclusively, information processing staff, needs to be carefully re-examined. Finally, management must be able to cope with a sceptical, and sometimes technically well-informed public on data security matters.

1.1.2 Sources of danger to data
Loss, disclosure, and contamination of data can arise from both accidental and malicious acts. Accidental occurrences can not only be directly deleterious to an organization, they can also reveal weaknesses in an organization's security and stimulate consequential malicious acts, particularly among company personnel.

FIRE   ESPIONAGE   THEFT OF DATA   BREAKDOWN

MALICIOUS ATTACK   FLOOD   COMPUTER FRAUD   ACCIDENTAL DAMAGE

POWER FAILURE   HACKING   LIGHTNING   TELECOMMUNICATIONS FAILURE

EXPLOSION   OPERATOR ERROR   VERMIN   THE UNKNOWN RISK

WARNING!
ONE OF THESE COULD BE YOUR DOWNFALL!

Fig. 1-2 Sources of danger to data (*source*: Hogg Robinson)

The greatest danger to data security lies in inadequate management procedures. The potential losses of data integrity in most
organizations can be listed:

- loss or disclosure of data associated with personal computer
  usage (see section 1.7.3 and chapter 3);
- incorrect data input into the system due to inadequate data entry controls (see section 1.6.3);

7

- existence of obsolete, misleading, or conflicting data due to inadequate ownership controls (see section 1.4.2);
- loss of data due to inadequate backup routines (see section 1.7.4);
- disclosure of information within the organization, or contamination of stored data, due to inadequate access controls (see section 1.5.3);
- disclosure of information during transmission due to inadequate communications security (see chapter 4);
- loss, malicious modification, or disclosure of information by personnel, particularly computing personnel with special access privileges (see section 1.3.2);
- disclosure to hackers (see chapter 4);
- loss, modification, delay/denial, or disclosure of transmitted data caused by malicious external individuals or organizations (see chapter 4);
- loss, modification, delay, or disclosure of stored/processed data, or interference with processing facilities caused by malicious external individuals or organizations (see section 1.7.2 and chapter 3).

1.1.3 Prerequisites for good data security

One of the most difficult aspects of data security, from a managerial viewpoint, is that it too often appears to comprise a confusing array of gadgets, computer and telecommunications jargon, and even the higher mathematics of cryptography. In fact good data security depends first and foremost upon good management. In many cases substantial improvements in data security can be achieved by improved management practices; the effectiveness of sophisticated gadgetry, software, and cryptographic systems can invariably be nullified by bad management.

The first rule is that the data to be protected must be worth protecting and the processing/communication system must be protectable; there is no point in surrounding a rotten egg with cotton wool.

If there has been no policy corresponding to data ownership in the organization then management may well be holding an amorphous information asset, with some data that is likely to be obsolete, conflicting, irrelevant, and/or inaccurate. If such data is included in a rigorous information security system various dangers exist:

- Inaccurate data will be given an enhanced status.
- Resources may be wasted in protecting a large mass of worthless data.
- The security system will lose credibility among employees.

8

In addition the processing/communications system must be protectable, i.e. the system must be well designed, well understood by management, and well documented. The task of information security systems is to:

- minimize occurrences outside system specifications;
- detect any such occurrences;
- discover the source of such occurrences;
- initiate actions designed to prevent similar future occurrences.

This task becomes virtually impossible if:

- the specifications are inaccurate or incomplete;
- the system contains insufficient internal checks on data accuracy (e.g. data entry controls – see section 1.6.3);
- the software contains bugs;
- documentation is inaccurate or incomplete;
- knowledge of the system is fragmented, and junior staff have a monopoly of such knowledge.

To summarize, if management intends to take information security seriously then it must ensure that it has a well-managed information asset and processing system at the outset. Data security can only be achieved within systems that are well designed and managed; imposing a requirement that an information system that is poorly designed or managed should conform to high standards of information security is wholly unrealistic.

1.1.4 Management action to protect information assets
Having ensured that its data is worth protecting and that the information processing/communications system is protectable, then management should turn its attention to the following areas:

- formulation of security policy (see section 1.2.1);
- allocation of information security responsibilities (see section 1.2.2);
- risk analysis of existing systems (see chapter 2);
- procedures for modifications of existing systems and design/ implementation of new systems;
- implementation of security policy (see section 1.2.2);
- contingency planning (see chapter 3);
- ongoing reviews.

The protection of information assets involves cost. The direct cost arises both in good information design and implementation, and in

9

the installation and operation of security systems. The indirect costs lie in staff induction and training, personnel problems arising from perceived user inconvenience, administrative overheads, etc. There is a natural reluctance of middle and lower management to invoke costs, or request funds, for an activity that does not, in itself, apparently produce a material return. This reluctance is even more marked when it might appear that security costs are consequential upon the installation of computer/communication systems originally recommended by the same management.

Top management should therefore take the responsibility for the formulation of its information security policy. This policy must be developed with security factors realistically weighed against costs. The policy must clearly establish the organization's stance in security matters, and the responsibilities appertaining to all levels of personnel in the security of information assets.

All members of staff in an organization must be fully aware of their responsibilities in security matters, and of the disciplinary measures following transgression of security rules. Overall responsibility for the implementation of the security policy must lie with a clearly designated member of senior management, hereafter termed the security officer; in many organizations it will be necessary to constitute a security advisory committee to assist the security officer.

The enhanced awareness of information security has generally arisen after the design and implementation of information systems. In many cases the security facets of an original system have been reduced, or nullified, by subsequent modifications or expansion. The security officer is therefore faced with the problem of designing and implementing the most cost-effective security measures to be retrofitted to existing systems. A risk analysis project (see chapter 2) needs to be undertaken to identify, and quantify, the risks and associated safeguards. The purpose of the risk analysis is to provide an indication of the cost-effectiveness of apposite security measures. The traditional concept of quantifiable risk analysis is quite straightforward, i.e.:

- estimate the value of a given information asset;
- postulate the threats to, and vulnerabilities of, the asset;
- estimate the probability of incidence of the set of threats associated with vulnerabilities;
- hence calculate the estimated potential annual loss, ALE (probability of loss per annum multiplied by asset value);
- postulate a safeguard to reduce the impact of the threat;
- estimate the annual cost of the safeguard;
- re-estimate the ALE with the safeguard in operation;
- compare the differences between the two ALEs with the annual cost of the safeguard.

In fact the performance of risk analysis can be a time-consuming and costly project.

The information processing and communications systems of organizations are subject to change. Such changes will necessarily have implications for the security officer. Procedures for the modification of old systems and design and implementation of new systems must be established from a security viewpoint, and consideration should be given to the impact of those changes on other aspects of information security, e.g. risk analyses, contingency planning, personnel security.

The implementation of a security policy involves the construction and operation of a secure environment. It will inevitably impinge on the activities of personnel; but it must not inhibit the functions of the organization to the point where the security produces more damage than the alleged threats. When it is enforced it must be effective, and seen to be effective. A security system that inhibits normal operations but fails to provide safeguards against attack is worse than no security at all.

Information processing systems will occasionally experience some degree of failure. Much damage can be caused by inappropriate actions to recover from the failure; worse damage can be caused by attempts to conceal it. The formulation of effective contingency plans (see chapter 3) is therefore an essential management activity.

The security situation in an organization is in a state of constant flux. The external environment changes continually: political, legal, economic, social, and technical developments will make an impact on the threats to an information system and on the costs of inadequate security. For example, the teenage hacker did not exist before the technical development of the microprocessor; data protection legislation massively increased the potential cost of inadequate security of personal data. There are also changes in the internal environment: staff will resign, carrying away knowledge and perhaps unrevoked security privileges; new untrained staff will be engaged; contented staff will become disgruntled; training will be forgotten; bad security habits will be seen to be tolerated. New systems will be installed; information will be received, stored, processed, and transmitted using new technologies. All these developments require systematic reviews of risk analysis findings.

1.1.5 First steps in implementing a security policy

While data and computer security have considerable technical overtones, the implementation of an effective security policy is a management issue. 'Computers don't steal, people do,' is a wise maxim: the major part of good data security involves the development of effective organizational controls, and the motivation of staff to operate

11

those controls. The success of this facet of data security depends heavily upon management skills.

A security policy is a statement by top management on the security stance to be adopted by the organization. Before committing themselves to such a statement, it would be as well to consider that it will not only explicitly set up safeguards for certain situations, it will also implicitly inform lower management that resources are not to be deployed in other situations. Before the formulation of such a policy, management should therefore take a fresh look at the risks, threats, and vulnerabilities of their organization. It could well be that traditional perceptions fail to give cognisance to the changes wrought by external technological, social, and economic developments. For example, a study of management perceptions of a bank revealed that management placed a major fraud at the top of their risk list, whereas the bank would probably have not survived a computer centre disaster.

In some instances technological or economic changes can affect the risk priorities, e.g. government departments may traditionally place disclosure of data high on their risk list, but the adoption of electronic money handling for (say) the collection of taxes can seriously enhance a previously low fraud risk.

Studies have also indicated that management tend to underrate threats that are traditionally associated with other organizations. It is commonly assumed that terrorist attacks are directed towards government agencies. In fact, as such agencies increase their perceived defences then it is likely that large commercial organizations, which can be viewed as part of 'the Establishment', can be more attractive targets for the terrorist.

It might also be difficult for management to admit to vulnerabilities which could, in some sense, be seen to result from organizational structure or management style, e.g. employee morale and loyalty.

Thus the first action of top management in the development of a security policy could well constitute a reappraisal and re-orientation of top management's view of the external and internal security stance.

1.1.6 Summary

The environment in which many managers operate is fundamentally different from that of a few years ago. There is now the potential for serious damage to the well-being of the organization for which they have a responsibility. This danger arises from the nature and importance of information processing and communication systems in modern organizations. Wise managers will review their organizations in the light of the threats and vulnerabilities of their systems and apply their management skills in reducing their risks to a level that is acceptable.

1.2 Security Policy and Organizational Structure

1.2.1 What should be contained in a security policy?
The security policy is a statement of top management's stance on information security. It must be capable of expansion by middle and lower management so that each member of staff has a clear, consistent, and unambiguous statement of their responsibilities towards the security of the organization's information asset, and the disciplinary consequences of any transgression. The statement should therefore deal with:
- the organizational structure and associated responsibilities for security matters. A senior manager could well be nominated for overall control and reporting to top management (see section 1.2.2)
- risk management (see chapter 2);
- personnel policy (see section 1.3.1);
- data ownership policy and data handling responsibilities (see section 1.4.2);
- access control and cryptographic controls (see section 1.5.1);
- information flow control (see section 1.6.1);
- security of stored data (see section 1.7.1);
- monitoring and audit trails (see section 1.8.1);
- fraud control (see chapter 7);
- design and modification procedures for computer/communication systems (see chapter 4);
- standards, ongoing reviews, and reporting procedures;
- contingency planning (see chapter 3).

1.2.2 What are the stages of implementing a security policy?
It must be stressed that data security is a management problem. The techniques employed in developing enhanced security may be sophisticated technically but they will only be effective if they are implemented and deployed within a well-designed and well-managed framework. The first step is to address the problem of overall security responsibilities and the nomination of a team, led by the security officer.

The most important factor in information security is people. A security expert once advised, 'Computers don't steal, people do.' The prime emphasis must therefore be placed upon personnel policy.
The second factor is the management control of information and

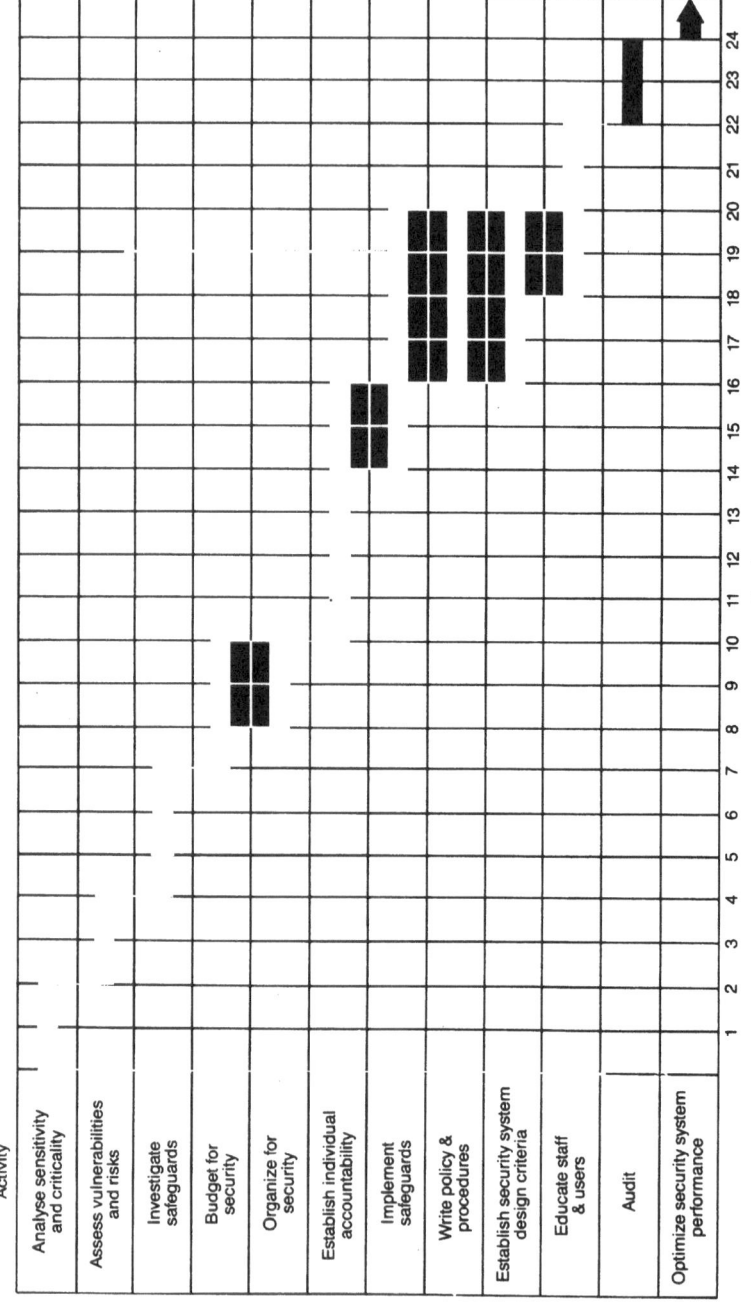

Fig. 1-3 A generalized security implementation plan

14

information flow. The flow of information within the organization is essential for its viability; the design of a good secure information system is predicated by the design of a good information system. Organizations employ considerable resources and managerial effort to ensure that their money is well deployed; it is just as important to ensure that information is well deployed. It must be made available to staff on a need-to-know basis, it must belong to clearly specified managers, its flow and storage must be subject to control, and it must be accounted for.

Given that the above factors are understood and the necessary systems implemented, then the more detailed, technical aspects of information security need to be considered and implemented. Policies and procedures for control of access and information flow must be formulated and implemented at this stage.

Having designed the system from the viewpoint of correct functioning it is then important to view the proposed system from the viewpoint of the potential attacker, and to consider what fraud control procedures need to be adopted.

The total system will not be static; it is the nature of information systems that they are subjected to continual evolution. The design and implementation of enhanced computing and communication systems must be viewed from a security viewpoint. Security should be designed into the system wherever possible: retrofitting is expensive and not always totally effective.

At this stage one has to admit that there exists the possibility of security incidents, both minor and major. There is no such thing as total security; at least not in a working environment subject to financial constraints. Contingency plans must be formulated to minimize the impact of those incidents that cannot be prevented.

Finally the message of information security must be continually reiterated, and management must produce a structure of ongoing security reviews.

1.2.3 What is an appropriate organization structure for security matters?

The development, implementation, and ongoing operation of a security policy will inevitably involve all departments concerned with information handling and physical security. The policy will impinge upon normal operating procedures, probably interfere with practices that have been developed to enhance efficiency or guarantee departmental autonomy, impact upon virtually all staff, and apparently not serve to improve the operation of the organization in terms of its profitability, performance, etc.

In these circumstances the responsibility for the security policy must be granted to a manager possessing sufficient authority and personality to overcome the inbuilt resistance among staff to security directives and initiatives.

The manager, hereafter termed the security officer, must maintain a difficult balance between organizational security and performance. This balance must, moreover, be achieved in an absence of feedback from a security viewpoint. If the security is good then there will be no security incidents to highlight its importance. Thus the security officer must possess a sensitivity to the operational needs of the organization to appreciate the potentially deleterious effects of proposed security measures.

The range of responsibilities of a security officer in a large organization is such that he should be assisted by an advisory committee to help in the development, implementation, operation, and review of the security policy.

1.3 Personnel and Responsibilities

1.3.1 What is the most urgent action that management needs to take in regard to the security implications of its personnel policy?
While it is important to ensure that security awareness is a responsibility of all staff, the most urgent action is in respect of those staff who are performing tasks that impact directly upon the information security of the organization, i.e. computing and communications staff. In particular the following must be recognized:

- Computing personnel – operators, programmers, systems analysts – may now be of such importance to the company that they are in a position to exercise considerable industrial power.
- The company may have become excessively dependent upon a few key computing personnel.
- Junior staff may lack sufficient supervision in the light of their potential impact upon system security.
- Staff may be put at direct physical risk from attacks on computer centres, or at increased moral risk of blackmail or external pressure to commit illegal acts.

The information-processing productivity of computer systems means that small teams operate the essential operations of large organizations, and hence can block them. More importantly, these teams can directly affect cash flows by inhibiting processing-associated billing operations. This situation was quickly recognized by trade unions; if such computer teams take industrial action then the impact on trade union funds, in terms of salaries paid to striking workers, is small, in comparison with potential financial losses to an employer. Successful industrial action was taken in the 1970s by UK trades unions exploiting this opportunity.

16

There has been a shortage of highly skilled computer personnel for some two decades. Organizations have often faced their computer development teams with unrealistic demands in terms of system design, deadlines, staff expertise, etc. This situation can result in computer systems that are not designed to the highest standards, and, more importantly, that are poorly documented. Moreover, the perceived importance of computer staff to the organization can all too easily be a function of their monopoly of knowledge of the idiosyncracies of the system. It has therefore not been difficult for some computer personnel to create a situation in which the organization is excessively dependent on their continued employment, availability, and integrity. Part of the solution lies in good design procedures that both remove local idiosyncracies from the system and ensure good documentation. The other part lies in good personnel procedures that discourage such attitudes and opportunities.

The advent of computerization often radically changes the opportunity for staff performing previously routine clerical functions to occupy security sensitive positions, or have enhanced opportunities to perpetrate fraud. In many cases these staff operate at the interface between the computer and the real world (e.g. data-entry clerks, warehouse workers receiving orders from terminals, etc.), and some computer crimes have exploited opportunities provided by these computerized interfaces (see chapter 7). Security staff themselves can form a seriously weak link in the security chain if they lack integrity, personality, training, dedication, or the ability to deal with unforeseen events. There is an apocryphal story that the security guard at a nuclear plant was heard to say to a colleague, 'There's no use in asking him for his pass, Charlie, he ain't got one'.

The changing environment in terms of information processing can also place the staff themselves at risk. Computer centres may be attractive targets for terrorist bomb attacks: disruption of processing facilities is likely to have considerable impact on government departments, public utilities, finance houses, etc., any of which may be considered to be part of 'the Establishment'. Enhanced physical access controls may also have an impact upon safe evacuation procedures. In addition, the advent of computerization may effectively transfer junior administrative and operational staff into areas that are targets for criminals. This can lead to temptations for the staff themselves, or to the possibility of blackmail from external agencies aimed at forcing employees to commit security breaches.

1.3.2 What principles should be observed in the formulation of responsibilities for staff who may hold security sensitive positions?
The three major principles are:
- separation of duties,

- responsibility for security,
- succession of key personnel.

An important tenet of data security is that no individual, or closely-knit group, should have sufficient privileges to undertake an attack. The requirement to form a co-operating team to undertake fraudulent activities not only serves as a deterrent but also greatly enhances the probability of detection through a weak link in the chain. Examples of the divisions that should be enforced are: systems development, programming, program maintenance, software support, data preparation, central and remote operation, control, and librarian.

In general, expertise and operation should be separated, so that those with the expertise to affect operations should be prevented from doing so, and operations staff should not have access to the knowledge, or expertise, necessary to modify systems. It is also important that knowledge of security controls should be restricted to a need-to-know basis. Some computer frauds have been detected simply because clerks were not aware of control actions performed elsewhere. The librarian who controls the movement of storage media should not have access to processing facilities, and programming/operations staff should only have controlled access to such storage media. No member of staff authorized to input transaction data should ever be given the opportunity to modify a master file.

There is naturally some objection to such separation of duties. It reduces the flexibility and autonomy of computing departments. It can certainly increase costs; a maintenance programmer needs to spend some time gaining the knowledge held by the original programmer before maintenance can begin. However, such costs are worth bearing. The communication between designer and maintainer produces a demand for good documentation. The designer is deterred from including time bombs or Trojan Horses in the software if such software will necessarily be subject to a later study by a maintenance programmer. The formal procedures will ensure that a clear record of all authorized modifications is available.

Management structures may not currently include security responsibilities; as mentioned elsewhere, an organizational security officer will have overall responsibility for security, but within the job descriptions of individual staff their responsibilities for security, in respect of themselves, their subordinates, and co-workers, needs to be specified. It is imperative that all security-sensitive staff are explicitly informed of their duties and responsibilities in security matters, and of the disciplinary consequences of security breaches.

An organization cannot afford to become totally dependent upon individual key personnel. All personnel with high levels of responsibility, knowledge, and expertise must have deputies who can take over if the occasion demands. This action not only safeguards against the loss of loyalty or integrity of such personnel, but also ensures that suitable alternative staff can be identified in disaster recovery plans, to obviate problems when key personnel are sick, on vacation, etc. The cost of such duplication of highly trained personnel may appear high. It involves at least a doubling up of expertise and up-to-date knowledge. If the cost is excessive then careful consideration must be given to the operation of the system that has produced the requirement for the particular key personnel.

1.3.3 What are the personnel procedures, for all staff, that should be reviewed in the light of data security?

Although very careful consideration must be given to staff with immediate access to sensitive information or processing/communication systems, it also needs to be recognized that such systems permeate most areas of the organization. Cleaners can have almost unlimited access to computer terminals, usually at times when there are no supervisors on hand. There are three phases in the employment of a member of staff, i.e. recruitment, on the job, and termination; the practices of each phase, together with those associated with external staff, need to be reviewed in the light of data security implications.

1.3.4 What aspects of recruitment should be reconsidered from a data security viewpoint?

Conventional recruitment policy is weighted to considerations of the applicant's potential performance in the appropriate post. The question of the degree of access to information systems needs also to be considered, since there is a possibility that the candidate may have character traits, or external pressures, that could lead to misuse of such systems. Character references tend to be accurate for very good applicants, and can be useful in separating out the high-flyer from the rest. However, such references can be somewhat bland at the other end of the scale, and cannot usually be relied upon to identify serious deficiencies. Some organizations employ both psychological and medical testing routines, particularly when the applicant may have access to sensitive data or facilities. Such psychological testing can assess social attitudes, political leanings, and general stability. Medical tests can indicate any problems that are likely to influence performance, ability to deal with stress, etc.

If a policy of insurance in the form of fidelity guarantees for key staff is undertaken, then an additional safeguard is supplied, inasmuch as the insurance company will often undertake its own investigation of the employee (see chapter 3).

The contractual arrangements for all staff (see chapter 7), whether employed or hired as independent contractors, must be given careful consideration in terms of:

- the handling of confidential information;
- copyright of organizational material;
- use of information acquired from the organization, at the end of the period of employment or contract.

1.3.5 How are staff working practices affected by data security?
The working practices need to be considered in terms of:

- incentives,
- job description,
- job rotation,
- training,
- peer group pressure,
- leave policy,
- personnel reviews,
- prosecution.

Security is all too often regarded in a negative manner. It has an impact upon working arrangements, departmental costs, etc. without apparently producing any positive benefit. Individuals will be exhorted to obey the rules and to put up with inconveniences, and yet be as efficient and productive as ever. Management needs to encourage staff to take a positive attitude to security; it could well introduce an incentive scheme to reward staff who are seen to co-operate fully with the security officer, report potential loopholes or incidents that could be of significance from a security viewpoint (e.g. evidence of experimentation with security controls, unusual events.

The job descriptions for individual staff need to be constructed in the light of good security procedures. Separation of duties (see section 1.3.2) is a principle aimed at maximizing the number of co-operating personnel required to commit a fraud or security breach. Separation of duties combined with job rotation (see below) introduces severe problems for potential attackers; they cannot be sure that the minimum-sized team essential to conduct the attack and subsequently cover up its tracks will have a constant membership over a given period of time. A policy of split control is essential in certain highly sensitive security areas, e.g. no single individual should have knowledge of a master cryptographic key. In such cases the complete key should be formed, by some mathematical operation, from constituent parts held by separate individuals, such that knowledge of one component is of no value to an attacker. Thus a system in which one manager knew (say) the first four characters, and a second manager the last four, is not advisable since knowledge of one component considerably reduces the effort in searching for the whole key. The job description should also emphasize the management's security stance, and its attitude to security discipline.

Vulnerabilities arise when a member of staff:

- has considerable opportunity to experiment with the security controls of a system;
- can develop a fund of knowledge and expertise placing him or her in a unique position relative to senior staff;
- can undertake tasks that will not be subject to examination by other staff;
- can implement private procedures or routines that are neither well-documented nor understood by others.

Such a situation effectively represents a loss of control by management. One solution is a firm policy of job rotation. If job rotation is operationally not feasible then management probably already has a serious security problem.

Certainly job rotation can be an effective safeguard against computer fraud. The perceived existence of the policy will serve as a deterrent, but its major benefit will lie in the assurance that existing frauds are likely to be of limited duration and severity. In many reported instances of fraud, the perpetrator only intended to commit a single act for a modest sum. However, the fraudulent acts were repeated, often over a significant period, either because they appeared to be successful and undetected, or because the process of covering the tracks became increasingly complex, and there appeared to be no alternative but to continue. In such circumstances, job rotation will set an upper limit on the period over which such frauds can occur.

There are, however, significant disadvantages in job rotation, even from a security viewpoint. In operational terms, job rotation demands a higher training budget, a loss of morale as amenable working arrangements are disturbed, and a resistance from management who do not like to lose staff with whom they have developed a good working relationship. From the security viewpoint, job rotation can provide feloniously inclined staff with a wider knowledge of security controls and undetected loopholes in security-interdependent sections of the organization. In such a case the job rotation may prove to be a training scheme for the attacker. It is generally considered, however, that the security advantages of job rotation outweigh its disadvantages.

21

In organizations that make a significant use of computer systems, training is a vital part of both operational efficiency and security effectiveness. The enhanced risk of physical attack on computer/communications systems and the security precautions that restrict access to such systems must be accompanied with a rigorous system of training in safety and evacuation procedures.

Inadequate training of users of sophisticated computer/communication systems can result in inefficient use of such expensive facilities, to the extent that such systems are needlessly overloaded or expensive to operate. An inadequate level of user expertise can result in security measures being negated, or evidence of attacks overlooked. Many users may be unaware of the security features of operating systems, the significance of log-on and log-off messages, etc., although careful attention to these features can often provide the first indications of misuse. For example, a user might well be informed of the last time and date of log-on and the number of unsuccessful attempts to log on.

The training problem is particularly severe in the personal computing area since hardware and software is often purchased with departmental budgets, and outside central control. Most casual personal computer users are not aware that file erasure on a floppy diskette actually leaves the magnetically recorded information intact. They will probably also not know of the serious dangers in relying on the results of large spreadsheet calculations, when such spreadsheets could be subject to modification (see chapter 3).

Peer group pressure is undoubtedly a powerful and continual influence on employee behaviour. It has probably been one of the most important factors in the reduction of smoking in the workplace. If the security routines are perceived to be obstacles, inhibiting the normal operations of the organization, then peer group pressure will tempt employees to bypass security procedures in order to enhance efficiency. If, on the other hand, individual slackness in data security is perceived to be a weak link in a section's or department's chain, negating the effects of others, then the peer group pressure will assist the data security stance of the organization. Management should seek means to ensure that peer group pressure operates in the direction of enhanced security.

A strict policy of requiring staff to take their leave entitlement should be introduced. Such a policy serves to minimize the danger that key staff will be subject to excessive stress, and it also ensures that no employee has a monopoly of control on some aspect of operation for an unlimited period. Computer frauds have been discovered, by chance, when unexpected circumstances arose during the vacation period of the employee undertaking the fraud. If an employee displays a marked reluctance to take leave, then management should consider the possibility that some illegal action is in operation or that some cover-up of operational inefficiency is taking place.

The security environment of an organization changes constantly: the changes may be caused by variations in the attitudes of employees, or the changes may themselves have an impact upon employee attitudes. In any event management should undertake regular reviews of staff attitudes and morale, thus ensuring that no significant deterioration has occurred. The reviews should not be solely concerned with security, but also deal with staff development, training opportunities, career re-orientation, etc. In this way they will be seen to have a positive benefit to staff, and hence be conducted in a co-operative manner.

The review should check for variations in pressures upon staff: financial, medical, domestic problems, difficulties in the workplace, friction among colleagues, social attitudes, etc. The attitudes to security measures and their perceived impact upon work practices should enter the review; such informal discussions will often give an indication of security measures that are being simply ignored or by-passed.

The question of prosecution in the case of computer fraud (see chapter 7) is a sensitive one, and has led to considerable cynicism. The comment is often made that firms are too embarrassed to prosecute, and that offenders, if caught, face at worst disciplinary action or a not dishonourable discharge. On the other hand, over-reaction to hackers who embarrass an organization, but do little actual harm, may greatly amplify the problem. Expensive, public legal wrangles ending in the discovery that no act had been committed that was illegal within current statutes (see chapter 7) can be a much more serious cause of embarrassment than the original incident.

The organization's policy in these matters is worthy of careful debate; there may be insufficient time for such a debate after a computer crime has been detected.

1.3.6 What precautions should be observed at the termination of staff employment?

When a member of staff decides to terminate employment, and particularly when the termination decision is made by management, the security status of that employee should be significantly altered. Access privileges must be fully revoked upon termination, preferably upon notice of termination; identity badges, access tokens, etc. must be collected, and all security/supervisory staff must be fully informed of the change in status. It is not unknown for ex-employees to be given free access to computer centres by security staff who recognize their faces, and for passwords to remain unrevoked. In the case of key personnel with high access privileges it may be wise to reduce access privileges during the period between the notice given and the actual termination. Some checkout procedures may also be necessary to ensure that essential documentation is still available, that no significant changes to files or software have been recently made, etc.

1.3.7 What precautions should be adopted in terms of external staff?
Staff external to the organization (e.g. contract programmers, computer maintenance engineers) can represent one of those inter-face gaps that severely weaken the effectiveness of control procedures. It is extremely important that the security privileges accorded to such staff be well defined, and that they do not have unsupervised access to sensitive material or facilities. If the workers belong to another substantial organization (e.g. maintenance engineers from a large computer manufacturer) then they will be part of an organizational hierarchy. In this case it is merely necessary to clarify lines of supervision and communication with that organization, from a supervision/responsibility viewpoint. Neverthe-less, it is still important, for example, that maintenance engineers should not be given privileges that grant them access to sensitive stored data or software. Contract workers who may be employed by small companies, or on their own account (e.g. contract pro-grammers) may present a significant security hazard, and the policies affecting their recruitment, job description, supervision, and termina-tion arrangements need to be carefully considered by the security officer. The contractual arrangements for such staff should also be reviewed (see chapter 7).

1.4 Data Ownership and Data Handling Responsibilities

1.4.1 How should management view information in an organization?
Information is an asset with quite unique characteristics. It can be duplicated indefinitely, and no single holder of the information can ever be sure to what extent it is held by others. The value of the in-formation may critically depend upon its exclusivity, or it may be en-hanced by sharing it among a team. Data may be considered as some physical embodiment of information and as such it is more amenable to control. Data is created, duplicated, transmitted, stored, and destroyed. Each of these processes must be carefully controlled. In particular the responsibilities for such data activities needs to be carefully defined.

Organizations have very clear guidelines for responsibilities in regard to money, down to very detailed levels. In particular, managers are required to develop budgets, allocate funds, authorize payments within well-defined overall guidelines, etc. A similar organizational framework needs to be developed for the information asset; it must be owned, it must be classified and rules for creating, duplicating, transmitting, storing, and destroying the data formulated.

1.4.2 What is meant by ownership of information?

The philosophy of information ownership is that every piece of data in an organization is the responsibility of a specified individual. That data can only be stored, viewed, modified, processed, or deleted with the permission of the owner. In particular the owner is responsible for making decisions, on behalf of the organization, and communicating those decisions in respect of:

- the classification and level of protection given to the data;
- approving application controls and authorizing access to the data;
- risk analysis (see chapter 2), risk acceptance, and contingency planning for the information asset.

The owner may bestow privileges to others, who may in turn further bestow privileges, but in no case can individuals bestow a greater level of privilege than they possess.

The levels of privilege are usually set at Read, Append, Write, and Execute. The Read privilege thus only allows the user to view a file, and no modification to it is permitted; Append enables the user to add more information to a file but not to alter any data already contained in it; Write allows for modification and deletion of a file; and Execute, which only applies to computer programs, permits only the execution of a program. Execute can be a significant privilege in a commercial environment since it authorizes the user to process data and transactions (see section 1.9.3).

Privileges will be commonly bestowed on a group basis and most mainframe computer operating systems provide mechanisms for privilege settings on individual files.

1.4.3 How should data be classified and handled?

Every organization has quite complex procedures for handling money; the uses of money are categorized and the manner in which money is budgeted, allocated, spent, received, internally transferred, and accounted are clearly specified. Information needs to be treated with the same careful forethought. From the instant that it enters the organization, to the time that it is discarded, the handling of that data by organization personnel should be clearly specified.

There are four areas of consideration:

- ownership,
- classification,
- access control and information flow control (see sections 1.5.1 and 1.6.1),
- disposal.

The first requirement is that ownership of all organizational data is clearly established (see section 1.4.2). There is little point in carefully controlling access to information if there is some confusion as to who has the authority and responsibility for the integrity of the data.

The second requirement is to provide classification labels so that data owners can unambiguously specify the manner in which their data is to be handled; military classifications: top secret, secret, etc. may appear to be comically dramatic. Nevertheless some form of well-recognized organizational security labelling will compel data owners to give serious thought to the classification of their data. This will avoid problems of communication between data owners and those responsible for processing, storing, and communicating the data. It will also provide the security officer with an immediate overview of the security stance adopted by middle management.

In the development of the classification labels careful attention must be given to the rules of handling information at each classification and to the problems of mixing data of different classifications. On the one hand, classified data must not be allowed to be incorporated in documents with a lower classification; but, on the other, the upward drift that results in the 'top secret' internal telephone directory must also be avoided.

The classification of information enables well-specified and appropriate controls to be applied to the files etc. It does not imply, however, a universal access for an individual with appropriate classification to information at that level. The data owner will grant access privileges to specific files on a need-to-know basis.

Access to information, information processing systems, physical media holding stored data, and most particularly to software processing the data must be strictly controlled in accordance with the classification rules.

The level of complexity associated with these processes can lead to a major organizational rethink, involving a team led by the security officer.

The use of cryptography to partition and protect data needs is directly related to access control (see section 1.5.1). Since it is often impossible to guarantee that only authorized personnel will have physical access to data, cryptography may be employed to ensure that such access does not lead to compromise of the information. Effectively cryptography changes the order of magnitude of the access control problem. Instead of having to limit access to a mass of stored and/or transmitted data, it is now only necessary to limit access to the cryptographic keys employed.

Such a development does not imply any reduction in the managerial responsibility for information security but rather imposes a strict discipline on all levels of management to operate within the demands of a cryptographically secure environment (see section 1.5.30).

Information will only be of value to an organization if it is transmitted to those members who will exploit it to the benefit of the organization. Information flow controls aim to ensure that such transmissions are consistent with the integrity requirements for the data and with the classification levels of the data and the communicating parties (see section 1.6.1).

The problem of disposing of discarded data must be given particularly careful consideration. There are innumerable instances when a search through a wastepaper-basket has enabled irreplaceable information to be retrieved. Some security consultants advise that trash should be aged as carefully as a good wine. A consistent policy of retaining waste paper etc. for a specified period may well provide an invaluable insurance policy against the unforeseen and potentially disastrous incident.

The other side of the coin, however, lies in the value of such waste material to the attacker. The term 'dumpster diving' refers to the treasures to be obtained from wastepaper-baskets. The collection of credit card vouchers from traders' garbage cans gave rise to instances of fraud, and cases of confidential information on discarded printouts have been well reported. Similarly the more technologically advanced attacker will seek for residues of information left on magnetic material or unerased portions of computer storage (see chapter 3).

1.5 Access Control and Cryptographic Controls

1.5.1 What are the main types of access control?
Access control can be divided into three categories:

- physical access control,
- communications access control,
- logical access control.

Physical access control is aimed at controlling access to the physical components of the information processing or storage media.

For example, access to rooms containing mainframe or mini-computers, and storage areas for magnetic disks or tapes are now controlled by guards or locked doors (see chapter 3).

Communications security seeks to control access into information processing systems, and their stored data, that can be provided by communications links (see chapter 4). The hacker traditionally attempts to use a personal computer and modem to gain access over the telephone network: the countermeasures to such telephone intrusion are now an important feature of communications security.

Logical access provides additional controls to users who have managed to log on to the computer system, by restricting access to sets of data or particular software.

Cryptography (see section 1.5.6) plays a vital role in access control, particularly with widely distributed information systems. If control to information is based upon physical access then major restrictions are placed upon the handling of the data; it must be stored, retrieved, transmitted, and returned to store, with each process undertaken in a physically secure environment. This is quite impracticable with modern information processing and communication systems, particularly those employing public communication networks. Cryptography converts meaningful text into garbled ciphertext, which may be handled in a physically insecure environment. Only authorized parties with knowledge of the appropriate cryptographic keys can retransform the ciphertext to its original form.

1.5.2 How can access control be made more effective?

There are few absolutes in data security; management can never be certain that their individual protective measures will be 100 per cent effective. The defensive depth philosophy aims to increase the number of hurdles offered to an attacker. This philosophy has a number of advantages:

- The potential attacker, e.g. a currently honest, contented employee, is less likely to stumble upon a loophole by accident.
- The actual attacker is provided with fewer opportunities to experiment with the system security.
- If an attacker is discovered after transgressing one or more of the security hurdles then there is a legitimate case for instituting appropriate early disciplinary or corrective action. In the absence of defensive depth there is a danger that an attacker, caught in the act, could provide some plausible excuse for the apparently single misdemeanour.

Access controls can provide the series of hurdles for a defensive depth philosophy even if no single one is foolproof. The access control, in whatever form, should be accompanied by some form of monitoring (see section 1.8.1) as an essential part of the defensive depth philosophy. For example, all attempts by computer users to access a directory, for which they have no privileges, should be recorded in a security log (see section 1.8.2).

1.5.3 How is logical access control applied?

Logical access control attempts to separate the legitimate user at a terminal from the attacker who may have gained illegal access, either physically or over a communications link (see chapter 3). There are three basic aspects of logical control:

- to identify and authenticate the user;
- to restrict user access privileges to the minimum required for the performance of that user's legitimate activities;
- to monitor all usage.

1.5.4 What mechanisms exist to authenticate legitimate users to systems?

Users requesting access provide details of their identity and some proof of that identity by means of:

- an attribute of the user,
- a possession of the user,
- knowledge held by the user.

Biometric sensors, e.g. fingerprint analysers, signature analysers, eye retina pattern devices, palmprint analysers, voiceprint devices, etc. seek to identify the user in terms of some unique biological attribute which can be reliably measured. Such devices are likely to come into common usage in the future (see chapter 3). They measure and store the user's characteristics at registration time, and on each occasion that access is requested the user's characteristics are measured by the sensor, transmitted to a controlling computer, and compared with the stored values. Although an attacker may be unable to mimic the characteristic, the possibility remains that the signals, representing that characteristic, could be recorded and replayed by the attacker. Thus some form of communications security is required to obviate such an attack.

A user may be granted access on the basis of a key, magnetic card, smart card, badge, or some other token. In this case it is important that duplicate tokens cannot be easily manufactured, and that some form of PIN be associated with the token to avoid use of stolen devices. Signals transferred between the reading and the con-

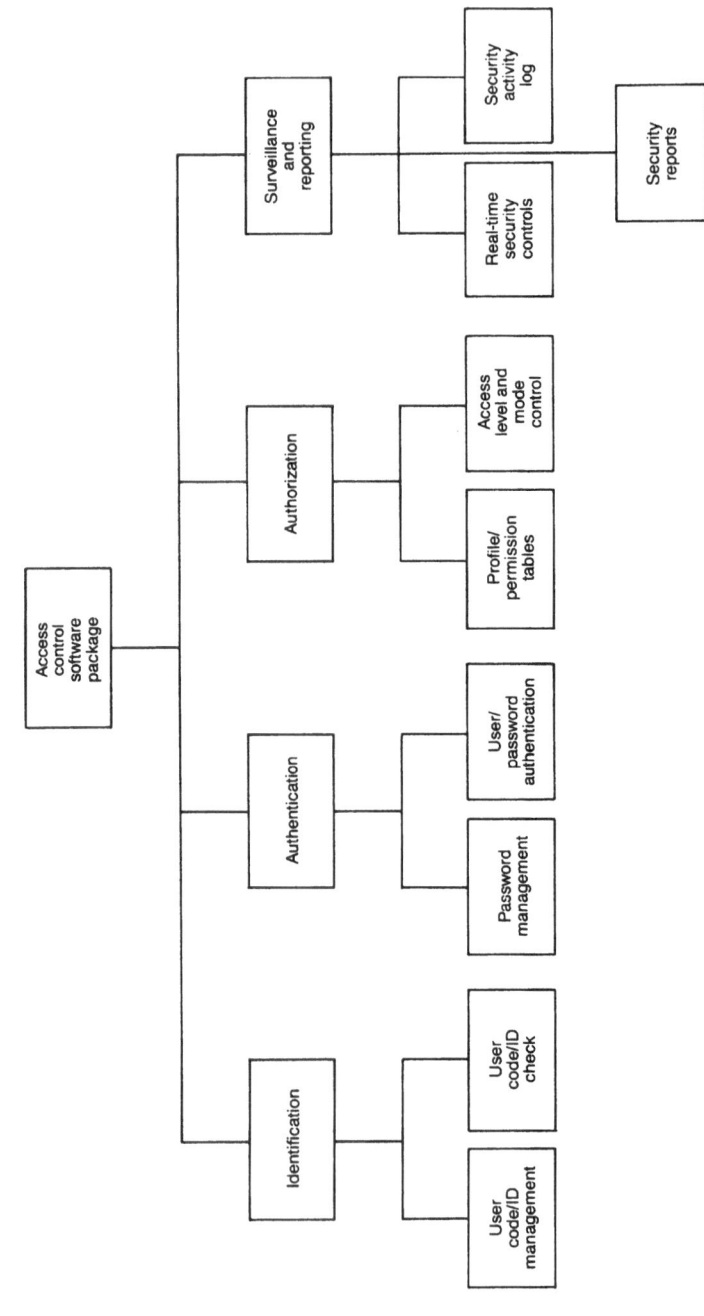

Fig. 1-4 Typical logical access control software features (*source*: J. Lobel, *Foiling the System Breakers*, McGraw-Hill)

trolling devices should not be susceptible to replay by an attacker. Smart cards which conduct a dialogue with a controlling computer use a different set of signals for each identification procedure. Dynamic password systems involve a token similar to a small calculator. At log-on time the user is presented with a random number which is entered via the keypad of the token. A second number is generated as a result of cryptographic transformation performed by the calculator, using a secret key known only to the calculator and the controlling computer. The same transformation is performed by the controlling computer and access allowed if the entered value equals the computer value (see chapter 3).

The most common form of access identification is, however, the password. The effectiveness of most common password schemes is so doubtful, however, it is unlikely that they provide any form of defence against a moderately intelligent attacker. There are two common approaches: either the user selects an easily remembered password (which can in turn be easily guessed by the attacker), or the user is given some random password (which cannot be easily remembered). The danger with a password that is not easily remembered is that the user immediately makes a written record and keeps it in a convenient place, e.g. on the side of the terminal.

There are plenty of mechanisms which can be used to enhance password security, and which make only realistic demands upon the user. Passphrases consisting of several words, checking programs which reject simplistic passwords, periodic changes of passwords, query programs which ask random questions likely to be known only to the user, e.g. the name of the teacher of one of the user's children. Password discipline is an area in which a determined security officer can make a substantial difference to access control effectiveness (see chapter 3).

1.5.5. What techniques are available to restrict user privileges once initial access has been granted?

The defensive depth philosophy requires that access should not open the Aladdin's cave to the attacker. A legitimate user will normally only employ the terminal for certain periods on working days and will normally only use a terminal in a given area. If access is then restricted on time of day, day of the week, and terminal location basis, then a hacker, who has learned the user's password, will be unable to log on over the public telephone network or use the terminal during the evening (see chapter 3). Operating systems provide a wide range of access privileges on a file-by-file basis. Thus files can be easily protected from other users who have no need to know, when access is granted it can be on a restricted basis, e.g. Read, which does not allow the user to modify its contents.

Operating systems have always provided a range of access controls, and in many cases they have been underexploited simply because users were inadequately trained, or were under no pressure to do so. The security policy should place a requirement upon computer centre staff and users to make full and effective use of such facilities.

The monitoring facilities of operating systems (see section 1.8.2) serve a dual role. They provide security staff with a detailed means of monitoring accesses, and their presence will also serve to warn staff that inadequate security awareness, on their part, can be detected by such logs.

1.5.6 What is the role of cryptography in access control?

Cryptography can ensure that an attacker who gains physical access to a terminal, and then logical access to data, is unable to exploit that data. The attacker cannot read the data because it is in the form of ciphertext. The attacker cannot make meaningful changes to the data because there is no way of knowing what the effect of changes to the ciphertext will be after it is deciphered. The attacker cannot make undetectable changes to the ciphertext because authentication checks will detect such changes.

1.5.7 What is cryptography?

Cryptography is defined as the art or science that treats of the principles, means, and methods for rendering plaintext unintelligible and for converting encrypted messages into intelligible form (FIPS). There are a number of terms with similar meanings, such as codes/ciphers and encipherment/encryption: their common occurrence in history and fiction has lead to some confusion.

Coding implies exchanging one form of information into another; it does not necessarily imply that any secrecy is involved. For example, each alphabetic character is encoded into a binary number before it is stored in a computer. If a secret code is used then there is no fixed limit on the length of each item of the original, plaintext, message that is changed into the secret codeword. Thus many military code books would provide short secret codewords for words or phrases such as 'tank' or 'divisional headquarter's staff'. *Ciphers*, however, always replace a given length of plaintext with a given, but not necessarily equal, length of ciphertext.

Encipherment is the action of converting plaintext to ciphertext; *encryption* is often used as a synonym for encipherment, but it also covers the act of encoding a secret message.

Cryptography was revolutionized by the advent of the computer; this is a somewhat ironic fact since the first electronic digital computer was built in order to crack a German military cipher. The major problems with early military, diplomatic, and commercial book and machine ciphers, were that they were extremely difficult to use and not too difficult to break. This is not true of modern ciphers: data encipherment and decipherment can be performed at high speed and be transparent to the user. No mathematical knowledge is required to administer and use modern ciphers, and many ciphers have withstood cryptanalytic attacks using supercomputers.

All ciphers use cryptographic keys for the encipherment and decipherment operations. A key is a comparatively short sequence of characters (e.g. AC8U0ZE). The key is specified by the user enciphering the message and must, of course, be kept secret. The original message (i.e. the plaintext) and the cryptographic key are fed into a computer, or cryptographic device, which performs the enciphering algorithm, producing a meaningless garble of characters comprising the ciphertext.

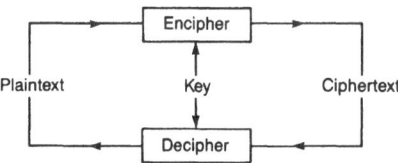

Fig. 1-5 Cryptography

With a well-designed cipher, to obtain the plaintext from the ciphertext without the cryptographic key is computationally infeasible, i.e. it would take an astronomical period of time to perform on the world's most powerful computer. It is also computationally infeasible to obtain the cryptographic key from the ciphertext even if the corresponding plaintext is available to the cryptanalyst.

In terms of data security the function of cryptographic control is to reintroduce partitioning of data held in common storage devices or transmitted over common communication channels. If the stored or transmitted data is enciphered with different keys then it is effectively partitioned. Only users with the appropriate keys can gain access to the data, even though all users have common access to the storage device or transmission channel.

1.5.8 Is it difficult to use ciphers?
Modern cipher systems are quite transparent to the user. In most cases the encryption/decryption operations are performed at high speed by special purpose microchips. Plaintext data entered by the user is encrypted by these chips immediately before local storage or transmission; encrypted data received from local storage, or over transmission lines, is decrypted before it is presented to the

33

authorized user. The microchips introduce a negligible delay in the processing. The complex mathematics of cipher systems are thus completely hidden from the user; there are none of the complexities or delays that were inevitably associated with book or machine cipher systems used in military, diplomatic, and commercial circles some years ago.

1.5.9 Can ciphers provide protection against forgery?

Yes. There are two types of protection: authentication and digital signature. Authentication (see section 1.5.16) aims to ensure that a message cannot be undetectably modified in transit between the sender and originator. Digital signature (see section 1.5.18) is a method of signing a message so that it can neither be undetectably modified between sender and receiver, nor can the signature be produced by anyone other than the sender. The receiver can thus check, but not produce or forge, the signature.

1.5.10 Does the use of ciphers impose additional responsibility on managers?

Information security is always a managerial responsibility. The manager need not be burdened with the technical or mathematical complexities of ciphers, but they must, nevertheless, accept the responsibilities of management in the information secured environment.

The degree of interaction between a manager and a cipher system will depend upon the manager's responsibility for the overall information system. In general the class of responsibility may be given as end-user, information system operator, and system designer/ implementor.

An end-user accessing data via a mainframe terminal or workstation linked to a network will not be aware of the encryption operations taking place. Most modern cipher systems use special-purpose encryption hardware which accepts plaintext and passes on ciphertext for storage or transmission, and vice versa. The encryption/decryption operations are performed by microchips and, as stated above, introduce negligible delays in the data-processing operations. Access to the data will be controlled and the users must provide evidence of their access authority; in general they will be required to enter a password or passphrase which is, or can be transformed into, the cryptographic key used in the encipherment/decipherment of the user's data. The user is absolutely responsible for the security of the cryptographic key. Any loss or disclosure resulting from poor password security (see chapter 3), failure to remember the key, loss of documents recording the key, informing other users of the key, allowing onlookers to observe password entry, etc. must be treated as a serious dereliction of duty. Failure to report a loss or disclosure of password, without delay, must be considered as a major breach of company discipline.

Any manager who has responsibility for a local processing system and associated off-line stored data, e.g. one using a workstation or personal computer with local backing storage, may be classified as an information system operator. An information system operator has rather more responsibility for the use of the cipher system than the end-user. In particular the operator may have full responsibility for the selection, storage, and allocation of passwords or cryptographic keys. Loss or disclosure of a key will probably compromise all data encrypted under that key, and the manager must decide what action needs to be taken to minimize the potential damage. At the very least this will involve re-encryption of the compromised data under a new cryptographic key; but it could lead to much more serious changes in (say) a company's marketing plans. Any information system operator must therefore have well-defined contingency plans, and such plans should be vetted by higher-level management, to cover loss or disclosure of keys. The re-encryption of compromised data, under a new key, should be performed from backup data, held in a secure store, rather than the compromised data. This safeguard will obviate the danger that the illegal acquirer of the lost or disclosed cryptographic key has modified, and re-encrypted, the compromised data.

The information system designer or implementor needs to be fully aware of all aspects of the selection and management of the cryptographic system. Fortunately this does not demand a detailed knowledge of the mathematics or cryptography, or a detailed study of cryptanalysis. It does require, however, a familiarity with the publications of international standards publications (e.g. FIPS) and an awareness of the modes of operation of cryptographic algorithms, of potential forms of attack (e.g. replay, masquerading, and spoofing – see section 1.5.28), and of the techniques of key management (see section 1.5.31). It is as well for the system designer/implementor to be better informed than the average hacker and attacker in these matters.

1.5.11 Are there different types of cipher?

Ciphers can be categorized as symmetric and asymmetric; they can also be categorized as block, cipher block chaining, and stream.

A symmetric cipher either uses the same key for encryption and decryption, or, if the keys are different, is such that, given one, it is possible to compute the other. If a symmetric cipher is employed for data communications then some secure means has to be determined to transmit the key from the encryptor to the decryptor (see section 1.5.31).

An asymmetric cipher uses different keys for encryption and decryption; moreover it is computationally infeasible to compute one key given the other. This type of cipher offers the facility of public key cryptography (see section 1.5.13), i.e. an organization can make its encryption key, and asymmetric cipher algorithm, publicly available; an individual wishing to send a secure message to that organization encrypts it with the public key and using the specified algorithm. The sender cannot, however, decrypt messages sent by other individuals using the same encryption key, since only the organization in question possesses the requisite private decryption key.

The classification of block, cipher block chaining, and stream cipher is one which often relates to the mode of implementation of an algorithm rather than the algorithm itself. With a block cipher the message must be split into fixed-size blocks; each block is then subjected to the algorithm and a ciphertext block is produced, The size of the ciphertext block is not necessarily equal to the plaintext block. Block ciphers can be subjected to a variety of attacks even if the attacker is unable to crack the cipher (see section 1.5.24). Cipher block chaining modes overcome some of the problems of block ciphers; the message is again split into blocks, but each block is combined with some function of the previous block before it is encrypted. This technique effectively removes repetitions in ciphertext blocks arising from repetitions in plaintext messages, e.g. if a phrase recurs several times or if a series of highly formatted messages are transmitted.

Stream ciphers are commonly used when it is inconvenient to assemble messages into fixed-size blocks before transmission. In this case a stream of random or pseudorandom data is produced by a keystream generator, and each bit, or character, of this data stream is combined with a corresponding bit, or character, of the plaintext stream. The resulting ciphertext is transmitted; the decryption process involves the generation of the same keystream, which is then combined with the ciphertext in an inverse manner to that used by the encryptor, to reveal the plaintext.

1.5.12 What are the most commonly employed ciphers?
The two most common current ciphers are DES and RSA. DES (Data Encryption Standard), also known as DEA (Data Encryption Algorithm), is a standard developed in the 1970s by the US National Bureau of Standards, and is widely used in commerce and finance. It will not continue to be supported by the American government indefinitely, but in view of its widespread use in international banking networks it is likely to be generally employed throughout the world for some time to come.

DES is a symmetric block cipher employing 64-bit blocks of plaintext which are transformed into 64 bits of ciphertext using a 64-bit key. There has been much discussion on the security of DES since the standard only allows 56 bits of the key to be independently selected. It is argued that in the future it will be computationally feasible to crack DES by searching through the 2^{56} keys. It is possible, however, effectively to lengthen the DES key at the cost of increased computational effort. DES may be implemented on microchips so that the encryption/decryption processes can be performed at high speed.

DES has a number of modes of implementation and can be used as a block, cipher block chaining, or stream cipher.

RSA (named after its inventors, Rivest, Shamir, and Adleman) is an asymmetric block cipher, and is regarded as the most promising algorithm for public key cryptography. It provides a particularly elegant method of signing messages (see section 1.5.18). The keys in RSA are several hundred bits in length and the blocksize varies with the parameters chosen. A user requires some assistance in the mathematically demanding process of setting up the block size, encryption, and decryption keys; moreover the algorithm is more computationally demanding than DES. However, microchips are now available for the RSA algorithm, and some form of key generation service will normally be provided to users.

1.5.13 What are the advantages of public key cryptography?
There are two areas for which public key cryptography may be employed:

- the provision of privacy of messages from a variety of dispersed senders to a central body,
- electronic signatures.

Public key cryptography uses different keys for encryption and decryption. Moreover it is computationally infeasible to derive one key given the other. Thus an organization can make its encryption key and encryption algorithm widely available; any individual wishing to send a secure message to the organization simply encrypts the message with the public key and transmits it. Only the organization holding the private decryption key can decipher the transmitted messages; thus even two senders using the same encryption key will be unable to decipher each others' messages. The major advantage of this technique over symmetric ciphers such as DES is that there is no requirement to make special secure arrangements for the exchange of keys between the sender and receiver before transmission of the message.

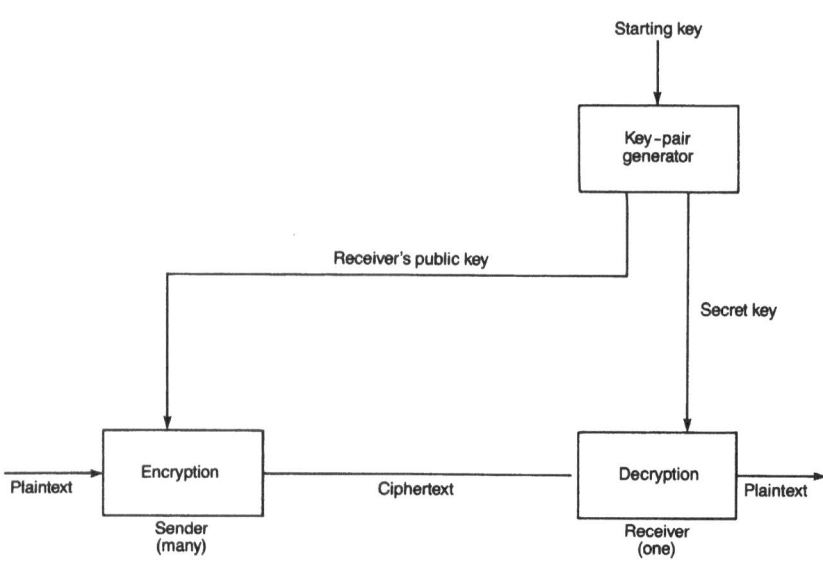

Fig. 1-6 Public key cryptography

An alternative use of public key cryptography is digital signature (see section 1.5.18). Not all public key cryptography can be used for this purpose, but RSA has the necessary attributes: the ciphertext and plaintext blocks are of equal length, and the same mathematical routines are used for encryption and decryption. In the simplest case the message is encrypted with the private (i.e. 'decryption') key. The signature can be checked by decrypting the ciphertext with the public (i.e. 'encryption') key.

1.5.14 What are the managerial implications of employing public key cryptography?

If an organization employs public key cryptography then it must ensure the integrity of its public keys, and of course guard the secrecy of the corresponding private keys. It must also warn its users against the danger of highly formatted, repetitive messages.

The organization must determine some secure means of providing its public keys, and must have some means of checking the public keys being made available in its name. If an attacker can supply an unsuspecting message originator with the attacker's public key, under the pretext that it is the public key of the organization for which the message is intended, then the attacker can decipher messages destined for the organization (see section 1.5.28). Thus an organization must ensure that the public keys published in its name cannot be modified. It must also monitor all sources of public keys to ensure that no attackers' keys are being published under its name.

If an organization is accepting signed messages, using the digital signature technique (see section 1.5.18), then it must be sure that the signee cannot revoke the signature by claiming that the private key had been discovered and used by some other party. Hence if public key cryptography is used then some trusted authority with responsibility for publishing public keys needs to be employed.

Management must also be aware of the danger of attacks on public key ciphers. An attacker can encrypt any plaintext message with the publicly available encryption key (see section 1.5.25). If highly formatted messages are transmitted then the attacker can simply produce a large number of such messages, inserting informed guesses for names, dates, quantities, etc. It might then be possible to correlate transmitted messages with this list of ciphertext blocks, and deduce their meaning.

1.5.15 How can data be protected against accidental corruption?

The simple answer is that data stored in electronic or magnetic media, or transmitted over communication lines, cannot be absolutely protected against modification or corruption. The whole purpose of representing data in electronic or magnetic form is to facilitate its modification for ease of recording and transmission. However, although it is virtually impossible to guarantee absolutely that computer or communications data is not corrupted or modified, it is possible to give a high level of guarantee that any changes, accidental or malicious, will be detected.

The problems of accidental corruption in data transfers, both within computers and over transmission channels, is commonly tackled with error detecting/correcting codes. A simple example of an elementary error-detecting code is the parity check. The number of 1 bits in a message are counted, and if they are odd then an additional 1 bit is tacked onto the message; if they are even then a 0 'parity' bit is appended. Thus the transmitted message always has an even number of 1 bits. The receiver counts the number of 1 bits: if they are even the message is accepted, otherwise it is clear that one of the bits has been changed and a retransmission is requested. This technique cannot detect all possible changes, nor does it allow the receiver to determine which bit in a faulty message is in error. If more comprehensive error detection is required then it is necessary to add more redundant bits to the message, and to use more sophisticated algorithms to determine the value of the checksum bits in terms of the original message. Error correcting codes enable the incorrect bits in the message to be determined so that the message may be corrected without retransmission, although such error correction is limited to specified number of incorrectly received bits.

1.5.16 How can data be protected against malicious alteration?

It is not possible to guarantee absolutely that data stored in electronic or magnetic form, or transmitted over communication lines, will be impervious to malicious alteration by a hacker or active wiretapper. Strict access controls provide some degree of assurance with stored data. However, it is normally impossible to guarantee that there is no point in a communication link that is not susceptible to the active wiretapper, even if fibre optics, or metal conduit protected lines, are employed (see chapter 4). Message authentication techniques are therefore aimed at ensuring that any such modifications can be detected before they cause damage. Such authentication techniques can also be used for data stored in files or databases (see section 1.7.6).

The techniques of message authentication bear a resemblance to error-detecting codes (see chapter 4); the message is subjected to a mathematical algorithm and an authentication block, similar to a checksum, is developed and appended to the message. The receiver performs the same algorithm on the received message and accepts it as genuine if the result is identical to the appended authentication block.

Consider for example an authentication block based upon a simple parity check (see section 1.5.15). Suppose that a message 1010 (101 and 0 parity bit) is received. The receiver checks that an even number of 1s exists in the message (corresponding to 0 parity bit) and then accepts the message as genuine. This is clearly a somewhat hasty decision since in fact there are three other messages that would also meet this requirement (000, 011, 110). In fact if an attacker, knowing nothing of the method used to determine the authentication block, modified the three message bits at random there is a 50 per cent chance that the change would not be detected.

It is clear that a single-bit authentication block provides no useful guarantee of authentication. If the message authentication block comprises three bits then we can divide transmitted messages into eight classes, and all the messages in a class will give rise to the same authentication block. For example, the messages in the first category will all produce authentication block 000, those in the second 001, and those in the eighth 111. In this case a random alteration to the original message will only have one chance in eight of avoiding detection. In general an n-bit authentication block will divide the message into 2^n partitions. In banking circles Message Authentication Blocks (MACs) normally consist of 32 bits (see chapter 5); giving a probability of 2^{-32} (i.e. one chance in 4.3×10^9) that a randomly corrupted message will be undetected by a check against the authentication block. The algorithm used to produce the checksum must be sensitive not only to the contents of the message but also to the order of those contents. If the words or figures in a message are transposed then the algorithm must produce a different checksum. For example, the simple parity check would be useless for authentication since the change of a message from, 011 to 110, would not be reflected in the parity bit.

Sophisticated error-detection codes in data communications meet the above mentioned requirements for the checksum but they still provide no protection against the active wiretapper. If attackers know how to compute the checksum then they can simply modify the message, compute the new checksum, and pass it on to the unsuspecting recipient. The sophistication of the authentication routine discussed above only provides protection against accidental corruption or mathematically inept attackers. The essential additional feature of message authentication is secrecy; the originator and recipient must, alone, share some secret knowledge which ensures that only they can produce the MAC for a given message.

Encryption algorithms using secret cryptographic keys provide the necessary secrecy for the MAC, and careful selection of the algorithm can also ensure that the necessary sensitivity to the ordering of items in the message can be achieved (see chapter 5). The use of an encryption algorithm to produce a MAC is not, however, the same as encrypting the message for secrecy (see section 1.5.17). In fact the actual text of an authenticated message may be sent in clear; it is only necessary that the means of producing the MAC is kept secret.

With all these precautions can it now be safely assumed that an attacker cannot interfere, undetectably, with transmitted messages? Well, no, not quite. Suppose a properly authenticated message is sent to authorize the transfer of a sum of money from Account A to Account B. If an active wiretapper recorded the message and replayed it later then two identical, apparently authentic, messages would have been received and processed, hence Account B would receive twice the due amount. This form of attack, known as a replay (see section 1.5.26), can be thwarted by putting a unique identifier, or a date/time stamp, in the body of each authenticated message.

Authentication can protect two parties against message modification by a third party; however, it cannot in itself protect one of the parties against the other. Thus the receiver can forge a message, or modify the contents of a received message, compute and add a MAC, and claim that it originated with the sender who shares the same secret key for the MAC generation. Similarly a sender can later revoke a message claiming that it was forged by the purported receiver. The problem of adding a digital signature to identify the sender unambiguously is discussed below (see section 1.5.18).

1.5.17 What is the difference between encryption and authentication?
Encryption is designed to conceal the contents of a message. Authentication is designed to ensure that the recipient can check the integrity of all aspects of a message, i.e. its contents, its originator, and its intended recipient, and that the message is not a replay. The process of authentication involves some knowledge that is secret to the message originator and some method by which the recipient can check the authenticity of the message. It is important that no attacker can inject or modify a message in such a way that it can pass the authentication tests used by the recipient. Encryption provides various methods of message authentication (see section 1.5.16). However, the fact that a message, or stored data, was encrypted does not guarantee its authenticity; moreover a message authenticated by encryption need not be secret, i.e. its contents can be in plaintext.

An encrypted message can be subject to attacks on its integrity:

- The message might be a repeat of an earlier message. Thus an active wiretapper could simply record the transmitted ciphertext and inject it into the communication link some time later; causing for example, a financial transaction to be performed twice (see section 1.5.26).
- The attacker could modify the message by rearranging the ciphertext blocks or by substituting ciphertext blocks from another message, where the same key had been used. This would be quite feasible if the messages were highly formatted. This technique could also be used in secure databases exchanging fields between records, hence, for example, exchanging diagnoses of two patients (see section 1.7.6).
- An old encrypted record could be substituted for its new value; thus replacing a 'employment terminated' record in a personnel database with an original 'current employee' record.
- The message could take the form of a random stream of data, such as a binary data stream produced by some measuring device, e.g. a seismic recorder used to monitor nuclear tests. In this case the ciphertext could be changed in some random fashion; the receiver would have no message redundancy to distinguish between genuine and garbled messages.

In all of the above cases the attacker does not need to decrypt the information in order to affect the integrity of the stored or transmitted data. In particular, public key cryptography messages can provide no assurance of integrity when the public key is used for encryption; since the key is publicly available the attacker is free to make any desired modifications to active wiretapped messages

A common method of authentication is to employ a cryptographic algorithm to produce a MAC (see section 1.5.16) and to append it to the message. In this case the encryption is only used in the production of the MAC, and the message contents can be transmitted in clear (see chapter 5).

1.5.18 How can public key cryptography be used to sign a message?
The traditional authorization of documents is based on the written signature, the value of which is that it can be easily checked, but not reproduced, by the recipient or any third party. In data communications a digital signature is a technique of processing the message by the sender using secret information, known only to the sender, such that the recipient can check the originator of the message. Moreover the recipient should be provided with some means of proving to an arbitrator that there was irrefutable evidence of the message originator's identity.

Message authentication techniques (see section 1.5.16) do not, in themselves, provide a digital signature. The MAC can be produced by the sender and recipient; only third parties (e.g. active wiretappers) are denied the means of successfully modifying a MAC for a transmitted message, or producing a MAC for a false message. Message authentication allows the possibility of the recipient changing a message, or producing a false message. This in turn opens up the possibility that the sender will revoke a message and claim that it was forged by the recipient. For example, a sender might attempt to revoke a message to a stockbroker if the transaction subsequently proved to be unprofitable.

Symmetric ciphers, such as DES, can be employed for message authentication but can only be used in digital signatures with rather complex and cumbersome methods. RSA on the other hand provides an extremely elegant method of digital signature, exploiting three features of the algorithm:

- It is virtually impossible to compute the decryption key given the encryption key.
- The encryption and decryption routines are identical, except for the keys used.
- The ciphertext block is the same size as the plaintext block.

The procedure of the RSA digital signature is simply to encrypt the message with a private 'decryption' key. The recipient then decrypts the received message with the public 'encrypting' keys.

Since no person, other than the sender, is capable of producing the ciphertext that can be decrypted into meaningful plaintext with the public encrypting key, then the authorship of the message is ensured. Moreover the recipient can hand the ciphertext to an arbitrator, and invite the arbitrator to decipher the message with the sender's published public key, giving proof of the message originator.

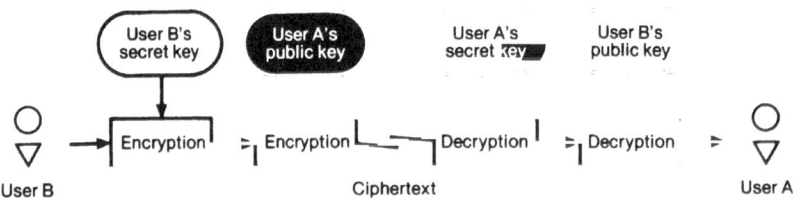

Fig. 1-7 Digital signature

1.5.19 Are there any pitfalls in the use of RSA digital signatures?
There are a number of factors to be considered in the use of digital signatures:

- The techniques of authentication must be applied to protect against replay and rearrangements of the constituent ciphertext blocks of the message.
- The signed message is not confidential since it can be decrypted with a public 'encryption' key.
- The integrity of the public and private keys must be subject to verification.

The encryption of the message does not in itself guarantee against malicious modification or replay attacks (see section 1.5.26). The message should contain a sequence number or time/date stamp to obviate replay attacks; also an authentication block or checksum that is a function of the whole message should be appended to it before encryption. The recipient will be able to check the authenticator block of the plaintext message but the encryption with the private key ensures that only the originator can produce the encrypted version.
The encryption with the private key ensures the authentication and signature but does not provide for confidentiality since any attacker can obtain the public key and decrypt the message. If confidentiality is required when Party A sends a signed message to Party B then the message must be encrypted with Party A's private key, for

44

signature, and Party B's public key for confidentiality.

Recipients must protect themselves against the situation in which they accept a signed message and then face a claim from the purported sender that disowns the apposite private key. If an attacker can persuade the recipient that a public key produced by the attacker is actually the public key of the purported sender then a forged message will be accepted by the receiver. Similarly an originator may later revoke a message on the basis that the private key was stolen and used by an attacker. The recipient must have access to a key registry which will attest to the authenticity of the public keys. A receiver can then check with the registry that the originator had not revoked the public key before the time/date stamp on the message.

1.5.20 Is data absolutely safe if it is encrypted?

Clearly encryption provides a high degree of protection against the intruder browsing through files or the wiretapper listening to data traffic. However, in the general case this question needs to be answered against the specific threats of data loss, modification, and disclosure.

Encryption provides no security against loss of data due to physical damage of data storage media, or accidental or malicious erasure of stored data. It is as easy to destroy disks containing encrypted files or erase encrypted files from storage as it is to destroy or erase plaintext data. Indeed, to some degree encryption can increase this danger. Loss of the means of decryption, e.g. permanent loss of cryptographic keys or loss of decryption facilities means that the plaintext data is no longer available to the legitimate user. Moreover the loss of decryption facilities also effectively renders any encrypted backup material unavailable.

Encryption also provides no protection against the actual modification of the data; ciphertext can be altered just as easily as plaintext, but it does increase the attacker's difficulty in making undetectable, meaningful changes to data. Thus a malicious random alteration to ciphertext will result in garbled plaintext providing the legitimate user with a clear indication of the loss of data integrity. It will still be necessary to resort to use of backup data to rectify the damage. The more sophisticated attack in which an updated encrypted file or section of a file is replaced by another earlier encrypted version is not immediately detectable unless some form of authentication (see section 1.5.16) is applied to the data.

Encryption does provide a high degree of protection against accidental or malicious disclosure of stored or transmitted data. Like all protective measures, however, it is important to recognize that the protection is relative and not absolute. It depends to a very high degree on the management techniques undertaken to protect the cryptographic keys and the decryption facilities. It also depends upon the encryption techniques employed (see section 1.5.21) and upon the care with which the encryption techniques are used.

1.5.21 Are ciphers safe?
This is really a series of questions:

- Is it theoretically possible for an attacker to derive plaintext from ciphertext for a given cipher? (See section 1.5.22.)
- How does one select a 'good' cipher? (See section 1.5.23.)
- Is it possible to get information from ciphertext without breaking the cipher? (See section 1.5.24.)
- What attacks can be mounted on cipher systems? (See section 1.5.24.)

1.5.22 Is it theoretically possible to derive plaintext from ciphertext for a given cipher?
If a message comprises a sentence from a natural language or is in a common format then, with one exception, it is theoretically possible to derive the original message, given a reasonable amount of the ciphertext. The one exception involves the 'one-time pad' concept. If the sender and receiver have access to the same list of genuinely random numbers, equal in length to the message to be transmitted, then the sender combines the plaintext with the numbers from the list (e.g. adds them together); the receiver performs the inverse operation (e.g. subtracts the random numbers from the ciphertext) revealing the plaintext. This technique provides perfect secrecy. However, it is totally impracticable for modern data communications since the users are faced with the problem of securely exchanging the cryptographic key which is of the same length as the plaintext message.

In other ciphers, with keys that are short compared with the total length of the message, it is theoretically possible to derive the plaintext from a given sample of ciphertext. For a given DES ciphertext message derived from plaintext English it is theoretically possible to derive the plaintext with less than three 64-bit blocks of ciphertext. However, although theoretically possible, this is, for all good ciphers, still computationally infeasible. The world's most powerful computers would require a massive period of computation to derive just one plaintext message, and the same amount of effort to derive a second message using a different key.

1.5.23 How can one select a good cipher?
Any individual user can only select a cipher algorithm on the basis of the reputation of the organization supplying it. Ciphers may be classified as:

- nonsecret algorithms supported by accredited agencies;
- secret algorithms supplied by an accredited body;
- proprietary ciphers.

Nonsecret algorithms such as DES can be subjected to intensive cryptanalytic attack by research bodies and the results published. If the cipher has been publicly available long enough for such an intensive study to be reported in the technical press, then it seems unlikely that it will be cracked by a hacker on a personal computer. On the other hand a secret algorithm would appear to have some attractions because the cryptanalyst is at a severe disadvantage. The advent of ciphers embedded in microchips, designed to prevent reverse engineering, enables secrecy of the algorithm to be maintained even though it is in widespread use. However, the user is in the hands of the chip supplier; for this reason the US government is handling through the National Security Agency the design and supply of cryptographic algorithms used by US organizations.

There is some debate as to whether greater security is attained if the algorithm is secret. If the security of the cipher is heavily dependent upon the secrecy of the algorithm then a serious situation arises if the secret is revealed by disgruntled employees, industrial espionage, or successful cryptanalytic attack. At best the users of the algorithm will be compelled to change to another cipher, a much more expensive operation than merely changing compromised keys. At worst the loss of security will not be revealed and the users will have a false confidence in their compromised data security.

With proprietary ciphers then it is a case of *caveat emptor*. The supplier is unlikely to provide details of the algorithm; the fact that the purchaser has neither the time nor the expertise to conduct a full-scale cryptanalytic attack does not necessarily mean that such an attack is infeasible.

1.5.24 Is it possible to attack a cipher system without breaking the cipher?
There are essentially four forms of attack on cipher systems:

- message exhaustion (see section 1.5.25),
- replay (see section 1.5.26),
- masquerading (see section 1.5.27),
- spoofing (see section 1.5.28).

1.5.25 What is a message exhaustion attack?

This form of attack involves the selection of a range of possible plaintext messages, enciphering them, and checking the corresponding ciphertext with enciphered traffic gained, for example, by wiretapping.

For this procedure to work it is necessary that there are a limited number of possible plaintext messages, hence message exhaustion, and that the attacker can gain access to enciphering facilities.

Normally the number of possible plaintext messages will be too large for this purpose. However, if an electronic codebook mode of encipherment is employed, and the messages are highly formatted or contain commonly recurring blocks (e.g. addresses, names of companies, etc.) then some blocks of the messages will meet the requirement for message exhaustion. The encipherment facilities are provided to the attacker if public key cryptography is employed (see section 1.5.13).

Thus suppose a firm's salesmen send back to home office formatted messages encrypted with the firm's public key. These messages might take the form: 'Today's must promising contact was Customer X'. The attacker merely has to produce a series of such messages substituting the names of likely customers for X and storing the ciphertext produced. A check of the salesman's transmitted ciphertext against the list of all possible ciphertext messages then effectively reveals the plaintext.

A similar attack can be mounted on some database systems. Suppose an attacker can browse through a database full of formatted, encrypted messages; some intelligent guessing and correlation can be quite revealing. If the browser is also permitted to enter data into the system then a guess can be checked out. For example suppose that the attacker suspects that a particular piece of data in a hospital's set of patient records corresponds to a diagnosis of AIDS. The attacker merely has to inject a plaintext record with AIDS in the appropriate field and observe the subsequent change to the encrypted records.

1.5.26 What is a replay attack?

If a message is protected with a MAC (see section 1.5.16) then an attacker will be unable to modify its contents, or produce another message and pass it off as a legitimate message. However, the attacker could simply retransmit the original message; if the receipt of the message causes the recipient to take some action, e.g. transfer a sum of money form one bank account to another, then at the very least some mischief will have been caused. The defence against such attacks is to ensure that all authenticated messages are unique by the inclusion of a message number or date/time stamp with the authenticated text of the message (see chapter 5).

1.5.27 How is a masquerade attack performed?

The essence of the masquerade is that the attackers successfully identify themselves to the system as legitimate users with rights of access to decipherment facilities. For example, in some systems employing remote terminals the traffic is encrypted but the terminal has all the necessary decryption facilities, including the stored cryptographic keys. A 'midnight attack' is performed by recording the traffic from the host computer to the terminal. Later, figuratively at midnight, the attacker gains access to the terminal and feeds in the recorded enciphered messages. The terminal assumes that they are derived from the host computer, deciphers them, and displays the plaintext message. Such attacks can be thwarted if the terminal enters into a handshaking procedure with the host immediately upon log-on.

1.5.28 What is spoofing?

In spoofing the attacker intercepts messages between two communicating parties; each party talks to the spoofer under the misapprehension that it is the other legitimate user. In this way the spoofer can gain access to confidential data and/or modify messages in transit.

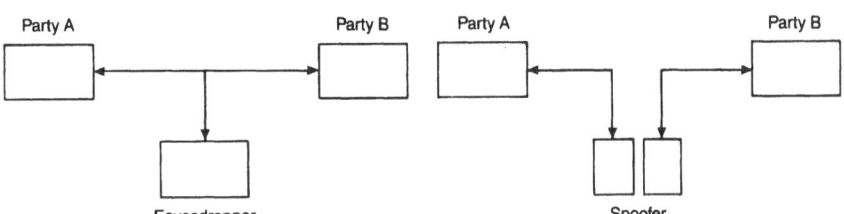

Fig. 1-8 Spoofing

In public key cryptography the spoofer persuades both parties to employ the spoofer's public encrypting key. The sequence of events is:

- Party A requests Party B's public encryption key.
- The spoofer intercepts the request, and
  - forwards the spoofer's public key to Party A,
  - requests Party B's public key.
- Party A encrypts data with the spoofer's key and this message is intercepted by the spoofer who:

- deciphers the message with the spoofer's private deciphering key,
- enciphers the original, or a modified form of the original, message with Party B's public key,
- forwards the re-enciphered message to Party B.

Spoofing can also be used by an attacker to persuade a user to interact with a system under the control of the attacker. For example, users may input passwords into an attacker's file because they are under the impression that they are performing a log-on sequence.

1.5.29 What security precautions need to be taken for encryption systems?
There are two main areas of concern:

- The data and keys must be protected before, during, and after the encipherment/decipherment processes (see section 1.5.30).
- Arrangements should be made for generating, distributing, transmitting, storing, and disposing of cryptographic keys, i.e. key management (see section 1.5.31).

1.5.30 How should data be handled during the encipherment/ decipherment process?
While it is certainly true that encryption considerably enhances the protection of data against disclosure, it needs to be emphasized that such techniques must be combined with effective management procedures. Even if the encryption technique employed is totally impervious to attack the data still exists in plaintext form both before and during encryption, and after and during decryption. It is essential that the data is fully protected against disclosure if it is stored before encryption, during transmission to the encryption facility, and during the encryption process. Moreover the plaintext must be completely purged from any temporary store as soon as it is encrypted. Similar precautions are required in the decryption process. It is important, for example, that decrypted data be sent only to printers in secure locations.

It is even more essential that the cryptographic keys are similarly protected since their loss would compromise not only the data in question but also any other data encrypted under the same keys. In general the encryption and decryption processes should not be performed in a multi-user computer system, since the security of the data and keys then becomes totally dependent upon the access security of the whole computer system. Special secure, tamper-resistant modules provide a safe environment for the storage of keys and the protection of data during cryptographic operations. If the encryption is performed on a single-user personal computer then a software package may be employed, provided that certain precautions are taken:

- The computer should be supervised during the operation of the package.
- The package must be checked to ensure that it contains no Trojan Horses which could write the plaintext or keys to a file.
- The plaintext must be purged from the disk after encryption. The conventional erase facilities do not actually remove the data from the disk.

In general, however, it is both more convenient and more secure to use hardware encryptor boards for personal computer security (see chapter 3).

1.5.31 What is involved in key management?

Key management is defined as the processes concerned with the generation, distribution, storage, and destruction of cryptographic keys. Encipherment effectively transfers the problem of ensuring the secrecy of a mass of data to that of protecting the secrecy of a cryptographic key. The problems associated with the various aspects of key management depend upon the range of the cryptographic techniques and the environment and applications in which the cryptographic keys are employed.

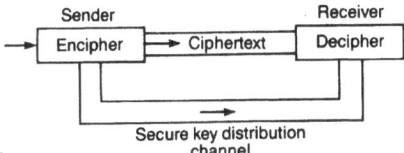

Fig. 1-9 Secure key distribution

Key generation must be undertaken in such a manner so as to ensure that:

- The result of the generation process is unpredictable.
- The range of keys that can be produced are equal to the full range of valid keys.
- There is no substantial skew in the probability distribution of the keys produced.
- An attacker cannot influence the generation process.
- An attacker cannot change the output from the generator.
- An attacker cannot monitor the generator output.

If the output from the generator is, to some degree, predictable then an attacker could independently produce the same key, or a set of keys, containing the generated key. If the range of key outputs is a subset of the valid range of keys, or if there is an increased probability that a certain subset of keys will be generated, then the strength of the generation process will be less than that of the cryptosystem.

Key distribution is one of the most complex problems in modern cryptographic systems. If a limited number of keys are to be distributed by manual methods then strict administrative procedures are required to maintain the security of the keying material. In many instances, however, the number of keys employed in the system, the frequency of key changes and the large, diverse user population demand that a variety of automated key distribution techniques be employed. Symmetric ciphers such as DES require that both the encipher and decipher processes employ the same key, and thus the cryptographic key must be securely exchanged between any two communicating parties. Public key cryptography imposes much less rigorous key management conditions, since the encipher key may be freely publicized, but precautions are nevertheless required to obviate specific attacks (see section 1.5.24).

Key management in database systems could be tackled by distributing to the users the keys used to encrypt the records. For example, such users could be provided with a plastic card with the key stored in a magnetic stripe; use of the card would also require the input of a password at the terminal to minimize the impact of lost cards. However, this method inevitably increases the danger of loss of database confidentiality arising from the compromise of user keys. A better approach is to store the keys within the database system and to rely upon access controls to ensure that only privileged users can gain access to the keys, and hence the deciphered records.

Key management for terminal–host communication commonly employ session keys to encrypt the messages in transit. These session keys have a lifespan restricted to the messages transmitted in an individual user session. Such session keys are generated by the host computer, upon request from a user, and are both stored in the host and transmitted, encrypted under a key encrypting key known as the terminal key, to the terminal. It is a principle of such systems that the session key is never revealed, outside system tamper-resistant modules, in plaintext form. Thus other key-encrypting keys, termed master keys, are stored at the host, while each terminal has its own terminal key.

EFTPOS networks pose particular problems of key management. The terminals will be located in retailers' premises, and there will be a large number of such terminals. The terminals must be not be

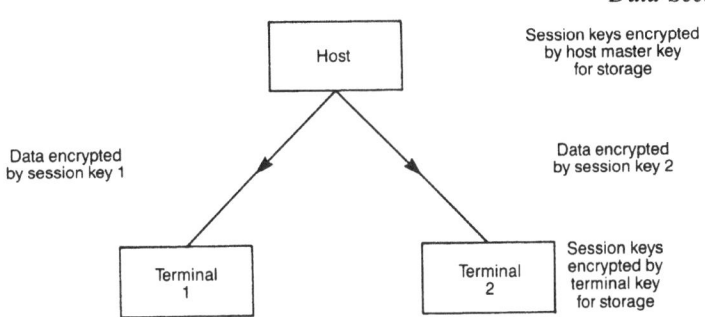

Fig. 1-10 Key management for terminal-host communication. Session keys are encrypted by terminal keys and transmitted to terminals; data is then encrypted by session keys for host-terminal dialogues.

expensive to manufacture, they will be unsupervised outside working hours, and they will be operated by relatively unskilled personnel. Moreover, the time to complete a transaction must be kept to a minimum, and the terminals should accept a wide range of customer card types. The network will probably include a variety of host computers operated by various financial institutions (see chapter 5).

Key distribution systems must not only guard against exposure of the keys by an attacker but also against the modification, insertion, or replay of keys by an attacker. Key notarization provides recipients with the guarantee that a data key originated at the communicating party initiating the transfer, and was intended for the recipient, i.e. an attacker has not transmitted a key intended for use between other communicating pairs.

1.6 Information Flow Control

1.6.1 What is information flow control?
Information flow control is defined as control over information as it enters a computer system, while it is within the system, and as it leaves the system. In general terms this means that control must be exercised to the flow of information into the computer system, between data items in the computer, and from the computer system to users.

1.6.2 How can the flow of data into a computer be controlled?
There is little point is exercising extreme care on the integrity of data within a computer system if one cannot be sure that it was entered correctly in the first place. Data entry controls are designed to ensure the integrity of data entered into the system by authorized personnel.

The most prevalent potential source of danger to data integrity lies in the accidental input of incorrect data; it is reported that 80 per cent of security breaches are due to errors or omissions rather than deliberate fraud. Not only are such errors a source of concern in themselves, but there is also the danger that naive attempts to re-cover from perceived errors can cause an even greater loss to data integrity.

This problem was well recognized in the early days of data processing when data was punched onto paper cards or paper tape by trained keyboard operators, and entered into the computer in batch mode. Control totals and verification techniques using double keying of data were commonly built into the mode of operation of data entry units. With dedicated staff employed solely for data entry, it was possible to maintain a high level of training, discipline, and supervision of data entry personnel.

The advent of transaction processing distributed the data entry task to personnel who had other tasks, e.g. direct interaction with customers. Such staff often operated in branch offices, airport terminals, etc., with little direct supervision of their data entry operations. The problems of minimizing data entry errors were tackled by good forms design for the computer screens, strict format controls for each field on the screen, checks for reasonableness of in-put data, etc. Good data entry input systems allowed staff to recover from error conditions, e.g. abort an incorrect screen, move back to correct fields perceived to have been wrongly entered, etc.

1.6.3 Is inadequate data entry control a source of danger to current systems?

Data entry is not a major source of concern while it can be strictly controlled; data processing managers have considerable experience of maintaining high standards within disciplined environments. However, when personal computers spread throughout organizations the problems of data entry integrity escalate rapidly. A transaction clerk has virtually no control on the type or form of data acceptable to the computer: all aspects of the user interaction are determined by the mainframe software. Personal computing on the other hand gives the end-user total control on the type and form of data to be en-tered into the system, and the processing to be performed on it.

Personal computers spread rapidly through organizations to provide private information processing systems for managers. In these circum-stances, and given good security of the personal computer (see chapter 3), the output of the managers continue to take the form of written reports, tables of data, etc. Given that competent managers are accustomed to check the accuracy of their written reports, it is likely that keyboarding errors will be detected and corrected before they infect the corporate information asset.

However, this safeguard disappears when the next logical step of information technology is introduced into the organization, i.e. the transfer of stored data by exchanging floppy diskettes or direct transfer of personal computer data into a local area network or mainframe computer. In particular, spreadsheets are notoriously difficult to control; the formulae in the spreadsheet are hidden during normal operation and the screen only gives a window on a small section of a large spreadsheet. Spreadsheets contained in floppy diskettes and handed from one user to another can easily hide and amplify any early data entry errors. Incidentally, an attacker who gains access to a spreadsheet on a floppy diskette can wreak havoc by making a few invisible changes to formulae.

If data entered into a personal computer is then processed by local software and downloaded directly into a mainframe computer, data entry controls into the central computer have flown out of the window. The potential sources of error are:

- accidental miskeying of data;
- software bugs in the personal computer software;
- malicious modification of personal computer data;
- a Trojan Horse (see chapter 3) in the personal computer software.

1.6.4 How can data entry control be improved if personal computers are widely used in the organization?
The necessary steps are:

- training,
- control of software,
- data ownership (see section 1.4.2),
- monitoring and audit trails.

In many cases powerful personal computer software packages, such as spreadsheets and databases, are being used with inadequate training and hence insufficient appreciation of the data integrity problem. A consistent policy of training to all personal computer users must be provided. The training should stress the potential pitfalls of packages, the importance of careful data entry techniques, effective file maintenance procedures, etc.

The control of software employed in an organization's personal computers is essential to ensure that:

- Software performs according to its specifications.
- Software is not susceptible to modification by attackers.
- Personnel are not required to operate too wide a variety of packages, or different versions of packages, to the extent that training policies are nullified.

- The organization is not subject to litigation due to the acquisition of pirated software (see chapter 7).
- Software does not contain malicious code (see chapter 3).

In particular, personal computer software developed in-house needs to be subjected to close scrutiny since it may not have been subjected to intensive testing and could therefore contain bugs that cause intermittent, undetected failures of data integrity.

In the last analysis it may be virtually impossible to exercise full control on locally produced and processed data. It is therefore essential that any problems should be localized to the source, and efforts should be concentrated on minimizing the impact on corporate data. The concept of ownership of corporate data places full responsibility for data integrity on every data item to a specified manager. Thus each data owner will be effectively responsible for ensuring data controls for his or her corporate data items. The degree to which this delegation of responsibility is effective depends upon the perceived security stance of top management, their readiness to specify security standards, the training provided, the discipline applied, and the monitoring performed.

While a data owner (see section 1.4.2) must accept responsibility for data controls on his or her own files it must be recognized that data will move from files belonging to one data owner to another. Data owners will therefore require that they be able to check on data entry and movements affecting their data. Controls on data access, monitoring of data changes, and audit trails (see section 1.8.10) must therefore be incorporated into the system.

1.6.5 How is control over data movements within corporate data effected?

Data is transferred from one file or database to another by read/write operations. Owners of a databases will wish to effect control on both the reading from, and writing to, their files. In the first case they need to ensure that confidential data is not leaked elsewhere; in the second they are concerned to maintain the integrity of their data against accidental or malicious contamination (see sections 1.5.15 and 1.5.16).

Both of these matters are properly the concern of the data processing manager. The security officer will wish to be assured, however, that an access control matrix effectively mediates all transfers between files so that only those transfers explicitly permitted by the matrix take place, irrespective of the applications software in the system. This raises the extremely complex problem of the security of operating systems (see section 1.9.2).

The question of software integrity is a major concern in organizations totally reliant on their information processing systems. If software is developed in-house then there exists the danger that a programmer has built in a malicious code for fraudulent or malicious sabotage purposes. Such malicious code can lie dormant for years and be triggered by time or by some specific event, e.g. the removal of the programmer's name from the payroll. Even if no deliberate malicious code has been implanted there are numerous bugs that only manifest themselves under rare combinations of internal data. In-house software developed under intense pressure, e.g. when unrealistic timescales have been insisted upon, is unlikely to have been subjected to the intense scrutiny essential for total assurance of software quality.

The post hoc detailed examination of source coding is invariably an exhausting and costly process, particularly if it is to be performed by a team other than the original designers. If the software documentation is in any sense inadequate or deficient (which again is quite common for software developed under severe time–cost constraints) then the examination process may be as expensive in manhours as the original program development. Software analysis tools exist for some languages, and such tools can provide a degree of assurance of software integrity. However, in general, cheap in-house software is a very expensive commodity.

Purchased software may provide more assurance of integrity, particularly if it is a widely-used package from a supplier with a high reputation. In some cases a fraudulently inclined, and talented, systems programmer may be able to effect a patch to the source or object code, but some method of checking the resident software against a copy of the original can usually obviate such dangers. However, the problem of computer viruses is causing an increasing degree of concern because previously reliable software may become infected with a virus between two successive invocations of the software (see chapter 3).

1.6.6 How is the flow of information controlled between the computer and the end-user?

There are two aspects to this question, i.e. the control over information flow in a communications network (see chapter 4) and the control of information to authorized users. The security of communications systems is a matter for negotiation between the user and the organization operating the network. The question of control of information to specific users is discussed under access control (see chapter 3), but it also raises the interesting problem of spoofing (see section 1.5.28) or masquerading (see section 1.5.27). When a computer can be accessed over a telephone network it is open to attack by hackers. Hackers or attackers will masquerade as legitimate users in an attempt to divert the flow of information to themselves. It is particularly important that they do not establish communication as legitimate receivers of cryptographic keys; many ingenious techniques exist for this purpose.

Information can also flow from the computer system to an electronic eavesdropper by the van Eck phenomenon (see chapter 3).

Many of these problems can be tackled by technological innovations, but in the final analysis it is a management problem. Some common-sense managerial actions (e.g. cutting off communication to the computer in periods after working hours when no legitimate users will be accessing the system) can be more effective than the most sophisticated gadgetry.

Ultimately the information will be transmitted to the end-user in the form of a printout or display on a terminal. At this stage the information must be in plaintext form and hence readily accessible to an attacker. There is little point in the use of sophisticated communication/computer security systems if the subsequent sensitive printout is itself produced in an insecure environment, or distributed through the internal post. The control on output must be such that sensitive data can only be directed to designated printers or VDUs subject to appropriate physical access controls (see chapter 6).

1.7 Security of Stored Data

1.7.1 Are there significant differences between the problems of data security of stored and transmitted data?
The principles of data security, particularly in regard to protection against disclosure, corruption, and modification are similar for both transmitted and stored data. The major differences lie in the opportunities provided to the potential attacker. Transmitted data is likely to be more accessible to the attacker but will usually have a limited life and be fragmented, i.e. data communications traffic will consist of many unrelated messages destined for multifarious files or databases.

Stored data can, on the other hand, be subjected to more rigorous access controls but it will remain relatively static over long periods and exist in files or databases, on-line and off-line, with a high degree of coherence.

1.7.2 What are the vulnerabilities of stored data?
In order to answer this question it is necessary to categorize stored data:

- data stored on personal computers or associated backup media (see section 1.7.3),

- mainframe computer backup media (see section 1.7.5),
- on-line individual files (see section 1.7.6),
- on-line databases (see section 1.7.7).

1.7.3 What are the potential dangers to personal computer data?

The data stored on personal computers, or associated backup media, is vulnerable to loss, disclosure, and modification from any person with access at any time to the computer or backup media (see chapter 3). The dangers of loss or corruption of the data are probably greater from accidental mishandling than from malicious acts. The threats are more numerous than with mainframe files because:

- Many legitimate users have inadequate training.
- Access, particularly outside normal working hours, is less restricted.
- The operating system will in many cases apply no logical access controls (see section 1.5.3).
- Many potential attackers have expertise on the use of personal computers, and stolen diskettes can be loaded into any other compatible personal computer.
- The information is likely to be a form that is of immediate commercial value, e.g. a database of customers, a spreadsheet of financial planning.
- Hardware and storage media are accessible and attractive targets for minor larceny.

The greatest danger to personal computer data lies in the actions of inadequately trained staff with legitimate access to the computer or storage media. Floppy diskettes are actually quite fragile devices. They are also in wide demand. Thus data stored on floppy diskettes is in danger from careless handling; they have been known to be stapled to listings and brochures, etc. They can be corrupted by spillages from coffee cups, by heavy-handed writing on diskette labels, by mishandling of the diskette surface accessible through the read/write slot, etc. They are also subject to 'borrowing' by other users. Once loaded in the computer the data can be accidentally erased or overwritten. Such erasure or overwriting can occur as the result of incorrect operating system commands, the action of locally produced software, or computer viruses.

Personal computers are most often purchased because they provide users with immediate access to data and processing facilities. They are portable and are commonly carried by office staff from one location to another, or taken out of the building. Organizations may have several hundred personal computers in one building with no rigorous periodic checks on their location. The range of staff working on personal computers is so diverse that in many environments an attacker using a personal computer in-house would escape attention.

Mainframe computers are multi-user devices and the operating system must provide logical access controls to inhibit interference, accidental or malicious, between users. Personal computers were conceived, and are still largely operated, as single-user devices, and in general have no form of logical access control. This situation is changing with security devices such as encryptor boards (see chapter 3) and the more powerful generation of microcomputers. In many organizations, however, the unprotected IBM (or IBM-compatible) personal computer is likely to remain in use for some years; it may be reckoned that anyone with physical access to the personal computer and its storage media is guaranteed access to the data contained therein.

Personal computer operating systems, software, and associated manuals are freely available in the market place. Courses on personal computers are provided by schools, colleges, commercial training organizations, etc. Knowledge of personal computer operations is becoming as much a part of growing up as learning to drive a car. Thus while access to mainframe computers is both controlled by limited physical access and the degree of expertise required to read or modify data stored on-line or in backup tapes, the same is not true of personal computer data. An attacker who can gain physical access will undoubtedly have the necessary skill to exploit that access. Damage can also arise from the employee simply trying out their imperfect skills on an unattended machine. The universal availability of personal computers and their operating systems also means that stolen storage media can be read at will.

Most senior management now have a personal computer for use by themselves or their personal staff, and they use it for report-writing, databases, spreadsheets, etc. This situation is extremely advantageous to the attacker. The location of specific types of data: marketing plans, customer lists, technical data, etc. will correspond to the offices of the appropriate senior management. Once located, the data is likely to be in a relatively final format and up to date. The attacker will not have the problem of sifting through a mass of mainframe computer directories, checking files with cryptic titles, misleading titles, etc.

Theft of microcomputers, their components, and storage media is rife in many organizations (see chapter 3). The computer itself, its peripherals, internal components, and boxes of floppy diskettes are attractive prizes to the legions of amateur home-computer users. The danger is that the loss to the organization may lie in the data contained therein rather than the hardware itself. Thus a larcenous teenager may steal a box of floppy diskettes for their face value and cause a major security problem for an organization due to the loss or potential disclosure of corporate data.

1.7.4 Do backup procedures provide a guarantee of data integrity?

The protection offered by backup must be considered against the dangers: loss, disclosure, and modification. Backup is designed to provide insurance against loss of data. It will be effective for this purpose provided that:

- The backup copies are not subject to the same incidents that produced the loss of original data.
- The backup data is not lost or corrupted.
- The backup data replaces the data that was lost.
- The original data is replaced by the backup data after loss or corruption.

Clearly, backup media that is subjected to the same fire, burglary, flood damage, etc. as the original data will serve no useful purpose. It is therefore essential that the backup data is stored at some safe place that is physically isolated from the location of the original data. This is common practice with backup tapes and disks for large computer centres. However, in the case of personal computers the floppy diskettes or magnetic tape backup used to insure against mis-handling of floppy diskettes or hard disk crashes are commonly stored in insecure locations conveniently close to the personal computer. This practice is generally unsatisfactory and some consistent policy of secure storage for personal computer backup media should be applied. If the personal computer is linked to a network or mainframe then a convenient centralized backup service should be provided for the personal computer users.

Separation of the store for backup media from the computer centre involves a secure method of transit, storage, and retrieval for the media. Any damage to the media will probably escape detection until the backup media is required, and this is clearly too late. Cases of malicious damage to backup tapes have been recorded. The back-up media must be held in secure stores (e.g. fireproof safes) and guarded against flood, vandalism, theft, etc. A librarian must exercise a strict control on the movement of tapes and disks. The data used for processing will necessarily be different from that contained in the backup copy, except for the period immediately after the backup. Thus a backup copy only represents a recent history of the information asset; to be brought up to date it must be subjected to the processing, transactions, alterations, etc. as the data being backed up. It is therefore essential that a record of processing, transactions, and modifications be maintained in an environment as secure as that of the backup copy.

The procedure of taking and storing backup copies, etc. will serve no purpose if the original data is not replaced by the backup version after loss or corruption. This not only implies that the backup material must be protected during transit to the store and while in storage. It also means that the backup data must be safely transferred back into the computer or personal computer. When the original data is lost, then the only copy is the backup; if an accident occurs in transporting the backup from its secure environment to the computer, or in loading the backup data into the machine, then all is lost. It is therefore recommended that two backup copies be maintained, preferably in different secure environments. Extreme care must be taken when using backup in a recovery from a computer virus attack (see chapter 3) since the only backup copy may be damaged in a similar manner to the original data.

Backup copies not only provide no insurance against disclosure, they actually increase the risk. Data contained in backup copies will be as useful to the attacker as the original; the temporary loss of backup tapes or floppy diskettes may well go completely unnoticed. The secure environment in terms of safety for the backup copy must also therefore provide access controls against the potential attacker. Floppy diskettes stored in a manager's desk or cupboard could be easily accessed by a dishonest or disgruntled employee.

An attacker is unlikely to bother to modify backup data since it is usually overwritten on the occasion of the next backup. The function of backup copies in case of alteration to computer is to enable the modifications to be eliminated. Integrity controls on the computer data (e.g. file authentication blocks) provide a warning of illegal modifications. When such modifications are detected the situation is akin to that of loss or accidental corruption of data; the function of the backup copies is then to enable the original data to be returned to the computer system.

1.7.5 What are the threats associated with mainframe backup data?
The sources of danger to backup data are these:

- physical damage during storage arising from fire, flood, vandalism, terrorist attacks, etc;
- corruption during transit;
- theft.

Backup data is most urgently required when a major incident, e.g. fire, flood, or terrorist attack, hits a computer centre. It follows that the backup data must be protected from the effects of such an attack at the centre. Secure, fireproof safes may be used to hold the backup tapes/diskettes at the centre, and such safes have survived major

fires destroying a whole building. However, there may be a considerable delay in retrieving the safe from the debris of the building, and
it is generally safer to locate copies of backup media at a significant
distance from the computer centre. At these remote locations the
data should be stored in environments compatible with the requirements of the media in terms of temperature, humidity, magnetic
fields, etc.

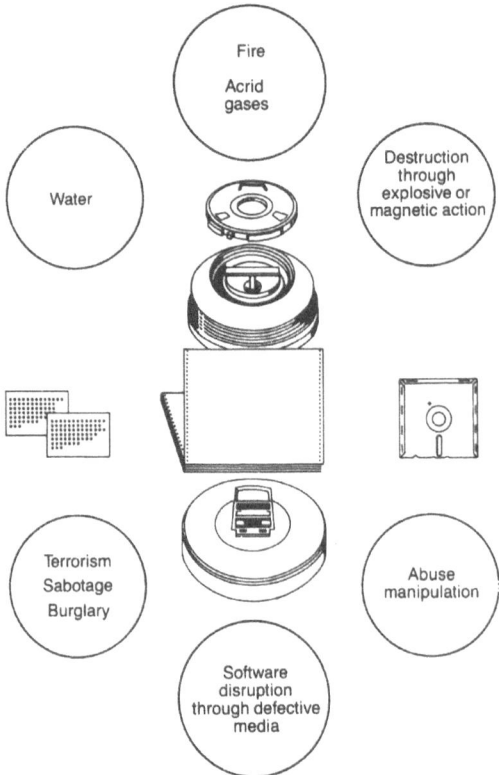

Fig. 1-11 Threats associated with computer centres and their data. No total
remedy can be provided for such wide-ranging threats. However, their
consequences can be mitigated. (*source*: Lampertz Systems)

The data held on backup media may be accidentally or maliciously
corrupted. There may be no evidence of that corruption until the
data is read back into the computer. It is therefore extremely
important that the personnel policy should seek to identify staff who
may be of doubtful loyalty (e.g. those under notice of dismissal) or
doubtful integrity and seek to isolate them from the backup media.
The backup media must be protected from malicious attacks during

storage, particularly those malicious attacks that produce no little external, physical evidence, e.g. exposure to strong magnetic fields, switching external labels on disks or tapes. Access to the backup data must therefore be restricted to trusted custodians.

The backup tapes or disks must similarly be protected during transit. If the backup media is damaged, either maliciously or accidentally, during transit to the store then the loss of backup data will remain undetected until it is required, and it will be too late to avert a disaster. The transit of backup data from the store after a major incident at the computer centre could present an ideal opportunity for a malicious attack, and a policy of duplication of backup media is normally recommended.

Backup media assumes a major value if the original data is lost and can then become a target for theft. Thus the movement of back-up tapes and disks must be strictly controlled by a library custodian. A ransom demand for hundreds of thousands of pounds sterling nearly succeeded because systems analysts were allowed to remove backup tapes from a store without authorization from senior management.

1.7.6 What forms of protection exist for mainframe on-line files?

There are three aspects to the protection of mainframe on-line files:

- log-on procedures,
- operating system and software packages,
- cryptography.

The operating system can only assume that the user who has logged on under a given user identity is actually the corresponding authorized person. All subsequent privileges will be granted to the logged-on identity on this basis. The first line of protection thus lies in access control. The problems of password management and the various techniques that may be employed to enhance access control (e.g. dynamic passwords) are discussed in chapter 3.

The security aspects of operating systems and software packages that interact with user files need to be considered in terms of the threats of accidental and malicious corruption of data. Operating system designers have paid careful attention to the problem of partitioning user work areas so that user input and command errors, program bugs, etc. do not spread from one user's data to that of another. Most good software packages will seek to minimize the impact of incorrect data input, e.g. good screen designs, opportunities for operators to examine and correct input data, reasonableness checks, etc. Hence in most well-designed large computer systems considerable care has been taken to minimize the accidental corruption of files. The problem of malicious corruption of data, however, still demands serious attention.

The operating system has the responsibility to control access to files according to the privileges associated with files and users. The security provided to users and files depends upon:

- the security features of the operating system,
- the use of security features by system programmers and users,
- flaws in the operating system.

Operating systems have been designed to provide a service to a population of users, and in recent years there has been an emphasis on providing an environment to a co-operating, communicating set of users. The ability to share files, exchange messages and data, exploit in-built software utilities, and provide users with comprehensive, user-friendly environments has been a feature of operating system design. Unix, in particular, was designed to serve a population of co-operating programmers and software developers. Such an operating system can, however, provide many avenues for the sophisticated attacker, particularly if the users do not fully appreciate its complexities.

Operating systems are extremely large and complex software packages. There are often many versions and updates of systems since such software is subject to continuous modification and improvement by the suppliers. The design procedures for such large software packages have been improving in recent years; the history of computing abounds with horror stories of operating system design disasters. However, it cannot be denied that flaws can still lurk in such large software systems, and such flaws may provide security loopholes to knowledgeable systems programmers, particularly those with direct experience of working with a particular installation. Information on such flaws, or potential security loopholes, may be provided by the manufacturers. However, such details can be easily overlooked by data processing staff operating under pressure. The security officer could well give serious consideration to the question of updating the expertise of data processing staff, and the measures designed to ensure that such updated expertise was made available to all apposite computing staff. A monopoly of such knowledge could well be a serious cause of concern in itself.

In recent years the security dangers inherent in operating systems have been recognized, and software systems are available to enhance the system security. These systems exercise sophisticated access control: access privileges may be associated with individual terminals and change according to time of day (e.g. access privileges are withdrawn outside normal working hours), users may be required to input passwords to access particular files, security logs (see section 1.8.3) may be maintained on all such accesses, etc. Thus the degree of security provided to on-line files will, in the first instance, depend upon the choice that was made at the time that the mainframe hardware and software was purchased. The degree to which the security of an operating system can be enhanced with security software packages will depend upon the existing hardware and software.

It is not unknown for the security of operating systems to be adversely affected by the failure of in-house system programmers to implement all the available security features. If the pressure placed on such staff was to get the system up and running in the minimum time, or on maximizing system performance, then there will have been a tendency to overlook such security features. Large operating systems are extremely complex software packages, and a detailed knowledge of all the inner complexities, particularly from a security viewpoint, will be limited to key computing personnel. The security officer may well pay serious attention to assurances provided by data processing staff on the implementation of operating system security features.

The privileges associated with individual files are allocated, either directly or on a default basis, by the user. Such privileges are usually granted to the user, members of a group, or any other user, and allow the person requesting access read, write, execute, and possibly append rights to the file. Users may deny themselves write privileges to avoid the possibility of accidental erasure or overwriting of a file. In some cases individual passwords may be required to access sensitive data. The effectiveness of these measures depends, of course, on the degree to which they are implemented by the user. If default privileges are always used, irrespective of the sensitivity of the file, then the security provisions provided by the software, system administrators, etc. will be of no avail. Moreover the user may well be unaware of the degree of access that is being granted to other users. It is clear therefore that adequate operating system training must be provided to all users. In particular those users with the facilities to create files must be made fully aware of the security procedures.

Highly sensitive data may require security precautions in addition to that provided by the operating system. Thus cryptography may be applied to secure against disclosure or modification. In the former case the whole contents of the file must be encrypted, but for security against modification the text may be in clear and a file authentication block, similar to a message authentication code (see section 1.5.16), is appended to the file. The file authentication block is checked each time that the file is accessed and thus the user is warned if any modification to file contents has been detected.

If cryptography is employed then the user must be guaranteed that the processes of encryption and decryption are performed in a secure manner (see section 1.5.30) and some form of key management (see section 1.5.31) will be required. The use of cryptography to guard against disclosure may, however, provide no guarantee against illegal modification (see section 1.5.16).

1.7.7 Can databases be made secure?

In general terms the question of database security is extremely complex. After all large databases were designed to provide answers to ad hoc queries from a wide variety of end-users. The design of efficient systems to provide such facilities has been a major consideration of computer scientists for over two decades. Having designed such systems, one is then faced with the problem of guaranteeing the denial of some categories of information to some end-users, who may well have authority to access other categories. In the most general case this security problem may well be insoluble with existing computer hardware/software systems.

Database systems comprise large, complex software packages, termed database management systems (DBMS) which interface the user and the operating system. The function of the DBMS is to analyse the user's query, call upon the operating system to access the file or files holding the relevant data, extract the required records from the files, and then use that information to form the answer to the user's query.

The accidental corruption of databases is a major concern in their design and operation, and database software is designed to cope with a wide variety of dangers, such as simultaneous updating by two users or system crashes that leave input transactions only partially completed. The problems of malicious corruption by system programmers or users with 'write' privileges is a matter for concern to system administrators and security officers. The security packages mentioned above can also be employed to protect the data files, under a DBMS, from illegal access by other programs running alongside the DBMS in a VM environment. A strict policy of access control and limitation of privileges to update databases must be applied. This is a matter of extreme importance if data can be uploaded from personal computers (see chapter 3).

Issues of security, particularly those concerning disclosure, that need to be considered in relation to databases are:

- Can the user bypass the DBMS and interact directly with the operating system?
- Does the system serve only one class of user, or is it required to determine whether or not to pass information according to the user's access privileges? (See chapter 3.)

• Is there a problem of inference control? (See section 1.7.9.)

1.7.8 Can the DBMS guarantee security of the database?

This question is most easily answered in terms of those situations in which the DBMS alone certainly cannot guarantee security of the database:

• when the user can bypass the DBMS and interact directly with the operating system;
• when the DBMS is required to perform complex accessing functions to data with varying degrees of sensitivity and serving a population of users with ranges of security clearance;
• when using statistical databases.

If the user can bypass the DBMS then the security of the database becomes entirely dependent upon that of the operating system. The problem then reverts to that of gaining access to on-line files (see section 1.7.6).

The security of complex multilevel databases has been the subject of considerable research. Most DBMS software is extremely complex; if security restrictions are applied then the complexity increases sharply. In this case it is virtually impossible to give cast-iron guarantees that no security loopholes exist, or that Trojan Horses cannot be inserted into the DBMS.

In some cases software filters are added to the database to separate out the security function from the normal access functions of the DBMS. In this case cryptography may be employed to give an indelible security classification to data. Such a technique is known as 'integrity locking' or 'spray paint'. The database contents may be protected from disclosure by encryption, but this technique has its own problems and dangers (see section 1.5.24). In particular if the security function is to be separated from the DBMS then the DBMS can only deal with plaintext data when it is extracting the required items from file records. If the DBMS is, however, dealing with plaintext data then Trojan Horses may be inserted and classified information leaked to unauthorized users via covert channels.

Statistical databases provide security problems since such databases hold detailed information about individual entities but should only answer queries about populations of users. For example a census database may hold financial information on the population of a state. A user may be given access to the average salary of a given town but should not be able to determine the salary of a given individual in that town. If inference control procedures (see section 1.7.9) are not applied then it may be possible for a user to develop a string of well-planned questions which eventually provide detailed information on an individual.

If we return to the original question – can a DBMS guarantee security? – then the answer is a highly qualified yes. Given the right environment for the DBMS, and severe restrictions upon the range of data and users, then databases can effectively provide users with schema that effectively provides each user with an individual database, containing only that information within the user's aegis of privilege.

If the database is guaranteed to be read only, then the security dangers are substantially reduced both from the aspects of corruption and disclosure (see section 1.5.25).

1.7.9 What is inference control?

Inference control is a technique applied for the security of statistical databases. In such databases highly detailed information may be held about individuals, e.g. census data, market research information, etc. The database operators may provide a service to research workers but, at the same time, be under an obligation not to reveal detailed information concerning a particular individual held on the database. For example, the database may legitimately be used to provide socio-economic information on average salary levels in an area but should not disclose the wages of a particular individual.

An obvious rule might be that no query will be accepted if it refers to an individual. However, careful questioning can overcome this restriction. If it is known that a particular town has only one female baker then questions on the average salary of all bakers in the town, followed by a second query on the average salary of male bakers in the town, would provide sufficient data for the female baker's salary to be computed.

Inference control techniques can be extremely complex, they may serious affect the performance of the database for legitimate queries, and they can lead to distortion of the statistical data provided for legitimate queries.

1.8 Monitoring and Audit Trails

1.8.1 What is the role of monitoring in information security?

The purposes of monitoring are deterrence, early warning, diagnosis, evidence, and correction.

- The visible presence of a monitoring system will act as a deterrent to attacks and to experimentation on security controls.
- An effective monitoring system will not only provide early warning of experimentation with the security controls, or changes in

the security environment, but can also allow a database of 'normal activity' to be developed. Such a database can give a model against which future patterns of activity can be judged; aberrations from 'normal' patterns may provide an early indication of security attacks.

- Effective security logs and audit trails are essential in the diagnosis of suspected attacks.
- The security logs and audit trails can be used as evidence against an attacker.
- The post mortem of an attack will require details of the mode of attack so that the security system may be strengthened.

1.8.2 What forms can security monitoring take?

There are essentially two forms of monitoring – physical and logical. The physical monitoring may be categorized as:

- physical environment of the processing hardware: fire and smoke detection, ingress of water, etc. (see chapter 3);
- access control: logging of access to computer rooms, storage areas, etc. (see section 1.5.1);
- personnel: monitoring behaviour patterns, changes in personal circumstances, etc. (see section 1.3.5).

Logical monitoring is concerned more directly with access and use by local and remote users of the computer system. It comprises three major types of monitoring:

- monitoring of attempts to log on to the system over public telephone lines;
- security logs of access to the computer system and information within the system;
- audit trails (see section 1.8.10).

Various port protection devices can provide a first line of defence against telephone intrusion and in this case the attack events can be monitored before the hacker ever gains access to the computer itself.

Once access has been gained to the system there will be two classes of security monitoring: security logs and audit trails. Note that there may also be some form of accounting monitoring so that users can be charged for their use of processing resources.

The function of security logging is to supervise the access to the computer system itself and the sensitive information within it. Such accesses are, of course, attributed to the identity associated with a particular user. If an attacker can masquerade as a legitimate user, e.g. by stealing or guessing a password, then the security log will assign all associated actions to the nominal user. This aspect of monitoring should encourage legitimate users to enhance their password discipline (see chapter 3).

The function of an audit trail is to assist in the post hoc examination of events that led to a particular situation. In general the data collected should enable the path of an event (e.g. from input data to file update) to be accurately reconstructed.

1.8.3 What are the important considerations in the development of a security logging system?
The major considerations in the development of the logging system are:

- restriction to system penetration attacks (see section 1.8.4),
- monitoring level (see section 1.8.5),
- protection of security logging data (see section 1.8.6),
- processing of security logs (see section 1.8.8),
- reporting and actions.

1.8.4 What type of attack is the security log concerned with?
The computer may be misused in one of two ways – conventional fraud or system penetration. An attacker may perpetrate a fraud or deal in confidential information while making only legitimate use of the computer (see chapter 7). For example, a manager might commit a conventional fraud involving only data within his access privileges, and performing associated calculations on a spreadsheet. In this case the use of the computer is only incidental to the attack; it could have been committed if the data had been stored in a filing cabinet and the computations performed on a pocket calculator.

It should not be a function of security logs to deal with such a situation; to do so would demand exhaustive data dealing with all legitimate actions and place prohibitive demands upon the computer and security systems.

The second type of misuse, system penetration, arises when the computer is a fundamental component of the attack. In this case the attackers will seek to misuse the system so as to gain access to information not within their aegis of privilege. The security logging system should be designed to counteract this form of attack by detecting attempts to access files etc. beyond the user's level of privilege and logging experimentation with the operating system commands, and by monitoring unusual uses of the computer, e.g. attempted accesses outside normal operating periods, excessive use of computer facilities, etc.

1.8.5 At what level should the data be logged?
Whenever a computer system is considered, the object described is essentially only a model of reality, or an abstraction of the true system. An attack will succeed if the attacker can operate at a lower level of abstraction than that guarded by the security system.

To illustrate this point consider the tricks played by illusionists. If the audience operates with a model consisting of a box only large enough to hold one person, and one woman (the illusionist's assistant), then the head protruding from one end of the box and the feet from the other must belong to the same person. Any attempt to saw the box in half and separate the two ends must therefore cause irreparable damage. The abstraction employed by the illusionist, however, comprises two boxes and two women.

In computing terms the model employed by normal legitimate end-users is that of a processing system which responds to a set of commands described in the operating system manual. In fact, large operating systems may be implemented in an imperfect manner or they may contain design errors which provide the skilled user with a different model. Since the security manager cannot guarantee that the system available to users is exactly that described by the data processing personnel, it is necessary to set the monitoring at a lower level of abstraction. For example, the action of accessing a file may be given by a single operating system command. This command will actually cause a sequence of lower-level actions, transparent to the user, to achieve the desired result. If the attacker can misuse other operating system commands to produce the same sequence of lower-level actions, then that illegitimate action will only be detected if the monitoring is performed on the lower-level actions.

There is, of course, a limit to the depth of level that can be sensibly monitored; eventually all computer instructions cause operations at a hardware level, but any attempt to monitor such events would not only seriously degrade the performance of the computer system, it would also provide a mass of detail that would be virtually impossible to correlate to the actions of users.

The selection of the monitoring level will necessarily involve a compromise between operating at a level of abstraction below that of the expected attack, and that of producing an excessive processing task for the security data. The detailed selection of monitoring level is clearly a matter for experienced computer personnel, but the security manager needs to be aware of the implications of the chosen scheme. The level chosen will effectively separate potential attackers into two classes; those who will be compelled to operate at a level subject to effective monitoring, and those who will have the expertise and access privileges to operate below the monitoring level. The security manager will need to be assured that the latter class comprises only a small and well-defined set of trusted personnel.

1.8.6 *What protection needs to be afforded to the security logged data?*

The logged data itself is an obvious target for the attacker. If it can be modified or destroyed then evidence of the attack will be lost to security personnel. If the audit data is stored on the same computer as that being monitored then it is vulnerable to the attacker who, it is presumed, has the capability to access files illegally. Even if the security log file is given a very high level of access security there exists the danger that the data can be modified by logical access (see section 1.5.3) or destroyed by a physical attack on the storage unit holding the data.

An alternative approach is to collect the data on a small computer dedicated to that security task. The 'security computer' can then be provided with more stringent physical and logical access controls than those possible with the multi-user system. In this case the remaining danger is that the communication lines between the two computers could simply be cut, or the attacker could mount a 'spoofing' attack in which an attacker's computer replaced the 'security computer', thus giving the main computer no indication of the loss of security log data.

The philosophy of guarding the security log file is thus similar to that of selecting the monitoring level (see section 1.8.5). It may be impossible to guard against all conceivable attacks, but any feasible attack should be restricted to a well-defined set of personnel with a high level of expertise and access privilege.

1.8.7 *What data should be logged for security purposes?*

The data collected for security logs should be that which indicates direct, illegal activity, or experimentation with controls which is likely to be a prelude to system penetration. In general the data collected and analysed may lead to one of two errors:

- a false indication of an attack,
- a failure to indicate an attack.

The second type of error is, of course, far more serious. In general the monitoring data should act as a filter, removing from consideration a large number of legitimate transactions and thus indicating a set of operations containing all security violations and, necessarily, some legitimate transactions.

One approach is to classify all normal transactions and then select logging data which does not conform to this normal pattern. A second approach is to postulate a number of security violations and collect monitoring data which is indicative of such transactions. In general the first technique is likely to highlight a large number of perfectly legitimate but slightly unusual transactions while the second will fail to indicate attacks other than those postulated.

The choice of some security logged data is self-evident, e.g. accesses to the system, accesses to privileged data, attempts to access the system and files without the necessary level of privilege, legitimate and illegitimate requests to browse through directories, failures to reconcile MACs, etc. All such events should be logged together with the user's identity and time/date. At log-on time all users should be informed of the time/date of their last log-on and of any incorrect entries of passwords, etc. This will forewarn users of any accesses gained by lost or guessed passwords, and of any experiments by hackers to determine passwords by experimentation.

Other features of security logs have been postulated:

- file sizes: to detect attacks by which a user attempts to bring down a system by occupying all available disk space;
- time of use: to catch hackers operating at the weekend, evenings, etc., as well as authorized users logging on at unusual times to abuse the system in some way or to experiment with security controls;
- CPU time usage on application programs: to detect excessive processing. Such activity might indicate applications browsing through a large mass of organization data, or attempts to overload the system, reduce response times for legitimate users etc.;
- memory usage: this test has proved to be useful in detecting attacks. It is not under the direct control of the attacker and it can indicate intensive processing activity;
- transmission speeds: to detect attacks from users having slow-speed terminals (300 baud) when the majority of traffic is at 1200 or 2400 baud.

1.8.8 How should security logs be processed?

Security logs will necessarily consist of a large mass of data relating, in the vast majority of cases, to perfectly legitimate usage. This data must be processed in such a manner that a high proportion of legitimate actions can be filtered out, thus allowing more detailed consideration to be given to data which may be indicative of attacks or experimentation towards attacks. One such approach is to develop a model of normal usage and to eliminate transactions conforming to this pattern. Such a model needs to be developed over a period of time and to be updated according to evolving patterns of usage and to sudden changes in the environment, e.g. the installation of terminals at a new site.

In addition the security logs, possibly after the filtering process mentioned above, need to be examined to detect patterns of activity which are consistent with attacks or experimental preludes to an attack. This examination might be performed by a manual review of the logged data or it may be possible to develop software to search for such patterns.

The selection of data to be monitored and the methods of processing it must be chosen to be compatible with each other. There is no point in logging a mass of data that cannot reasonably be processed and examined, nor is there any point in performing sophisticated processing upon an inadequate quantity of logged data.

The security log will also be required for post mortem examination and possibly for evidence against an attacker. The log needs to be organized so that the relevant information can be extracted quickly from the archives; the material stored needs to be sufficiently comprehensive for this purpose but on the other hand it must be such that it can be reasonably processed and examined for post mortem purposes. The organization's legal advisers should also be consulted on the collection and storage of the log if it is likely that it will be presented as evidence in legal proceedings.

1.8.9 How should the information from security logs be used?
The security log performs two distinct functions, to provide warning of a potential attack and to provide post mortem evidence of an actual attack. It is therefore essential that the security log be subjected to a regular examination and analysis (see section 1.8.8). The organization security policy should specify the manner in which security logs are collected, processed, examined, and reported. Misuse of the system by staff needs to be promptly reported to appropriate management to discourage experimentation, misuse of computing resources, etc. at an early stage; such a policy is consistent with good personnel procedures (see chapter 7) and it serves to emphasize the managerial stance on security.

In some cases there may be a temptation to refrain from informing staff of detected security violations, on the basis that they may later provide evidence of other, more serious wrongdoing. All such procedures should be considered in relation to advice from legal and personnel staff on the implications from the viewpoint of staff morale and possible allegations of entrapment.

1.8.10 What is an audit trail?
A series of definitions exists for audit trails in computing:

- a set of records that collectively provide documentary evidence of processing used to aid tracing from original transactions forward to related records and reports, and/or backwards from re-

cords and reports to their component source transactions (US Department of Defense);
- a chronological record of system activities which is sufficient to enable the reconstruction, review, and examination of the sequence of environments and activities surrounding or leading to each event in the path of a transaction from its inception to output of final results (FIPS);
- a clerical or automated method for tracing the transactions affecting the contents of a record;
- in banking, the ability to view what the system has completed in the past.

In general the purpose of an audit trail is to enable the current file records to be traced to the input data that caused them to assume those values. Audit trails can provide some degree of defence against the anonymity of computer data; unlike handwritten ledgers, computer data leaves no trace of changed digits or the hand-writing of a forger. Thus the trail data can include the identity of the user making the transaction its corresponding time/date.

The contents of audit trails will usually be decided by internal and external auditors. However, audit trails may also be used to provide some defence in circumstances where the accuracy of organizational data has been questioned. Information held by or supplied by an organization may well have been subjected to significant processing; if the accuracy of data is under question, e.g. as a result of a complaint relating to personal data (see chapter 7), then the question of negligence may arise. In some cases the organization may have accepted data from an external source in good faith and processed it accurately. If the final form of the information is inaccurate, due to an error in the input data, then the organization will wish to trace the information back to its source and demonstrate that it took all reasonable precautions to maintain the accuracy of the data. A set of audit trails will enable such tracing back to be undertaken.

1.8.11 What protection should be afforded to audit trails?
An audit trail is an obvious target for attack by anyone undertaking a computer fraud. If the audit trail can be undetectably modified then the forger who has access to the original data is granted the means to cover the trail of the fraud. Audit trails can be protected by authentication (see section 1.5.16) such that any modification is subsequently detectable. However this safeguard does not provide a defence against malicious erasure of audit trail data. In general such data should be held in an appropriate secure file, i.e. an on-line file with a high-privilege access classification or on a separate secure computer system.

1.9 Military and Commercial Security

1.9.1 Introduction
The military have a long tradition of concern with the confidentiality of their information and the budgets to protect their information. The military also make extensive use of complex computing/ communications systems. It is therefore not surprising that a significant amount of research and development effort has been expended by the US Government on theoretical aspects of data security. In particular, results have been published on formal models of data security and the security of software and operating systems.

The Bell–La Padula model describes a theoretical approach to rules for the protection of confidentiality of information; the model proposes mandatory rules for classifying, reading, and writing information, such that users are unable to gain access to information beyond their aegis of privilege, or to leak information to unauthorized users.

The security of software and in particular, operating systems, is described in a US Department of Defense document, the Orange Book. This document gives specifications for classes of secure operating systems, i.e.

- Class D systems, which have been formally evaluated but fail to meet the requirements of higher classification levels;
- Class C systems, which meet the requirements for discretionary access control;
- Class B systems, which satisfy requirements for mandatory access control;
- Class A systems, which provide no more functionality than Class B systems but which have been designed to permit formal verification of the security principles of the system.
- Within each system there are subcategories, e.g. Class C1, Class C2.

An essential feature of these systems is the evaluation procedure in which the operating system is subject to an extensive, and expensive, examination by an accredited body.

These developments were until recently of virtually no interest to the commercial world. Much of the research effort was directed to a highly theoretical aspect of computer science, concerned with the formal proof that program code satisfied the specifications for software. However, major computer manufacturers were involved in such military research effort. The increasing concern of the commercial sector on data security matters has now led such firms to bridge the gap between military and commercial approaches to data security.

Manufacturers are promoting operating systems with various Class C and Class B classifications.

1.9.2 Should an organization invest in a secure operating system to enhance its data security?

It is important to differentiate between two classes of secure operating systems: Class A, Class B, and Class C systems on the one hand, and proprietary software packages such as RACF, ACF/2, and CA-Topsecret on the other. The former are designed to meet the requirements for certain levels of access control (e.g. discretionary access control, mandatory access control), while packages such as RACF serve to provide security functions within an operating system used in a commercial/industrial environment.

There is an important distinction between the focus of data security effort in military and commercial systems. Much of the research effort for military systems has been directed to the problem of data confidentiality, whereas the commercial world will tend to place data integrity as its highest priority. Of course, military systems are concerned with the integrity of their data, and commercial systems are likewise concerned with the confidentiality of much of their data; nevertheless the formal models developed for military systems may not provide a good theoretical basis for commercial systems.

The decision on the purchase of a secure operating system must therefore depend upon the data security requirements of the application area for which it is to be purchased. If the prime requirement is for data confidentiality then an Orange Book classification is appropriate. If the security policy on such confidential data is based upon a discretionary access control policy then a Class C classification is adequate. If, however, the data and users are classified within a mandatory access control policy then a Class B system will be required.

1.9.3 Does a formal model exist for the security of commercial systems?

An interesting approach to the extension of formal models to commercial systems has been proposed by Clark and Wilson. This model was designed to meet the specification that no user, 'even if authorized, would be able to modify the data items in such a way that the assets or accounting records of the company could be lost or corrupted'.

The philosophy of the model was that certain categories of information were to be separated out for special treatment. This category of information had valid states which corresponded to an accounting situation in which all the books were balanced. A category of integrity verification processes would check if a given set of data were in a valid state, i.e. equivalent to the action of an auditor. Subcategories of this data could only be processed by certified programs, and such processing would always transform the data from one valid state to another. In accounting terms a transaction could only be performed in such a way that if the books were balanced before the transaction then they would be balanced after the transaction. Only authorized users would be permitted to execute processing of specified transactions on specified data items. This rule provides for a separation of duties, so that no individual would have sufficient privilege to perform the complete set of transactions necessary to perpetrate a fraud.

It was recognized in the model that no system can, in itself, differentiate between fraudulent and legitimate processing. However, the system required certification by duly appointed security staff. The certification involves statements that:

- a given section of program code, if applied to a given category of data, would confirm or deny that the data was in a valid state;
- a given section of program code, if applied to a given category of valid data, would transform that data in another valid state;
- a given user, with authority to execute specified processes on specified data items, would be unable to perpetrate a fraud without the collusion of other authorized users.

With this type of certification the system applies enforcement rules, similar to mandatory access control. The enforcement rules do not permit unauthorized users from being given access to processes, i.e. there is no mechanism for a security officer to exercise discretion and grant access to an unauthorized user. The data items can only be processed by authorized programs, and these authorized programs can only be executed by users with authority relating both to the programs and data items. Additional enforcement rules ensure that processes are applied sequentially to data and that one process must terminate before the next commences. Systems to ensure that processes were only performed in a given sequence are also required, see figure 1-12.

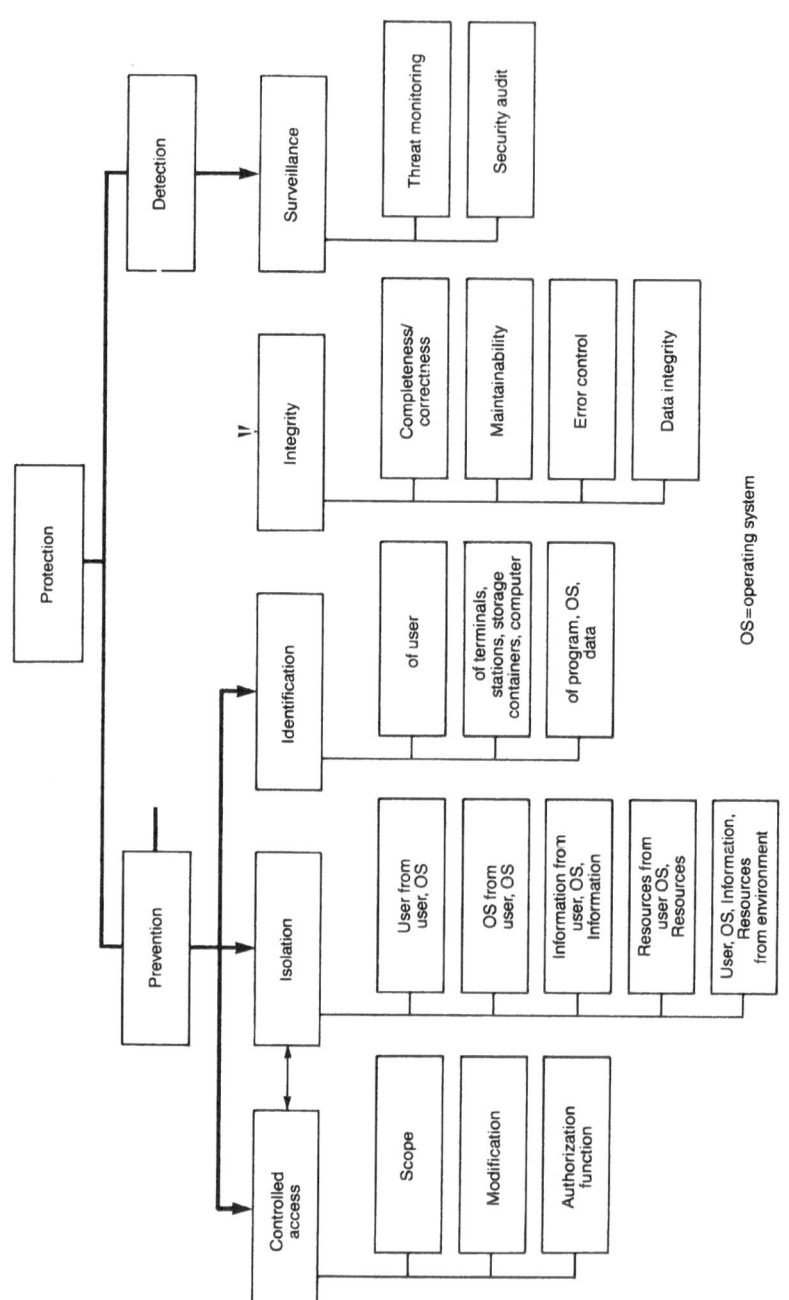

Fig. 1-12 Elements of secure operating systems

2 Computer Security Risk Analysis and Management

M. Shain and A. Anderson

2.1 Overview

2.1.1 Introduction
This chapter deals with the techniques and tools associated with:

- evaluation of the effectiveness of existing computing security measures;
- estimation of the cost to the organization if current defences are inadequate;
- selection of appropriate, cost-effective countermeasures.

Risk analysis is a familiar concept in business as well as in everyday life. The fundamental problem is universal: how much should I pay now to reduce the possibility of some hypothetical event costing me dearly? Which one of several possible outlays reduces the likelihood most?

The problem may be as simple as deciding whether to take out comprehensive insurance on a very old car, or as far-reaching as a proposal to move a manufacturing plant from one country to another. Clearly, individual judgment of the problem's context is important: how likely is it that the car will be involved in an accident?; is the destination country likely to have future political problems? Both situations involve guesswork. The only differences are those of scale – the number of different factors affecting the guess and the amount of information available to the guesser concerning the behaviour of these factors over time and in concert.

2.1.2 Risk Analysis
When you take a risk, you are betting on the likelihood of some

outcome in the future. What you risk is loss – of actual or potential income, of reputation, or of any other asset. In business terms, all of these mean loss of money. People take risks when, in their opinion, there is a reasonable chance that some unpleasant outcome (a car crash or a civil war, in the previous examples) will *not* take place. Thus, they decide not to tie up assets in hedging their bets.

Whatever the benefits in taking risks, it is had at the expense of safety. The task of risk analysis is to discover:

- How much is being risked;
- How dangerous the environment is;
- How much should be paid for safety;
- What the best level of safety is that can be obtained for a given level expenditure;
- At what point it becomes cost-ineffective to spend more on safety;
- How reliable selected measures of safety are;
- Where security should be introduced;

In the context of this chapter, the 'risk' of concern is the risk to a computing resource, whether this is a computer, a network, or both. Organizations are more reliant than ever on their information systems and computing resource to the point where many organizations would be ruined if the resource were damaged in some way. In the context of computer security, risk may be defined as the probability that a specific threat will successfully find a vulnerability in the system's defences (or safeguards), so as to cause a specific kind of damage to some object in the computing resource.

2.2 Risk Analysis and Management: an Overview

2.2.1 What are the terms used in CSRAM?
This definition contains several terms with a 'standard' meaning in Computer Security Risk Analysis and Management (CSRAM):

- risk analysis (see section 2.2.2);
- threat, vulnerability, and safeguard;
- computing resource (see section 2.2.4);
- security auditing (see section 2.2.5);
- risk management (see section 2.2.6).

2.2.2 What is the purpose of risk analysis?
Risk analysis is a technique for reducing the overall level of exposure of a computer centre or network to a wide variety of threats. The objective is to enable management to balance the cost

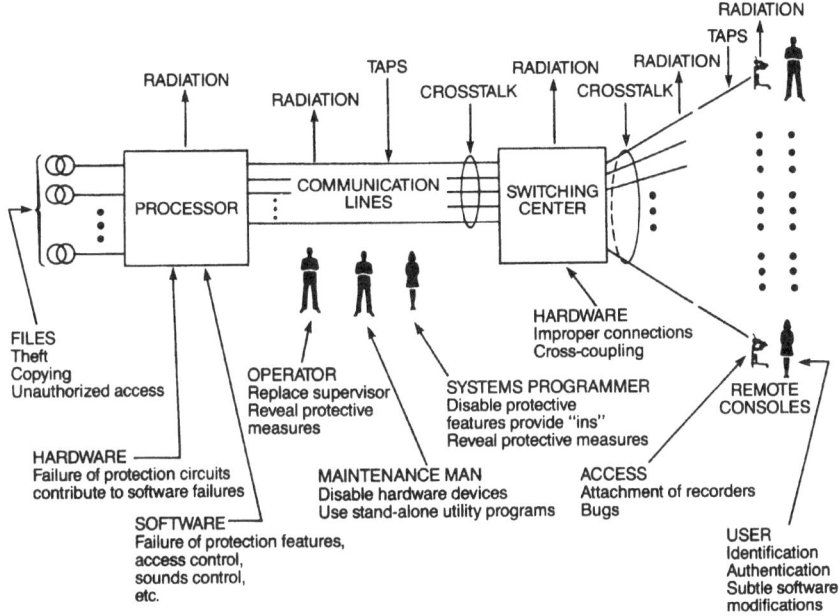

Fig. 2-1 Some of the many possible threats to the security of a computer system. (*source*: *Journal of Computers and Security*)

of proposed security countermeasures against a realistic estimate of the risk impact.

Risk analysis should not be considered to be a once-and-for-all activity. If possible, it should be performed at the design phase of a system or subsystem, since security measures integrated within a system at the outset are more effective than those superposed at a later stage.

2.2.3 What is being analysed in risk analysis?

In this context the analysis is directed at the risk to the organization's computing resource. Organizations are more reliant than ever on their information systems and computing resource, to the point where many organizations would be ruined if the resource were damaged in some way.

In the context of computer security, the risk relevant to this discussion may be defined as the probability that a specific threat will successfully find a vulnerability in the defences (or safeguards) so as to cause a specific kind of damage to some object in the computing resource. A threat is defined as any circumstance or event with the potential to cause harm to the system in the form of destruction, disclosure, or modification of data, or denial of service. A vulnerability is a weakness in the physical layout, organization, procedures, personnel, management, administration, hardware, or software that can be exploited to cause harm to the system. A safeguard (or countermeasure) is a protective measure designed to mitigate against the effect of a vulnerability; it may also serve to reduce the frequency of occurrence of a particular threat.

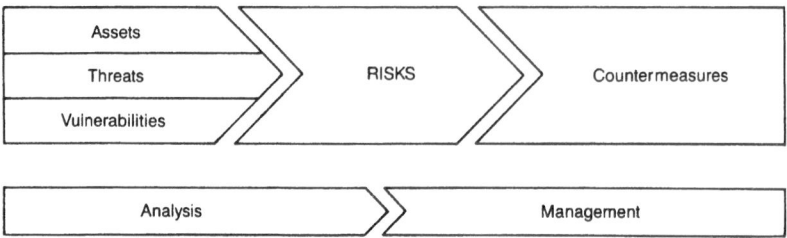

Fig. 2-2 Traditional simple risk analysis model

2.2.4 What is covered by the term 'computing resource'?

'Computing resource' is a blanket term covering the collection of people, procedures, operations, programs, hardware devices, files, input data, output results, networks, or databases that support the computerized part of an organization. It is convenient to think of a company's computing resources as a collection of assets subdivided into physical and information assets.

Clearly the computing resource covers a myriad of components, and a consideration of each one would be a daunting task. In practice, however, risk analysis is less formidable than it may at first appear, because:

- In most cases operational guidelines already exist and CSRAM examines the adherence to these guidelines.
- Only a proportion of the functions of the computing resource are of crucial importance to organizational objectives, and CSRAM determines these functions.
- CSRAM supplies heuristic and common-sense guidelines that reveal crucial deficiencies early, reducing the scope of later analysis.
- Analysers can specify the systems of interest: CSRAM techniques can be applied globally, or to a particular information system or operation determined by the client.

2.2.5 What is the difference between risk analysis and security auditing?

The terms 'risk analysis', 'risk assessment', 'security auditing', and 'security evaluation' are often used interchangeably by non-auditing personnel. Certainly they all address the same problem. Security auditing, however, is more strictly applied to the examination of how well the organization adheres to existing auditing controls (computing and otherwise). Risk analysis or assessment includes in its scope an evaluation of those auditing controls themselves, set against an array of possible threat scenarios. In short, security auditing implies that the necessary levels of safety are already known; this may well not be the case.

2.2.6 How does risk management relate to risk analysis?

A risk analysis project performed through to completion, as described below, represents the first stage of risk management. Its successful completion ensures that risks have been identified, their impacts assessed, and their likelihood documented. Risk analysis recognizes that:

- Security procedures are costly and often involve some compromises with company profits, user convenience, and turnaround times.
- Complete security, whether of a computer system or any other business activity, is never attainable. Acceptable levels of risk must therefore be postulated.
- Computer systems are complex, and many of their aspects, from the database to application programs, are subject to risks.
- Of the many, varied hazards involved, some are self-evident, others are obscure.

The main purpose in undertaking a risk analysis is to assess the potential losses that could occur from intentional or accidental events. It therefore underpins an effective risk management program by providing the basis for risk management decisions. The question of which risks may be tolerated and which must be addressed is complex and must be considered in the light of corporate goals and budget constraints – parameters of no relevance to risk analysis. In the overall risk management process suitable steps have to be taken to reduce the risks to a level acceptable to the client, and methods implemented to ensure that the risk remains at that level.

2.2.7 Where is risk management used?

Risk management, in its formal context as an element of management science, has provided the basis for underwriting decisions in the insurance industry. Underwriters have access to well-established tables on the frequency of untoward events within a defined community, e.g. fires in certain types of buildings, or crime statistics for breaking-and-entry in certain districts. Using these historical data, and given a large population of policy holders, underwriters can estimate with a considerable degree of accuracy the expected total loss to their policy holders from these untoward events within a specified time. This enables the insurance company to set premium rates so that the expected loss is shared proportionately among their policy holders, and at the same time ensuring that the company makes a reasonable profit.

In 1980, the US federal government, conscious of the importance of cost-effectively protecting its computer and information assets, mandated that these assets should be subject to a risk analysis at each of its computer centres. This directive provided the impetus for applying the techniques used in insurance to the computer industry at large.

2.2.8 What is involved in risk management?

In spite of variations in terminology, individual examples of risk analysis/management methodologies all adhere to the following paradigm. Risk management consists of:

- identification of the different information assets represented by the computing resource;
- identification of the importance of each to the organization;
- determination of the current level of risk in the environment;
- a decision on how much reduction in risk the organization requires;
- implementation of the safeguards or countermeasures that reduce the risk to the required level.

Once the hard work of setting up a 'risk-conscious' organization is complete, it can be managed with minimal effort by timely reviews. This cyclic maintenance is summarized in figure 2-3.

Over time, the list of assets and/or the costs associated with losing an asset will change. However, most organizations do not have a very volatile asset base in information technology: hardware and software are planned and acquired on an annual basis rather than weekly or monthly. In any case it is far easier to make adjustments to the overall model represented above (i.e. to evaluate the incremental effect of new hardware and software) than to repeat the entire exercise from scratch. Thus it can be seen that the risk model itself represents a valuable collection of information for the organization, as long as it is kept up to date by regular reviews.

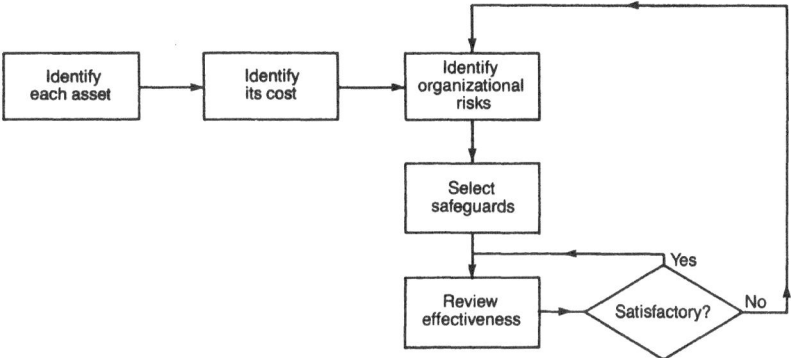

Fig. 2-3   The cyclic nature of risk maintenance

2.2.9 What is the difference between CSRAM and conventional business risk management?

Most management decisions involve the assumption of risk. Indeed if there were no risks involved in decision-making there would be no need for managers. However, the biggest problem in computer security risk management, as opposed to conventional business risk management, lies in the fact that there are far more empirical data available to reduce uncertainty in the latter.

The reasons for this are obvious. Recognition of the computer resource as an asset in its own right is a comparatively recent advance, whereas the theory of business risk has existed as long as business itself. It is comparatively straightforward, for example, to identify assets and potential losses when these are recognizable objects such as buildings, stock, or investments. Likewise, businesses generally have access to, or can develop the probability distributions governing factors in the typical business environment, e.g. demand, labour costs, seasonal variations, etc.

Business can, therefore, in principle draw on the distilled experience of many similar organizations as well as detailed internal statistics in its conventional risk analyses. Analysis of computer security risk has few comparable aids. Actuarial tables relating to the life-expectancy of systems are not readily available, nor are probability distributions of expected level of computer fraud versus type of business. Organizations may be reluctant to disclose their computer fraud losses, whereas they must legally publish ordinary business statements.

Thus, although CSRAM uses ordinary risk analysis techniques where applicable, and empirical data where available, the state of play at this point is that it must draw heavily on techniques for managing uncertainty and for manipulating value judgments rather than figures.

2.2.10 Can CSRAM be performed in the absence of detailed actuarial data?

It must be recognized that the alternative to performing CSRAM with inadequate statistical data is no analysis at all. Further, any forecasting is uncertain, and the key to success often lies not just in the willingness to accept uncertainty, but in the ability to recognize and qualify the elements of risks so that they can be treated in a systematic manner.

CSRAM involves guesses, but these are informed guesses guided by the knowledge possessed by the owners of the information asset in question, and all guesswork is performed in the same context – that of efficient and profitable business objectives. The risk analysis techniques described in this chapter are similar to all forecasting inasmuch as they begin by creating a representation of some aspect of reality – in this case, the security aspects of the organization. This representation is not always expressed in mathematical or statistical terms, but is nonetheless a model. (Most security risk analysis models are semantic rather than scientific; the model can then be easily manipulated in terms of its behaviour when various environmental factors are changed.) Risk management (including computer security risk management) is no more, or less, than an integral part of general organization and project management. It deals with the identification, measurement and control of uncertain events.

2.2.11 Summary

This section makes the case for treating computer security risk analysis as another technique in rational business management, one severely neglected and undervalued in today's information dependent world. Its lack of 'scientific' theory and models arises mostly because the information technology development has left conventional business risk management methodologies behind. Nevertheless the risk of adopting these approaches is less than the risk of ignoring the problem.

Risk analysis is most cost-effective if it is undertaken at the design stage of a new system: the security countermeasures so identified may then be most readily incorporated. However, it must be remembered that these countermeasures may add to the overall cost of the project, and so it is necessary to present clearly to management the case for spending more money. The methodology for this is discussed in sections 2.4 and 2.5.

2.3 Conventional Computer Security Risk Analysis and Management

2.3.1 What are the stages involved in CSRAM?
The basic processes of CSRAM are:

- identifying and valuing assets,
- identifying threats,
- identifying vulnerabilities,
- relating safeguards to vulnerabilities,
- determining the cost-effectiveness of proposed safeguards.

2.3.2 How are computer assets identified and valued?
As defined previously (see section 2.2.4), an information asset is some component of the overall computing resource. CSRAM has to find some means of categorizing these components so that the cost or impact associated with their loss or compromise can be estimated. In fact, it is a method of grouping objects that are unlike in kind, so that they may be treated by the same methodology. For example, a communications processor is an asset in the traditional sense: its replacement cost is known, its mean time between failures is also (probably) known, so conventional methods can be used to determine the cost of its loss as an asset in its own right. But this does not accurately depict its significance in information terms. To the organization at large, the asset is not the processor itself but rather the information it handles – the systems for which it provides an essential service. If its only two tasks were to handle both electronic funds transfer and an on-line personnel system, in most cases its loss would be more financially significant in the former case.

The above trivial example gives the clue to the way assets are defined in CSRAM: by information function or by system. Fortunately, most managerial staff view information assets in this way: the processor is usually immaterial to them; most users do not know or care how many communications processors handle the task. However, they are perfectly able to value the significance of the information they use in everyday working life. Technical and computer staff, on the other hand, have no interest in information content and value (unless they are contemplating an attack).

From this starting point of defining assets by information function or system, each system can be subdivided into its system features (from the user's point of view) and the benefits of its data. Table 2-1 shows an example of this division for a small stock control system.Although this represents a very simple example, it illustrates how users could realistically put a value on, for example, loss of the maintenance subsystem, or severe damage to file 3. Most CSRAM methodologies use a system-based approach to asset identification. As pointed out previously, this facilitates identification of those systems that can be removed from the analysis on the basis that their information value is not high.

The basic asset elements of any computer system are:

programs that make the system features available:
- live programs in memory,
- live programs on storage media,
- backup copies,
- program documentation;

files containing the system data:
- live data in files,
- input documents,
- output in readable form,
- backup files,
- archived files;

hardware involved in providing the system:
- processors,
- disk and tape drives,
- communications links;

devices used to capture input and receive information:
- terminals,
- printers,
- other display devices.

All these objects have one property in common: they can be lost, damaged, or misused.

2.3.3 What kinds of damage to systems does CSRAM recognize?

The three categories of damage found to be useful in CSRAM can be defined as follows:

- damage to data integrity: the intentional or accidental modification or destruction of system data, in any of the forms described in section 2.3.2 (live, backup, etc.);
- damage in the form of loss of data confidentiality: intentional or accidental disclosure of information;
- damage in the form of unavailability of any system components.

These concepts are appropriate because they encompass the effect of every possible type of threat (see section 2.3.4) and can be applied at any level of granularity, i.e. to a whole system or to its high- or low-level components, to a particular file, or to any item in that file.

Table 2-1

	System features	*Subsystem*
1	create a new stock item	maintenance
2	delete an obsolete item	maintenance
3	change item reorder level or supplier	maintenance
4	record stock movements	daily transaction
5	highlight fast-movement stock	daily transaction
6	produce reorder list	reporting
7	stock-taking report	reporting
9	post-stock-taking reconciliation	maintenance
10	maintain supplier details	maintenance

	Database (or files)	
1	information about items:	number, location, supplier, level, movements
2	information about suppliers:	name, address, reliability, terms
3	information about movements:	date, time, responsibility

2.3.4 What threats are considered in CSRAM?

A threat in the context of computer security is any circumstance or event with the potential to cause harm to an ADP system or activity in the form of disclosure, modification, unavailability and destruction. The following is an extract from a 'threat list' – the enumeration of possible sources of damage in CSRAM:

- small fire,
- large fire,
- wiretapping,
- break-in and theft,
- earthquake,
- hackers.

A threat is a potential for harm, although the presence of a threat does not mean that it will necessarily cause actual harm. Threats exist because of the very existence of the system or activity and not because of any specific weakness. For example the threat of fire exists regardless of the amount of fire protection at a facility. However, the facility is not vulnerable to fire unless its fire safeguards are not adequate.

2.3.5 How is the concept of vulnerability used in CSRAM?
A vulnerability is any weakness or flaw existing in an information system that may be exploited to cause harm. The presence of a vulnerability does not in itself cause harm; a vulnerability is merely a condition or set of conditions that may allow the system or activity to be harmed by an attack.

CSRAM, however, uses this concept less vaguely than the above might imply. In many CSRAM methodologies (including those conforming to the approved standards of the US Department of Defense) a vulnerability can be thought of as the existence of a three-way relationship among a type of damage, an object (or system component, as described above), and a threat, for example:

- loss of documentation for the maintenance program due to theft, resulting from poor access controls (vulnerability);
- alteration to a bank account deposit statement by intercepting (active wiretapping) an update transaction, resulting from a lack of message security controls;
- loss of the backup tapes for the entire stock control database in a fire because of inadequate disaster-recovery plans.

Only those damage–object–threat triples that are possible in a given environment are of interest to CSRAM.

2.3.6 What are safeguards in CSRAM, and how are they related to vulnerabilities?
Essentially, a safeguard is some kind of filter. It may be physical, such as key cards, locks, alarms, Halon gas; programmed, like access control systems or cryptography; or procedural, such as the use of control totals or counter authorization. Safeguards may act in different ways. They may:

- reduce the impact of harmful occurrences (see section 2.3.3),
- reduce the likelihood of threats,
- detect the occurrences of damage,
- facilitate recovery from these occurrences.

Computer security safeguards may be generic, providing protection against whole classes of threat, or specific to a certain vulnerability. In this way, different degrees of protection can be suggested for a particular computer facility, so that management can get cost benefit figures for different levels of protection. The following is an extract from a typical safeguard list used by a CSRAM methodology:

protection of messages in transit:
- end-to-end acknowledgement,
- serial numbering for transactions,
- message authentication,
- encryption;

log usage:
- console log,
- log of security table changes,
- log of unauthorized log-on attempts,
- terminate continued log-on tries,
- report on continuous log-on tries,
- audit trails;

procedures:
- review console logs,
- review audit trails,
- collect statistics on traffic.

2.3.7 How can cost benefit be measured in CSRAM?

This question addresses an important concept in the nature of risk evaluation and costing, summarized in the following equation:

$$R = P \times L$$

where R denotes the risk, P is the probability of a threat occurrence, and L is the one-time loss produced by the occurrence of a threat.

Since the controls themselves usually reduce operational efficiency to some degree, the total cost of a given set of controls is given by the cost of installation of the controls plus the cost of lost efficiency. Hence there is a trade-off between the costs of security measures and their benefits, represented by risk reduction. This relationship is summarized in the graph shown in figure 2-4. The graph shows the cost–benefit trade-off curves as applied to security controls. The actual expected cost per loss (or per security breach) is the sum of the cost of the particular set of controls and the cost per loss remaining after applying these contols. Thus, for example, control set CS1 reduces the maximum loss to C1 pounds for a control cost of C2 pounds. The actual expected cost per loss minimizes between CS2 and CS4.

A security measure, or countermeasure as it is sometimes called, is considered to be cost-effective if the annual saving so gained is greater than the annual cost of security control. This calculation involves:

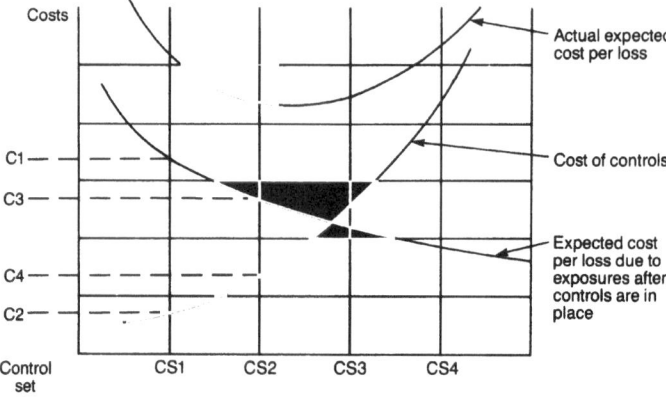

Fig. 2-4 The optimal cost-benefit trade-off in security controls

- the annual expected loss from the exposure to be protected, i.e. the Annual Loss Expectancy (ALE) (see section 2.4.5);
- the annual cost of the proposed security countermeasures;
- the annual expected loss from the exposure after the counter-measure is in place.

Thus the proposed control can be justified on cost grounds if the annual cost of the countermeasure is less than the reduction in ALE produced by its implementation (i.e. $b < a - c$).

2.3.8 Summary
The basic concepts of computer security risk analysis, i.e. assets, costs, threats, threat likelihoods, vulnerabilities and safeguards, have been introduced and defined in this section; it has also been shown how the relationships between them can be expressed in a structured way. Although terminology may vary, all CSRAM methodologies use the same basic ideas for arriving at a description of a particular computing resource's 'dangerous environment', by distinguishing between the threats to a system object and the strength or weakness of its defences. These structured relationships provide a basis for performing security cost comparisons. The next section considers these concepts in more detail and discusses a particular standard risk analysis technique using 'annual loss expectancy' estimates (ALEs). An alternative methodology (CRAMM), which was developed by the IT and Privacy Group within the Central Computer and Tele-communications Agency of the UK government is presented in section 2.5.

2.4 Courtney Technique of Risk Analysis

2.4.1 Introduction
In this section a well-known CSRAM technique popularized by Robert Courtney is described with examples. From this description, it can be seen that the basic paradigm outlined in previous sections is employed in this technique. This approach collects a 'model' of the case at hand so as to evaluate its current security; escalating uncertainty is controlled by breaking the elements of the case down into familiar, tractable problems which can be related to everyday life.

2.4.2 The stages of risk analysis
The stages are concerned with:

- assets,
- threats,
- vulnerabilities,
- quantification.

The first step in risk analysis is the identification and evaluation of assets subject to loss. Regardless of the cause, any harm that occurs in information processing manifests itself as an asset loss to the organization. As discussed earlier (see section 2.3.3) all loss can be ascribed to the impacts of disclosure, modification, unavailability, and destruction. The purpose of the first stage is to assess the loss suffered by each asset in the above impact areas.

The second step is to identify the likely or most pertinent threats to the assets so identified, and to estimate their likelihood of occurrence over the year. The threats must then be associated with the loss areas they are most likely to impact.

Next it is required to assess the vulnerability of each asset or group of assets to the threats identified above. Unlike threats and assets that are relatively stable, vulnerability can change almost on a daily basis. However, unless a vulnerability can be shown to exist, a threat is probably not meaningful, regardless of how prevalent it might be.

Finally there is the risk assessment process. This involves the quantification of the levels of risk indicated by the output of the first three stages:

- levels of threats,
- existence of vulnerabilities,
- values of the assets.

This process recognizes that there has to be some motivation for certain types of threat to be translated into harmful actions. For example, a water bed factory probably gives less consideration to terrorist threats than a government installation would. Likewise, some information systems (e.g. credit systems and military installations) are intrinsically more 'interesting' to hackers. Stock control systems (see section 2.3.2) are prone to the depredations of fraudulent *bona fide* users. Depending on the context, the impacts could range from insignificant to catastrophic.

The main approaches to risk assessment can be classified broadly as quantitative and qualitative. The conventional method relies on ALE calculations based on numerical data from the previous stages, particularly the asset valuation (step 1) and the frequency of occurrence of threats (step 2). Data from these evaluations are used in the derivation of ALEs.

The other approach to risk assessment relies on a more qualitative approach, such as CRAMM, developed by the IT and Privacy Group of the Central Computer and Telecommunications Agency (CCTA) of the UK government (see section 2.5.1).

2.4.3 Asset loss exposures

The first step in a risk analysis is to assess the financial impact of an undesirable event on an organization's assets (see section 2.4.2). Table 2-2 shows a simplified risk analysis worksheet in which an organization's data files are to be listed for each application in the first column. The advantage of cataloguing company assets in this way is that it instils an organized and systematic approach in the team carrying out the work.

Each asset to be listed in the first column of the worksheet is subject to a variety of threats resulting in losses which could fall in one or more of the other columns:

- data integrity (modification and destruction),
- data confidentiality (disclosure),
- system availability.

Data integrity is the assurance that processed data is the same as that in the source documents, or has been correctly computed from source data; and has not been exposed to accidental alteration or destruction. Incomplete data, unauthorized changes, or additions to the data are all considered violations of data integrity.

Data confidentiality is the assurance that sensitive data is held in confidence and is protected from unauthorized disclosure. Misuse of data by those only authorized to use it for limited purposes is also considered to be a violation of data confidentiality. Data may be confidential only at certain times, or even sensitive only in conjunction with different data.

Systems availability is the assurance that vital system functions and features can be performed within an acceptable time period even under adverse circumstances. As pointed out previously, non-technical staff often do not consider their total information technology resource in terms of separate 'systems'. This is why it helps to present these to the user as 'features' or 'tasks'.

In carrying out this first stage, it is not necessary for the team to know precisely the extent of the damage a threat might cause. This can be estimated using a combination of historical data, the team's knowledge of the system, and their own experience and judgement. Estimates within an order of magnitude are usually sufficiently accurate in most cases, but later, at the time of selecting safeguards, specific items can be refined if it becomes important.

Table 2-2

System name or data set	Accidental			Deliberate			Exposure (Breach) (if unable to process for) Hours					Comments
	Des	Mod	Disc	Des	Mod	Disc	2	4	8	12	18	
	Int		Conf	Int		Conf						
I F L												

I = impact, F = frequency, L = loss, Des = destruction, Mod = modification,
Disc = disclosure, Int = integrity, Conf = confidentiality

2.4.4 *Estimation of likelihood of a threat*

With threat impact evaluation, it is impossible to determine, accurately, the frequency of many undesirable events. Some threats occur only once in a number of years, while others happen many times in a day. With systems that have been operating for many years, the task of assigning probabilities for some threats is relatively straightforward because historical data is often available on the frequency of such events.

It is, however, more difficult to assign probabilities relating to the dishonest behaviour of employees. Even if all white-collar crimes were reported, as opposed to the estimated 10 to 15 per cent of detected instances, there would still not be a sound statistical base of reliable data on which to draw. It must be recognized, however, that such estimations for risk analysis are concerned with orders of magnitude; it is not required to distinguish between frequencies of (say) 10 or 30 events a year. Informed judgement based on a thorough knowledge of the environment under consideration is the best approach to obtain an order-of-magnitude estimate.

2.4.5 Derivation of I (impact), L (loss), and F (frequency)
If the impact of an event (the precise amount of damage it could cause) and the frequency of occurrence of that event (the exact number of times it could happen) are known, then the product of the two defines the loss:

$$\text{Loss} = \text{Impact} \times \text{Frequency}$$

However, because neither the impact nor the frequency can be specified precisely, it is only possible to approximate the loss with an Annual Loss Expectancy (ALE), which is the product of the estimated impact in pounds or dollars (I) and estimated frequency of occurrence per year (F). To take a simple example, the stock control system (see section 2.3.2) could cease to be operational for 18 hours, and it would cost $2,500 in overtime for recovery procedures. However, this event has occurred only once in the last ten years: so the annual loss exposure is only $250. The calculations, using the order-of-magnitude measures, can be simplified by indexing the estimated impact and estimated frequency of occurrence, as shown in table 2-3.

Table 2-3

Estimated Impact Cost	*I*	*Estimated Frequency*	*F*
$10	1	Once in 300 years	1
$100	2	Once in 30 years	2
$1,000	3	Once in 3 years	3
$10,000	4	Once in 100 days	4
$100,000	5	Once in 10 days	5
$1,000,000	6	Once per day	6
(etc.)			

The basis for calculating these is the formula :

$$L = 1/3 \times 10^{(I+F-3)}$$

Hence if the estimated impact cost is $10,000 and the estimated frequency is once in three years then $I = 4$, $F = 3$, and the ALE is given by:

$$L = 1/3 \times 10^{(4+3-3)} = 1/3 \times 10,000 = \$3,333$$

With this technique tables are supplied giving the value of L for specific values of I and F, thus considerably reducing the effort of computing ALEs. The computation is easily automated.

2.4.6 Risk analysis project using ALE calculations
A risk analysis project based on these techniques involves a project team, a time-scale, management support, an objective, and a set of people committed to the project's aims. However, if the CRAMM technique is used (see section 2.5) the size of the project team is considerably reduced because of the use of automated techniques.

2.4.6.1 Project team
The selection of the risk analysis team is critical to the outcome of the project. Where possible it is important to obtain members from those parts of the organization responsible for:

- data processing operations management,
- systems programming,
- internal auditing,
- physical security,
- data files under consideration (including users),
- programming support of the files under consideration.

These entities should be represented on the team by people who are well informed both of their own department's mission and its relationship to the overall organizational mission. The task team leader should be equally knowledgeable and should come from one of the first three groups listed above, but should not be their representative. None of this should be taken as precluding others from participation on the team, and departments such as legal and personnel must be consulted.

2.4.6.2 Time-scale
Risk analysis based on the ALE approach is a time-consuming process and one that cannot be hastened. Previous experience or availability of documentation for a previous risk analysis project will be of considerable value, and reduce both effort and time-scale. The ready availability of all the necessary information is essential to minimize the duration of the project. The consideration of each file, in the light of the hazards which beset a system, is a critical task. It should only be delegated to experienced staff in view of the level of knowledge and experience required in the decision process.

Software packages (see section 2.5.1) can reduce manual clerical effort on the project, but they do not reduce the demand for careful judgement and evaluation.

A lengthy time-scale will create difficulties for the team members. The assignment of some individuals to the team may create difficulties for their departments, which will temporarily lose their services. Team members may feel compelled to rush through the project to get back to their normally assigned duties. An agreement that the team will meet only (say) half of each day would alleviate some of these burdens.

2.4.6.3 Project reviews

Top management should review both the preliminary findings and the final results of the risk analysis team for reasonableness, policy adherence, and organizational unity before a protection plan is formulated. At the very least, the plan will require co-ordination with financial and administrative departments, and will probably be included in the organization's long-range planning.

2.4.6.4 Preliminary security examination

The US National Bureau of Standards, in their guidelines for 'Automatic Data Processing Risk Analysis' suggest that in order to establish a firm basis for conducting a risk analysis, the team should start by surveying the organization's existing computer security, the cost of replacing assets, and the actual threats to which the organization's information technology systems are vulnerable. The benefit of this preliminary phase is that it determines the scope of any subsequent detailed review, by pinpointing the most significant information assets.

This preliminary phase helps to focus on the more significant issues that have to be highlighted in steps 1 and 2 (see section 2.4.2), i.e. the potential asset losses and the list of threats that could bring these about. Identifying actual threats will give the risk analysis team a feel for the vulnerabilities or possibilities for damage of the facility and the systems they will be analysing. Unless a vulnerability can be shown to exist, a threat is probably not significant, regardless of how prevalent it might be.

One objective of the preliminary review is to ensure that time resources are not wasted in carrying out a detailed review on a system that contains a minimal number of low-value assets likely to be at significant risk. Such a system should only require a baseline level of security countermeasures.

Direct involvement with management at the outset of the preliminary review is essential. The purpose of this initial meeting between the managers and members of the review team is to:

- ensure management authorization for the review;
- establish the boundary of the system to be reviewed;
- document or arrange the provision of specific system information;
- identify data owners or those who can speak authoritatively about the data.

If, as a result of the preliminary survey, it is concluded that all data assets have a low value, then the risk analysis plan need be taken no further, and instead baseline countermeasures should be evaluated (see chapter 3).

If the risk analysis is being undertaken in the system design stage, an effort should be made not only to identify existing threats but to predict any future threats which might result from the implementation or operation of the system.

2.4.6.5 Threats
Once the major assets have been listed, in the preliminary survey, the likely threats to these assets must be identified. Experience indicates 'target areas' of the organization where significant threat is usually found:

personnel:
- areas of concern: hiring and termination procedures, scope and amount of training, quality of supervision at all levels;
- threats include: bomb threat, data alteration, data denial, data entry (error or fraudulent), access allowed to a disgruntled employee, embezzlement, injury or death, post-employment access, privacy violation, strike, theft, unauthorized disclosure;

environment of the computing resource:
- areas of concern: neighbourhood, quality and reliability of utilities, building design, operation and maintenance, physical access controls;
- threats include: airborne particles, air conditioning failure, earthquake, explosion, fire (minor or major, external or internal), flood, hurricane, ice and snow storms, landslides, lighting, liquid leakage, mechanical shock, power (failure or transient), static electricity discharge, riot, terrorist actions, unauthorized personnel access, volcanic eruption;

hardware and software:
- areas of concern: its operational availability, procedures for controlling change, software features, documents;
- threats include: tampering with hardware, denial of hardware services, hardware and software malfunction, software alteration, software denial, operating system flaws or alterations;

101

communications links:
- areas of concern: hardware and transmission circuits, procedures to validate and control distribution of messages;
- threats include: communication malfunction, communications outage, eavesdropping, wiretapping, electromagnetic interference, emanations interception, insertion and deletion of messages, vandalism;

computerized application systems:
- areas of concern: their technical design, their documentation standards;
- threats include: inadequate testing, programming errors, inadvertent modification or destruction of files;

operations surrounding the computing resource:
- areas of concern: standards and procedures for source document protection, information dissemination, I/O control, tape library forms, computer room processing, housekeeping and maintenance, production control, contingency planning;
- threats include: improper handling of data and media, improper marketing of media and output, sabotage.

The lesson gained from comparing this long (but not exhaustive) list with the simple ALE form given above (see section 2.4.3) is that the numerous threats which might cause damage are divorced from considering the effect of the damage. Threats cause damage; damage causes loss. The former is known from experience; the latter is collected independently.

2.4.6.6 Vulnerabilities

As part of the preliminary study, the threats to which the system may be subjected have to be evaluated in the light of any system vulnerabilities. For example, if effective physical access controls are in place, then there is little risk of an intruder damaging or destroying magnetic media storing files, and so the threat of this can be discounted.

Each vulnerability in a system can be associated with one or more threats, and, of course, each threat can be associated with more than one asset. Recall that a vulnerability is a security deficiency that makes it possible for a threat to materialize, and/or exacerbates its adverse affects on assets. A prime objective of risk analysis is to identify and overcome those vulnerabilities that might lead to significant losses (see figure 2-5).

Vulnerabilities are as important to the risk determination as a detailed list of threats. In recognizing system vulnerabilities the risk team will be able to concentrate only on those threats that are

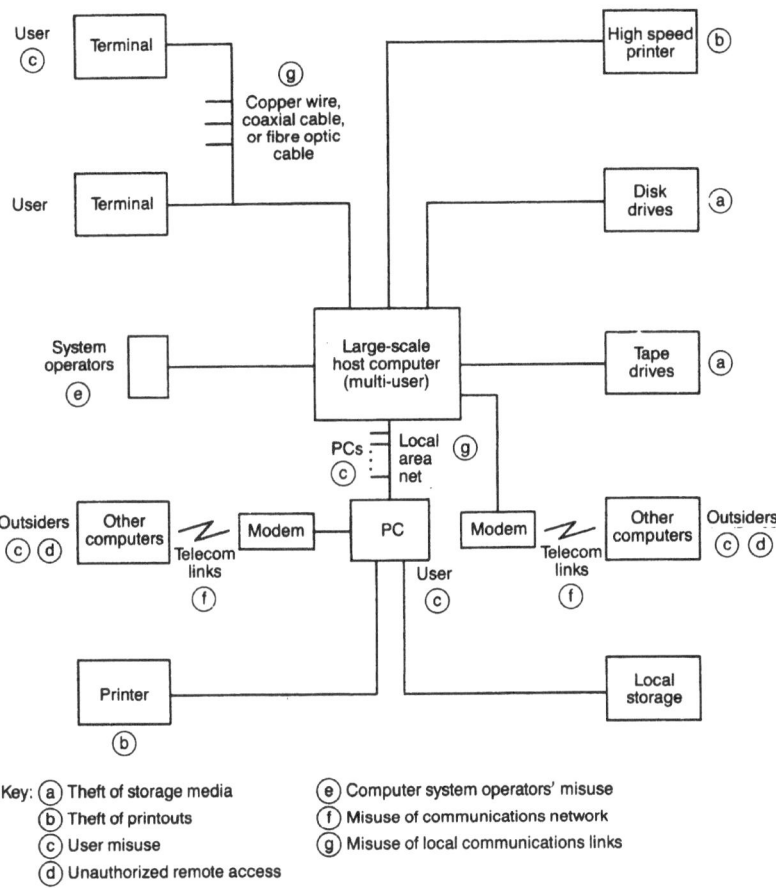

Key: (a) Theft of storage media   (e) Computer system operators' misuse
     (b) Theft of printouts   (f) Misuse of communications network
     (c) User misuse   (g) Misuse of local communications links
     (d) Unauthorized remote access

Fig. 2-5 Typical vulnerabilities of computer systems (*source*: US Office of Technology Assessment)

pertinent to the job in hand. However, vulnerabilities are seldom discrete and unrelated, but again experience indicates the susceptibility to losses are typically caused by:

- lack of management support for security,
- ineffective security organization and/or protection,
- inadequate security training and awareness,
- disloyal or unreliable personnel,
- ineffective risk management,
- inadequate housekeeping,
- unreliable environmental support equipment,

103

- inadequate audit procedures,
- insecure document control,
- insecure recovery procedures,
- ineffective error detection,
- insecure applications software development,
- inadequate hardware/software maintenance,
- insecure software acceptance procedures,
- obsolete hardware/software,
- lack of organized operating procedures,
- inadequate contingency planning,
- insecure or unreliable communications,
- insecure input/output procedures,
- ineffective physical access control (internal or external),
- inadequate systems and terminal access control,
- opportunities for liquid leakage.

2.4.6.7 Evaluation of preliminary findings

The last part of the preliminary phase should be a list of all security safeguards currently in effect, whether or not the original purpose of such features (e.g. storage media logs, control of printout distribution, data entry quality control) was security.

The results of these surveys should be evaluated and presented to management. As mentioned earlier, a code of good security practice may be adequate for the system under review because for assets of low value, even if a threat occurs and the system is vulnerable, the resultant impact would almost certainly be insignificant.

However, if the value of one asset is high for one of the four impacts (disclosure, modification, unavailability, or destruction) then one needs to proceed to a full review (see section 2.4.6.9).

2.4.6.8 Risk analysis worksheet

Having completed the preliminary survey, and reviewed the results with management, the team will need to proceed in a structured way in filling in the risk analysis worksheet. All the organization's application systems or data files arranged by application should be listed on the worksheet(s).

By tracing the flow of data through a system, the team will be able to pinpoint where in the flow of the data the threats identified in the preliminary study are likely to occur. With the preliminary vulnerability study, and the team's collective familiarity with the systems/applications/files, they should be able to assign reasonable estimated frequencies to such events. If a file is used with more than one application system, it should be listed under each, because it can be vulnerable to different hazards under different systems.

In the initial risk analysis, organizations with a large number of files will tend to consider their data on an application basis, rather than on a file basis, because of the size of the tasks awaiting them. Such an analysis should be followed by the more detailed file-by-file consideration, in any instances where there is an indication that protection requirements differ radically among the files, in any one application system.

The values of I and F should be filled in at each intersection on the worksheet, as should the value of ALE, or it will be impossible to reconstruct the basis for a particular ALE. A running total of the ALEs, attributable to each threat on the list of actual threats, should also be kept. The final total is used in the safeguard selection process (see section 2.4.6.9.) (If additional threats surface, they should be added to the list). A note in the 'Comments' column linking the ALE to the particular threat, or threats, will be useful at the time of selecting remedial measures.

It is not appropriate to deal with the current security measures at this stage; it is more efficient to consider them later, when selecting safeguards.

Where more than one circumstance can affect data integrity, data confidentiality, or processing availability, the I and F values for these events should be noted separately; this will be an aid in deciding on security measures. Use should be made of the 'Comments' column to note the steps or functions in a system where problems can occur. When the team is considering data confidentiality, their task can be simplified by first eliminating the files which are known to contain no personal, proprietary, or other information of a confidential nature.

The further division of data integrity into modification and destruction is necessary because the two will not always have the same impact, nor occur with the same frequency.

The 'Comments' column can be used as shown to indicate the processing step in which a vulnerability arises. It can also be used to refer to additional notes which may be needed to explain certain situations more completely.

The time periods in the 'Exposure (Breach)' column are 'mission dependent' (i.e. they could be hours, days, or months depending on the organization's business objectives) and will have to be determined by each organization for itself. They will be important in the selection of backup facilities and should be subject to review by top management. The destruction of equipment should be considered under 'Exposure' because the ultimate effect of destroying equipment will be the inability to process data, unless backup contingency is available. The impact will be the cost associated with the inability to process rather than the cost of replacing equipment. Replacement is a possible remedial measure, the cost of which should be subject to the same analysis as any other measure.

105

2.4.6.9 Security safeguards
It is seen from the above that risk analysis yields a value for the average probable loss that an organization might sustain in any one year. The process of risk management is first to determine protective measures that will provide the best overall security. Subsequently, these measures must then be costed to determine the most cost-effective controls. This is performed first by noting the ALE reduction produced by the safeguard on the total ALE attributable to this threat type (see section 2.4.6.8), then considering the total cost of the combined measures in relation to the net ALE reduction. Finally, the additional ALE reduction by each measure should be compared to its share of the total cost.

By constructing such a matrix (see table 2-4) the threats and the protective measures which could affect one or more of them can be displayed. The threats should be arranged in order of total ALEs attributable to them (highest to lowest). Each intersection in the matrix should contain three pieces of information:

(a) the estimated ALE reduction,
(b) the annual cost of the measure,
(c) the resultant annual cost reduction.

There is no significant precision in these figures. The annual cost of a measure is listed opposite the most serious threat which it addresses; when it is listed opposite any other apposite threat, only the increase in cost to cover that threat is noted. Table 2-4 shows a comparison of three safeguard measures under consideration for the stock control system – database encryption, a user authentication procedure, and an after-the-event log of unauthorized attempts to access the database. The threats under consideration (not an exhaustive list) are hacking, visual eavesdropping, and physical theft.

An additional effect of completing this matrix is that the value of existing security measures to the overall security of the facility may be determined. All safeguards should be included in the matrix but only the annual maintenance costs need to be considered; the initial installation costs have already been expended. The cost of those which are not solely for the purpose of computer security should be proportioned if possible. Replacement costs should also be considered at this stage. Replacement of equipment should be treated in the same way as any other remedial measure. It may prove to be the case that the cost of replacing equipment is less, in some cases, that protecting it.

Comparing all the measures which remedy the same threat (or lesser included threats) will indicate which is the most cost-effective in the given circumstances. In the matrix in table 2-4, protective measure 1 (encryption), costing $9,000, provides a $12,000 saving against threats 1, 2, and 3, while measure 2, costing $15,000, provides only a $5,000 summed saving. The two measures together, at a cost of $24,000, provide an ALE reduction of $25,000. On these figures, the additional benefit of measure 2 is arguable. In some circumstances it may be determined that the additional reduction is necessary; in other less sensitive situations, the cost saving will be adopted instead. In addition care should be taken to ensure that the measures chosen to counter certain threats do not increase the estimated frequency of other threats.

With all of the ALE reduction and cost figures arrayed, various combinations of safeguards can be considered until a satisfactory aggregation of security measures is achieved. The matrix will be useful in explaining to management why particular safeguards should be selected.

Table 2-4 Remedial Measures vs Threats

Threats		*Safeguard measures*		
		(1)	(2)	(3)
		Encryption of data	Authentication procedure	Log of unauthorized attempts
	(a)	20,000	20,000	18,000
Hacking	(b)	9,000	15,000	8,000
	(c)	11,000	5,000	10,000
Visual	(a)	10,000	5,000	0
Eavesdroping	(b)	9,000	15,000	8,000
	(c)	1,000	0	0
Physical	(a)	0	2,000	2,000
Theft	(b)	9,000	15,000	8,000
	(c)	0	0	0

(a) = ALE reduction, (b) = annual cost of measure,
(c) = resultant annual reduction

2.4.6.10 What are the most cost-effective safeguards?

In the process of deciding which protective measures will provide the best overall security, management should consider first procedural and physical safeguards, since people represent the most significant generic threat type.

Procedural controls, especially when used in combination with physical barriers, produce the highest degree of security for the lowest cost of all forms of protection. They will serve to satisfy the requirements of the US *Privacy Act* of 1974, and the UK *Data Protection Act* (see chapter 7) as well as many other demands either dictated by prudence or mandated by regulations.

Procedural measures are essential for filling the gaps between manual and automated processing, between human beings and systems hardware and software. They are very effective against accidents resulting from human negligence and against amateur theft. They promote an atmosphere of managerial concern for data and processing security that tends to discourage all but the most determined felons. It should not be forgotten, however, that the biggest threat to computer security comes from the legitimate insider.

Most measures are effective against more than one threat (see chapter 3). Maintaining facility access logs is a method of controlling who goes into a facility, of knowing who is in a facility at a given time, and of preventing unauthorized removal of material from a facility. Encryption (see chapter 1) protects data both during transmission and while in storage. Audit trails furnish information for backup and recovery and also provide a basis for detecting abnormal processing events.

System security measures should be contemplated only after it has been established that physical and procedural safeguards are insufficient to meet the organization's protective requirements. If an organization's needs dictate the use of software or hardware protection for some systems, then those measures can also be incorporated in the protection plan for systems with lesser requirements, provided the operating costs of those systems are not thereby inordinately increased.

2.4.7 Summary of the ALE approach

The components of risk analysis and management are:

- asset identification and valuation: the identification and evaluation of an IT system's physical and data assets to determine the effects of vulnerabilities impacted by threats, in terms of the impacts of disclosure, modification, unavailability, and destruction;
- threat assessment: the identification and assessment of the likeli-

hood of unwanted deliberate or accidental incidents impacting on IT systems;

- vulnerability assessment: the assessment of the extent to which IT systems could be susceptible to identified threats;
- risk assessment: the assessment of the levels of risks indicated by the perceived interaction of threat presence, high impact on high value assets, and highly likely vulnerabilities;
- countermeasure selection: the selection of security counter-measures justified by, and to reduce to an acceptable level, the levels of risk assessed.

The last step, and its regular review, is the risk management part of the process.

2.4.8 What are the main issues with the ALE approach to risk analysis?

While at first glance the ALE-based quantitative approach appears attractive, the way in which both the frequency of occurrence of threats and asset impact values due to these threats are derived is to a high degree subjective. The merit of the approach is that it calls for system in evaluating risks and helps with the selection the most appropriate countermeasures.

However, neither the asset impact values nor the estimated frequencies can be qualified by the estimator, and the certainty associated with each estimate is not recorded. Naturally, this increases management scepticism about the results. Further, it is difficult with ALEs to evaluate several sets of safeguards against each other for a given level of risk; the determinism of the model works in only one direction (i.e. threats determine risk, not vice versa).

Moreover, if there is more than one reviewer carrying out a risk analysis, then one might expect inconsistencies to arise in attributing values to data assets. To overcome this problem of standardization, and the requirement for staff with a security background, the CCTA have devised a personal computer-based support tool, known as CRAMM (see section 2.5.1). The benefit of CRAMM is that it provides a common metric guidance for qualitative valuation of data assets and for the assessment of threats and vulnerabilities. CRAMM is able to calculate numeric representations of risks based on qualitative estimates, and to match a given level of risk to specific counter-measures.

CRAMM thus automates the process of risk analysis and removes the need for security judgments from the reviews. It does this by relying on lookup tables with predefined values reflecting the experience of its authors. So even with CRAMM the results are based on subjective assessments. However, they are consistent, which is a prime requirement for risk analysis.

2.5 CRAMM Risk Analysis and Management

2.5.1 Origins of the CRAMM Methodology

The importance of CRAMM (CCTA Risk Analysis and Management Methodology) in the UK arises from the recognition by HM Government of:

- the increasing reliance of its departments on information systems;
- the high cost of many of these systems;
- their increasingly interdependent and distributed nature;
- the fragmented and highly varying approaches among departments to information security control.

Establishment of CRAMM as a government-wide formal, structured approach to risk analysis and management represents a significant improvement in standards of control. CRAMM is now the preferred CSRAM methodology in all HM Government departments and agencies for the protection of unclassified but nevertheless sensitive information.

CRAMM was specially developed in response to formal criteria set by HM Government:

- It should be adaptable for use with organizations and systems of all sizes.
- It should encompass all technical and non-technical aspects of security.
- It should be compatible with existing government security guidelines.
- It should be usable during new system development as well as in existing system review.
- It should be automated, easy to use, and fast to apply by people who have IT experience but not necessarily a security background.

2.5.2 How does CRAMM differ from the ALE approach?

The CRAMM methodology comprises a staged or modular approach. The first two stages address analysis of the risks, and the third deals with the management of risks through the implementation of countermeasures. Each stage is supported by questionnaires and guidelines, and sets out to answer a major question:

- Stage 1: Is there a security need above a certain baseline level?
- Stage 2: Where and what is the intent of the security need?
- Stage 3: How can this be met?

Stage 1 parallels the preliminary security examination mentioned earlier (see section 2.4.6.4), and if the findings are that the asset impact values are low, there is no need for a full security survey.

2.5.3 Stage 1 of CRAMM

2.5.3.1 Initial information
The first part of stage 1 is the important task of precisely determining the nature and boundary of the system under review, and its various components. This is accomplished by the acquisition of information on the user community and the manner in which they use, or will use, the system, together with an outline system configuration diagram. This information is obtained from interviews with senior installation or project and user managers and their staff, and is essential in providing the reviewer with the understanding necessary for the specific boundary of the review to be agreed and later for the questionnaires and guidelines to be put into perspective.

Stage 1 also provides a level of detail, e.g. on the number of owners of (and/or those who can speak authoritatively about) data for the review to be scheduled. Stage 1 then continues with its major function: the determination of qualitative values for assets, both physical and data.

The CRAMM documentation provides detailed advice on how the reviewer should schedule for interviews with data owners and personnel responsible for physical assets, how to conduct and record them, and how to review the results with system or project management.

A carefully structured questionnaire enables the reviewer to establish the selection of qualitative data asset values on a scale of 1 to 10, without user bias, for the four possible impacts of disclosure, modification, unavailability, and destruction, by both accidental and deliberate means.

This selection is aided by detailed 'common metric' guidance for data valuation. This covers such issues as political embarrassment, commercial confidentiality, personal privacy, personal safety, and financial, legal, and user disruption. Physical assets such as hardware, documentation and air-conditioning plant are first valued on the basis of replacement or reconstruction costs (i.e. quantitative measurement). These costs are then converted to the same qualitative scale as that used for data assets. Following this the dependencies of data assets on physical assets are ascertained.

111

2.5.3.2 Abbreviated threat and vulnerability assessment
An advantage of the methodology is that time and resource wastage can be avoided when all asset valuations are low (3 or lower on the scale). In these circumstances what is in effect an abbreviated version of stage 2 would be used to check whether there are any threats or vulnerabilities of sufficient level to justify greater than baseline (or code of good practice) protection for low-value assets. If the value of all assets is low, and only baseline protection is justified, then the review will move directly to stage 3. Only where asset values are medium or high is stage 2 recommended.

2.5.3.3 Stage 1 management review meeting
At the end of stage 1, as with the subsequent two stages, there is a comprehensive management review. The main objective of this meeting is to agree the valuation of the assets. This is often very interesting since management may not previously have had a clear perspective of the values of the assets within their systems. It is worth emphasizing that CCTA feels that the need for management involvement and commitment to a review from its inception is fundamental to a successful outcome.

2.5.4 Stage 2 of CRAMM
The extent of the security needed by a system relates not just to the values of assets but also to the levels and nature of threats to which the system could be subjected, and the likely vulnerabilities of the system assets to those threats. The first part of stage 2 is concerned with identifying how assets can be conveniently grouped together for consideration of threats and vulnerabilities. This grouping is another means to avoid wasting resources and time. For example, where two assets (say two identical hardware units in the same room) are to be subject to the same threats and vulnerabilities, there is no point in conducting two identical exercises.

2.5.4.1 Threat and vulnerability assessment
The next step is to identify which potential threats relate to which asset groups. Then, in accordance with the outcome, well over 30 generic threat types (convenient categories or groupings for considering threats and vulnerabilities, e.g. fire, water damage, system infiltration, and misuse of resources) are used as the basis to assess the qualitative threat and vulnerability levels for each asset group, using pairs of structured questionnaires which incorporate the knowledge of HM Government security experts.

These questionnaires enable input where relevant of such items as frequency of event statistics and up-to-date 'intelligence' and motivation information. As far as possible questions are framed so as to prompt a 'yes' or 'no' answer to avoid bias, with each answer afforded a particular score. Total scores per questionnaire indicate a high, medium, or low threat or vulnerability.

2.5.4.2 Measurement of risk
For each particular asset group, the combination of asset value and assessment of the levels of vulnerabilities and threats is used to calculate a security requirement (or measure of risk) number. Numbers calculated will be on a scale of 1 (baseline) to 5, for each of the four possible impacts (i.e. disclosure, modification, unavailability, and destruction).

2.5.4.3 Stage 2 management review meeting
The completed analysis of risks at the end of stage 2 is reviewed in detail with management before moving to stage 3. At the end of stage 2 management has a clear view of the levels of threats to, vulnerabilities of, and thus risks to, particular asset groups. The expression of risks in a numerical form enables the reviewer to direct and identify the appropriate countermeasures in stage 3.

2.5.5 Stage 3 of CRAMM
With risk analysis completed, stage 3 is concerned with the management of the identified risks. In other words stage 3 determines how the identified security need can be met by countermeasure selection. Taking the determined levels of risk (i.e. the security requirement numbers established at the end of Stage 2) for each asset grouping, countermeasures (covering all aspects of security, i.e. physical, personnel, hardware, software, communications, etc.) are selected from a large 'library', which is referenced by, among other things, security aspect, and is further annotated by the type (e.g. reduce threat, reduce vulnerability, reduce impact, detect, recover).

If the review is of a current installation, details of existing countermeasures are now recorded. (This activity is deliberately kept until the end of the review to avoid prejudging the justification for existing countermeasures.)

A comparison is conducted to ascertain which additional countermeasures are to be recommended, and which existing ones are not justified. As the list of countermeasures is produced, it is annotated with the likely levels of cost (from information held in the library). Costs specific to the actual or likely countermeasures can then be added, and a further management review held.

2.5.5.1 Prioritization
A management help facility in CRAMM enables prioritization of countermeasures. This process takes account of such items as cost

level, the measure of risk for which a countermeasure is required, number of threat types addressed, number of impact types addressed, and the relative contribution a countermeasure will make to achieving the objective of its subgroup (of similar types). (The countermeasure library is grouped and subgrouped.)

2.5.5.2 'What if?' scenarios

If management is unhappy about some aspect, for example the likely overall cost is outside the budget, account can be taken of the countermeasure priority list, and also a 'what if?' question exploration facility. This facility can be used, for example, to see the effect of reducing the levels of threat and vulnerability by moving locations, or removing one very sensitive file from the system (therefore transferring the risk outside the boundary), or to gauge the effect of a new application. In other words, parameters can be changed and CRAMM rerun. This is also an essential feature for the consideration of change within a system.

2.5.5.3 Backtracking

CRAMM also offers the manager the ability to backtrack to see exactly what contributed to the recommendation of a particular countermeasure or countermeasures. This would identify the impacts of concern and the scenarios that led to those impacts; the threats and vulnerabilities addressed and the justification behind why particular levels were identified; and the related assets which the countermeasures are designed to protect.

2.5.5.4 Follow-up reviews

The final step is to determine when a subsequent review should be carried out. It is obvious that much of the information gathered during a first review can be used in subsequent reviews, and thus greatly speed them up. Particularly as each life-cycle stage is reached, security can always be considered when changes are proposed to the system or potential system, with each subsequent review enabling a check that all information is accurate, and accounting for such items as changes in technology, threats, and vulnerabilities.

2.5.5.5 Project life-cycle

As mentioned earlier, it is much easier at the design stage to introduce the more effective countermeasures which avoid or transfer the risk, or reduce the threat. Retrofitting countermeasures to an existing system is more costly and less efficient, and such countermeasures tend to be those which reduce vulnerability, reduce impact, detect, or enable recovery. To highlight the life-cycle approach CCTA is ensuring that the British government-sponsored IT system project control (PROMPT) and analysis and design methodologies (particularly SSADM) have the right 'hooks' in them to relate adequately to risk analysis and management, to security in general, and to CRAMM in particular.

2.5.6 Summary of CRAMM
The main CRAMM concepts are as follows:

- There is 'common metric' guidance to assist reviewers to obtain objective qualitative valuation of data assets for the four major impacts.
- There is objective qualitative assessment of the threats to, and vulnerabilities of, specific groups of assets.
- There is a combination of qualitative values for assets, and threat and vulnerability ratings, to form numeric indications of risks.
- Numeric indications of risks are matched to specific detailed countermeasures. (This has been particularly popular with government users.)
- No presumptions are made as to the need for previously implemented countermeasures: for an existing installation not only justified but also unjustified countermeasures are identified.
- There is always a baseline (or code of good practice) level of countermeasures. (This is based on the premise that all systems must have some 'value' even if it is minimal – otherwise why have them?)
- Extensive and readily understandable management help facilities are provided.

Information collected during a CRAMM review could be used to identify particular hardware/software evaluation needs and to construct security policy and requirement documents. Indeed, CCTA feels that CRAMM, with its automated support tool, will be invaluable to management in presenting easily understandable results in the form of countermeasure lists that are justified in accordance with the real security need (and for existing installations identifying countermeasures that may not be justified and which could be removed, probably with cost-saving and easing of operational constraints). It is further considered that management will thus be able to review submissions for money spent on security supported by a logical, properly constructed, and justified case. This will be with a wide coverage of security, with all aspects and all impacts considered, and with countermeasures related to many facets, from contingency planning to software security needs and to 'pure' (or financial) audit.

2.6 Conclusions

2.6.1 Is this consensus approach to estimating uncertainty common among CSRAM methodologies and automated tools?

Until far more empirical data on system security are available, some similar kind of uncertainty controlling technique will be necessary. Another semi-automated methodology, SBA (Security by Analysis), structures its risk analysis techniques in a similar series of modular reviews, identifying crucial and vulnerable systems early in the review process, and providing scenario analysis tools for examining the effect of safeguards in terms of hypothetical future events. Again, the approach to impact estimation is qualitative, but the uncertainty is moderated by consensus. The thrust of modern CSRAM methodologies is threefold: to reduce the hackwork of collecting the patterns of information and system usage; to control, or at least add plausibility to the multiple estimates in risk analysis; and to provide the distilled knowledge and theory of computer experts at large in automated methodologies.

This knowledge takes the form of heuristics about threat likelihoods and interactions, good patterns of security safeguards versus bad, special measures for particular kinds of application such as banking and electronic data interchange (EDI), better analyses of the nature of threats, etc. (See figure 2-6).

2.6.2 What are the trends in CSRAM?

It is hoped that this chapter has convinced the reader that CSRAM is necessary to provide a consistent method of finding the most cost-effective security countermeasures. Since many organizations have also recognized this, we can expect progressively more objective data on the outcomes of risk management. CSRAM models can use this in risk evaluation. Secondly, there is a considerable trend toward using artificial intelligence in CSRAM. It is, after all, only another application of expertise capture and policy evaluation. Software aids of this type will considerably lessen the work. However, the implementation and control of the advice given by these 'software experts' will remain firmly in the hands of management.

Note: The CRAMM 'product' is Crown Copyright; 'CRAMM' is in the process of being registered as a trademark.

References
Experiences of the Use of the SBA Vulnerability Analysis for Improving Computer Security in Finland, IFIP Sec (1988)
Fisher, R. P., *Information Systems Security* (Englewood Cliffs, NJ: Prentice-Hall, 1984)
Perry, E. E., *Management Strategies for Computer Security* (Butterworth Publishers, 1985)

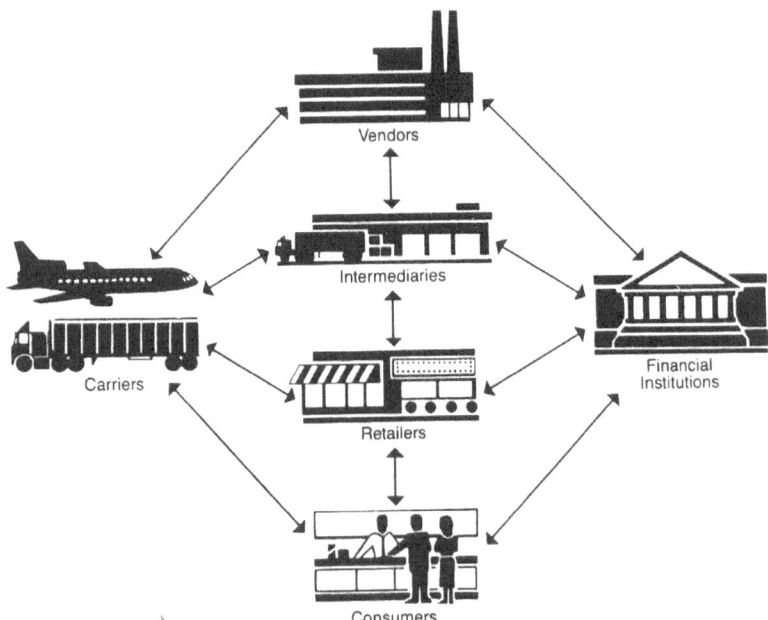

Vendors

Intermediaries

Financial
Institutions

Carriers

Retailers

Consumers

Fig. 2-6 Security in electronic data interchange (EDI). Documents in a common format are transmitted over a network linking companies and their trading partners - customers, vendors, carriers, and financial institutions. Risk analysis, which may be applied at the level of an individual company or to the overall network, provides a systematic approach to the complex security considerations.

Acknowledgement is given to Mr Robin Moses of CCTA for his assistance in producing this section.

3 Countermeasures

M. Shain

3.1 Overview

We have seen that the key elements in achieving information security involve the detection of threats, reduction in vulnerability to such threats (see chapter 2), and the ability to recover in the event of an impact. The controls and procedures that form part of a security programme should ideally have been established through the process of risk analysis.

Security involves both the protection of information and the equipment required to transmit and process that information. Six basic factors have to be considered in establishing and maintaining a secure information processing utility:

- physical security (see section 3.2.1),
- access control (see section 3.3.1),
- administrative controls and procedures (see chapters 1 and 6),
- personal computer security (see section 3.4.1),
- contingency planning (see section 3.5.1),
- insurance (see section 3.6.1).

The purpose of this chapter is to review the controls and procedures that have been established in the light of experience. Although perfect security is generally regarded as being unobtainable, security mechanisms are effective and do work well. The issue lies in selecting those countermeasures that best suit a given computer centre or information processing facility.

Security mechanisms are effective because a particular threat has a low probability of occurrence while the associated mechanism has a high probability of detection, so preventing any serious loss. For example, fire protection systems prevent loss by both detecting and extinguishing fires (see section 3.2.5). In most case there is a low

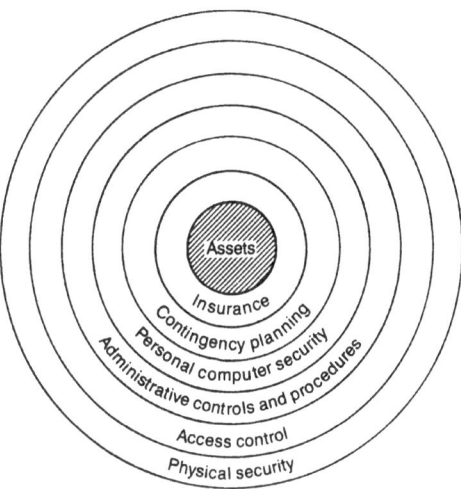

Fig. 3-1 The layering of security countermeasures for protection of information assets

probability both of a fire starting and, if one does start, of its causing much damage.

The purpose of a security system is to reduce the probability of loss to an acceptably low level at reasonable cost (see chapter 2), and to ensure adequate recovery. It is up to management to decide what assets are to be secured and what threats need to be met. This chapter reviews the security measures that can be evoked to counter a variety of hazards. The information is not intended to be exhaustive from a technical viewpoint, but rather to indicate the factors that have an impact upon management in the design of the security systems.

Regardless of the means used to protect an installation, two elements must have primary emphasis:

- The staff in the information processing environment must be made 'keepers of security'. They must be motivated and trained to evaluate, to take decisions and to respond quickly when required (see chapter 1).
- Access to information must be limited only to those with a need to know.

3.2 Physical Security

3.2.1 What are the main factors of physical security?
Many factors contribute to adequate physical security, and they are generally interrelated. For example, building construction, access con-

trol, and fire protection cannot be considered in isolation; often measures taken to counter one threat may in fact be sufficient to detect or inhibit other attacks.

A plan that caters for the physical security of an information processing/communications installation will need to cover the risks of fire, rising and falling water, and intrusion. These issues are closely related to the location and design of the building where the computer equipment is housed. The primary factors affecting the physical security of computer centres are:

- location (see section 3.2.2),
- construction (see section 3.2.4),
- fire prevention (see section 3.2.5),
- water damage (see section 3.2.6),
- radiation (see section 3.2.7),
- eavesdropping (see section 3.2.8),
- access control (see section 3.3.1),
- intrusion (see section 3.2.10).

3.2.2 Why is location important in physical security?
Location of an information processing system can influence many of the threats to which it might be subjected. For example, any site is subject to natural threats such as storms and flooding, as well as to man-made threats such as the danger of chemical or even radioactive pollution.

Often there is little choice in the selection of a computer site; the threats inherent in a location need to be evaluated, and the site protected from natural hazards. The costs of protection, the ease with which it can be provided, the extent to which damage can be inflicted by industrial accidents or by fires in the adjacent areas, etc. are directly related to location. Similarly, ease of access to and surveillance of an installation is affected by the immediate location. The general social, economic, and political environment of the location can also influence the threats of vandalism, terrorist attacks, loss of services due to industrial action, etc.

3.2.3 What are the physical security considerations of a computer centre location?
The factors to be considered in the location of a computer centre are:

- concealment of the function of the building,
- perimeter control,
- water damage,
- access,

- telecommunications,
- power supplies.

If the nature of the building is to be disguised then signs outside the building, and directories within it, should not reveal the location of the computer centre. Perimeter control, such as a continuous secure wall or fence, gives a degree of protection against a direct assault. The risks of attack from a vehicle are minimized by a dry moat and a bank; this will also limit damage that might be caused by an uncontrolled vehicle, especially if the site is near a busy road.

If possible the computer equipment should not be located below ground level. More insurance claims from computer installations derive from water damage and flooding than from almost any other cause.

The safety of computer staff should be borne in mind when planning emergency exits for cases of fire, terrorist attack, or bomb warnings.

Good external lighting helps to reduce the probability of attacks on staff at night, and is also an effective means of deterring would-be intruders. It is also important that good access roads exist for fire and emergency services.

When a computer site is selected consideration must be given to telecommunications requirements. If there is likely to be a significant volume of data communications or telephone traffic the common carrier needs to be consulted to ensure spare capacity is available. If possible the site should be served by two or more dedicated communication lines to the local telephone exchange in case one is out of action.

The supply of electric power to the site should be protected against natural hazards. Ideally the site should be served by two independent supply routes so that there is a fall-back if one should fail. Although the supply of electricity rarely fails by accident in the UK, it cannot be taken for granted. The possibility of accidental damage to supply lines or substations (particularly in storm-force conditions), industrial action, and load-shedding at peak periods all need to be evaluated. If this is an issue then the provision of standby power may have to be considered, although this is very expensive. Alternatively, uninterruptible power-supply equipment is designed to take over the load automatically in the event of failure, thus permitting a controlled shut-down of the installation.

3.2.4 What are the significant security factors in design and construction of a building housing a computer centre?
Failures or deficiencies in the design and construction of the building will increase the vulnerability of the information processing system.

The factors that need to be assessed are:

- fire resistance,
- toxic fumes,
- shared premises,
- access,
- support services,
- evacuation.

Ideally, a computer installation should be housed in a dedicated building made from fire-resistant materials. The use of modern materials, which produce toxic fumes in the event of fire, should be avoided. A serious hazard arises from fires involving electrical transformers in which PCB is used as an insulating fluid. The chemical is highly toxic, even in small amounts, and if it is discharged into the atmosphere near a computer centre, the building would have to be evacuated and the area decontaminated. This represents a potential hazard to both staff and data security.

A dedicated building housing information processing/communication facilities is not subject to risk from fire and water damage caused directly or indirectly by other occupants. If the premises are shared then the computer centre should be separated by fire- and flood-resistant walls, floors, and ceilings. Cables for power and communications should be supplied through special ducting and properly protected, especially against deliberate interference. Small holes should not be made in the computer rooms walls for cables and other services, since they will increase the vulnerability of these services, and reduce the effectiveness of gas-flooding in the event of fire (see section 3.2.5).

Access control needs to be considered at the outset (see section 3.3.1). Limiting the number of entrance and exit points to the installation is important, and these should meet the requirements of the appropriate fire authority. All perimeter entry and exit points should be monitored (e.g. with closed circuit television) to prevent unauthorized entry.

Support facilities outside the building ought to be protected. The following, for example, may need special attention:

- generator fuel supplies;
- power and communication cables;
- air-conditioning units and cooling towers;
- underground services: gas, water, power, and sewers.

If the installation is performing highly sensitive operations, alarm sensors might be located underground and embedded within walls,

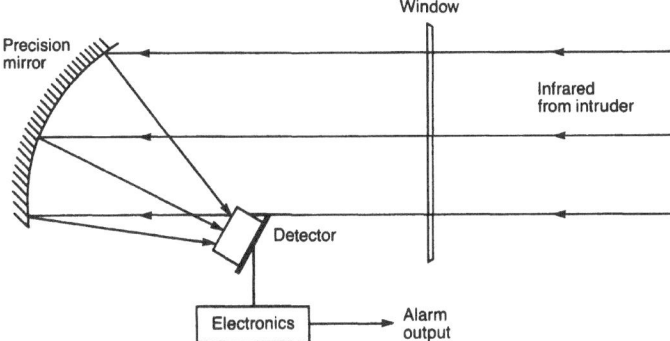

Fig. 3-2 Intruder alarm. Passive infrared sensors used with electronic signal processing ensures that ony a combination of both infrared heat detection and movement will result in an alarm.

floors, and ceilings, to detect tunnelling and other types of intrusion.

Emergency evacuation routes and procedures require special attention. There should be well-considered guidelines for handling bomb threats: should staff be evacuated or not? Staff may in fact be less vulnerable dispersed around the installation than if they are all gathered at one assembly point.

3.2.5 What precautions need to be taken against fire?

The result of a fire in a computer centre may be extremely serious, but fortunately such fires in the centre itself are comparatively rare. The most common cause of fire is a breakdown in electrical insulation resulting in a short circuit or arcing. The heat in the area of breakdown can be quite intense. However, the fire is normally localized and only lasts as long as the cause. But there always exists the threat of a fire emanating in another part of the building, e.g. in a manufacturing area, and spreading into the centre.

The factors in fire damage prevention are:

- fire detection,
- fire extinguishers,
- fireproof materials,
- combustible materials,
- suspended ceilings,
- staff training,
- liaison with fire service.

Automatic fire detection equipment should be installed in any space where a fire could develop or spread undetected, especially in floor and ceiling voids. The threshold of smoke detectors must be

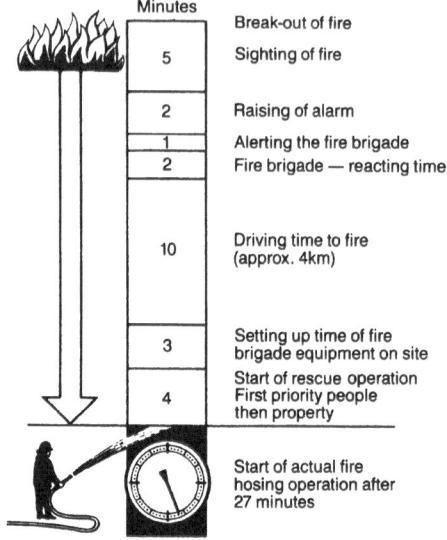

Minutes

	Break-out of fire
5	Sighting of fire
2	Raising of alarm
1	Alerting the fire brigade
2	Fire brigade — reacting time
10	Driving time to fire (approx. 4km)
3	Setting up time of fire brigade equipment on site
4	Start of rescue operation First priority people then property
	Start of actual fire hosing operation after 27 minutes

Fig. 3-3 How quick is the fire brigade? Many computer centre managers overestimate the speed of the fire brigade. (*source*: Lampertz Systems)

sufficiently sensitive to provide the earliest possible warning of fires, non-smoking regulations should apply in all computer centres, and such smoke detectors are therefore unlikely to be falsely triggered. Nevertheless a high concentration of detectors may be needed to minimize the possibility of a false alarm arising at an individual detector.

The detectors should be of a type that respond to both temperature and smoke, and be linked to an alarm system with a direct connection to the fire brigade. British Standards lay down the type of detectors to be used and the density of their distribution (typically one for every 10 to 30 square metres in ventilated installations).

The first line of defence against fire in the computer room is provided by hand-held extinguishers designed to cope with small fires; they should be positioned so as to be visible and within easy reach. All computer operators should be trained in their use.

Sprinklers and automatic gas-flooding systems are all used in modern installations. Water is suitable for quenching stationery fires, particularly in areas containing only peripheral equipment, but near the computer equipment portable carbon dioxide or Halon extinguishers should be used.

Gas-flooding extinguishing systems work by smothering the area where a fire has broken out; such systems are advantageous in-

124

asmuch as they leave no residual damage. Carbon dioxide gas is commonly employed because it is relatively cheap. However, it requires a 30 per cent level of concentration to extinguish a fire, at which level it becomes lethal. For this reason, carbon dioxide systems should be locked-off when people are present. Halon, although more expensive, will extinguish a fire in much lower concentrations and has little toxic effect.

Water sprinklers are useful as a fail-safe precaution when everything else has failed. Their main purpose is to provide disaster protection and to stop major fires from spreading and causing total destruction. The water itself can, however, be a major source of damage, although pure water will do no permanent damage to major hardware components.

Fire prevention commences with the construction of the building (see section 3.2.4). Walls, ceilings, and floors should be manufactured from fireproof materials. This care should also be extended to furniture. In particular any such furniture should not emit toxic fumes if a fire breaks out.

Experience shows that fires are aggravated by a combustible environment. Lint from moving line-printer stationery, particularly from bursting operations, can ignite easily and burns very rapidly. The space under the raised floor of a computer installation acts as a trap for lint and should be cleaned frequently, unless there is a controlled and filtered air-flow in the void. Good housekeeping and cleanliness are vital to maintaining a non-combustible environment.

Suspended ceilings and raised floors are commonly installed in computer rooms. The voids produce concealment spaces in which fire could develop, and be difficult to locate without special equipment. Ideally, the construction materials used in ceiling fittings (e.g. ventilation grills and light diffusers) should have self-extinguishing properties.

Staff training in fire precautions, raising alarms, and evacuation procedures is an essential part of management responsibilities. Smoking should be banned in computer centres. If necessary a rest room, isolated from the computer centre, should be provided to reduce the temptation to ignore anti-smoking regulations. The computer facility should have a valid fire certificate; the installation, and its procedures, must comply with government Health & Safety regulations. In addition the computer equipment manufacturer's recommendations concerning fire precautions should be obtained and implemented.

3.2.6 How can management protect installations against water damage?
Water damage represents the most common insurance claim for

computer centres. A significant portion of claims arises from broken water mains, blocked-up sewer lines, flooding from storms, heavy rains, rising streams, and flooding arising from fire-fighting on a floor above the computer installation. It is clearly wise to avoid natural flooding by siting the installation above the high-water level. However, flooding can arise from many other causes, including leaking roofs, burst pipes, overflowing tanks, and faulty fire sprinkler systems. In fact the writing of this section was undertaken to the sound of a pump emptying water from a college computer centre: a water valve had broken in a photographer's laboratory on the same floor as the computer centre during the weekend and resulted in ankle-deep water in the equipment room. Ideally, shut-off valves for the water supply to the premises should be clearly marked and tested regularly so that they can be operated in an emergency. The threat of rising water can be minimized through the use of under-floor water detectors, and the threat of falling water can be reduced by ensuring the ceiling is free of holes and defects that might permit water or other substances to penetrate from above.

3.2.7 Can electric or magnetic fields cause damage?

It is almost inconceivable that a magnetic or electric field generated outside the building could have any effect on recorded media located inside the building. A large permanent magnet has no measurable effect on a disk or tape held twenty inches away. At 6 to 8 inches it may begin to cause errors that render records unreadable, and at three inches a very strong magnet would have erased data for all practical purposes.

Strong radar signals can interfere with the operation of data processing equipment, but only if the signal that reaches the equipment is greater than about 5 volts per metre. Such a signal could only transpire if a radar antenna were sited next to the computer installation and pointed directly at it.

Radiation and radioactive particles are not a threat to information processing systems, but are, of course, a very serious hazard to computer personnel.

3.2.8 Is it possible to eavesdrop from outside a building?

Modern surveillance techniques are very sensitive and it is possible to gain access to information without actual entry to the premises. Many electronic devices emit electromagnetic signals that can be received from some distance with standard detecting equipment. Most microcomputers have video displays that radiate sufficient power for the information on the screen to be reproduced using relatively unsophisticated electronics (see section 3.4.7). Terminal keyboards also radiate distinctive signatures when keys are depressed.

126

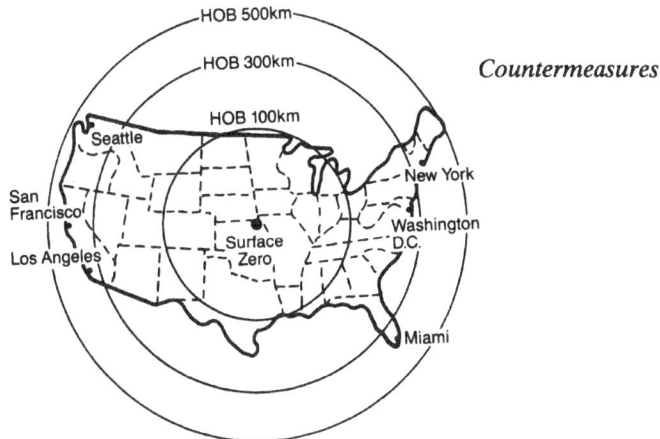

Fig. 3-4 Nuclear electromagnetic pulse (NEMP) ground coverage for high-altitude bursts at 100 km, 300 km, and 500 km. A single exo-atmosphere burst could cover the entire area of the United States, causing considerable damage to all unprotected electronic equipment, including computers. (*source*: Elgal Systems)

If data privacy is of sufficient importance, then computer equipment may have to be operated in a specially screened room, known as a Faraday cage, to prevent information-bearing signals from leaving the building. Alternatively, specially protected microcomputers can be purchased working to Tempest-proof standards (see figure 3-5).

If encryption equipment is used to protect data transmitted over links into the building, then some form of Tempest-proofing of terminals and printers may be required. Display terminals should always be sited facing away from windows, to avoid the danger of photography of screen images by a camera with telephoto lens.

3.2.9 What precautions should be taken to ensure good access control?
Many techniques exist for controlling entry, whether to a building or a room. to sensitive facilities should be through one properly controlled and monitored door, and be limited to people who work in that facility on that shift.

The right balance of physical access controls (see section 3.3.1) should be applied to ensure that they are effective without being too burdensome. Where visitors are permitted they should wear visible identification, such as a badge, and be accompanied by a member of staff, who should also wear an identifying badge with a photograph.

For sensitive installations a two-stage entry system may be considered. The purpose of this is to isolate individuals by using an outer and inner door so that their identities may be checked by a guard. Also within the installation, the area can be partitioned into

You may require shielding for one of several reasons:

1. To exclude unwanted electro magnetic radiation or signals — for instance, in order to carry out sensitive electrical measurements or prevent malfunction of vital equipment. Shielding will allow systems to function correctly.

2. To contain radiating signals which can disrupt other equipment elsewhere.
Operating interference generating equipment within a shielded environment will protect susceptible equipment in nearby laboratories, calibration facilities, computer systems etc.

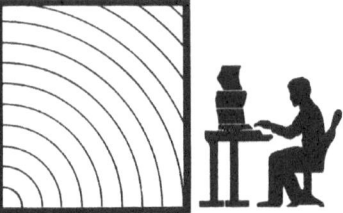

3. To protect confidential data from interrogation.
Lines can be tapped and radiating signals from computer and data handling systems can be read by sensitive espionage devices. Shielded systems are necessary for secure operations and information confidentiality.

4. To protect systems from damage due to a large electro-magnetic pulse. This threat should be considered if an installation must continue to function after a nuclear explosion.

Before practical recommendations can be made, it may be necessary to conduct a specialized investigation including measurements to evaluate the electromagnetic pattern around the equipment under consideration.

Fig. 3-5 Why electromagnetic shielding may be needed (*source*: Belling Lee Intec)

security zones so that greater protection can be afforded where necessary (see figure 3-6).

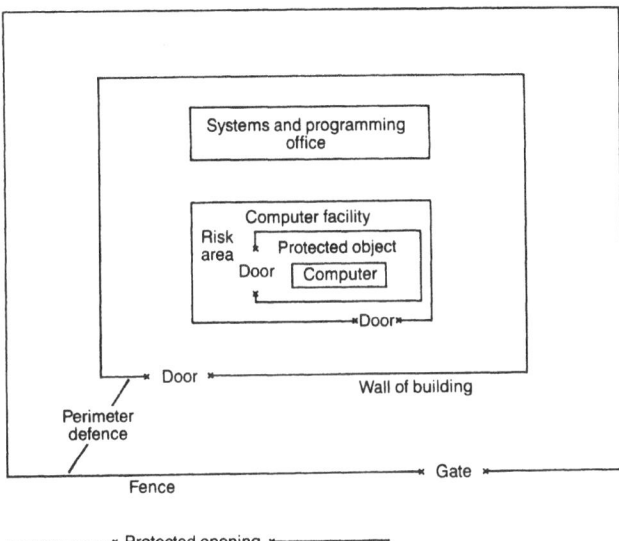

Fig. 3-6 Zone approach to physical security

Access to a building area or room can be limited, controlled, and audited using card locks which are opened by a card which contains an optical or magnetic code. Systems can be set so that different card holders are allowed access at various periods and even to one or more controlled doors depending on the circumstances.

In microcomputer-based access control systems, entrance authorization can be controlled dynamically by door, time of day, day of week, and security classification of the individual to whom the card was issued. Authorizations can be readily added or deleted and audit trails on entrance activity be maintained. Door status can be monitored and attempts at unauthorized entry can be detected.

A card key can be confirmed with the owners's photograph to form an identification badge, making it look less like a key. One advantage of this is that passback is less likely to occur when the card is also a badge that must be worn. Although electronic locks offer a great deal of flexibility, they can be bypassed just like mechanical ones. Cards are often used in conjunction with locks having a keypad so that the individual must know the correct code to gain entry. Cards may, however, be left in the slot and codes written on walls.

Where passes are used they should be inspected regularly. This helps to reinforce security awareness and reduces the risk of passes being lost or mislaid. If passes are inspected on leaving then there is little chance of a visitor keeping his pass, and an intruder stands more chance of being caught.

3.2.10 How can intrusion into the building be minimized?

A good access control system (see section 3.2.9) must be complemented by adequate building design so as to minimize the risk of forced entry. To this end, detectors to monitor the sound of intrusions should be installed.

Any security wiring must be protected and terminated within the secure area. Automatic doors should be set into robust frames to withstand the heavy stress involved.

Windows should be made of break-resistant materials, be alarmed, and be inaccessible from the outside. Control perimeters and approaches to sensitive facilities should be kept under observation, either directly or else by closed circuit television. Automatic surveillance systems can also be used to detect unwanted movement, and can be used in conjunction with other detector technologies to maximize detection: vibration and sound detectors, infra-red beam and body heat detectors, microwave systems, and ultrasonic beams.

3.2.11 What action should be taken if an intruder is detected?

Procedures must be established so that security and reception staff have instructions for all eventualities. The guard must know when and how to summon help unobtrusively, and the help may involve operations personnel, building guards, and even local police to cope with problems of varying complexity. The possibility that the guard may be compelled to grant access needs to be considered; some access control systems have ambush codes to enable a guard to give warning of such duress, while apparently conforming to the intruder's demands.

When premises are left unattended an intruder could be scared away by a loud alarm or by the sudden glare of external lights when they are switched on. The alarm can also be linked to the police or to a security company.

3.3 Access Control

3.3.1 Does access control provide good data and computer security?

Access control is the traditional means of securing assets against loss or damage, and of maintaining the confidentiality of information. If the physical components of information systems are effectively isolated then no loss or malicious damage can occur. Similarly if access is controlled to all the physical devices that interact with the stored information, or control the information processing, then the confidentiality and integrity of stored data is guaranteed. There are, however, aspects of information security that either complicate the implementation of access control or mitigate against its effectiveness. These facets of access control are:

- limitations of effectiveness of physical access control,
- policy on granting access privileges,
- identification and verification of users,
- integration of physical and logical access control,
- effectiveness of defences against intruders,
- spoofing.

For many years physical access control also provided a denial of access to stored data. When there were only a limited number of computer terminals connected directly to a mainframe computer then guarding such terminals against illegitimate usage gave a high degree of assurance on the security of stored data. This safeguard disappeared when computers were interconnected with data communication networks, and users were allowed to access computers over public telephone networks. In most current information systems it is not possible to deny initial access to the computer system; one cannot prevent hackers from using their own microcomputers and modems. In fact current hacking is commonly performed from overseas countries.

The second facet of access control is concerned with the problem of determining the basis on which potential users are given, or denied, access rights. When a few senior management are permitted to open the company safe the decision is straightforward; with a complex organization and an extensive information asset, however, the security officer is faced with a massive list of requested access privileges, effectively in the form: user – data item or software – type of access (Read, Write, Append, Execute) (see chapter 1).

A set of ad hoc decisions, on an individual basis, is likely to lead to inconsistencies, administrative overheads, security lapses, etc. Some clear access policy needs to be thought through for access control; there is little point in denying access to unauthorized personnel if one is not clear who should, and should not, be so authorized (see section 3.3.3).

Having decided whom one wishes to have authorized access, how can the security officer then be sure that the system will always grant the desired access to that person, and deny access to all unauthorized personnel? This is the problem of user verification. The most commonly used system, which relies upon passwords (see section 3.3.7), has often proved completely ineffective. More sophisticated user-verification systems are now available; they need to be carefully evaluated by the security officer (see section 3.3.5).

The actual form of access control has traditionally been divided into physical and logical. The first refers to a restriction placed on access to a location or a piece of equipment. Logical access control is concerned with granting users of communications or computing systems access to facilities, files, programs, etc. This distinction may become blurred as security systems integrate both forms of control. For example, some operating systems can restrict a user's access to files according to the terminal under use and the time/day of the access. Thus physical access to a specific terminal, during specific time periods, is required before logical access to the files can be granted. In other integrated security systems biometric sensors may control access to a building. When a user has been verified by the sensor then a set of access privileges will be automatically granted; e.g. lights and air-conditioning are switched on in the user's offices; a terminal in the office is connected to the computer; access is permitted to, and only to, the user's files; all accesses, both physical and logical are automatically logged, etc.

The next area of concern is the strength of the 'company safe'. There is little point in having extremely sophisticated user-verification systems if the intruder can open the safe with a penknife. Unfortunately information technology has completely revolutionized the means of accessing and processing information. It has opened a Pandora's Box of tools for the attacker. The illicit modes of access of current concern are:

- physical intrusion,
- wiretapping (see chapter 4),
- the van Eck phenomenon (see section 3.4.7),
- a computer virus (see section 3.3.16),
- spoofing (see section 3.3.10).

The physical security of computer centres is now taken very seriously indeed. The days of operating the centre on a ground floor, with large external windows to allow the general public to admire the company's gleaming technology, are now past. The defence of computer centres against physical intrusion is discussed above (see section 3.2.10).

Wiretapping can provide direct access to information transmitted over communication lines. Such wiretaps may be made at telephone junction boxes on or off the organization's premises. Local area networks can all too easily facilitate unauthorized access (see chapter 4); in many cases spare access points are provided throughout the network to facilitate the connection of additional workstations, and these may be freely available to the attacker. Who would question another workstation appearing in an office building (see chapter 4)? Encryption is an effective means to counteract such attacks (see chapter 1). Eavesdropping does not even demand the physical connection of a wiretap. The van Eck phenomenon relates to the electromagnetic radiations from computers and VDUs which can be picked up from some distance away. The confidential screen display presented to a company executive can be viewed by an attacker sitting in a van parked outside the building. The equipment required for this purpose can be assembled by an electronics handyman for a few hundred pounds. Note that encryption of data flowing to the terminal is no defence against this form of attack because the data is decrypted before it is displayed on the screen (see section 3.4.7).

The computer virus is potentially deadly to organizations totally reliant on information processing power. It effectively allows a vandal systems programmer to strike from a distance, with a guarantee that widespread damage will be caused to software and data in a whole network of computers. The internal software access control system needs to ensure that each piece of software is checked against infection by another piece of software before it is executed on the computer (see section 3.3.20).

In access control the emphasis is usually upon users identifying themselves to a distrustful system. On the other hand, users need to be concerned that they are not entering confidential data, or authorizing transactions, on an attacker's computer, i.e. a spoofing attack (see section 3.3.10).

3.3.2 How can an outsider make a connection to the organization's computer system?

This can be done very easily if the computer is connected on a communications network, or staff can dial up the computer over the telephone network. Many managers are often unaware of the communication facilities connected to their computer systems. Sometimes they are reassured that sensitive data (e.g. payroll) is handled on one dedicated machine and (say) all engineering design work is confined to another. They do not realize that both machines are interconnected with communication channels that allow files to be transferred easily from one to another. Electronic mail provides interconnection of computer systems, sometimes across the world. Internal postal systems still query bulky envelopes due for airmail delivery, while files can be transferred from one organization's computer system to another, over an international network, with just a few keystrokes.

The hacker's entry point is a home computer and a modem. With knowledge of the requisite telephone number, an authorized user's identity and password, then many systems will grant open access. Stories of telephone numbers and passwords displayed on bulletin boards are part of the common folklore of hackers.

Defences against misuse of computer networks are discussed more fully in chapter 4. In general careful control of user privileges to communicate over such networks, and monitoring of network traffic, is the first step of good security. It must be emphasized that the existence of such communications facilities strengthens the case for strong user-verification techniques (see section 3.3.5); an attacker who can masquerade as a legitimate user, with extensive communication privileges can, at the very least, run up a massive telecommunications bill.

Defensive depth is a good philosophy when dealing with the hacker attempting access over the telephone network. Port protection devices can intercept the incoming call and conduct a dialogue with the user before allowing even the first connection to the computer. Call-back techniques can thwart the less sophisticated hacker but there is evidence that one should not consider such defences to be invariably effective (see chapter 4). There is never going to be a single completely effective technological defence against the experienced, well-equipped intruder. A series of good security management practices can discourage most hackers and limit the damage that they can inflict. Nevertheless, the security system, even with sophisticated user-verification facilities, can never cope with legitimate users who make their access privileges available to the hacker through sheer carelessness. Nor can the security system prevent losses due to errors and omissions of operating staff. That is a job for management.

3.3.3 How should access privileges be granted?
In many cases access privileges are granted on the basis of requests from users, possibly with endorsement from their superiors. A designated person (e.g. the security officer) is given the task of administering these requests and granting or refusing the requested accesses. In some cases accesses are granted on a single-user or group basis, e.g. all members of a given department form a group and automatically receive authority to access group designated files. In most cases a user is allowed to bestow privileges to other users without recourse to the security officer; no users are permitted to bestow more privileges than they possess. The computer operating system is then required to control accesses to files, programs, etc., and only grant access according to the stored privileges of the user. This form of access control is termed discretionary access control.

A disadvantage of such discretionary access control is that there is no overall strategy; each request is considered on its merits and granted or refused. It is extremely difficult for the security officer to maintain close control of information flow under these circumstances, or to impose a control strategy. Even if every request is judged on a strictly need-to-know basis, then it is likely that access privileges will remain valid after such need to know has disappeared. It may be quite in order for an employee to view a particular file during the lifetime of a given project, but there is often no automatic means of removing the privilege when the project is completed.

Military circles have always tended to have more formal access control systems to protect the confidentiality of their information. Mandatory access control systems classify both files and users. The terms 'objects' (for files, data items, etc.) and 'subjects' (for users, calling programs, etc.) are commonly used in this context. With this formal classification a user with a given classification will only be permitted certain specified accesses to certain classifications of files; the operating system imposes the rules of such accesses and they cannot be overridden even by the security officer. In some cases discretionary access may be embedded within mandatory access, i.e. if the mandatory rules allow a given form of access then reference is made to granted access privileges as in discretionary access control.

In commercial circles the function of the access control has a different emphasis from that of military systems. The main consideration may be the integrity of commercial data, rather than its confidentiality. It may for example be much more important to ensure that transaction processing software is not activated by unauthorized users than to ensure that such users do not browse through the accounts files (see chapter 1). Thus attempts to transfer some of the more formal access control models from military to commercial systems could be inappropriate. Nevertheless it is suggested that the security officer should be in a position to declare and impose a structure on the granting of access privileges.

3.3.4 How is physical access control effected?

There are three stages to the access control process:

- identification of user,
- user verification,
- granting/refusal of access.

In some access control systems the three stages merge together; holders of door keys identify themselves as the holder of a key, authenticate themselves by placing the correct key in the lock, and gain access by turning it. In more sophisticated systems the three phases are quite distinct. For example, with a plastic card system, users first insert their cards, which contain details of their identity; then enter a PIN or password to prove that they are the legitimate holders of that card; and then an electric lock is activated, or an ATM proceeds with the transaction. User verification may be based on:

- something the user knows, e.g. a password (see section 3.3.7);
- something the user has, e.g. a key (see section 3.3.8);
- an attribute of the user, e.g. a fingerprint (see section 3.3.12).

In developing access control systems one must also take into account the possibility that access data may be wiretapped and later used by an attacker; some form of randomization of data may therefore be required (see section 3.3.7).

3.3.5 What factors need to be considered in the specification of a user-verification system?

The specification of a user-verification system will naturally vary with the nature of the system to which access is being controlled. In general the factors affecting such specifications are:

- cost;
- ruggedness, reliability, and maintenance;
- user throughput;
- tailgating;
- system errors;
- user acceptability;
- administrative overheads;
- local versus central control.

Clearly cost is a significant factor if the system is to be used in (say) a retail EFTPOS system with multiple outlets; many biometric sensors (see section 3.3.12) are currently too expensive for multiple use. The ruggedness, reliability, and maintenance factors are of prime importance in any proposed access control system. The device will be roughly treated by impatient users, and is likely to be subject to attacks by vandals or intruders. If the reliability of the device is low, then it will either have a serious impact upon the normal operations of the information processing system that is to be protected, or it will be bypassed with consequent loss of security. Intruders may well seek to render the device sufficiently unreliable to ensure that operators get into the habit of bypassing it.

The device must not cause significant delays in user operation; most users will accept a delay of the same order of magnitude as that of unlocking a door, but will not wait for extensive biometric pattern-matching to be performed. Clearly the acceptability of the delay will depend upon the users; high-security area users are likely to be more tolerant than supermarket queues.

Tailgating refers to the practice of getting through the system on the basis of another user's verification. It can arise when the legitimate user obligingly holds open the door, or fails to log off when vacating a terminal. Most defences against tailgating aim to detect its occurrence and discipline the careless legitimate user. Photoelectric beams across doors can detect if two people enter, and hence log security lapses by the identified users. Security logging of file accesses (see chapter 1) will place responsibility on careless users who leave 'live' terminals for use by intruders. Incidentally, some operating systems do not allow users to log off if they currently exceed their disk storage allocation; users are expected to delete files until their storage demands fall within their allocation. In practice impatient users simply walk away from their live terminals leaving them available to an attacker. Access control systems that also control exits can ensure that a token, such as a magnetic card, used for entry cannot be re-used for entry, e.g. handed back to another user, before it is employed at an exit.

Some access control systems, particularly biometric sensors, can sometimes exhibit Type 1 or Type 2 errors, i.e. refuse entry to a legitimate user or allow entry to an unauthorized user. Manufacturers will often quote the probability of a Type 1 and Type 2 error; the specification of a system needs to consider the implications of occasional unauthorized accesses, or user frustrations, and set the permitted probability levels for such errors.

User acceptability is a factor that will be of prime importance if the system is to be employed by customers or clients, and is a major consideration for employees. Some biometric systems may be considered obtrusive or socially unacceptable, e.g. fingerprinting is an activity that is commonly associated with criminals. Some token devices may require complicated keypad operations, some devices may be inconvenient for classes of disabled users, etc. At the very least management needs to investigate the potential reactions of the user population, and to investigate if particular individuals may be seriously disadvantaged before committing themselves to the system (see section 3.3.6).

A user-verification system will involve administrative overheads at the time users are accepted to the system and when their access privileges are revoked. From a security viewpoint it is important that such administrative procedures are clearly specified, performed in a secure environment by designated personnel, and cannot be misused by attackers (see chapter 5). If some form of a token (e.g. a plastic card or key) is part of the control system then revocation of privileges may lead to the problem of recovering the token; a system in which access privileges can be revoked centrally and without the co-operation of the user is clearly preferable. The acceptability of the administrative overheads will depend upon the access control system, user population, number of devices, etc. The overhead must not be so high that it is likely to lead to poor practices, which will in turn reduce the security offered by the system.

The decision to grant or refuse entry may be made locally or by a central computer. There are a number of factors which render the one or the other more appropriate in any given circumstance, e.g a need for central monitoring of accesses (see section 3.3.6).

3.3.6 How are the user's interests catered for in an access control system?

Many members of the public are now quite versed in the discipline of plastic card access systems operated by banks (see chapter 5). This experience has not always been a happy one, and it is reasonable to anticipate that users will be increasingly aware, and critical, of their rights vis-à-vis such access control systems.

There are a number of factors which will need to be given careful consideration before the access control system is imposed upon employees, clients or customers:

- acceptability of the control procedures,
- administrative procedures,
- amount of user training required,
- security from a user's viewpoint,
- responsibilities of user and system.

The acceptability of the control procedures will depend critically upon the relationship between the organization and user. One would expect that management would be prepared to undertake more complex security procedures than manual employees, customers, etc. In general simpler procedures are more acceptable than complex ones. Biometric sensors may offend susceptibilities, e.g. retina scanning, fingerprinting, etc. Other biometric devices may cause difficulties for classes of users, e.g. disabled people. Any form of token needs to be convenient to carry, but not so small that it can be easily lost.

The administrative procedures must be performed in a secure manner by trusted, designated employees. It must not be possible for an intruder to impersonate a legitimate user at the stage that passwords, keys, etc. are supplied; nor should intruders be able to intercept them. Whenever possible, separation of duties should be enforced so that, for example, the member of staff dispensing plastic access cards should not be entrusted with the corresponding PINs (see chapter 5). All transactions involving the granting of access privileges should be recorded in a secure store, together with the name of the employee administering the procedure. It is preferable for the system to be such that access privileges can be revoked centrally without the co-operation of the user. Thus if an access token is lost, or the security status of the holder is changed, then it should be possible to ensure that the token cannot thereafter be used to gain access.

Most access control systems are so simple that no user training is deemed necessary. However, this has led to situations in which extremely poor security habits developed; many users are totally unaware of their responsibilities of the potential effects of their actions. Systems that demand some form of user training or require a contact with security staff for administration provide an opportunity to stress the importance of good security.

The plastic card used for banking has created an awareness among users of the potential hazards of access control systems; it is likely that future systems will come under scrutiny from consumer organizations, trade unions, etc. The user may well require assurances on two issues:

- Failures in system security will not disadvantage the user.
- Users' rights are protected against system security failures.

The action of an attacker may well be ascribed to a user; this is, from the organization's viewpoint, an advantage of the system. It means that a terminal user who carelessly walks away without logging off may be held responsible for the actions of the intruder who exploits the oversight, thus providing a deterrent against lax security. On the other hand, users can reasonably demand that they should not be held responsible for actions arising from system security failure, e.g. system programmers gaining access to lists of passwords. Management must therefore guarantee the security of the system and be prepared to discuss the security provisions with user representatives.

Biometric devices may well be a source of contention from the viewpoint of user rights. Suppose, for example, that fingerprint analysers became commonly used for access control. Users might well provide banks, employers, clubs, etc. with their fingerprints. Generally these patterns would be encrypted during storage, but again suppose that the security of one system was lax, a cryptographic key was revealed, and an attacker managed to obtain fingerprint patterns and the owners' identities. Suddenly those users might find that they were not acceptable as employees, bank

139

customers, etc. because their identity had been stolen by an attacker. Fingerprints, unlike passwords, cannot be changed, and the organizations would not be prepared to set up alternative access control systems for the unfortunate few. In this case the solution would be to encrypt the stored fingerprint pattern irreversibly. The general nature of the problem remains, however, and again users will at least need to be reassured on this point.

The operation of the access control system effectively forms a contract between the user and the operating organization. As described above, failures on one side can have serious effects on the other. It is important that the responsibilities on both parties be clearly spelled out by management. The users should be fully and carefully informed of their obligations when access privileges are granted, and they must be made aware of the likely consequences of security lapses.

3.3.7 How effective are 'something the user knows' types of access control?

'User know' systems such as passwords, PINs, etc. are extremely popular in mass access control systems, e.g. ATMs, campus computer systems. They are also responsible for some of the more notorious hacker successes. The major disadvantages of such systems are that:

- attackers can gain the knowledge required for access by experimentation, observation, or wiretapping;
- there is no means of knowing if the security has been breached before an attack;
- there is no sure method of assigning responsibility for any security lapses;
- the user can share the access privileges, knowingly or unknowingly, with others while continuing to have access privileges;
- there is normally no means of proving that an attacker has gained the requisite knowledge;
- it is difficult to persuade users to adopt good security practices.

Good password management procedures can improve the security of such systems. For example, the common hacker technique of trying various guessed passwords can be detected by security logs which record all unsuccessful log-on attempts. Users and security staff should be informed of such experimentation, and action should then be taken to change passwords. Users can be supplied with easy-to-remember but meaningless phrases to assist them to remember random passwords, e.g. 'Unhappy Monks Eat Rusty German Bicycles' is probably easier to remember than UMERGB. Password validation programs should check and reject passwords that are too short, have been used previously, or are meaningful in the context of the user, etc.

Wiretapping or shoulder surfing (i.e. observing a user inputting the password) may be thwarted by sensible physical design and systems that change the user dialogue for each log-on. For example, the system may hold a database concerning the user (e.g. wife's maiden name, place of birth, etc.). At each log-on the user is asked random questions and the answers are checked against the database. It has also been suggested that word association could form the basis of a knowledge test. A series of word pairs would be stored for an individual user; at log-on the user would be presented with a random selection of words and required to enter the corresponding association words. The word pairs would need to be individualized, e.g. New York–Manhattan would not be acceptable, but a particular user might associate New York with Carmen because he first saw the opera at that city.

Such complex systems are however probably unacceptable in terms of user convenience, throughput, storage requirements, etc. for most access control systems. In general if the security requirements are such that simple password systems are unacceptable then the 'user knows' technique is probably not the answer. On the other hand this technique is commonly used in conjunction with 'something the user has' systems and thus good password/PIN (see chapter 5) procedures will continue to be required for some time to come.

3.3.8 What are the characteristics of 'something the user has' access control systems?
Access control systems in which the user must provide some form of access token (e.g. badge, plastic card, key) overcome some of the limitations of password-type systems (see section 3.3.7), namely:

- attackers normally need to steal or find the token;
- a user normally knows if a token is lost;
- responsibility for lost tokens clearly belongs to the user;
- the users cannot normally share access privileges with others while simultaneously retaining them;
- possession of a token by an unauthorized person may sometimes be proved;
- users holding tokens may be more aware of their security responsibilities.

Some of the distinctions between password and token systems are not absolute. For example, an attacker may be able to gain access without stealing the token, by interfering with the access control mechanism or by manufacturing fake tokens (see chapter 5). Users may be unaware that they have lost the token for some time, allowing attacks to be undertaken in the meanwhile; however, users cannot hide the loss of a token since they will themselves thereafter be denied access. It is, of course, still possible for a user to lend a token to an unauthorized person, who may, in turn, pass it on to an even less authorized person.

If tokens are employed for access control then the following considerations apply:

- Use of the token should be combined with either a password/ PIN or a biometric access technique.
- The token should provide identification of the user at access time.
- Enhanced security is achieved if the dialogue between the sensor and the verification system changes for each log-on.
- Manufacturing set-up costs should be high but unit production costs of the token should be low.
- Manufacture of fake tokens, or modification of genuine tokens, must require a high degree of cost and technical expertise.
- Administration of the supply of tokens must observe strict security precautions.

The traditional access token, i.e. the door key, fails every one of these criteria. A token should always be used in conjunction with some other verification technique (e.g. badge with photograph, plastic card with PIN, smart card with biometric sensor – see section 3.3.12) to obviate the danger of loss or theft. The token should identify the user to the system at access time so that accesses may be logged and access privileges changed without the co-operation of the user. Thus access privileges may be revoked centrally when staff leave employment.

An attacker may attempt to gain access without the token by injecting signals that simulate the normal dialogue between the token receiving unit and the verification system. This type of attack may be prevented by changing the dialogue on each occasion; dynamic password (see section 3.3.10) and fiat–shamir techniques (see section 3.3.11) can overcome this form of attack.

Clearly the production of the false tokens, or the modification of genuine tokens, must be inhibited. This is a major problem when it is necessary to minimize the cost of the token (e.g. customer plastic cards for EFTPOS and ATMs) while recognizing that organized crime will find it profitable to produce such plastic cards (see chapter 5).

An advantage of the token is that it demands some formal administrative system to arrange for the handover of tokens, and an opportunity to provide users with a security awareness. The combination of password and token provides an opportunity for enhanced overall security if separation of duties is enforced, so that staff handling tokens are not provided with the corresponding PIN or password (see chapter 5).

3.3.9 What forms of access token are available?
There are four classes of access tokens used in conjunction with automatic devices:

- keys,
- plastic cards with user identity,
- see-through security devices,
- supersmart cards (see section 3.3.11).

The key class covers a number of physical entities which have the characteristic that they enable access without either requiring any additional verification, or indicating the identity of the user. The device may be a simple door key, a plastic card with some coded information, recorded optically, on a magnetic stripe, with punched holes, etc. These tokens provide only minimal protection. If lost or stolen they can be used by an intruder. Some systems permit recoding of the card reader (say) so the lock can be effectively changed. Thus it can be arranged that the tokens are only valid over defined time periods. A second limitation of these systems is that it is difficult to revoke privileges without the co-operation of token holders; recoding the access device to revoke privileges of one user may involve the reissue, or recoding, of the tokens held by all similar users. Finally, these systems do not provide for any central monitoring of accesses by individual users.

Plastic cards with magnetic stripes are universally used as credit cards and access devices for ATMs and EFTPOS. They have the advantage that their use is well understood by the general public and they are subject to international standards (see chapter 5). Such tokens are used in conjunction with PINs and can hold encoded information on user identity etc. on the magnetic stripe. It is possible to manufacture fake plastic cards or to re-encode the data on genuine cards. The access decision may be made locally if there is some relationship between the data encoded on the card and the PIN (see chapter 5), otherwise the data from the card and the PIN is transmitted to a central computer where the PIN is checked against the card-holder's identity. Encryption of PINs is essential during these transactions to avoid wiretapping attacks, etc.

See-through security systems (see section 3.3.10) combine the advantage of token devices with variable password systems:

- they do not require equipment to 'read' the token;
- users cannot log on without use of the token;
- attackers cannot gain knowledge of the requisite password by observation, wiretapping, or eavesdropping;
- they provide a defence against spoofing.

Supersmart cards (see section 3.3.11) are a further development of the smartcard (see chapter 5), i.e. a plastic card with in-built microprocessor and memory, containing access control algorithms, keypad, and display. They can provide facilities to permit off-line authorization of transactions and cope with the problem of mutual distrust between the user and the verification system.

3.3.10 What is see-through security?
See-through security is a token-based access control system which effectively generates a new password for each log-on. The device has the form of a pocket calculator, and thus log-on can be performed at any conventional user terminal. There is no requirement for a card reader.

There are two techniques of see-through security: automatic password generators and dynamic passwords. In the former case an electronic clock in the token is synchronized with a corresponding clock in the system; at log-on time the user enters the number shown on the token's display and this is checked by the central computer.

With the dynamic password systems the following sequence of steps is performed at log-on (see figure 3-7):

1 User enters user identification at the terminal.
2 The verification system generates a random number and displays it on the terminal.
3 The user enters a PIN, or some biometric data (see section 3.3.12) into the token which then verifies the user to the token.
4 User enters the random number, displayed at the terminal, on the token keypad.
5 The token performs a mathematical calculation, based upon some local secret data (e.g. DES encryption with in-built token cryptographic key) and displays the result.
6 User copies the response from the token display and enters it at the terminal keyboard.
7 The verification system meanwhile has selected from a secure store the secret data (see step 5) corresponding to the user identity, and performed the identical computation on the random number. If the result corresponds with that entered by the user, access is granted.

144

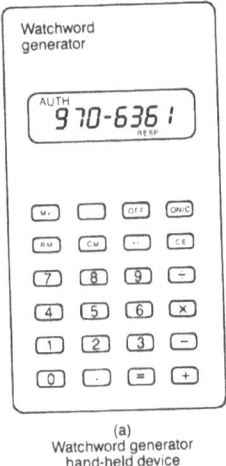

(a)
Watchword generator
hand-held device

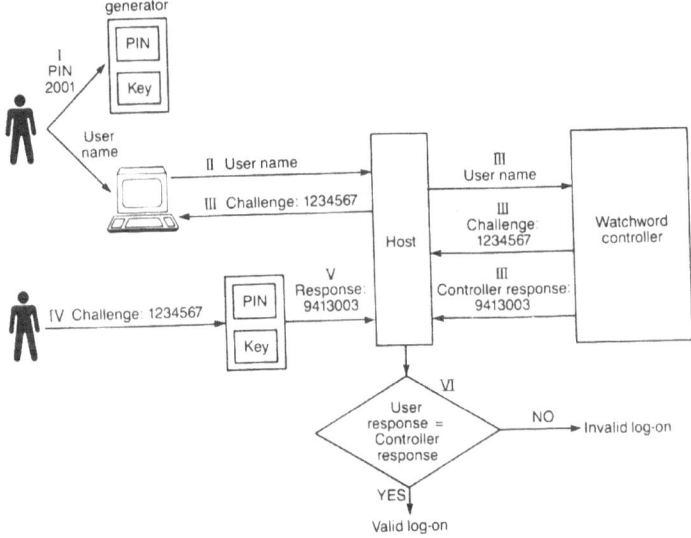

(b) Operational scenario of Racal's Watchword system

Fig. 3-7 Dynamic password. The user enters the challenge into the Watchword, which automatically calculates a seven-digit user-response, using the challenge and the secret key stored within the Watchword. If the user fails to present the correct PIN to the Watchword, it will generate an erroneous response.

145

In some systems the random number generated by the computer can be automatically read into the token; a coded graphic pattern is displayed on the screen and the user places the token against this display. Photosensors then read the random number directly into the token. This provides enhanced security and greater user convenience. In addition the system can be designed to issue a further challenge during a session after successful log-on. This is known as mid-session verification and is used to check that the authorized user is still at the terminal.

The challenge–response approach of the dynamic password can also be used in the opposite direction so that the computer verifies itself to the token. This provides a defence against spoofing in which a user is persuaded to enter confidential information, or authorize a transaction, on an attacker's computer.

3.3.11 What additional facilities can supersmart cards provide over see-through security devices?

There are two situations in which more complex demands are being made upon access control systems, and the techniques employing supersmart cards have been developed to meet these demands. These situations are:

- off-line authorization of transactions (see chapter 5),
- mutual distrust at log-on,
- anonymity of user.

Conventional plastic cards are not considered to be sufficient, in themselves, to authorize transactions when the status (e.g. bank balance) of the user is variable. Similar situations can arise in other areas. The authority of an employee to perform transactions may vary from time to time, or the employee may have authority only to undertake a given 'value' of transactions. One solution is to refer all transactions to a central location and check the current status of the user. The smart card and the supersmart card (see chapter 5) can store the current status, and update it after each transaction, thus permitting off-line verification.

Access control devices may provide more than just access to a system; they may be employed to authorize the user to perform sensitive transactions or electronically sign significant documents. Most traditional access control devices assume only that the system distrusts the user. If the users, however, give personal authorizations at terminals then they may, not unreasonably, seek assurances that they are dealing with legitimate terminals. Moreover, the user may also wish to ensure that the system cannot use information provided by the user at log-on, and later to exploit that information to create fake log-ons or authorizations.

This situation arises most commonly in EFTPOS systems. One would like to be sure that the retailer cannot create a number of fake transactions on the basis of information supplied in the conduct of a genuine one. However, it is not difficult to envisage similar circumstances facing managers. Financial and legal transactions may be performed at terminals located in the offices of clients etc. The system granting access will wish to verify the user, but the user will want to ensure that information supplied at the terminal could not be used to enable the verification system to collaborate in a subsequent fake transaction. With the dynamic password, for example, the system generates the random number and knows the secret data in the user's token. This information would enable a dishonest system to create a fake log-on.

Access techniques of mutual distrust can be developed using public key cryptography. The fiat–shamir algorithm involves a dialogue between the terminal and the user's supersmart card in which both parties make selections of data. Given suitable algorithms and secret keys embedded in the supersmart card then the terminal can verify the user; but at the end of a transaction, or after many transactions, never has sufficient information to determine the secret data contained in the user's card, and cannot therefore masquerade as a user, even to itself. The need for a keypad and display on the supersmart card arises from the mutual distrust aspect of the transaction. It would be much easier and cheaper to use a keypad and display on the terminal. However, the user could not be sure that data supplied to the card, or the data entered into the card by the user, had not been altered by the terminal display/keypad system (see chapter 5).

The fiat–shamir algorithm can also provide anonymity for the user, i.e. users can prove that they are authorized, but their identity is not necessarily revealed to the system.

3.3.12 What are the characteristics of biometric sensors?
There are two classes of systems that may be more accurately described as biometric and physiological/behavioural devices. The first measures some biometric attribute (e.g. fingerprint, retinal blood-vessel pattern, or hand geometry) while the latter deal with dynamics of signature, voice print, keyboard rhythm, etc. Biometric access sensors are likely to be of increasing significance in access control technology. The potential advantages of biometric devices over 'password' or 'token' systems appear to be that:

- biometric characteristics are unique to an individual: they cannot be copied or faked by an attacker;
- biometric sensors do not necessarily require the user to carry a token, or remember a PIN/password.

In addition passive biometric devices such as fingerprint analysers are less demanding in terms of users' action. The disadvantages of this class of devices (see section 3.3.6) are:

- cost,
- false rejections and acceptances,
- low throughput,
- susceptibility to external factors such as injury,
- user acceptability,
- disadvantaged users.

If biometric sensors are employed then the characteristics of the user (i.e. biometric signature) must be stored. At log-on these characteristics are measured and the resulting signature produced by the sensor is then compared with the stored value. The two potential modes of operation of biometric access control systems are:

- host-based biometrics,
- stand-alone biometrics.

In the host-based system the user accesses a biometric sensor located at the terminal; the biometric signature is encrypted and transmitted to the host computer for comparison. The advantage of this system is that a single sensor may serve multiple users; if the sensor fails then the user could normally seek out another. Problems will arise, however, if centrally-stored signatures are compromised. In this case there is no future guarantee that the access information is not a masquerade signal from an attacker, and, unlike a PIN or password, the user is not free to select a new signature (see section 3.3.6).

Alternatively a combination of token with biometric sensor technique may be employed. In this case the user carries a token which stores the biometric signature, and also acts as a biometric sensor. Users then identify themselves to the token, instead of inputting a PIN. If they are accepted by the token, log-on proceeds as for the case of see-through security systems (see section 3.3.10).

The advantage of this approach is that there is no danger of a compromise of centrally-stored biometric signatures; the tokens would require designing so as to be sufficiently tamper-resistant to defy a local attack on their stored data. Access could also be provided at any terminal since there is no longer a requirement for a local sensor. The disadvantages are that each token would require an individual sensor, which is likely to be expensive. Moreover, failure of a token would lock out the user from the system since there is no alternative sensor. It is also possible that the security officer would be concerned that the integrity of the identification system would be delegated to a multiple of token/sensors some of which could be captured by attackers. A slight modification of the system would involve storage of the biometric data in the token and the use of a biometric sensor at the terminal. In this case the user would plug the token onto the sensor and the signature produced would be compared with the stored value on the token. The token would then identify itself to the system.

3.3.13 Is there now a sharp distinction between physical and logical access control?

Two developments are tending to erode the distinction between physical and logical access control. First there is considerable advantage in re-establishing physical security as an integral part of logical security. It is, in theory, extremely convenient to allow users to access systems from any location: other branches, overseas offices, hotel rooms, etc. However, the cost of such convenience is that it opens the door to hackers. If the vast majority of users access the computer system from fixed locations, during office hours, then the security cost of total open access, to provide for the occasional user, may be too high. Thus a policy of restricting logical access to information on the basis of computer terminal location, and time/date of use, will enhance security if appropriate physical access control is applied to the terminals.

A second factor which may impinge on this question is the increasing sophistication of controls in large modern buildings. Some such buildings use computer control of access, lifts, lights, air-conditioning, etc. There may well be a case for linking such systems into the logical access control of computer information used by workers in those buildings.

3.3.14 If the access control system is totally secure can an attacker compromise the information security?

There are at least two methods by which an attacker can affect information security without logging on to the computer:

- electronic eavesdropping (see section 3.4.7),
- computer viruses (see section 3.3.16).

The problem of electromagnetic radiations from computer equipment has been well recognized in military circles for many years, and Tempest-proofing has been a standard form of defence. However, it had been generally assumed that the equipment required by the eavesdropper was so sophisticated that this was not a matter of concern in commercial environments. More recently, however, van Eck reported that electronic eavesdropping on computers was possible using cheap, readily-available electronic components. Demonstrations of eavesdropping outside finance houses were given in a television documentary. There are various protection devices available to combat this problem (see section 3.4.7).

The computer virus is a much more insidious problem. It has been widely recognized (see chapter 1) that organizations were always at risk of attack from their own programmers; various forms of malicious code (e.g. Trojan horses, time bombs, and logic bombs) were described in the past. This form of attack, however, has always involved the direct change of code of a given program, usually in the form of a patch. Thus the only programs at risk were those that could be accessed by the vandal programmer; once they were detected and removed then the danger was past.

The computer virus is a piece of code that can not only do damage in its own right, but it can also cause itself to be written to another program. Thus one can not only import malicious code produced by somebody else's vandal program, but also such importation can be second-, third-, or fourth-hand, etc. Moreover, having found and eliminated the virus, there is no guarantee that other software has not been infected. Defence against viruses may well be a major issue for computer security for some time to come (see section 3.3.15).

3.3.15 How can software have an impact upon information security?
There is no way of differentiating between a legal and illegal act within the context of program code. Reading information from one file, writing to another, deleting a file, changing a number in a file of financial transactions, etc. may be perfectly legitimate actions, or they may cause serious breaches of information security. One can only deduce whether a piece of code is performing a legitimate or illegitimate act by considering it within the context of the specification of the program. Programs are commonly changed during their lifetime to remove bugs, enhance their effectiveness, etc. Such minor changes are termed 'patches'. It is absolutely essential that patches to software be fully authorized, kept to a minimum, and fully documented.

Programmers, particularly systems programmers, have special access rights to software, and it is often possible for them to insert patches for illegal purposes. Such modifications are usually termed 'malicious code'. The reported forms of malicious code are:

- time bombs,
- logic bombs,
- Trojan Horses,
- viruses (see section 3.3.16).

Time bombs are sections of code that are triggered at a specified time/date; during execution they check the time/date from the operating system and either remain dormant or perform some malicious act, e.g. delete files, depending upon the data.

Logic bombs are similar to time bombs except that the trigger is some event, e.g. the payroll file is checked and the trigger is the removal of the programmer's name, indicating that he or she has terminated his or her employment.

Trojan Horses use the privileges of the program to perform some illicit act, e.g. access a confidential file and write the contents to an unclassified file.

Viruses are a new form of malicious code that can cause themselves to be written to other host programs in computer store.

3.3.16 How does a virus work?

A computer virus operates during execution of the host program by:

1 checking other software in the computer store;
2 writing itself to a program that does not already contain it;
3 checking its own time bomb or logic bomb trigger, if any;
4 performing some malicious act according to the state of its triggers, if any.

The virus will thus spread to any program held in computer store, usually backing store, that is not protected against a write action. Thus a floppy diskette with a write-protect tab would be safe against the spread of a virus among its stored programs.

The deadly effect of the virus is that its spread rapidly accelerates as each infected program is executed, causing the infection of other programs. The initial program causing the virus need only be executed once for the infection to begin and spread. Viruses may therefore appear to remain dormant for long periods and then spread rapidly throughout the computer system. The virus can easily spread from one microcomputer user to another. If the virus infects the operating system then the following sequence of event can occur:

1 User unknowingly loads diskette with infected program into microcomputer.

2 Virus infects operating system resident in the computer RAM.
3 User removes diskette and vacates computer without switching it off.
4 Second user loads diskette into the microcomputer without re-booting the operating system.
5 Virus in the resident operating system infects second user's diskette.

Thus although the initial design of the virus is a deliberate act, its propagation through a system is caused by the inadvertent actions of innocent users.

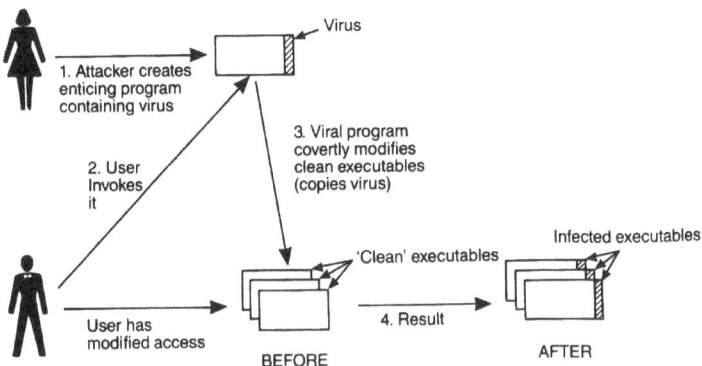

Fig. 3-8 Computer virus

3.3.17 How does a computer catch a virus?
Someone, somewhere produces a section of code which has a virus action, and either executes that piece of code, or embeds it in a legitimate program which is then executed on the computer. Other programs are then infected with the virus, unbeknown to the operators of the computer. These programs are then copied onto floppy diskette, downloaded over computer networks, e.g. by electronic mail, or written on bulletin boards. The copied programs are then transferred to other computers, infect programs on their new host; copies of these infected programs are then transferred to other computers, and so on.

3.3.18 What categories of computers are most vulnerable to viruses?
A major factor in the development and transmission of viruses is the operating system of the computer. Viruses are most likely to be injected into a program in object code form; as such the programs can

only be executed on computers that have compatible operating systems.

The transfer of viruses is likely to arise predominantly in the personal computer field for the following reasons:

- the standardization of the market into a few operating systems, and the proliferation of personal computers;
- the widespread use of pirated and borrowed software;
- the ready availability of bulletin boards, hobby magazines, etc.;
- the widespread use of personal computers in schools and colleges;
- the environment in which personal computers are used.

The standardization of personal computer hardware and software has created a large international population of programmers with extensive knowledge and experience of personal computer operating systems. A very high proportion of these programmers are hobbyists, and some of them will inevitably experiment with a concept as fascinating as a virus. Inevitably some experimenters will pass on their viruses to other computer users.

There is a common tradition of usage of pirated software in the personal computer field. In addition games, useful routines, etc. are produced and passed around. This provides a ready means of distribution of floppy diskettes; a personal computer is also likely to be used by a variety of different categories of users, so that it is not difficult for a virus to be brought into the home on a games diskette by a teenager, and then infect the software of a small businessman. Perhaps more seriously, the integrity of a computer network is threatened if a manager uses a portable computer at home, and then loads infected diskettes into an office personal computer connected to the network. Bulletin boards provide yet another means of distribution of infected programs, so that it is no longer necessary for there to be immediate contact between users, or the exchange of floppy diskettes. Hobby magazines, however responsible the editors, will inevitably carry articles on viruses and assist in the dissemination of interest and expertise.

The introduction of personal computers into schools and colleges was designed to produce a generation who were completely at home with the computer; this is, however, an environment in which the temptation to experiment with viruses, pass around expertise, and play pranks will prove to be stronger than the disciplinary procedures to prevent the misuse of computers.

The greatest vulnerability of the personal computer arises, however, because it was designed to be operated by non-computing professionals with the minimum of administrative overheads. Most personal computers are operated with a complete lack of organizational controls. The users are unlikely to adopt the sort of rigorous precautionary procedures that it will be necessary to adopt if virus infection becomes widespread (see section 3.3.21). The virus position for the mainframe computer is somewhat different. On the one hand there are far fewer experienced systems programmers with the expertise necessary to develop a virus for a mainframe operating system, and, it is to be hoped, less prevalence of pirated software. Moreover mainframe operating systems automatically provide protection of files against unauthorized access by other users. On the other hand a virus could cause appalling damage if it entered the computer complex of an organization. The main danger to mainframe computers arises if there is substantial development of software, with teams of co-operating programmers, or if software is routinely moved around computer networks.

It is also likely that more viruses will be reported in the personal computer field because it will be more difficult to deny their existence than in the corresponding case of organizational mainframe computers.

3.3.19 Are some viruses more dangerous than others?
There are two impacts of a virus:

- increase of storage requirements of infected programs;
- action specified by the triggered virus.

When a virus is written to a program then the program occupies more space in backing storage. Some viruses were detected on a college campus simply because users found that they were running out of diskette space without writing any more files to diskette.

The real damage produced by a virus, however, depends upon the action performed when it is triggered by the time bomb or logic bomb action. This could cause major inconvenience, or damage, e.g. files may be deleted or program operation affected or halted. On the other hand the damage may be as trivial as a 'Gotcha, arf, arf' message displayed on the screen. It has even been suggested that some viruses could be developed to have a beneficial action, e.g. a virus that caused programs to compress themselves during storage, to minimize memory requirements, and to expand themselves prior to execution.

Another factor in the danger associated with a virus is its host program. Viruses that are only resident in application programs may be easiest to detect and eliminate. Viruses in system utilities will be much more difficult to handle because the very actions to deal with the virus may invoke software which itself spreads the virus. For example, if the object code of an application program is found to contain a virus then one would delete that copy of the program and produce another version by re-compiling the original, 'clean' source code version of the program. Suppose, however, that the system utility required (i.e. the compiler), contained the virus and immediately wrote it into the new object program.

The situation is even worse if the virus is hidden in software that is invisible to the programmer; there are many items of software that are invoked during the operation of a computer which are not listed in directory searches and are not normally accessible to the user.

A network virus with a delayed action, so that it is propagated and then, at some point in time, goes into an infinite loop would cause programs to gobble up CPU cycles and storage; everything would then seize up instantaneously.

3.3.20 Can viruses be automatically detected and killed?
There is no foolproof method of ensuring that a program is free of all viruses. Clearly if the virus is known then it is possible to search through the program code, detect the existence of the known virus, and delete it. However, there is no method by which an automatic routine can guarantee to detect a section of code which has the action of a virus. Filter programs which can, at least, detect some viruses, are already available. However, one can anticipate a continual battle between the designer of the virus and that of the filter.

It is possible to detect the changes that occur in a program when it has been infected with a virus, and this is a source of protective routines. If the amount of code in a program is noted and recorded before the program is infected, then it is possible to check the program for increased code immediately before execution. It may be wise to employ message authentication techniques (see chapter 1), with secret keys, to guarantee the integrity of the program. It might not be too difficult for the ingenious virus developer to arrange for the virus to recompute a checksum automatically; the use of a cryptographic key in the calculation of the checksum would ensure that this form of virus was thwarted. Unfortunately programs will be born with the virus if the system utility software is itself infected (e.g. the compiler) in which case even the previously mentioned protection is ineffective.

3.3.21 What defensive measures should be taken by management in the light of computer viruses?
Computer viruses will cause most damage in environments with poor information security. There is no guaranteed software defence or vaccine against virus attacks. Current software defences are only effective against a known class of current viruses. For every software defence package or vaccine, there will be a systems program with a new virus to defeat the package.

The virus must be seen as further evidence of the importance of the need for good information security management. It will be seen elsewhere (see section 3.4.1) that the uncontrolled use of personal computers is a major source of concern from the viewpoint of information security, and the computer virus is further evidence of this problem. Software must not be freely imported into the organization; it is becoming increasingly clear that tight control must be exercised by the security officer on all software used within the organization.

It may be time to re-evaluate the use of personal computers in their current form. Most personal computers are much more versatile than necessary from an operational viewpoint. Suppose that they were replaced by workstations with fixed functionalities, would this really bring the organization to a standstill? The forms of protective measures that might be considered:

- non-removable encryptor boards installed in all personal computers,
- workstations with only ROM-based software,
- diskless workstations.

If an encryptor board is fixed in the personal computer, such that all data and software is decrypted before it is read into, or encrypted before it is written by, the personal computer, then no unauthorized software can be loaded into the personal computer. Authorized software would have to be encrypted by the security officer; hence the flow of software into the organization would be controlled. Of course it might still be possible to key in software via the keyboard, but this is an extremely time-consuming and error-prone operation which is unlikely to be undertaken lightly.

The second approach would recognize that the majority of personal computers are purchased for word processing, spreadsheets, or database applications. If these packages are supplied in ROM, or on a compact disc, then no virus infection can occur. It would also be possible to remove the capability to run any software other than the specified packages.

The third possibility is to fix the functionality of the personal computer, and control the flow of data, by employing diskless workstations linked to a file server. In this case the workstation user would be offered a fixed set of functions only; having made the selection the software would be loaded into the workstation from the file server. Similarly data would be transferred between the workstation and the file server on demand. Requests for data to be loaded onto floppy diskettes, for collection from a service point could then be security logged, similarly data could only be loaded into the system from a service point and security logged.

3.3.22 What are the recovery procedures following a virus attack?
The recovery procedures must be designed well in advance and written into the contingency plans (see section 3.5.14). To date very few computing staff have any experience of virus attacks and recovering from them. It is said that the worst effect of a virus attack is the state of panic that it induces. Above all backup data must be protected. If the backup data is loaded into the computer after an attack then there is a significant danger that it will itself be damaged. If the very first action is to create to an additional version of backup data one must reckon with the possibility that the 'copy' utility is infected.

The full recovery procedure may involve the use of a sterile backup computer, with a minimal set of sterile software. Gradually additional software is loaded in and checked for evidence of infection before it is executed.

It is imperative that the contingency plans for a virus attack be developed well in advance and that computer operator staff are fully aware of the recovery procedures, and their actions monitored closely if there is a chance that an operator was responsible for introducing the virus.

3.3.23 When were viruses first reported?
An early paper on the concept of viruses was produced by Cohen in 1985. Little interest was shown in this development originally and first serious reports of viruses came from the Hebrew University in Israel. LeHigh University, Pennsylvania also reported a microcomputer virus, and IBM had an attack on its electronic mail system. Now viruses have been more widely reported but the situation is not dissimilar to that of computer crime: there is clearly considerable concern in the computing community, and there are suspicions that organizations are not reporting attacks.

3.3.24 Should organizations be concerned with the dangers of viruses?
Yes. If a virus strikes an organization that is both unprepared for a virus attack and heavily dependent upon its information processing system, then the effects could be disastrous. The most dangerous aspect of viruses is that they may render normal recovery procedures inappropriate. While computer centres may have some experience of disaster recovery almost none will be experienced in recovery from virus attacks, when software utilities used in recovery operations may themselves be infected with the virus. It is essential that contingency plans be reconsidered in the light of possible viral attacks (see section 3.5.14).

3.4 Personal Computer Security

3.4.1 Introduction

Personal computers represent the Achilles Heel of data security. They are often employed in unsupervised locations, used by inadequately trained and unsupervised staff, carried from one location to another together with any resident data, and are targets for theft. Their data is stored on floppy diskettes which can be easily stolen, damaged, misused, or simply lost. The software employed can originate from unauthorized sources (e.g. software pirates), be subject to illegal modification, or carry viruses.

This situation would be bad enough if the data handled were less sensitive than that held on corporate databases. However departmental data processed by personal computers may be very attractive to an attacker because it can represent a coherent, complete picture of a functional area, e.g. a research project or marketing plan.

This somewhat depressing picture takes a turn for the worse when the personal computer becomes a workstation linked to a host computer or communications network. It then becomes an access point into corporate databases or expensive communications facilities. Not only can data or services be misused, but contaminated local data can be passed directly into a corporate database. The personal computer can also be linked into the public telephone network, allowing the hacker to dial up the personal computer and then gain illegal access into the corporate network (see section 3.4.8).

3.4.2 What are the essential differences between personal computer and mainframe security?

The essential attributes of personal computer security, which differ from mainframe security are:

- access control (see section 3.3.1),
- in-built security mechanisms,
- nature of processed data,
- users.

The phenomenal growth in personal computing was largely due to the high degree of guaranteed accessibility that they provided to the individual user. The first reaction of mainframe data processing managers to growing concerns on security was to create a protective shell around their equipment. However, this solution would negate the whole concept of a personal computer. This guaranteed accessibility to personal computers not only creates a vulnerability to hardware and data theft, and unauthorized modification and disclosure of data, it also renders any security mechanisms themselves vulnerable to direct attack. Thus expansion cards designed to impose access restrictions may be removed or rendered inactive by an attacker who simply opens up the computer.

The operating systems for personal computers were designed to be user-friendly and thus provide a high degree of functionality to non-technical users. They also tacitly assumed that they were single-user systems so that there was no requirement to protect one user from the accidental or malicious depredations of another. Thus the in-built security mechanisms of multi-user mainframe systems are absent from most personal computer operating systems. In general anyone who logs onto the system has access to all data and software. There are also normally no security logs or audit trail systems. Even the time/date stamp on files can be reset to any value specified by the user.

The information stored on personal computers is likely to relate to some well-defined organizational role (see chapter 6) and an intruder in the marketing manager's office may well be able to collect from a single hard disk device highly coherent spreadsheet, word processing, and database information relating to a given project. A similar attack on a corporate mainframe computer would involve sifting through vast quantities of relatively unprocessed data.

The most significant security hazard associated with personal computers, however, is the user. The hazards arise both from authorized office staff and the attacker. The former are often exploiting the power of the personal computer with inadequate training and security awareness. The attacker, on the other hand can easily acquire significant knowledge and expertise of personal computer operating systems from readily available documentation and unlimited experimentation on home computers.

3.4.3 What are the main aspects of personal computer security?
The four main considerations of personal computer security may be listed as:

- physical and communications security (see section 3.4.4),
- data security (see section 3.4.10),
- procedural security (see section 3.4.15).

Personal computers, their peripherals, and their associated storage media are expensive, portable, and widely used. They are therefore attractive items for the thief. They are essential for efficient operation of an office, and since they are easily damaged they are potential attack areas for vandals and saboteurs. The greatest threat associated with theft or damage of personal computer systems, however, may lie not in the direct loss or damage to hardware, but rather in the consequent loss or disclosure of sensitive stored data. A

159

petty theft of floppy diskettes, with a retail value of a few pounds, may result in significant organizational losses if the diskettes hold irreplaceable data, or if sensitive stored information were subsequently disclosed.

Physical security of personal computers is thus often primarily directed at the protection of stored corporate data and/or access to communications facilities; in such cases the cost of protective measures needs to be weighed more against the effect of data losses or misuse of communications facilities than the retail value of the hardware.

Personal computers were conceived as stand-alone devices but it was soon realized that their full potential lay in their use as local processors of information received from corporate databases or other users at local or remote sites. The physical security of individual personal computers can thus easily affect the overall security of corporate data or communications. This not only means that local departmental security can have an impact upon corporate security, but also that the personal computer must, in these circumstances, satisfy the security requirements of communications systems (see chapter 4).

Data security is concerned with the protection of both software and data. Data security is related to physical security, but the potential sources of loss, contamination, and disclosure of data, both accidental and malicious, together with associated protective measures, need to be fully understood by management.

Personal computers are widely used by office staff with virtually no technical training or expertise in the functioning of computers. Indeed the growth of personal computers is largely ascribed to the user-friendly nature of their hardware and software. This situation, however, has created many vulnerabilities for organizational data processed by personal computers. Since one cannot rely upon all users being fully acquainted with the security implications of their actions, it is essential that careful forethought be undertaken by management, and procedures developed, to minimize the possibility of accidental or malicious damage to personal computer data.

3.4.4 How can microcomputers be physically protected?
Lockdown devices are available to secure the computer to a bench and thus prevent the casual thief from simply carrying it out of the office. Such mechanisms need to be augmented with locks which prevent the pilferer from removing expensive internal components, floppy disk drives, etc.

It may also be necessary to prevent access to the power switch to avoid deliberate power removal during processing, e.g. unattended backup. One should also ensure that power leads do not trail over the office floor: data may easily be corrupted by an accident that drags the power lead from the power point. Some software systems can lock out access from unattended personal computers, which may be temporarily left unsupervised while still switched on.

The computer should not be located in hazardous environments, e.g. under sprinkler systems, in close proximity to heavy electrical equipment, or connected to power lines subject to power surges or frequent power failures.

The computers should not be available to unauthorized staff who could operate them without supervision. Hard disk systems are particularly vulnerable to misuse since their data is permanently resident. Given that staff are likely to make unauthorized use of microcomputers during unsupervised periods (e.g. lunch breaks) for personal word processing, course assignments for part-time students, etc., it may be wise to set aside a personal computer for that purpose, and then absolutely forbid the use of official personal computers for unofficial business.

3.4.5 What are the vulnerabilities of magnetic storage media?

Floppy diskettes are commonly employed to store data and software; care must be exercised both to prevent physical damage to such media and to ensure that the stored data is well administered.

Floppy diskettes are now so common in office environments that they are likely to be handled by staff with no technical training; it is not unknown for floppy diskettes to be stapled to printouts, brochures, etc. The diskettes need to be handled with care: the slot in the plastic envelope, provided for contact between the magnetic disk and reading head, leaves a section of the diskette vulnerable to damage from direct contact with fingers, sharp instruments, etc. The diskettes should always be placed in the protective paper envelopes as soon as they are removed from the machine, and then securely stored in diskette container units. The 3.5 inch microfloppy diskettes are less vulnerable to damage because they have rigid covers and the magnetic surface is completely protected from accidental contact. Diskettes left lying on desks may be lost, borrowed, stolen, or damaged by a spillage from a coffee cup. Floppy diskettes are also widely used by home computer hobbyists and there exists the danger that diskettes will be stolen for their intrinsic value resulting in the loss of invaluable organizational data; use of distinctive diskette labels and protective envelopes is recommended (see section 3.4.10).

The diskettes must be correctly labelled with an indication of their contents, and it is wise to set departmental standards on the generic titles to be given to diskettes. It can be difficult to determine an appropriate short title covering multifarious files on the diskette, and duplication of titles for different diskettes may lead to confusion within an office. Similarly, containers for floppy diskettes should be specified, and labelled for functional areas. Backup floppy diskettes should never be stored in the same containers as the originals.

3.4.6 What precautions need to be taken when a hard disk system fails?

Clearly it is important regularly to backup data on a computer with a hard disk drive; unlike floppy diskettes any failure of the disk drive immediately renders the hard disk data inaccessible to the user. However, the data on a faulty unit will be available to the maintenance personnel; such work will normally be conducted off-site and therefore beyond the control of the organizational security officer. The disk data may not be protected by software access controls during repair unless it is encrypted.

Organizations with sensitive data should investigate the security precautions taken by microcomputer repair companies, and insist that such firms give a contractual undertaking to protect the data on machines under repair.

3.4.7 Can one eavesdrop on microcomputer transactions?

Electronic equipment gives off electromagnetic signals that can be picked up from a distance with surprisingly unsophisticated equipment (see section 3.2.8). This phenomenon has been well known in military circles for some time; expensive Tempest controls have been specified to combat the problem. Van Eck published details of the vulnerability of microcomputer systems; demonstrations have been publicized in which the data on terminal screens, located in an office block, were captured and displayed in a vehicle parked outside the building. The total equipment required cost a few hundred pounds and could be readily assembled by an electronics handyman. Electronic countermeasures equipment is available on the market to combat this problem (see figure 3-9).

3.4.8 What are the security exposures associated with the connection of a microcomputer to host systems or networks?

Personal computers are now commonly connected into networks or host computer systems; the security stance associated with the personal computer environment can have an impact upon the security of corporate data or networks. The main considerations are:

- local processing power and storage facilities of the personal computer workstation;
- access control to the workstation;
- injection of data or software from the workstation;
- misuse of communications facilities.

162

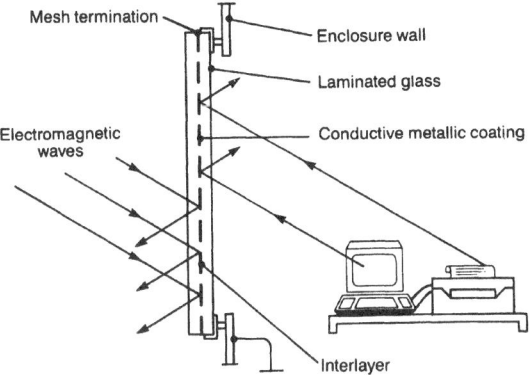

Fig. 3-9 Shielding against eavesdropping. Specially made laminated glass provides an effective barrier to radiation from microcomputers.

It is possible to program a personal computer workstation to run through a complex set of procedures to access corporate data or to make a network connection. The workstation can store telephone numbers and passwords, so that a few keystrokes will automatically dial up a host computer, log-on, undertake password dialogues, and then select mainframe files for downloading into the personal computer. Moreover, it may even be possible to dial up the workstation itself from a remote location to initiate the aforementioned routines. Such facilities may be timesaving for the manager but they represent a major security weakness, providing an open sesame to an intruder. Passwords, confidential telephone numbers, etc. must never be stored in personal computer log-on sequences.

In some mainframe systems access to data is restricted to certain terminals at specified times; these systems thus assume that access to the terminals is controlled. Personal computers connected into such systems should therefore be adequately supervised; it should not be possible to access the mainframe by dialling up the personal computer from a remote location. The major source of access control vulnerability will always lie with poor password discipline (see section 3.3.7) and this matter must be firmly policed by management.

The security of data and communications is not restricted to the unauthorized receipt of data; increasingly there is concern at the injection of unauthorized transactions, or software that may contain viruses (see section 3.3.16). There is a trend against the use of versatile personal computers in corporate networks because they represent an uncontrolled source of local processing power within the system, subject to abuse by an attacker. Diskless workstations, in which the software and data is downloaded from a file server, can provide all the facilities required by managerial workstation users but render the total system less vulnerable to injection attacks (see section 3.3.21).

When a personal computer is connected to a communications line the legitimate, or unauthorized user, can run up some expensive call charges, and management needs to ensure that such access is restricted to authorized users, that it is rendered inoperative outside working hours and that communications costs are monitored and controlled.

3.4.9 Is it necessary to protect programs on a personal computer?

Programs, particularly proprietary software, are not unique to an organization, and may therefore be considered to be at less risk than organizational data. However, there are two good reasons for restricting access to software:

- contractual responsibilities to the supplier of the software;
- danger of contamination of the software.

Software is normally supplied under licence and the purchaser has a responsibility to protect it against use or copying outside the terms of the agreement (see chapter 7). Given the widespread use of word processing packages, spreadsheets, etc. and the high cost of some proprietary software, there will always exist the temptation for staff to make illegal copies of software.

Another security aspect of software that is of increasing concern is the contamination of software. Software may be deliberately modified for malicious purposes with the injection of time bombs, Trojan Horses, etc. (see section 3.3.15). In addition software can be damaged by viruses (see section 3.3.16) inserted unwittingly by authorized users.

3.4.10 How can one control access to data processed by a personal computer?

The data may be resident in the personal computer (e.g. on a hard disk) or stored on floppy diskettes. The data may therefore be subject to unauthorized use from:

direct access to the data resident in the computer:
- by accessing the computer while the data is being processed;
- by accessing the data on the hard disk when the computer is unattended;
- by accessing the hard disk during repair or maintenance of the computer (see section 3.4.6);

164

- by electronic eavesdropping (see section 3.4.7);
access to the data on floppy diskettes stored apart from the computer;
access to data residues (see section 3.4.12).

In the case of computer resident data the access may be controlled by physical access control to the computer itself, or logical access control which protects the data from unauthorized computer users (see section 3.3.1).

Personal computers are designed to be freely available, and it will be difficult to control access by methods which inhibit free access to authorized users. The control of physical access to the computers will therefore depend upon the control of access to offices in which they are located. If a personal computer provides a general service to a group of workers then it should be located either in a controlled area, or one that is sufficiently supervised to ensure that unauthorized access does not go unnoticed.

The logical access control required for a personal computer will depend upon whether it is:

- a stand-alone floppy disk drive system,
- a stand-alone hard disk system,
- connected to a mainframe or network (see section 3.4.8).

Stand-alone floppy disk drive systems only have resident data during processing. Thus the only form of logical access control that may be required is some form of software lockout if the computer is left unattended while processing data.

Hard disk systems may well be attractive to an attacker since the data are permanently resident, and relate to a given functional area, e.g. personal computer for the marketing manager. In such cases the computer may be protected against unauthorized log-on by access control devices such as a badge or card reader (see section 3.3.8). The data may be further protected by encryption so that the user will require knowledge of a password before access is granted to the data (see section 3.4.11).

Sensitive data stored on floppy diskettes requires that users are aware of the sensitivity of the stored data and the regulations governing the handling of such data. Diskettes containing sensitive information can be marked with special labels and brightly coloured jackets (see chapter 6). Such marking will ensure that legitimate users are aware of the nature of the diskette, and are likely to observe attempts to remove such diskettes illegally from the office, or the possession of such diskettes by unauthorized persons. Unfortunately the marking is also useful to the attacker, and such diskettes need to be held in secure cupboards when not in use.

Data may be protected from disclosure or from undetectable modification by encryption. The encrypted data may be held on hard disk or floppy diskettes and can then only be read or meaningfully modified by an authorized user with access to a computer containing the requisite cryptographic facilities and a knowledge of the associated cryptographic key. Encryption does not, however, protect the data against malicious destruction (see chapter 1).

3.4.11 How can personal computer data be encrypted?

Encryption of personal computer data may be performed with a software utility or hardware encryptor board. A computer program can be developed to perform encryption/decryption operations using proprietary or standard algorithms such as DES (see chapter 1). The user creates a plaintext version of the data to be protected, invokes the encryption algorithm, and enters a cryptographic key known only to authorized users. A ciphertext version of the data is then produced and stored on magnetic disk. The user must then completely overwrite the plaintext version of the file, the simple 'Erase' facility provided by the operating system is not sufficient for this purpose (see section 3.4.12). Decryption of the data is similarly performed by invoking a decryption software utility and entering the required cryptographic key. Bulk file utilities may be provided to encrypt all data on a disk in one operation.

The software utility requires no special hardware and it enables each user to decide whether to encrypt the data, moreover each user may have an individual cryptographic key. On the other hand this approach makes demands upon the user which may be inappropriate in an office environment. The alternative approach is to fit an encryptor board into the microcomputer. With this device the user is required to enter a password at log-on if the encryption facility is to be used. Thereafter each block of data, to be written to disk, is first encrypted; similarly each block read from disk is decrypted before it is passed to the requesting program. Thus the cryptographic process is almost transparent to the user.

3.4.12 Does the 'Erase' or 'Delete' command on a personal computer actually destroy the stored data?

It is commonly believed that the 'Erase' or 'Delete' command actually removes a file from a magnetic disc. In fact this process merely sets a 'delete' flag in the file directory: the data still exists on the disk until some time later when the disk space may be required for writing another file. Although deleted files are inaccessible from normal operating systems functions, they can be resurrected by competent programmers. This residues problem can be solved by using a program to overwrite all file data as part of the deletion process. Although such programs are relatively easy to write, they are usually not provided as standard features of personal computer operating systems. They must therefore be acquired or written by the user.

3.4.13 What are the security aspects of personal computer accounting applications?

Accounting packages are commonly run on personal computers and their financial connotations render them vulnerable to attack. This fact must be also be considered in relation to the general rule that the majority of computer crime is committed by inside staff. The factors that need to be considered are:

- separation of duties,
- lack of in-built controls,
- lack of control of software design and modification.

The personal computer enables one person to perform in the roles of programmer, systems analyst, data entry clerk, computer operator, and accountant. This situation completely negates the separation of duties (see chapter 7) considered essential as a protection against computer fraud.

Accounting software developed internally, or acquired from producers lacking well established reputations, may not only contain undiscovered bugs, or deliberately implanted malicious code, it may simply not conform to good security procedures. For example, such packages may lack audit trails, records of activity, effective data entry controls, input and output validation checks, etc. Such design shortcomings are even more significant if the application involves substantial transaction processing.

The maintenance and operation of personal computing accounting packages also may not conform to the level of standards implemented by a security conscious computer centre. Thus documentation may be inadequate, backup and recovery plans not well understood or implemented, program modifications may not be subject to stringent control or sufficiently tested, etc. The software may leave the files in some undefined state if processing is interrupted by a power failure or simply accidental removal of power (see section 3.4.4).

It is clearly important for management to recognize the security hazards associated with accounting packages and to ensure that guidelines are developed and implemented.

3.4.14 Are security logs and audit trails provided in personal computer systems?

Given the sensitivity of data often processed on a personal computer, security log procedures and audit trails (see chapter 1) may well be required by management, but such facilities need to be expressly requested in most cases of personal computer software.

Organizations with substantial investment in personal computer equipment may wish to monitor the usage of such equipment and the monitoring can have security benefits. The types of event that may be of interest include:

- system startup,
- user session initiation and completion,
- program initiation and completion,
- access to specified data files.

An audit trail provides a means of identifying changes made to data files or actions taken during processing of data. Much business application software, particularly financial statement application software currently available, allows accounting data to be modified easily without producing any audit trail. Not only should audit trails be provided by the software, there should also be safeguards against the subsequent modification or deletion of such audit trails (see chapter 1).

3.4.15 What are good security practices for individual users?

Personal computers used in office environments by staff with limited technical expertise may well be subject to accidental or malicious misuse. It is important to ensure that minor incidents do not cause major damage to data. The three important principles are:

- backup (see section 3.4.17),
- isolation,
- administration.

Data must be backed up regularly during and at the end of each processing session. Never spend long periods at a workstation without periodically saving the file being processed. All the work between 'Save' sessions is subject to loss due to miskeying, power failures, etc. Never leave the computer during a session without saving the data, and never leave the computer unattended such that data can be changed or inserted by a passer-by. At the end of the session ensure that backup routines are undertaken (see section 3.4.17).

Always ensure that the impact of an incident is isolated and prevented from spreading. The data held on diskettes is normally far more valuable than the diskettes themselves. It is a mistake to load many files onto one diskette; loss or damage to the diskette will destroy all the files on it. In general only load files onto the same diskette if it is necessary, i.e. to avoid continually changing diskettes during processing. A software incident during processing may affect all the files on-line to the system and therefore it is wise to minimize the potential impact of such events.

It is even more important to isolate one user from another. Each user should have his or her own diskettes; if one person's data is to be passed to another then it should be copied onto the other's diskettes. Similarly, application software should be isolated; users need to ensure that they only use authorized versions of software. Data can be transparently modified by programs and thus an attack on the program can produce hidden changes to data. The advent of viruses (see section 3.3.16) highlights the dangers of interchange of software.

Users must take care in the administration of their data. It is absolutely essential to set the correct time/date stamp on sensitive files, to record the time/date stamp after each session on a written log, and to check it on the next occasion that the files are loaded. This precaution will at least indicate any accidental, and possibly malicious, changes to files. Unfortunately an experienced attacker, and some viruses, reset the time/date stamp of files to the original values after the attack. It is also important to develop a personal standard, or conform to a departmental one, on the naming of files and diskettes (see section 3.4.5).

3.4.16 What contingency plans should be formulated for personal computer systems?

The contingency plans for departmental personal computers should be integrated with those for any host computers and networks to which the personal computers are connected (see section 3.4.8). If the personal computers are only used as stand-alone devices (see section 3.5.12) then the contingency plans should address:

- loss of processing power,
- loss of stored data or software,
- compromise of data or software,
- loss of key personnel.

Given the wide availability of personal computers the loss of access to a given computer, or a small set of computers, does not normally present the same problem as that of loss of mainframe computing facilities. However, attention needs to be paid to this problem if an isolated site has a single workstation and it is essential that the computing facility be continually available. Moreover, some personal computers tend to become highly personalized with the addition of expansion boards; this can lead to problems when software can only be run on the personalized computers (see section 3.5.13).

Precautions against loss of stored data or software must be taken with backup routines (see section 3.4.17). In some cases the loss may be due to theft and there is an associated danger that sensitive data will be available to unauthorized personnel.

The disclosure of sensitive data may present a very serious situation. However, the failure to take cognizance of the event may be even more disastrous. In some situations the value of stolen data is considerably enhanced if the proper authorities are unaware of its disclosure. The contingency plans must therefore address both the problem of ensuring that data is accounted for, and the reporting and remedial actions to be taken in such cases. Compromise of software from virus attack needs particular attention in contingency plans; inappropriate recovery routines may result in the loss of backup data or software (see section 3.3.22).

The use of personal computers should never be so idiosyncratic that the absence of a key person renders the stored data inaccessible, or halts the processing of data. The data ownership policy must allow for the possibility of absence of the owner and specification of appropriate deputies.

3.4.17 How frequently should backups be taken?

The normal practice in taking backups on diskette is to write only those files that have been updated since the last scheduled backup. This backup facility is usually provided by the microcomputer operating system. Frequency of backup should be selected so as to keep the time required to perform backup balanced against the time to re-key the updates that could be lost. Given the low incidence of failure of microcomputers, running the backup program once per day or once for each session is a useful rule of thumb.

Backing up to diskette is both easy and economical, and this is the preferred practice for copying relatively small files. However, floppy diskette backup can be a time-consuming chore for large files, particularly if a substantial quantity of data is copied from a hard disk, and in such cases the use of a tape streamer is recommended.

For personal computers connected to larger systems, the opportunity may present itself for using the larger system for storage of backup copies of files. This use can vary from simply uploading a file to complete applications involving schedule management and security.

3.4.18 What are the risks associated with backup?

It is important for users to understand the threats addressed by backup procedures (see chapter 1). The obvious reason for backing up files is to enable recovery of data after loss due to media or hardware problems or accidents, e.g. unintentional erasure of files. This aspect of data loss tends to encourage users to store backup copies in a convenient nearby location. The other threat of concern, however, is loss resulting from a fire, theft, flood, etc., which might involve an entire office or building. In these situations, locally stored backup copies would be lost along with the originals. It is also wise to retain two backup copies; if the original data is lost, then damage to the only backup copy during transit or loading would be disastrous.

The backup copy must be sufficiently well documented so as to identify it uniquely with the personal computer on which it was made; otherwise in the event of a serious incident (say in an office fire) it may not be possible to read the file if the right computer is not used. This situation arises because personal computers become even more personalized by their users with the addition of expansion boards.

If the backup data is sensitive then it may well be subject to an attack, and needs therefore to be held and transported in a secure manner.

3.4.19 What guidelines should be adopted by management covering the use of personal computers?

Personal computers represent the most vulnerable information processing facility in organizations, and there is often extremely strong resistance to any centralized control of such facilities. Management must therefore ensure that staff using personal computers are aware of the security consequences and hold them accountable for their actions. The guidelines must be developed to ensure that:

- staff are fully aware of their responsibilities;
- staff are adequately trained in the use of the equipment;
- staff and equipment are adequately supervised;
- the impact of incidents is limited;
- the incidents are fully reported.

The guidelines should specify:

- password discipline (see section 3.3.7);
- restrictions of use of hardware (see section 3.4.10);
- data ownership policies (see chapter 1);
- rules on access, copying, distribution, and storage of magnetic media;

171

- rules on the acquisition, introduction, copying, distribution, and modification of software (see section 3.3.21);
- documentation standards, recording of activities on files, backup routines, security logs, etc.;
- physical security of hardware and magnetic media;
- rules on the connection of workstations into networks, mainframe computers, dial-up facilities;
- rules on the use, and recording of use, of communication facilities;
- standards for naming files and diskettes (see section 3.4.5);
- backup routines (see section 3.4.17);
- reporting routines for security incidents;
- hardware maintenance routines and policy (see section 3.4.6);
- contingency plans (see sections 3.4.16 and 3.5.12).

3.5 Contingency Planning

3.5.1 Introduction
Most information systems managers understand that their data and their data processing centres are critical organizational resources. They also appreciate that these resources may be subjected to natural disasters and to malicious attack. Nevertheless surveys in the USA have shown that fewer than one data processing centre in four has a current, tested contingency plan.

In the UK, Hogg Robinson Ltd carried out an analysis on the findings of 50 surveys undertaken by professional risk management auditors on information processing systems. The companies in the sample fell within the better end of the risk spectrum. In these surveys they found that disaster and recovery planning rarely extended to the computing area. Such recovery plans that were shown to the auditors consisted of lists of telephone numbers, gentlemen's agreements, and letters from hardware suppliers stating that they would do their best.

Thus the most common strategy for dealing with a catastrophic event is total risk acceptance. This lack of planning is the result of several factors. First, the lack of appreciation by operational management of the strategic role of information systems; second, the lack of appreciation by senior management of the extent of reliance upon these systems, and their complexity.

A contingency is any event that causes an unscheduled interruption to data processing capability. A contingency may vary from a few hours' downtime, for a hardware fault, up to the complete destruction of the computer and the building housing it. The type of events of interest are characterized by low rates of occurrence, high levels of uncertainty, and devastating consequences. Spectacular losses following computer disasters are rare, so the subject is not regularly publicized. Most managers will not see a disaster in their careers, the typical frequency of occurrence being less than once every thousand years. However, because there are many thousands of computer installations, catastrophes do occur, and if the business has no contingency plan then experience has shown they do not survive long without backup facilities. There is no way of scheduling a contingency. When they arise they must be met in a way that is as well planned as possible. Contingency plans will certainly need to be invoked after a disaster such as a fire or flood.

There are three kinds of contingency plans: emergency plans, backup plans, and recovery plans. Emergency plans attempt to contain the damage caused by the disaster in order to preserve the essential working of the installation. This plan will call for the provision of the type of controls mentioned in section 3.2.1.

Extensive damage requires backup and recovery plans. Backup plans provide for continuing critical portions of the mission between the disaster and the completion of the recovery process. Recovery plans provide for more permanent restoration of the information processing capability. This section will concentrate on backup plans, including the dumping and off-site storage of company files.

3.5.2 What are the benefits of a contingency plan?
The benefits derived from contingency planning are:

- The actions to be taken in an emergency can be formulated in a non-stressful environment, over a period, and carefully reviewed before implementation.
- The expertise of staff can be captured for use in the emergency.
- Written authority will be provided to junior staff to undertake requisite actions during the emergency.
- The contingency plans will provide an intrinsic form of communication during the emergency.
- Management will not be concerned with formulation and supervision of routine working arrangements during the emergency. They will therefore be available for unforeseen tasks.
- Suitable plans can be formulated to cater for the needs of staff operating in adverse conditions.
- A database of essential information can be made available for workers during the emergency.

The formulation of a contingency plan compels management to give detailed consideration to the types of emergency situations of which they would most probably have had no experience. By anticipating such events, and having time to plan what action to take, management is better prepared to act swiftly and surely should the need ever arise.

A good contingency plan will have captured the experience and expertise in emergency procedures of those in the organization who have it, and will have made it available to those who will need it in the emergency. Periodic updating of the plan, to take into account new applications and new procedures, provides the opportunity for consolidating the current expertise. This is particularly important in an environment where there is a high rate of labour turnover; otherwise knowledge of these skills would not be available if it were ever needed. In addition the plans will capture the expertise of current staff who may simply not be available at the initial stages of the emergency.

An important aspect of the contingency plan is that it provides authority for operational staff to assume the additional responsibilities necessary in an emergency. A relatively junior member of data processing operations may be charged with the initiation of the emergency procedures. The plan will authorize and encourage such junior staff to use their initiative in crucial circumstances. Such perceived delegation of tasks may well enhance staff morale and confidence.

Copies of the plan held by individual workers will provide an inherent form of communication during the emergency situation. The plan will indicate where staff are located, and what actions they are taking; thus it should not be necessary for staff to disturb other workers with unnecessary questions of 'who is doing what?'

The contingency plans will not be able to cover every management action required during the emergency, but it can at least deal with a host of routine tasks. Junior staff will therefore be able to operate autonomously, leaving management to concentrate on those matters that could not be foreseen within the plans.

Disaster recovery may also require staff to operate under difficult circumstances (e.g. in damaged buildings) and over extended periods. Contingency plans that recognize this situation and lay down procedures for catering, transport, accommodation, etc. will greatly improve morale at a time when it may be all-important.

The emergency may not only render access to normal documentation more difficult, it may also produce a situation in which rarely accessed information (e.g. wiring diagrams, communication cabling, staff home telephone numbers, building construction plans, etc.) become vitally important. The contingency plans must be accompanied with a good database to ensure immediate availability of such information.

3.5.3 What are the levels of responsibility associated with contingency plan development?

The range of staff associated with contingency planning are:

- top management;
- data processing management;
- user departmental management;
- legal, finance, and/or internal audit staff;
- personnel and trade unions/professional organizations.

Contingency planning is a corporate issue. Most prudent senior managers do it as part of their job when they hedge against currency fluctuations, take out corporate insurance, etc. They put controls in their business to mitigate the effects of undesirable and uncontrollable events. Top management must be made aware of the sort of risks that are faced in the event of a computer centre disaster. The consequences that may follow include loss of customer goodwill or competitive advantage, and the inability to administer many aspects of the organizations's day-to-day operations. Corporate support is essential in the contingency planning process to ensure that there are sufficient resources to tackle the problem.

The data processing staff must provide the technical expertise on proposed plans, e.g. suitability of alternative processing facilities, implications of loss of communications links, time estimates of changeover to backup systems, number and expertise of staff required, estimate of proportion of normal operations that can be undertaken in the various stages between the onset of the emergency and complete recovery, etc.

The user departments need to specify the relative impact of loss of facilities on application areas so that tasks may be sensibly prioritized during the post-emergency period. The individual departments can then formulate their internal contingency plans to cope with the loss of processing/communications capacity.

Finance and internal audit staff are required to provide a measure of the relative costs of contingency plans, that of loss of facilities, and to indicate the controls that need to be applied during the operation of the contingency plans. A disaster situation could present an ideal opportunity to exploit a relaxation of controls in order to perpetrate a fraud etc. Legal staff need to consider the implications of the contingency plans in terms of meeting legislative requirements, e.g. provisions of the *Data Protection Act*, responsibilities to staff in potentially hazardous circumstances, etc.

The successful implementation of contingency plans will demand the wholehearted co-operation of staff who will be required to undertake new tasks, work in adverse conditions, often outside, and in excess of, normal working hours. The plans must be vetted by personnel and staff representatives to ensure such wholehearted support.

3.5.4 What is management's role in the overall formulation of a contingency plan?
Management must ensure that:

- contingency plans are formulated, vetted, and tested;
- the plans are consistent with corporate objectives;
- changes in the organization that have an impact upon the effectiveness of contingency plans will cause such plans to be updated;
- staff are fully trained to implement the plans;
- the necessary facilities for the implementation of the plans are always available;
- the plans are regularly reviewed.

3.5.5 What strategies should be considered by management in the formulation of a contingency plan?
There is no single strategy that is suitable for every organization. Each organization must formulate a strategy that is appropriate for its own needs, based on a cost versus protection trade-off.

There are, however, two matters that need careful forethought:

- information processing/communication procurement,
- backup strategies.

The overall procurement strategy for computing/communication systems can dramatically affect the magnitude of problems arising from the loss of such facilities. An owner of an exotic car may find him- or herself at a distinct disadvantage, compared with someone running a Ford, if the car breaks down in a country district and spare parts are required. Similar considerations apply to computer/communication systems.

- Ensure wherever possible that hardware and software systems are compatible within sections of the organization, and with a range of neighbouring users.
- Processing facilities at a remote site should be of a type and capacity that could provide backup for critical processing.
- Use proven technology where possible.
- Conform to standards; avoid bespoke hardware and software.
- Ensure that there exists a sufficiently large population of staff trained to operate systems in the perceived emergency.
- Use distributed processing or networking.

The information processing and procurement strategies should consider the implications of loss of facilities due to an adverse event, and balance the cost of backup against those of policies, which either facilitate the transfer of jobs to a backup facility, or provide inherent backup within the organization. If the applications are designed to be compatible with those of a range of other organizations, then there will be many fewer problems in transferring jobs to a backup computer. Inherent backup is provided by a policy of decentralizing processing activities; thus processing loads may be distributed between sites or processing performed by a network of computers linked with telecommunications facilities. These solutions may be expensive in terms of operating costs but should be considered for critical processing tasks.

The backup strategy needs to determine and address critical functions, short-term contingency requirements, and long-term requirements. The backup facilities must be sufficient to meet the immediate requirements of the critical functions and then extended to the short-term contingency requirements, the long-term requirements will not normally be addressed by the backup system. The backup strategy may opt for provision of all backup facilities within the organization, a mutual agreement with another organization, or use of a commercial backup site. If in-house facilities are developed so that a remote site can undertake the critical and short-term contingency requirements of the organization, then it will provide a guaranteed backup totally under the control of the organization.

If the backup is organized on a shared basis, either through a cooperative plan with organizations having similar equipment, or through a commercial service, then the important considerations are:

- provisions for joint use of the backup if two organizations simultaneously lose their primary systems;
- number and location of subscribers to the scheme;
- nature of the commitment to provide backup;
- review of backup facilities.

Shared backup systems may be provided on the assumption that no more than one organization will require the service at any one time. This assumption may prove to be wrong, through sheer bad luck, or an unwise mix of subscribers, so that two or more are affected by the same external incident. An individual subscriber needs to be sure that such occurrences do not bar them from the facility when they require it, e.g. a clear understanding of subscriber priority or some facilities for joint use.

Clearly the backup facility should not have so many subscribers that there is a significant probability of double booking. Nor should the subscribers be located in such close proximity that two or more are likely to be affected by the same fire, flood, toxic spill, etc. On the other hand a commercial facility with a very low subscription may indicate a lack of commercial viability, with an associated danger that the facility will not be maintained at the necessary level of readiness. A total of 20–30 subscribers for a single backup facility is a good rule of thumb.

It is essential that an organization has a firm guarantee of a back-up facility. The provision of the facility must be legally binding and the organization providing the facility must have sufficient stature to render such legal obligations meaningful. Gentlemen's agreements between individuals in two different organizations are not sufficient for this purpose.

Backup facilities must be regularly reviewed. If the backup provider is another organization then it is possible that changes in their primary system may have rendered it less compatible for back-up purposes. If the provider is a commercial organization, established specifically for that purpose, then the commitment and ability of the company to provide the agreed service should be checked on a regular basis (see section 3.5.9).

3.5.6 What are the options for backup?

Applications must be run in environments compatible with their home environment in terms of both operating systems and hardware. The options for backup are:

- application portability,
- operating system portability,
- compatible operating systems,
- manual procedures.

With application portability the software is designed to run in a variety of environments; with multi-user systems such applications can be added to the workload of the backup system. This is a wise strategy from a contingency plan viewpoint.

Operating system portability involves loading the operating system into the hardware at the backup site. This may be achieved with the use of a virtual machine interface; however, this approach may result in comparatively inefficient use of hardware, a factor that must be borne in mind when estimating capacity requirements. The compatible operating system strategy overcomes the need for such a virtual machine interface, and the backup jobs are run on the normal operating system of the new host computer operating system of the host installation.

Manual procedures may well be appropriate for some tasks when processing facilities are lost; given the flexibility of operating such procedures they may prove to be an attractive alternative to the double transfer of software/data to and from the backup computer. A stock of stationery, forms, operating manuals, etc. should be held at an appropriate backup location.

3.5.7 How is backup planned at an application level?

It will not be possible to replicate the organization's normal information processing activities in the period of backup operation, and once all the applications have been identified they need to be classified into three priority levels:

- critical,
- important but not critical,
- discretionary.

Critical applications are those for which there is no scheduling flexibility, e.g. cash flow (paying suppliers, payroll, dividends, etc), product flow (production work orders, shipping orders), or a billable service (invoicing). Critical jobs normally represent a limited portion of the total workload and they vary with the time of year.

In the second level are classified those jobs that are important to the extent that the organization would suffer if they were not performed, but are such that they could be deferred for a week, or even up to a month. Finally there are the discretionary applications which can be shed until normal resumption of work thus making capacity available for the aforementioned job categories.

The priorities, having been established the phased backup facilities required following the emergency need to be specified in terms of type and capacity. The individual sections then need to lay detailed plans on the changeover to backup systems, e.g:

- storage of backup data;
- operating procedures for changeover during backup, and return to normal operation;
- specification of personnel required;
- backup materials, forms, stationery, etc.;
- communication links to be established.

3.5.8 How is an organizational backup plan developed?

There will be a hierarchy of contingency plans with individual sections providing the requisite level of detail. In developing the overall organizational contingency plan, management must ensure that the following requirements are satisfied.

- A review of all contingency plans, by a common level of management, has been conducted.
- The plans satisfy corporate objectives, and meet audit, legal, personnel requirements.
- All plans are properly documented and distributed.
- Plans are periodically tested and reviewed (see section 3.5.9).

Plans should exist for all functions and levels within the business. Each department must be cognizant of the contingency plans of others to ensure compatibility, reduce duplication, and check that no essential functions are omitted. Potential clashes on usage of backup facilities must also be checked out.

The backup plan should be developed application by application, and job by job. Users should be asked to specify the relative importance of the various applications, given a disaster has occurred. Backup capacity should be available from sufficient alternative sources so that no single source will be over stressed. Attempting to identify backup strategies for entire systems complicates an already difficult task, and emphasis should be placed on identifying the back-up environment required for each application, rather than the need for having identical hardware operating systems and communications.

The total set of contingency plans then needs to be reviewed by the contingency planning team. The total contingency plan must be costed and compared with corporate objectives. In some cases departments may tend to overrate the importance of their applications, with consequent disproportionate demands for backup facilities. Some reconsideration of priorities may well be called for, in order to bring demands down to sensible cost limits, while still ensuring corporate objectives.

The plans must be considered in terms of technical feasibility and audit, legal, and personnel requirements (see section 3.5.3).

The next phase is to ensure that all plans are properly documented and distributed. Given that the plans need to be accompanied by a database of factual information, required by staff in the emergency (see section 3.5.2), there is a good case for the plans and database to be stored on floppy diskettes. A laptop computer with such diskettes will be invaluable to management during the emergency.

3.5.9 How frequently should the contingency plan be reviewed and tested?

The contingency plan is a form of insurance, and it must be effective when implemented. Thus the plans must be subject to regular review (e.g. annually) and significant changes in the organization may also demand a review of the plans soon after the implementation of the changes. The effectiveness of the contingency plan depends upon:

- the environment immediately before the disaster;
- the state of the backup system at the time of the disaster;
- the personnel who implement the contingency plans.

A strategy that is appropriate for the company at a particular phase in its development may not be adequate at some later time. Changes in business strategy, business acquisitions, hardware, or software will all require that the plan be kept up to date and reflect the requirements of critical applications.

The state of the backup facilities must all be carefully reviewed; if reciprocal arrangements have been established with other organizations, then one needs to check that they have not made changes affecting compatibility of systems, and failed to inform the organization of possible impacts upon backup arrangements. If commercial backup sites are employed it would be wise to check that they continue to offer the agreed level of service, e.g. they have not oversubscribed a limited service with the possibility of clashes in demand for backup (see section 3.5.5).

Management should check, on a regular basis, that those with a critical role to play in the contingency plan are kept up-to-date with any changes. Any changes in personnel will also have implications for awareness and training on contingency plans.

In addition to reviews of the plans, existing plans need to be tested on a regular basis. Some organizations test their backup facilities on a scheduled basis, up to four times a year. These tests will include the use of the backup site and monitoring of the effectiveness of backup procedures. Key members of the operational team must be familiar with the procedures, and ensure that they are up-to-date.

A full-scale disaster simulation may be staged in order to test and evaluate all aspects of the disaster plan. The cost and disruption of such exercises will, however, preclude their frequent repetition.

3.5.10 What action should be taken following a disaster?

Once a contingency has arisen there is a need to delegate as speedily as possible. The first stage of the plan usually requires that pre-designated key emergency staff be contacted; the emergency staff in turn call up nominated staff to carry out the second and subsequent stages. This 'bootstrapping' of emergency procedures may well be initiated by on-site security personnel, and it represents one of the more crucial aspects of the contingency plan.

The first people contacted will already have been trained in disaster recovery, and will know what part of the plan they have to play. It is important that copies of the plan are up-to-date and available, so that if any copy is destroyed in the disaster others are at hand; key personnel should have copies of the plan securely stored at home to minimize delay at the outset if the disaster occurs outside working hours.

The standby site should be contacted and arrangements for access, transport, and accommodation put into play. Backup data must be retrieved from store; such a store should be remote from the disaster site. Tapes stored in fireproof safes may be protected from damage, but they can be inaccessible if they are in a fire- or bomb-damaged computer centre.

Experience of those who have had to recover systems suggests that one should expect problems in re-starting at the host site, even though software and hardware standards have been agreed. Even basic utilities may be of different versions. One therefore needs to call on skilled system programmers who can isolate and patch round teething problems.

It is also important that a member of staff accepts responsibility for actions in relation to subsequent insurance claims (see section 3.6.9).

3.5.11 What procedures should be followed for making backup copies of data and software?
Records are one of an organization's most valuable assets. Their protection is a responsibility of management and involves more than protection against loss or damage; such data has to be reconstructed or replaced should the need arise. A backup of all key records which can be used to reconstruct or replace master files is necessary (see chapter 1).

It is normal practice to keep at least three generations of magnetic tape files (grandfather, father, son). A record of the transactions linking each generations is maintained so that it is possible to go back and reconstruct all but the most recent transactions. A similar procedure holds for disk files. At least one backup copy of all application programs operating systems and utilities should be stored in a separate location. One approach is to dump the object program library on a periodic basis as well as retaining source program listings and documentation of program changes made since the last dump.

In the event of a major catastrophe, stationery supplies may be lost. With the possibility of delays in obtaining a fresh batch of pre-printed stationery, emergency supplies should be held at another location.

3.5.12 Are special precautions required for personal computers?
Most people do not plan for the loss of personal computers and diskettes in the event of a fire. Even if hard disks are regularly backed up onto floppy diskettes, a serious fire would destroy both personal computers and diskettes alike. Moreover, much of the personal computer data becomes personalized because there is often a lack of company standardization; expansion cards are commonly added to personal computers, e.g. graphics cards, multifunction boards etc. An additional difficulty is that some users employ access control software in which the backup data is password-protected and encrypted. Trying to recover data in these circumstances can be virtually impossible.

The solution is to have a viable backup program for personal computers with off-site storage, along with configuration details of each personal computer. For example, the fire at the headquarters building of the US Postal Service was the second biggest in the history of Washington, with damage estimated at about $20 million. At the time floppy diskette backups were kept in supposedly fireproof containers, but they did not withstand the heat. It transpired that the Postal Service had many more personal computers than it had realized, and the combined data stored on them was at least equal to that of its mainframes. Now the authorities require that staff backup their personal computers on a weekly basis, and that the backups are stored off-site.

3.5.13 What procedures should be followed for storing backup data and software?
Good physical security is essential to prevent damage theft or unauthorized access to stored data. Whatever the cost of storage it is likely to be insignificant when weighed against the consequences of not having backup data. It is also important to store magnetic media, particularly diskettes in a controlled environment.

Many installations rely upon computer room libraries for their disaster storage because of convenience. In so doing, the possibility of total loss is being overlooked. The safest approach is to store the material at completely different locations. A bank vault offers good security but it is not suitable for large volumes. Many organizations use the services of security storage companies for their valuable records. In the event of disaster a telephone request using a preselected security password may be made for the transfer of selected tapes to a stand-by site.

Regular auditing of the flow of materials to off-site storage must be maintained and fixed schedules established. It is all too easy to assume everything is in order just because the security storage company's van calls on schedule, tapes are taken away and others returned. A periodic audit of the records against the stock of the off-site stores is necessary.

3.5.14 How can one recover from a mainframe virus attack?

Fortunately, virus attacks (see section 3.3.16) on a mainframe are still rare, but their effects can be more devastating than a fire or flood. A virus may lie dormant for a long time before it is suddenly triggered into action, but during this period it may well have multiplied and infected a number of files and programs. The problem is that the various generations of program file backups may themselves have become infected, so a recovery cannot be made from this source.

Obviously, if a mainframe is hit with a virus, then one has to assess how far it has spread: what programs have been infected, how much data has been corrupted, and what was the source of the infection. When one reloads software into the program library as part of the recovery process it is essential that each program is clean and uncontaminated. This means that the organization may have to isolate and store original versions of its source code, and that updates and modifications to the programs are stored separately. This is to guard against the virus having been planted in an update to an existing suite.

If a contaminated application has to be reconstituted then it may have to be recreated from the source material, an unenviable task for a large suite of software. At each stage in the reconstitution the presence of the virus must be tested.

Reported virus attacks on mainframes have been perpetrated via computer networks. The viruses in question were designed specifically to attack mainframes. Because personal computer viruses have to exist in an MS-DOS, or equivalent, environment it is unlikely that a personal computer virus could infect a mainframe. However, a personal computer linked to a mainframe via a network could be a source of the infection.

Prevention is better than cure with viruses, and adequate access control provision in the mainframe environment is essential. The most sensitive aspect is ensuring that access to the program libraries on the mainframe is tightly controlled and that only authorized personnel with the appropriate rights are permitted to make software changes. Any update tape containing revisions to an operating system must be checked for authenticity; did it come from the proper supplier (manufacturer, software house, etc), or is someone masquerading as the authorized distributor?

It is clearly prudent to ensure that all program updates to a mainframe are carried out centrally, and not over an insecure network, so that the right physical and logical controls are in place, and can be constantly monitored.

3.5.15 What should a contingency planning checklist contain?
The development and review of contingency plans should check:

- Do the overall goals of the contingency plan reflect the corporate requirements?
- Is the contingency plan part of an overall risk management program?
- Is the contingency plan up-to-date? Does it prioritize applications? Have individuals been allocated specific responsibilities?
- Have the legal, personnel, and audit aspects been checked with the appropriate staff?
- Has adequate consideration been given to hardware and software failures?
- Have risks from accidental and man-made threats been adequately covered?
- Have risks for natural disasters been adequately reviewed?
- Has due consideration been given to the various options for off-site processing?
- Is the plan kept up-to-date and tested, at least in part, on a regular basis?
- Have the insurance aspects been considered? e.g. cover for staff during the recovery period, notification of insurance company, recording costs, etc. (see section 3.6.9).

3.6 Insurance

3.6.1 Introduction
One objective of risk analysis (see chapter 2) is to determine how much insurance cover a business enterprise needs. The controls and countermeasures that form part of an overall risk management strategy are designed to make the enterprise less vulnerable to the impact of threats such as fire, flooding, and malicious damage. It is never possible, however, to mitigate completely the destructive consequences of some threats, nor is it sensible to protect against every conceivable threat. The only way to protect against these residual exposures, after the implementation of a risk analysis programme, is through insurance.

Insurance is not a substitute for loss prevention and disaster recovery planning. It is, in fact, the final stage that has to be taken after the physical controls (see section 3.2.1) have been analysed, and some, if not most, have been implemented. This section describes the types of protection available to information processing users, and reviews the essential elements of an insurance policy tailored to the organization's needs.

Insurance does not reduce the likelihood of a mishap occurring; it can only provide financial redress if one occurs. It is a method of transferring the consequences of loss from the insured to the insurer. The insurer operates by sharing the losses among many enterprises; the premiums charged are intended to reflect the insurance company's estimate of the risks. These premiums must be sufficient to cover the liabilities, and to make a reasonable profit, otherwise the insurance company will not be able to meet its commitments, thereby putting all its clients at risk.

The benefit of insurance to the insured is that it will provide funds to reduce the financial impact of a loss of information processing. The main concern arising from this loss is not so much the material damage to hardware as the more significant impact such losses have on the ability of the organization to continue trading. The likelihood of loss, and the extent of the loss when it occurs, will depend to a large extent on the precautions taken. If an organization's loss record is good, with in-house prevention procedures and contingency planning implemented then insurance will be more readily available and less costly.

Insurance for information processing/communications systems is, however, bedevilled by the same problems facing managers protecting their facilities. If the data security situation for the organization is such that it is unable to guarantee the protection of its information assets, then the insurer will be reluctant to assume those risks, or will charge high premiums which reflect that reluctance. Rapid changes in the nature of vulnerabilities and threats (e.g. the advent of viruses) create entirely new situations and render the task of estimating the probability of loss virtually impossible. If insurers are unable to estimate the probability of loss, and spread the risk over many premium holders, then they will have no sound basis for accepting the liability. In short the use of insurance to cover those risks that cannot be dealt with by internal controls may not be possible for some sophisticated attack scenarios (see section 3.6.8).

3.6.2 How should the main areas of risk be covered with insurance?

There are three main categories of loss:

- material damage, e.g. to hardware, buildings, etc.;
- consequential damage, e.g. business interruption and loss of data;
- personnel, liability for compensation, and losses arising from malicious actions.

As a rule, standard forms of insurance for data information

processing do not exist, and one must examine to what extent the business requires protection against each of the main categories of loss indicated above. One of the problems for insurers is that computer insurance is still a relatively new field, and the traditional methods of separating insurance into fire, accident, and life are not apposite. This difficulty is compounded by the rapid advances within information technology, and the increasing dependency of organizations on their information processing facilities.

The best approach, in deciding what potential losses should be subject to insurance, is to contact the organizations's insurance broker. Although it is unlikely that such brokers are experts on computer insurance, they can at least relate this problem to the general insurance stance of the company. In this way the broker can ensure that:

- the general insurance and computer insurance do not overlap, to avoid duplicate payment of premiums;
- the general insurance and computer insurance between them cover all exposures, and that there are no gaps in the policy provisions.

The insurance broker will need full details of the physical and logical controls, standards, and procedures in place at the computer centre, along with details of the contingency plan. This will enable the broker to estimate the cost of recovery from a serious mishap, and so justify to the underwriters the cost of underwriting; i.e. the premium is more likely to be reduced. A good broker may seek to spread the risk of the insurance across several underwriters in order to obtain the best terms.

3.6.3 How can one insure against material damage?
Material damage is the most obvious kind of insurance. It covers loss or damage to such items as the computer hardware, ancillary equipment, media, and the building itself.

It is advisable to keep an inventory of all equipment, software, and data, for the purposes of insurance cover. Indeed this should be at hand following the risk analysis exercise. If the analysis was carried out some time ago, the list should be updated as new equipment is installed and old equipment removed.

The ownership of all items on the list should be established, since some computer equipment may be rented or leased. Clearly, everything owned by the company should be insured; liability for leased equipment may still fall to the company, and not to the manufacturer or leasing firm.

Once the list of insurable items has been completed, a decision has to be made about the threats for which insurance protection is required. An All Risks policy may be taken out; this will cover the insured for all risks except those that are specifically excluded, and since the wording of the insurance policy is crucial, advice from the broker about the extent of cover is advisable. Cheaper cover can be had by excluding some risks. This is called Selected Perils, and is a more cost-effective instrument for protection, if considered in the light of a risk analysis study. Included in the category of all risks is the chance that computer equipment may be unavailable for use because of events happening in the vicinity of the computer centre, e.g. toxic spills and other forms of contamination, and even long-term power or communications failure.

Damaged equipment can be repaired, be replaced with similar equipment of comparable age, or replaced with new equipment. If a replacement, or new, cover is obtained, it is usually much more expensive since the sum at risk is the full new replacement cost of the asset. If the insured equipment is to be replaced by second-hand machines, it may subsequently prove to be impossible to find a suitable replacement. In practice, the insurers would most probably pay only the value of the old equipment.

Breakdowns in equipment are normally covered by the rental or maintenance agreements. However, separate cover should be taken out for loss arising from a prolonged breakdown, which might well call for implementing some parts of the contingency plan. The All Risks policy should cover this.

3.6.4 How can one protect against business interruption losses?

Experience indicates that the majority of small and medium-sized firms do not survive a catastrophic loss of information processing. The consequences of prolonged computer failure are often far reaching and the loss of information handling capabilities may cause:

- loss of sales because customers cannot be served;
- loss of revenue because customers cannot be billed;
- loss of production arising from lack of material planning etc.;
- competitors to gain a market lead because of better service.

These losses are quite separate from the costs associated with re-placing damaged equipment and recreating lost files. Even for very large corporations the loss of data processing facilities, just for a short while, can be harmful, particularly if the corporate treasurer is unable to transfer funds or carry out cash management. Business interruption insurance covers the loss of net profits caused by computer and media damage. Income lost after damage to the premises should also be included in the cover. The amount of business interruption insurance needed depends largely on the organization's recovery measures. The faster normal operations can be resumed after a disaster, the less insurance is required.

Business interruption insurance belongs to a class of insurance known as 'Consequential Loss Insurance' and 'Loss of Profits Insurance'. It is naturally very expensive. The best protection against consequential loss is prevention rather than cure, i.e. an effective contingency plan that offers a rapid resumption of service.

Cover for this class of insurance is provided for a fixed period, called the 'indemnity period'. This is defined in the policy. During this period the insured is covered for specified costs and losses. Thereafter, there is no protection. The usual period for indemnity cover is twelve months, but this is often inadequate.

A related cover is extra-expense insurance, which covers the cost of continuing operations while normal processing is being restored. Like business interruption insurance, it is directly related to the organization's recovery measures. Replacement of the simplest equipment can take as long as twelve weeks. If outside data processing services are purchased in the interim, the cost can be twice that of normal processing.

Extra-expense insurance should be part of the policy that covers equipment, media, and business interruption. The amount of extra-expense insurance needed is based on the availability and cost of backup facilities. These costs may include:

- charges for use of standby site,
- charges for moving equipment,
- accommodation and travelling expenses of computer staff,
- overtime charges,
- cost of installing additional lines,
- use of bureau service.

If equipment has to be moved during a contingency, additional insurance cover may be required, since equipment is usually insured for use at one site only. Insurance cover should also be extended to cover the employment of staff at the contingency site. Other examples of consequential loss for which cover might be required are: delays in gaining access to data, and the cleaning and restitution of equipment after the crisis.

3.6.5 What protection should be obtained in respect to staff?
The UK employer must, by law, insure staff against loss or injury suffered at work, and a certificate of employer's liability must be displayed at every place of work. It is also prudent to extend it to staff working away from their normal place of work. This cover is

particularly important during contingency working, since staff may be exposed to an unfamiliar environment, be working long hours, and hence be more prone to accidents. The employer is also liable for loss or injury inflicted on members of the public. This is covered by a Public Liability Policy, and it would be extended to damages caused by unauthorized disclosure or inaccuracy of data, e.g. as claimed under the UK *Data Protection Act* (see chapter 7).

3.6.6 How can an employer be protected against his staff?

There is always the possibility that a disgruntled employee may try to inflict damages on the computer installation. Indeed the experience of computer security is that most attacks are performed by internal staff (see chapter 7). A fidelity guarantee is used to cover the computer installation against damage caused by the negligence or fraud of staff (see section 3.6.7). Deliberate sabotage is usually covered in the All Risks policy.

The employer may seek protection against claims by customers having a contractual relationship with the company, arising from the negligence of the computer installation and its staff. Additional cover may be required during the actual period of a contingency. Insurance of this type is very expensive.

3.6.7 Is it possible to insure against computer crime?

We have seen that a company can, by having a fidelity guarantee, protect itself against any fraudulent activities of its staff. Most fraud on computing and networked systems takes place through the collusion of two or more individuals, at least one of whom is an employee used to provide 'inside' knowledge. Again, the fidelity guarantee may well be the best investment for protection here. However, what happens when a computer crime occurs and an employee is not involved? Can a firm obtain cover, say to protect against fraud on a money transfer transaction? This is a relatively new area and is compounded by a lack of clear definition as to what constitutes a computer crime (see chapter 7). Underwriters also have difficulty with defining what constitutes a computer system! For example, are distributed CPUs or network switches included? The real problem is that computer crime loss does not really fit the traditional characteristics of an insurable event, i.e:

- the loss must be common to a large population so that it can be averaged over a significant number of premium holders;
- the event that causes loss at any one time should apply at most to only a few within the large group;
- the event causing loss must have a very low chance of occurrence and apply equally to any member of the insured group;

- the event causing loss should be random and unpredictable;
- the extent of the loss should be clearly definable;
- the extent of the loss should be statistically identifiable and bear a direct relationship to the claim expense, premium income and profit margin.

A loss resulting from a computer crime may not fulfill all these criteria: it may not be random; the loss itself may not be clearly definable, especially if malicious damage is involved, and the probability of loss may not occur equally throughout the group.

Some groups of businesses are clearly more susceptible to computer crime than others, e.g. those involved in money transfer. Predicting criminal intent to defraud is not statistically based, like many types of insurable risks. Also certain types of software packages, operating systems, or fourth generation languages that are widely used in commercial installations may have undocumented vulnerabilities that make the risk of fraud much higher. The computer criminal can therefore attack a whole class of insured organizations on an unequal basis. All these considerations have the effect that very few underwriters are prepared to offer cover against losses from computer crime, and where they do, the premiums are likely to be very high.

The message here is that given elsewhere in this book: the only solution lies in good security management deploying the technological and procedural controls available against misuse of information processing/communications systems. The insurance underwriter will be reluctant to provide insurance against a potentially massive loss when there is evidence that insufficient controls are in place, and the loss cannot be spread over a large population only a few of whom are statistically likely to suffer the loss.

3.6.8 Is the damage that viruses produce covered by insurance?
It is unlikely that an insurance cover will extend to damage produced by computer viruses (see section 3.3.16). The virus is an example of a sophisticated attack scenario in which the insurance companies are currently unable to establish the internal controls that would minimize the probability of the attack, or the extent of the consequential damage.

3.6.9 What actions are required in relation to insurance claims during the post-disaster situation?
During a contingency it is important to know who is responsible for making the insurance claim. Someone should be nominated for maintaining records and collecting information to support the claim,

otherwise its submission and settlement might be delayed. The list of items covered under the All Risks policy will be invaluable here.

With any insurance claim, the insured is required to prove loss. At the beginning of the recovery phase someone needs to be appointed to maintain a special cash book of all receipts and expenses relating to recovery, as well as overtime records etc. It is advisable to set up a special bank account to deal with all transactions related to the recovery.

The insurance company or broker will need to be notified immediately once a contingency arises. Brokers may be very helpful in view of their business contacts and experience of recovery operations. The insurance company will appoint a loss adjuster to act as their representative and it is his job to advise the insurance company on the applicability of the policy. If the controls and procedures outlined in this chapter have been enforced then it is most unlikely that any claim would be rejected on the grounds that the level of security fell below the standard specified by the policy.

References

Broadbent, D., *Contingency Planning* (NCC Publications, 1979)

Hearnden, K., *A ˙Handbook of Computer Security* (Kogan Page, 1987)

Hutt, A.E., Bosworth, S., Hoyt, D.B., *Computer Security Handbook* (Macmillan, 1988)

Lobel, J., *Foiling the System Breakers* (McGraw-Hill Book Company, 1986)

Wood, Michael B., *Computer Access Control* (NCC Publications, 1985)

Wood, Michael B., *Introducing Computer Security* (NCC Publications, 1982)

Wood, Michael B., *Physical Computer Security* (NCC Publications, 1986).

4 Communications Security

W. Caelli

4.1 Overview

In 1982 it was predicted in a *Scientific American* article that by 1990 '40 to 50 per cent of workers in the USA will use electronic terminal equipment' (Giuliano 1982). Such electronic terminal equipment will not be restricted to processing local data, but will provide access to corporate and global data over communication networks.

Certainly a high proportion of organizations now commonly employ computer networks in their day-to-day operations, and the control, management, and protection of such networks has now become of paramount importance to management; disruption of the network may mean disruption of the business of the organization. The security features of communication networks are affected by:

- the complexity of the network,
- the services available on the network,
- the nature of the data transmitted,
- national and international standards,
- the volume of network traffic.

Computer networks are becoming larger and more complex, providing numerous types of services over the same system. These new networks are providing for more users, more access points, and for more host computer systems and databases. In a current network, electronic mail may be mixed with facsimile data, EFT transaction messages, telex data, and general computer data relating to computer applications operating in host systems. Moreover the technology of the data network is changing. User workstations may be connected to a local server unit via a local area network (LAN). This server may provide all information services needed to meet the demands of, say, an individual department within a larger organization. Increasingly, for example, factories are being wired with local networks conforming to internationally recognized communications standards, such as the Manufacturing Automation Protocol (MAP), and these networks may interconnect with the enterprise's main information system and office automation networks. If more global information is required then the server may be connected to a larger database through a wide area network (WAN).

In the future there may be another intermediate communications network between the LAN and the conventional telecommunications network. This new type of network has been called the municipal area network (MAN), which will provide for the connection of information units over, say, a 20 kilometre radius (e.g. within a city area) and at very high speed (generally in the order of 100 to 200 million bits per second). The MAN may then connect to a nationwide and international WAN at lower speeds, say 64 kilobits per second to 2 million bits per second respectively.

The integrated services digital network (ISDN), due to be widely introduced in the late 1980s, will integrate all forms of user services: voice, facsimile, telex, on-line access to external databases, etc. All such services will be supplied by digital transmissions over the network. This integration will have an impact upon the user devices, and a single workstation will replace the telephone receiver, facsimile terminal, personal computer, and on-line database terminal. ISDN may be considered to be the backbone of the so-called 'wired society' of the 21st century, with services extending beyond the office to the factory, home, and school. This high level of integration imposes a higher level of concern for information security; illicit access to the network now implies access to all aspects of an organization's communications and data.

The development of local and wide area network technology has provided the user with more than just an enhanced communications service, it has provided the opportunity to offer new services. A widespread user population may now have access to coherent corporate information assets over public communications networks. The information requirements may also lead to demands for access to global information databases. Initially interest focused on bibliographic databases providing access to a wealth of published material, but increasingly the trend is towards full text services, or to sources of rapidly changing information, stock market prices, worldwide financial data, etc. These developments spread beyond the mere accessing of data to transaction-based systems in which users transfer money, order goods or services, etc. from a variety of office, home, or publicly available workstations such as ATMs, EFTPOS terminals, or enhanced television set (e.g. Minitel and Prestel terminals).

These developments in the technology of networks and the associated expansion of services have been accompanied by a change in the nature of the data transmitted through networks. The data will represent more than just the output of a database of past facts; it may comprise information that would result in substantial losses to the organization if it were revealed to another, lost in transit, or merely delayed by a few minutes. The transmissions may constitute authority to perform financial transactions or to undertake substantial contractual commitments. The development of such powerful networks has considerable social and economic implications for countries; government legislation will impinge both upon the nature of such traffic (e.g. the flow of data across borders) and the consequences of poor security (see chapter 7). It has been estimated that, using electronic funds transfer, the entire financial reserves of the UK government could be transferred out of the country in a matter of minutes.

Probably the most significant development, from a security viewpoint, was the widespread adoption of national and international standards. This adoption of national and international standards for interconnection by many computer manufacturers, the Open Systems Interconnection model, has been referred to as the major trend of the 1990s as evidenced by S. T. McClellan in his 1984 book, *The Coming Computer Industry Shakeout: Winners, Losers and Survivors.* He states that: 'any company that hopes to survive and compete over the long haul will have to sell more than discrete computer products. It will have to offer systems compatibility ...' Such compatibility is a boon to the user of communications facilities, since it reduces the complexities associated with interconnecting equipment from various manufacturers. Moreover individual manufacturers will no longer be able to 'lock-in' their customers, and organizations can exploit the marketplace in getting the best deal when purchasing systems. On the other hand such international standards are also of considerable benefit to attackers; the ready availability of standards documentation means that technical information is no longer locked away in manufacturers' manuals, and hackers can gain the necessary expertise to undertake wide-ranging network attacks.

The recent developments in microelectronics have increased the power and sophistication of computer and communications technology; simultaneously price has been decreased to bring it within the range of the consumer. This factor, combined with widespread training of schoolchildren and adults in computer programming and data communications, has created a situation in which the expertise for sophisticated attacks on communications facilities is readily available.

The data flowing in networks must be protected from computer-related criminal activity, from network disruptions, from loss of integrity, and loss of privacy. In order to achieve this level of security a balance must be achieved between management procedures and hardware, software and communications control mechanisms. These security mechanisms must be matched to the sources of data, the access and communications technologies, and the processing software/user workstations on the organization's premises. Concern for data network security has risen to such an extent that the term COMSEC (Communications Security) is now widely used. The term covers security in all forms of communications, such as voice/telephone communications, facsimile units, telex, satellite, and other related radiated services (e.g. microwave communications links).

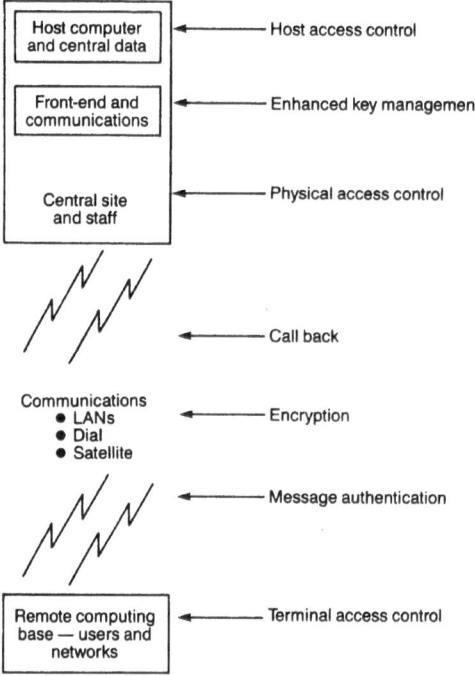

Fig. 4-1   Technical safeguards in communications security (*source*: *Personal Identification News*)

Planning for network security must occur at the same time as that for network development or enhancement. Not only will costly mistakes be avoided but cost savings may occur as security is integrated into network components from the outset. This applies particularly to architectural planning of buildings for corporate office use. The location of cable ducting, its ease of access, and its protective covering all take on new meanings once the office is wired. Fire and water protection for LAN as well as for PABX cables is of vital concern and must be planned from the outset (see chapter 3). The protection and location of the main telecommunications interconnection closets is vital since these present the lifeline of the organization to the outside communications world.

Methods employed to enhance the security of a network are likely to impinge upon its efficiency and traffic throughput. This will have major implications for networks which are operating with traffic volumes close to their maximum capacity.

Data communications security can be introduced today, and if planned from the outset may not present a major cost burden to the information systems development budget. The products and educational services are available now from a number of companies worldwide. The main problem may be management acceptance of the need to protect the information resource.

4.2 Network Security

4.2.1 *What are the main concerns in data network security?*
The concerns related to communications network security are:

- authenticity of users and systems,
- integrity of messages,
- privacy of information,
- availability and performance.

Each must be perceived against an acceptable level of risk and cost of countermeasure implementation.

Authenticity is concerned both with the identity of users and terminals on the network, and whether they are permitted to use the network facilities. At this level it may even be a question as to whether terminal audit trails are themselves authentic (see chapter 1).

The logical and physical integrity of the network must be preserved at all times, together with the integrity of transactions. At the privacy level some or all complete sessions on the network, as well as individual transactions, may require protection from eavesdropping.

The network must of course continue to be available: the most devastating attacks can result from unsophisticated, malicious damage to cables. Moreover any security scheme implemented must not degrade the performance of the network below acceptable levels.

These concerns may be summarized as the five Ss in communications security:

- Secret   confidentiality ('not been read')
- Sealed   integrity ('not been opened')
- Sequenced continuity ('messages received as transmitted')
- Signed   identity ('the sender of the message')
- Stamped   receipt ('confirming acceptance of message')

4.2.2 How can the network be attacked?

Data networks may be subject to various forms of malicious activity:

- line-tapping,
- introduction of spurious messages,
- replay attack,
- disruption of service,
- modification of messages,
- introduction of illicit terminals or host systems.

Line-tapping involves the recording of message traffic on the network, possibly combined with storage of associated parameters, e.g. date and times of transmission, location of circuit. Such line-tapping may be followed by the introduction of spurious messages to be delivered to users, host computers, etc. The spurious message may be produced by the attacker or it may take the form of a replay, i.e. the retransmission of a previously valid message (see chapter 1).

Disruption of service can be disastrous to an organization highly dependent upon the timely communication of data, e.g. stock exchanges. Such disruption may take the form of a selective loss or delay of legitimate messages, or a complete breakdown of communications. The attack may be achieved by simply occupying a communications line at the expense of a legitimate user, even though the attacker may be incapable of creating legitimate transactions. Another form of disruption is the deliberate modification of legitimate messages, either for the benefit of the attacker, or for purely malicious purposes.

A spoofing attack is performed by connecting an illicit terminal to the network and masquerading as a legitimate terminal to the host system, or as the host system to other users.

4.2.3 What are the major parameters of network security?

There are four major parameters that should be assessed when developing guidelines for investment in security equipment for an enterprise's data network:

- the level of security technology,
- safety margin,
- limitations of flexibility,
- security against continuous, automated attacks.

The level of security technology employed should be matched to the level of the technology available to an attacker. For example it must be assumed that an attacker today may not only possess modems, personal computer systems, communications connection equipment, etc., but may also have access to sophisticated data line analyser equipment, capable of determining the communications formats and protocols used in a data network.

The network security design team must also allow a safety margin for higher-level attacks. The user will be restricted to the defences offered by current technology, while the attacker will be in a position to exploit any future technological advances. It is also wise to recognize that automated security systems for network protection are more reliable and enforceable than manual systems, but they lack the inherent intelligence and flexibility of human vigilance.

Finally, most effort should be expended on the prevention of automated and continuous attack on the network. Such an attack may well follow an initial, successful penetration on an apparent one-off basis.

4.2.4 Is there more risk associated with dial-up, or switched, lines as compared with dedicated or leased lines?
There are two factors in assessing the comparable risks of dial-up and leased lines:

- identification of the user and telecommunications line;
- asynchronous versus synchronous transmission.

In both cases one should view the problem from the attacker's viewpoint. Consider an attack against a user dialling out from an organization. The user, who may be any one of a number of workers in an office, requests a line from the PABX, i.e. the local in-house exchange. A line is available and the user can dial the appropriate number, e.g. one for a remote database, to be interrogated with a personal computer. If the organization had, say, eight external lines and 24 internal phones, then an external eavesdropper keen to monitor this user's call would not know which of the eight external lines had been allocated by the in-house PABX. In this case the attacker would need to monitor all external lines.

In contrast, data communications via a private, or dedicated, telecommunications line always occur over the same path or circuits.

199

Once the attacker has identified this circuit, then future attacks are simply a matter of monitoring it continuously.

The problems of monitoring the line are, however, different in the two cases. Switched lines will tend to be voice or low-speed data circuits, largely confined to asynchronous mode of transmission; whereas dedicated lines are normally used for high-speed data flows, in synchronous mode (although synchronous mode may be used on some switched lines, particularly in IBM-based networks).

Thus, in low-speed, switched circuits, data transmission is normally restricted to asynchronous mode, and this mode is also widely employed for local connections (e.g. to printers) in the broad range of personal and minicomputer systems. The operation of such communication links is therefore widely available and well understood by personal computer enthusiasts. The user's personal computer may be connected to the line via a 300 to 2400 bit per second modem unit, and at these speeds the data transmissions can be easily recorded on standard audio cassette recorders. Thus while the attacker may have more difficulty in identifying a particular line, the low-speed dial-up access facilitates the recording of the data transmissions; it is even possible to intercept and modify them. The attacker can also record the number at the receiving end of the data transmission, thus permitting lines to be selectively monitored on the basis of specific conversations between an identified user/terminal and a host computer system.

At the receiving end, the host computer or terminal must be able to accept dialled connections over the general network. This is the situation commonly exploited by hackers, who attempt to bypass the access control system and thus gain illicit entry to the computer system. Even if such attempts to thwart the access control system are unsuccessful, the action of the hacker may block legitimate access to the system (see section 4.2.2).

Dedicated lines are normally only used for higher-speed data transmissions, usually in synchronous mode; the data transmission rates on such circuits normally vary from 4,800 to over 64,000 bits per second. The recording, modification, and/or insertion of data may present the attacker with far more complex technical problems than with low-speed circuits. However, as mentioned in section 4.2.3 it is wise to allow a safety margin for developments in attacker technology. Even personal computer systems can now accept expansion cards which enable such microcomputers to make a connection to high-speed circuits operating in synchronous mode. Monitoring of these fixed lines has thus become accessible to more people, and the risk of attack has risen markedly in the last year or two.

4.2.5 Do call-back modems provide the necessary protection of dial-up lines?

A call-back, or dial-back, modem is designed to ensure that users can only access a computer system from specified locations, and is therefore intended to provide protection against telephone intrusion. When users dial up the computer, they are required to supply their identification. If this identification corresponds to an authorized user, the dial-back unit automatically requests the caller to hang up, and then dials a preset number for that user. The call-back may be dialled out on the same line as the previous incoming call, or it may use a second line. The latter technique can overcome one reported form of attack, in which a tone is sent down the line indicating, incorrectly, that the user has hung up. The modem then remains connected to the original caller while it believes that it is dialling up the specified number.

With a call-back on a separate line, an attacker may simply 'clamp-on' to that line, intercepting the outgoing call. Some advanced forms of call-back modems are designed to thwart such attacks.

The major disadvantage of call-back modems, however, is that they restrict access to specified locations; mobile authorized users with laptop computers are thus denied access from public telephones, hotel rooms, etc. In this case access should be restricted by the use of encryption techniques such that only user terminals, or personal computers, with the requisite cryptographic keys, can communicate over the network. Such systems may operate in conjunction with advanced access control systems such as dynamic passwords (see chapter 3).

4.2.6 How can cryptography be used in a data communications network?

Cryptographic systems (see chapter 1) are commonly employed to provide effective security in data networks. However, since such networks are used to interconnect a population of users, as compared with a simple connection between two parties, there are a number of ways in which encryption is performed on network traffic:

- link-by-link encryption,
- node-by-node encryption,
- end-to-end encryption.

With link-by-link encryption (see figure 4-3), data is encrypted on each communication link e.g. telecommunications line, microwave link, fibre-optic data line, connecting two nodes in the network. Each link on the network requires two data encryption/decryption units in this mode of operation; large complex networks may thus requires the installation of hundreds, or even thousands, of encryption

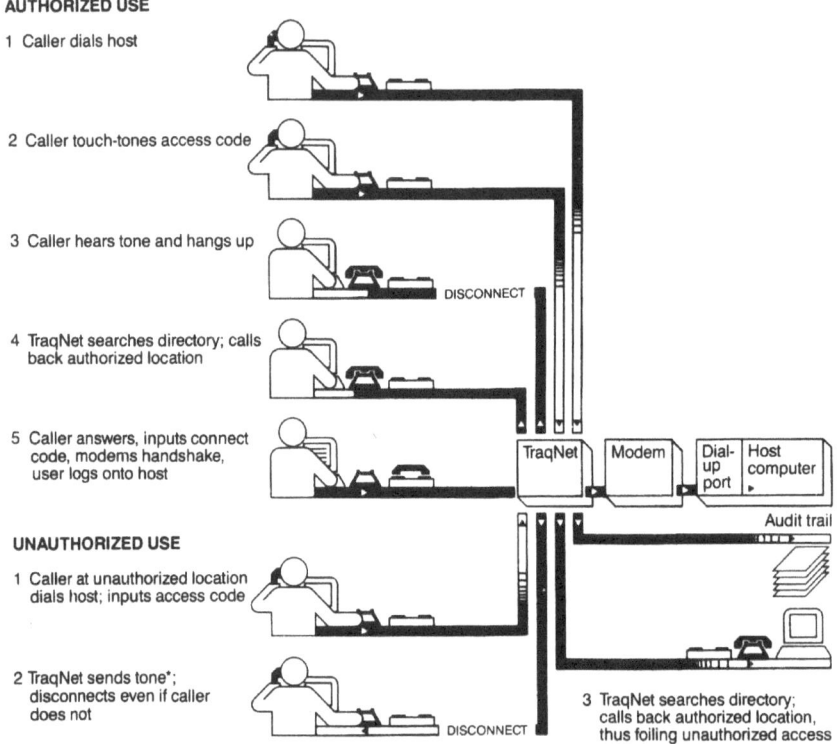

AUTHORIZED USE

1 Caller dials host

2 Caller touch-tones access code

3 Caller hears tone and hangs up

4 TraqNet searches directory; calls
back authorized location

5 Caller answers, inputs connect
code, modems handshake,
user logs onto host

UNAUTHORIZED USE

1 Caller at unauthorized location
dials host; inputs access code

2 TraqNet sends tone*;
disconnects even if caller
does not

3 TraqNet searches directory;
calls back authorized location,
thus foiling unauthorized access

Fig. 4-2 Dial-up control. The LeeMah TraqNet 2000 System.

units. This approach may simply be too expensive, and difficult to administer, for large networks.

Node-by-node encryption provides a more cost-effective solution for large networks. In this mode incoming data to a node are decrypted, with a cryptographic key corresponding to that used in the previous source node, and re-encrypted with a different key, prior to onward transmission. Such cryptographic functions, and the storage of the keys, is undertaken in security modules, and not in the node computer.

Both link-by-link and node-by-node techniques are vulnerable to attack by line-tapping between the data terminal equipment (DTE) and the data encryption equipment (DEE), i.e. between the network node, host computer, or terminal and the encryptor, since the traffic is in plaintext over these links. Such illicit access may be achieved with data monitor probes in a front-end communications processor of

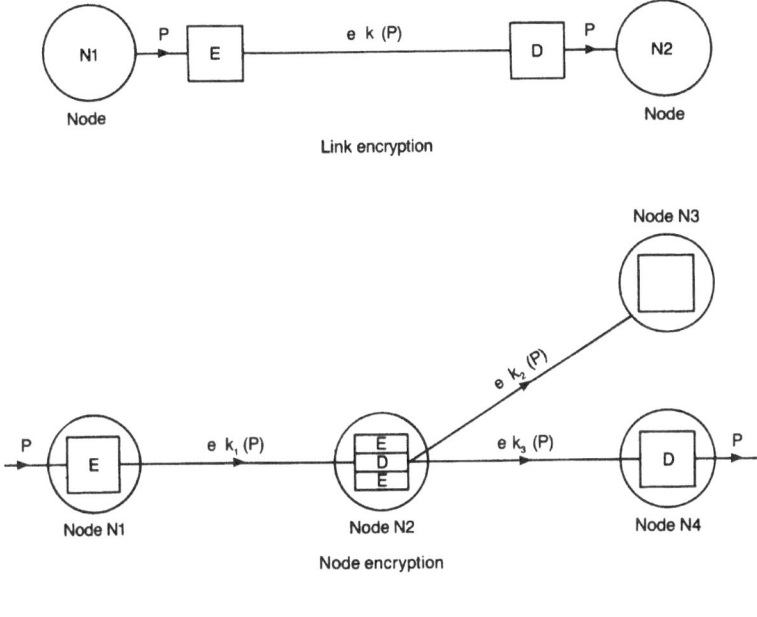

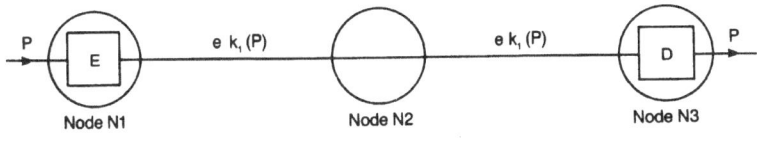

Fig. 4-3 Network encryption

a mainframe computer, e.g. the IBM 3725/3745 communications processor. Thus physical access controls are required for such areas.

With end-to-end encryption the data is encrypted by the sender and decrypted by the receiver. Thus it is never revealed in plaintext form at any intermediate node. In this mode of operation the encryption equipment normally forms part of the node equipment, e.g. the terminal and host computer. This form of network encryption is normally used, for example, in X.25 packet switching networks, but it assumes that the act of encryption will not affect the correct operation of the network. For example, in the X.25 case it may be that the information in the message relating to the source and destination addresses transmitted on the network must not be encrypted (though a solution to this problem does exist).

The three modes have their individual advantages and disadvantages. In some cases a combination of these modes may be employed. For example it may be necessary to disguise the fact that any communication at all is taking place between certain parties, but end-to-end encryption must supply in clear all message headers, containing sender and receiver addresses. Link-by-link encryption can then be used on critical links, thus encrypting all message traffic, including addresses.

End-to-end encryption probably presents the safest and lowest-cost solution to network security; it is likely to be the predominant mode employed in the 1990s. It is inherent in the application layer security services specified for the Open Systems Interconnection (OSI) model (see section 4.4.1). The number of points where encryption and decryption must take place is minimized, with ensuing savings in the number of encryption devices or sub-systems. The overheads imposed by the encryption process will have minimum effect on the overall performance of the network – an important consideration whenever encryption is contemplated. Moreover, the problem of key management may be relegated to those users for whom security is a prime concern (see chapter 1).

4.2.7 What is the most significant problem associated with the use of encryption in a corporate network?
The use of encryption implies that authorized users, and only authorized users, of the network have access to the requisite cryptographic keys. Key management has been defined in draft ISO documents (ISO DIS 8732, *Banking – Key management, Wholesale*) as the process concerned with the secure generation, distribution, and eventual destruction of cryptographic keys. The draft standard indicates that key management is concerned with the generation, distribution, storage, custody, monitoring, destruction, and backup procedures of keying material. The provision for audit trails is also aided by the formalization of such procedures.

It will be impractical to handle such procedures manually for most geographically distributed networks; particularly when keys need to be changed frequently and in response to network traffic flows.

The particular key management scheme chosen will be a function of the topology of the network, but in any case the management technique chosen must meet the following requirements:

• The network must be operated as an open network in order to facilitate the introduction of new nodes, terminals, etc.;

- It must allow for different connection options within the network.
- It must be implemented with the same level of technology as the encryption system.
- It must be independent of any particular network conventions for message and data types, formats, etc.

In regard to various connection options, the key management scheme must not impose upon the network user the requirement to connect a terminal or host computer via a specific communications technique dictated by the encryption scheme, nor should the scheme limit the number or types of hosts or nodes to which a user may have legitimate access. At the same time, there exists the requirement to complement the encryption system with a similar level of technology for the key management scheme. If there is a mismatch in this area then overall network security may be jeopardized. For example, if encryption hardware is used then the keying data must also be protected via hardware techniques, and not be stored in software form in a node, where illicit access is feasible (see chapter 5).

4.2.8 What physical problems exist for network security?
Every computer security manager must be able to inspect and obtain full information on the following:

- location of all internal data and telecommunications cabling;
- location and accessibility of the main telecommunications interconnection box, usually installed by the PTT or public network company;
- type and nature of all connections to the network cabling.

This requirement extends even to the cables connecting the network to a mainframe's front-end data communications computer system, e.g. an IBM 3725/3745 unit. The problem of eavesdropping on data cables must be emphasized; the same techniques apply as for any simple voice-level tapping operation. Probes may be inserted onto the cable at numerous points, but certain areas are under particular risk, including the main telecommunications closet for a building. This closet forms the principal point of connection of the internal data network within a building to the external, wide area public data network. It houses the main junction points for connection.

Location and control of the main communications closet is paramount. The following checklist may assist in assessment of the security of this vital corporate link:

- Is the closet clearly identified and its location known to the data

205

processing manager and the security managers, including the main security officers for the building? Is there more than one closet?

- Is the closet regularly inspected for any suspicious extra wires or other forms of connectors? (A radio emitting bug may be quite small and use its connecting wires as an aerial.)
- Are the circuits labelled in a compromising way (e.g. leased/ fixed data lines marked with pieces of tape with numbers etc. on them) that does not form part of the normal PTT identification scheme?
- Does the security manager know what identification scheme is used by the PTT?
- Is the closet securely locked with a steel door having a sufficient locking device and non-removable door hinges?
- Is the closet well fixed to the wall?
- Is the closet visible to a company officer (e.g. in the main reception area) and thus able to be monitored by a company representative, or is the closet located in an obscure area, e.g. in an underground car park?

All data links must be available for inspection. Even if encryption equipment is used in a network between, say, a DTE and a DCE, a listening bug may still be planted between the encryption equipment and the DTE. For example, a radio-transmitting data probe could exist between a data encryption unit, the telecommunications link connector, and card in a front-end processor, even though the front-end processor and the data encryption equipment may both be located in a controlled entry main computer room.

In an extreme case the problem of illicit insertion of data bugs into data communications and terminal/computer equipment must be considered. The existence of these so-called 'Red Cards' has been suggested for some time, but it has been difficult to confirm actual attacks. This particular form of attack involves the illicit placement of a special data probe card, an electronic sub-assembly, inside the computer or terminal equipment itself. The scenario suggests that such placement could be performed by corrupt service technicians, computer operators, users, or, indeed, anybody with access to the systems. The bug-board may be an active or passive unit. In the active case it may radiate data via radio signals to a waiting receiver, while in the passive case it may simply collect data, possibly selectively, in battery-backed memory, for later removal and collection of the data by the penetrator. At present, systems using a commonly known bus structure appear most vulnerable, e.g. IBM PC-based workstations, RS232C/V.24 communications connectors, etc. In this latter case the bug may actually be inserted into the small plastic or metal connector that terminates the cable connecting the terminal to a modem, or a modem to a computer system, etc.

4.2.9 Is a local area network (LAN) more secure than the wide area data communications network?
Risks to a LAN appear to be much the same as for the wider data communications network, although the level of technology required by an attacker for full penetration of a LAN may be somewhat higher. The LAN normally operates at some 10 million bits per second, as compared with 64,000 bits per second for a wide area data communications network. The security of terminals and workstations are, however, the same for both types of network. The threats associated with LANs are similar to those of other networks:

• introduction of false messages into the LAN,
• eavesdropping,
• disruption of service,
• attaching an illicit terminal or node to the LAN,
• re-routing of messages to fraudulent terminals or nodes,
• illegal access via gateways.

Information related to cabling, and physical access to it, is not normally available in the case of telecommunications services supplied by the national carrier. However, with LANs the introduction of false messages, eavesdropping, and disruption to service are facilitated because internal staff have ready access to the cabling and details of such cabling, type, location, etc., both for office LANs and factory automation systems. Thus LAN co-axial copper cable may be tapped, both actively and passively, either on the cable directly or at termination and connector points. Hence LAN cable should be physically protected (e.g. using steel cable ducts with key locks), yet it should be capable of being regularly inspected. Optical fibre cable is less vulnerable, although not entirely immune to attack, but the initial purchase price may be higher. Fibre optic cable does have the advantage that it is not susceptible to magnetic and electrical interference from within the building, nor does it radiate signals to the eavesdropper, except at the point of connection of the optical fibre to the electrical world of the workstation. If LANs are to be extensively used in the organization then management must consider the purchase of the necessary test equipment for the appropriate LAN for security as well as backup and maintenance purposes.

Illicit terminals may be easily connected to most LANs since simple, office-level connectors are commonly employed: indeed, such ease of interconnection for additional workstations is one of the purported advantages of LANs. An attacker may cause LAN messages to be re-routed by the insertion of illicit LAN driver software at a workstation. Such software may also contain Trojan Horse routines to monitor and record selected traffic on the LAN. The development of such illicit software is greatly facilitated if personal computers are employed as LAN workstations, since attackers are likely to have extensive knowledge of the operation of the network, its workstations, and servers. Cryptographic systems, located at the workstation and server, can provide a degree of protection against unauthorized access to, and misuse of, LAN data.

If the LAN is connected to a wide area network through a gateway then management should be vigilant on the operation of the gateway, since it may provide an entry into the LAN to hackers, and grant opportunities for expensive, unauthorized use of WAN facilities by internal staff.

4.3 Security on IBM Systems

4.3.1 How is security maintained in an IBM mainframe-based system?
There are three aspects of security implementation on IBM mainframe systems:

- SNA network security,
- cryptographic systems,
- access control software.

The IBM System Network Architecture (SNA) was one of the first commercial-level computer network schemes to incorporate data security from the outset. Messages on individual terminal-to-host sessions may be encrypted for data transmission. The SDLC data communications protocol that forms the communications base of SNA contains indicators that specify whether or not an individual message (or packet) is encrypted: this indicator may be used to activate automatically any necessary decryption at the receiving mainframe system. These schemes usually function under the IBM MVS operating system on the mainframe, with appropriate encryption hardware and/or software at the host computer and terminal device. For example, the encryption sub-system for the IBM 3274 or allied terminal controller, and the IBM 3848 encryption sub-system for the host computer system. At the host computer system operating under IBM's MVS/XA the encryption system is supported by either the Program Cryptographic Facility (PCF) or the IBM 3848 Cryptographic Unit and its Cryptographic Unit Support Program (CUSP) (see figure 4-4).

The IBM 3848 (or its equivalent) or PCF are required for the

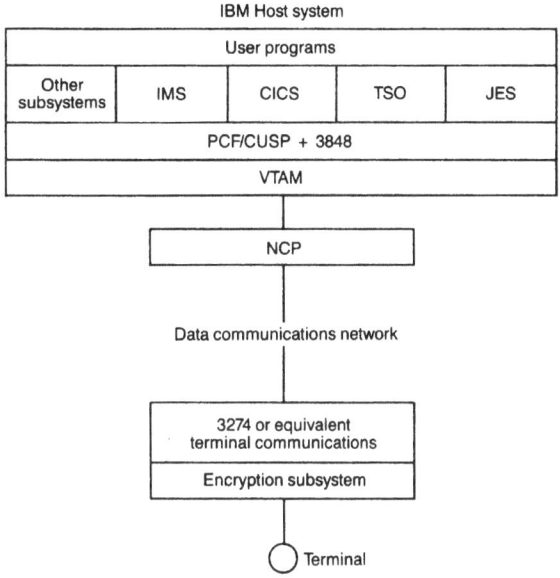

IBM Host system

User programs				
Other subsystems	IMS	CICS	TSO	JES
PCF/CUSP + 3848				
VTAM				

NCP

Data communications network

| 3274 or equivalent terminal communications |
| Encryption subsystem |

Terminal

Fig. 4-4 IBM mainframe security

creation of a secure network in that environment. These are then used by the Virtual Terminal Access Method (VTAM) to provide the session-level encryption services needed for confidential data transmission. These same cryptographic services are again used by the IBM REPRO program to encrypt and decrypt data sets when they are copied.

There is also increasing use of access control packages on IBM mainframe computer systems operating under MVS/XA and its equivalents to enhance security (see figure 4-5). These packages, such as IBM's own RACF (Resource Access Control Facility) or RACF/VM (Resource Access Control Facility/Virtual Machine) for both MVS/XA and VM operating system environments, and Computer Associates' ACF/2, are normally quite separate to the establishment of encryption services on the data network, although this may change in the near future. Access control facilities are also provided on the IBM System/36 and System/38 computers. The Data Security Monitor (DSMON) that is available with RACF and RACF/VM maintains the data set required to control the groups of users with extraordinary privileges. It also permits the overall access control strategy of the system to be reviewed on a regular basis and required changes to be made.

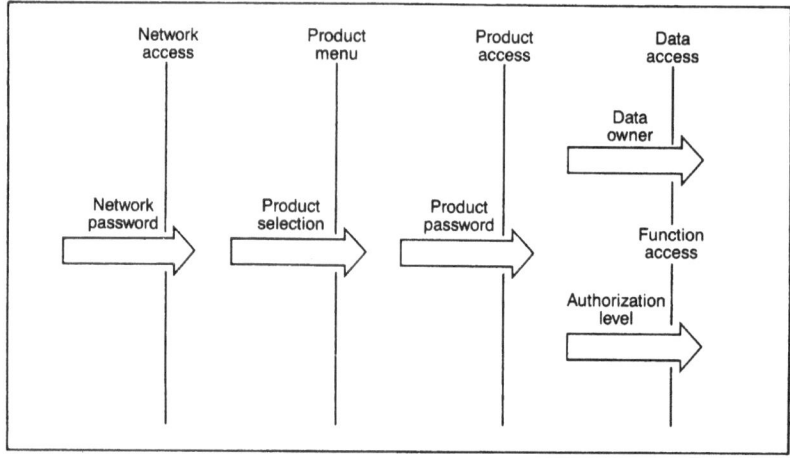

Fig. 4-5 Security mechanisms for controlling access in an IBM environment

In the future, however, it is almost certain that the access control packages, and in particular RACF, on the large mainframe computer systems will become further integrated with the overall security programme for the main IBM host mainframe computer and the associated data network. In March 1988 IBM made a statement of commitment that its mainframe operating systems MVS/ESA, VM/SP, and VM/XA would conform to the so-called B1 level of secure functionality as set out by the US National Computer Security Centre's *Trusted Computer System Evaluation Criteria* report, the 'Orange Book' (see chapter 1). It also made a commitment to enter into the formal evaluation cycles needed with the US Department of Defense to verify the compliance of the systems at the B1 level. By mid-1988 IBM had two systems under evaluation by the NCSC. These were RACF Version 1.8, for a C2 classification, and a special version of Xenix, for its personal computer-level products, at the B2 level (see chapter 1).

In a 1988 paper (IFIP/Sec'88) an IBM expert stated in relation to these Department of Defense evaluations of its products that 'while many users may not need a US DoD-evaluated system, the assessment is stringent and many of the required functions will be beneficial to all users'.

4.3.2 Can a personal computer participate in a secure IBM data network?

Data, programs, and text are now commonly transmitted between personal computer-based user workstations and mainframe applications programs. An organization's main database (e.g. an IBM DB2 database system on an IBM-308X mainframe operating under MVS/ESA) may be the source for data files to be used with a spreadsheet program on the workstation (e.g. Lotus 1-2-3 under PC-DOS or OS/2 on an IBM PS/2 Model 50Z personal computer). An IBM, or indeed any other personal computer-based workstation, usually participates in an IBM network scheme by emulating one of the earlier IBM terminal units and/or controllers, e.g. an IBM 3274 controller and IBM 3278 paged visual display unit with associated printer. The terminal emulation is normally provided by an expansion card in the personal computer, used in conjunction with emulation software. The personal computer is connected to the network via a synchronous data modem, such devices being supplied by the user or a particular telecommunications supplier (e.g. a PTT).

If the workstation is to be used for secure transmission with an IBM host computer the terminal emulation subsystem in the personal computer must also contain cryptographic facilities similar to those available with the encryption options in IBM's terminal controllers. Packages are available to enable such secure terminal emulation to be performed on the IBM personal computer, or compatible microcomputers.

With the move by IBM to its Systems Application Architecture (SAA), application programs operating on the personal computer workstation will be able to converse over a data network with other application programs on an IBM host computer. The exact methods that will be used to perform encryption in such an environment have not yet been defined.

From an application viewpoint a personal computer package may simply encrypt data to be sent to a host application package, and present that encrypted data to a transport subsystem in the workstation for forwarding to the associated application on the host.

At the host the associated program can receive the data and apply appropriate decryption techniques. This end-to-end (see section 4.2.6) or application-to-application mode of encryption makes minimal demands on the architecture of the SNA-based (or similar) data network. However, the important problem of cryptographic key management (see section 4.2.7) must still be tackled either by the co-operating secure applications or the network.

4.4 OSI Security

4.4.1 What are the security implications of using the principle of open systems interconnection (OSI)?

The basic concept of the OSI model is to structure the extremely complex operations involved in passing data from a user's application program to a receiver's application program that is located on another computer connected to the data network. The purpose of the structure is to provide a series of levels, at the sending and receiving end, so that each sender level is only concerned with communicating with its corresponding receiver level. In the sending computer a particular level has interfaces only with the level immediately above and below, and these interfaces enable information to be sent to the corresponding level at the receiving end. As an analogy, manual telephone systems involved switchboard operators in one company who established relationships with corresponding operators in another. The operators received requests from the managers and made connections on the switchboard. They were neither concerned with the nature of the messages nor the technology of the telephone network. Similarly OSI defines logical levels that will interact in well-defined ways.

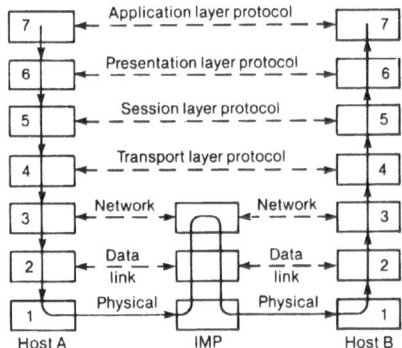

Fig. 4-6 The OSI model

The OSI model defines seven such levels or layers. From the user's viewpoint down, they are:

7 application layer,
6 presentation layer,
5 session layer,
4 transport layer,
3 network layer,

2 data link layer,
1 physical layer.

The lower the layer, the closer it is to the physical reality of the computer system or network, e.g. the physical layer is concerned with the cables on which data will flow, the particular connectors used, etc. The layers must exist, and be identifiable in co-operating open systems, to enable information to flow.

The development of the set of standards that comprises the OSI model will enable computer systems from different manufacturers to participate in enterprise-wide data networks, and even in networks linking different organizations. From the user's viewpoint this development has a major advantage: manufacturers will not be able to 'lock-in' their customers with protocols and equipment incompatible with other systems on the market.

The development of standards is a sign of a maturing industry. There is, however, an obverse side of the coin; standards open up networks to a wide variety of users, and can create opportunities for illicit penetration. A hacker's home computer could, in principle, use the same set of procedures to gain access to networks based upon DEC, IBM, Nixdorf, and other manufacturers' computer systems. In 1986 it was realized that the specifications for control, management, and security requirements were lagging as the OSI standards gradually emerged. The overall aims of Open Systems Interconnection (OSI) and their relationship to the security of OSI networks have been set out in the OSI documents of the International Standards Organization (ISO). The appropriate standard document (ISO 7498 Addendum 2) states:

The objective of OSI is to permit the interconnection of heterogeneous computer systems so that useful communication between application processes may be achieved. At various times, security controls must be established in order to protect the information exchanged between the application processes. Such controls should make the cost of obtaining data greater than the potential value of obtaining or modifying the data.

4.4.2 How will security in OSI systems be established?

The main concept in OSI security is one of network-wide 'pervasive security mechanisms'. These mechanisms must be present in the network nodes whenever any form of network security is required.

The pervasive security mechanisms will provide the basic security management functions for the open network. They will control the distribution of security related information to various open systems:

- providing required security services;
- reporting on security services provided in the network and by its hosts;
- reporting on security relevant events that may occur.

Security measures, which are to be accepted by a diverse range of users, must comprise subsystems which are trusted in a technical sense, i.e. they must be well designed, rigorously tested, evaluated, and then accepted by all members participating in the network. The basic mechanisms listed above must therefore be trusted and accepted by management.

The pervasive security mechanisms in the network will, for example, need to provide all security-related event-detection and handling services. For example these services may include:

- all aspects of recovery procedures;
- logging of the events (security audit trails) (see chapter 1);
- local or remote reporting of the event;
- the facility to disconnect unilaterally the systems when a security breach has been encountered.

At the audit trail level, agreement on the recording techniques will be required, together with the formats to be used for interchange of the audit log records.

The more detailed security services in an OSI network may be separated into mandatory and discretionary controls (see chapter 3). The mandatory security policies are those imposed by the administrators of communicating computer systems. In mandatory systems individual users or systems will be restricted to communications with a specified group of other users or systems, using specified protection services. On the other hand discretionary controls may enable a particular system or user to determine the group of other systems or users with whom communications are to be established, and the level of security services to be used on the channels, e.g. proof of identity, privacy of messages, etc.

4.4.3 How will security facilities fit into the OSI scheme?

The overall definition of security facilities for OSI systems and related networks will cover the security services and the mechanisms to provide those services. These services and mechanisms will be provided by the various separate layers of the OSI model (see section 4.4.9). The main activity in the creation of security standards in OSI will then comprise the definition of the positions within the OSI layers where these security related services and mechanisms will be provided or reside. It is to be hoped that this activity will result only in additions to the concepts and facilities set out in the OSI model, and not in any modifications to the overall OSI model itself.

4.4.4 What types of security services are planned for OSI compliant systems and networks?

A number of security services have been identified for OSI systems and networks. These services have been discussed for a number of years and appear to be a well-accepted base set of services. The services currently identified are:

- confidentiality,
- integrity,
- non-repudiation,
- peer entity authentication,
- data origin authentication,
- access control,
- traffic flow security.

Data transmitted on the network may need to be protected from accidental or deliberate disclosure. Privacy of message content may need to be guaranteed, given the assumption that eavesdroppers may be present on the network, particularly if the computer network makes use of the public telecommunications services. There is a requirement for assurance that data sent and received are the same, i.e. without insertions, modifications, deletions, duplications, or replay. In commercial networks this aspect of security is often more important than the maintenance of confidentiality. Although integrity services ensure that no unauthorized person can insert or modify messages, they do not, in themselves, prevent the recipient of data denying receipt of that data, or the sender repudiating transmission of the message. In an open network some form of non-repudiation service may be required to guard users against such abuses.

A peer entity authentication service ensures the identity of a remote OSI device, such as a computer system, terminal, workstation, etc. with whom communication, using defined OSI communications protocols, is to be established. Data origin authentication is similar to peer entity authentication; this service provides assurance that the source of transmitted data on the network is as it purports to be. For example, an application running on a remote personal computer workstation in an OSI network may need to label securely the data it generates, while peer entity authentication validates the originating 'terminal' or application program itself.

Access control (see chapter 3) ensures that only authorized entities can gain access to host OSI systems and their applications programs via the various data communications links of the network.

A traffic flow security service will disguise or hide message traffic patterns on networks connecting OSI systems. Such patterns may be of value to an attacker in that the mere knowledge of the existence of messages exchanged between users at particular times may be of significance, e.g. regular EFTPOS payments between parties.

4.4.5 How are security mechanisms related to security services in the OSI model?

A security technique or mechanism is one that exists in a lower layer of the OSI model to provide some of the security services (see section 4.4.9) required by a higher layer. For example, a security service for layer 7 (application layer) may be provided by a mechanism at layer 3 (network layer). Some of the mechanisms that have already been identified by the OSI committees are:

- encryption,
- cryptographic key management (see chapter 1),
- data integrity (see chapter 1),
- digital signatures (see chapter 1),
- notarization,
- authentication exchange,
- access control (see chapter 3),
- routing control,
- traffic padding.

Encryption may be employed with symmetric ciphers (e.g. DES) or asymmetric public key systems. Any such use of ciphers requires effective cryptographic key management, particularly among a diffuse user population of an open network (see chapter 1). Conventional use of cryptography protects the confidentiality of messages, but these techniques need to be extended to protect against undetected tampering with messages (see chapter 1). In the banking and finance industries this technique is termed 'message authentication coding' (see chapter 5); a checksum, based on the contents of the message and protected by encryption, is added to the message by the originator. This MAC is subsequently tested for validity by the recipient. A non-repudiation service can be provided, with digital signatures appended to the messages, thus serving the same purpose as conventional handwritten signatures on documents (see chapter 1).

Notarization provides a method by which communicating entities on an OSI network can effectively consult with an independent and trusted third party, a digital equivalent of a notary public or justice of the peace. This technique can provide an independent verification of their identities before exchanging messages, and is designed to prevent spoofing attacks (see chapter 1).

Authentication exchange mechanisms provide communicating OSI entities with a secure mechanism to authenticate each other's identities. Access control mechanisms can be employed to ensure that users and systems on the network prove their identity and authorizations before using network facilities. For example, the location and type of a particular workstation in the network may dictate the host systems, host applications, and databases that are available to that terminal (see chapter 3).

Messages in a network may be transmitted from the sender to the receiver via any one of numerous paths within the network. The choice of these paths may be left to the discretion of the network control systems, but this may not be acceptable from a security viewpoint, in which case a routing control mechanism will often be used to restrict the paths for certain classes of messages.

Traffic flow security can be aided by traffic padding, which prevents eavesdroppers determining traffic patterns on the network. In this technique traffic flow is padded out with null messages so that the presence of a genuine message is disguised: this may incur additional traffic charges.

4.4.6 *How are the security mechanisms managed in an OSI network?*

Overall security management in OSI networks needs to provide a number of specific management functions. These functions should be assessed before any OSI system participates in a network environment, and appropriate communication protocols should be devised. Typical management functions are:

- cryptographic key management,
- authentication and integrity management,
- access control management,
- security controls and event handling.

Encryption services demand the secure management of cryptographic keys, in terms of key generation, distribution, and deletion. This will involve the generation of keys at time intervals dictated by the level of security demanded. The determination of those OSI entities authorized to receive the keys must be performed in accordance with the overall access control parameters set up for the network. This key management function must also cope with the various principles and methods involved in the use of symmetric and asymmetric ciphers (see chapter 1).

The authentication management function must provide for the distribution of descriptive information, passwords, and cryptographic keys to all OSI entities in the network concerned with the integrity of exchanged messages. Thus a suitable protocol must be defined for those OSI communicating entities and for any other entities in the network that wish to provide authentication services.

217

The security management function must also provide for the creation and updating of all access control and capability lists for OSI systems in the network. This involves, for example, secure distribution of passwords, tokens, and similar identification parameters. This function must be supported with appropriate communications protocols.

The overall security management system for the OSI network may involve the collection of remote audit records, or even deal with the enabling or disabling of audit trail logging for selected events.

4.4.7 What data are required by the OSI security management system?
The main security management system for an OSI network will require access to a security management information base (SMIB). This database will contain a set of files or tables that store security relevant information. It may be centrally located, or could be distributed over a number of hosts or control systems in the OSI network.

Each layer in the OSI model will consult the SMIB for the information required in the provision of the security services. The SMIB itself must also be created and updated by security management application programs operating on network nodes; application level protocols for this task also need to be defined.

4.4.8 How does the OSI security management scheme relate to other management functions in OSI systems and networks?
Security management forms one of a number of overall management concerns of OSI networks and systems, e.g. fault management, configuration management, accounting management, performance management.

Users of OSI networks (i.e. networks of corresponding OSI systems and appropriate network controllers or relay systems) expect network managers to plan, organize, supervise, control, and account for the usage of interconnection services in the computer network. This means that the network and its management system must be able to respond to changing information and communications requirements. Facilities should exist to ensure predictable behaviour in the network while maintaining information protection, and also to ensure the authentication of all sources of, and destinations for, transmitted data.

The overall impact of security requirements on these management aspects must be determined for each network. Moreover, overall management standards need to be defined for OSI networks involving aspects of the type of management information services to be provided, the network management communications protocols to be used, and the structure and data definitions for the management information to be provided. It is likely that by the early 1990s standards for all of these aspects of OSI system and network management will be defined and published. However, there will be an intervening period when only parts of these management standards will be in existence: management will need to work with the security and network managers for corporate information systems in order to determine the best solutions available to meet the identified risks.

4.4.9 In which layers of the OSI model will the various security services be provided?

There is a problem in this area. While there appears to be general agreement on the types of services and mechanisms that are required to create secure OSI systems and networks, the exact placement of the services in various layers appears to be contentious. There are varying views on this topic among the groups responsible for defining standards.

The general principles to be observed in the allocation of services and mechanisms to layers in OSI seem to be agreed:

- The number of alternative ways in which a security service may be achieved should be minimized.
- Security services may be provided in more than one layer.
- Wherever possible security functions should not duplicate OSI functions already defined in other areas.
- The independence of the OSI layers that forms the basis of the OSI model must be retained.
- The number of overall network security management functions that must meet trusted requirements should be minimized.
- When a higher layer depends upon a lower layer for a security mechanism, then any intermediate layers must be constructed so that security violation is impracticable.
- Security features, added to systems in an OSI-compliant network of OSI systems, apply not only to the end systems in the network that contain all seven layers, but also to any intermediate or relay systems, e.g. network controllers.

The location of security services and mechanisms in the layers of the model may occur over three broad levels:

level 1: network hardware level:
- layer 1: physical layer;
- layer 2: data link layer.

This level could essentially classify the security services and mech-

219

anisms in terms of network hardware. This may not have any major effect on the level of integration of OSI systems into the network.

level 2: sub-network level:
- layer 3: network layer;
- layer 4: transport layer;
- layer 5: session layer.

Security services at this level will essentially be concerned with the control of the various communications services in the network.

level 3: application-to-application level:
- layer 6: presentation layer;
- layer 7: application layer.

Security in the network at this level will be essentially concerned with information flow from one OSI application to another.

The final text of the appropriate OSI document (DIS 7498-2) sets out the allocation of security services to the various layers of the OSI Reference Model as shown in table 4-1. This illustrates the further addition of security services to OSI, e.g. the security problems arising when no distinct connection is established between entities prior to the exchange of messages, i.e. connectionless security. This is a normal mode of operation in transaction networks, e.g. EFT systems in the banking industry.

The non-repudiation services provided in layer 7 (application layer) protect senders of messages against receivers who later falsely deny receipt, and recipients of messages against senders who later falsely claim that the received message did not originate from them. The definition and location of security services as above will play an important role in the future, as users have access to host computers, databases, and other users operating on different networks. This means that networks themselves will create networks of networks and the problem of secure data transmission between them will become even more pressing. The problem today is that the matter of security in OSI networks may be at the same level of acceptance as the OSI model was itself some ten or more years ago.

4.4.10 Are there any current standards for the incorporation of encryption equipment into a network?

The OSI model provides a framework around which particular standards may be created; it enables individual standards to be related and interlocked within an overall architecture or plan. Some standards for the incorporation of encryption security equipment do exist. One such standard is the ANSI (American National Standards Institute) X3.105-1983, which is entitled a 'Data Link Encryption'

Table 4-1 Allocation of security services to OSI layers

	layers						
	1	2	3	4	5	6	7
peer entity authentication			*	*			*
data origin authentication			*	*			*
access control service			*	*			*
connection confidentiality	*	*	*	*		*	*
connectionless confidentiality		*	*	*		*	*
selective field confidentiality						*	*
traffic flow confidentiality	*		*				*
connection integrity with recovery				*			*
connection integrity without recovery			*	*			*
selective field connection integrity							*
connectionless integrity			*	*			*
selective field connectionless integrity							*
non-repudiation origin							*
non-repudiation delivery							*

(*source*: ISO DIS 7498-2 July 1988)

standard, and covers the link-to-link network encryption mode (see section 4.2.6).

The standard sets out the requirements for the incorporation of data encryption equipment (DEE) into a link in a data communications network. Thus the standard applies to Layers 1 (Physical) and 2 (Data link) of the OSI model. In communications terms the DEE is introduced between the data terminal equipment (DTE) in the network (e.g. a terminal, host computer system, or workstation) and the data circuit terminating equipment (DCE) (e.g. a modem or network terminator unit). The standard assumes that the network is insensitive to the content of the data messages and thus will not alter any parts of those messages, a network property defined as bit-configuration transparent. All data sent from the DTE to the DEE is encrypted and passed onto the DCE; similarly all data received by the DCE is passed to the DEE for decryption, and subsequent plaintext transmission goes to the DTE. In this mode of network security the encryptor is said to be 'protocol insensitive'. In fact the DEE may be physically part of the DCE (e.g. an encrypting modem) or part of the DTE (e.g. a personal computer with an encryption subsystem).

The main aim of the ANSI X3.105 standard then is to ensure that 'equipment produced by different manufacturers can successfully exchange encrypted data that can be secure only if all other related security precautions have been met'.

Data encryption on a network alone is insufficient to guarantee an acceptable level of security for a complete information system. Other techniques including management procedures are necessary.

The ANSI standard also discusses the manner in which the data encryption algorithm (DEA), itself an ANSI standard (ANSI X3.92-1981), shall be used in the DEE to encrypt and decrypt the data bit stream in the network. These methods of usage, called 'Modes of Operation', are also an ANSI standard (X3.106-1983). The standard defines:

- the start-up procedures for the DEE;
- the methods required to bypass the operation of the DEE should network testing be required without encryption;
- specific techniques to be adopted for various communications formats, e.g. synchronous and asynchronous communications modes.

Thus from a management viewpoint a standard already exists for the incorporation of cryptographic security into an enterprise's data network, at least for two individual points in the network. An attacker eavesdropping on the connection between the two points will only be able to observe ciphertext data. If the encryptor continuously feeds data onto the line, whether or not messages are being transmitted, the attacker will not be able to determine traffic patterns (see section 4.4.5).

It must be borne in mind that it has taken some ten years for the OSI scheme and some of its standards definitions to be created, fully defined, and accepted. The development of security in the OSI scheme is very recent, and unfortunately it may be some time before OSI security standards at the various levels are set out. The security and management standards may first appear as part of application layer (layer 7) standards, such as those for Electronic Document Interchange (EDI), X.400 message systems and X.500 network directory services. The security considerations will then form part of those applications as indicated in the March 1988 OSI security table shown above.

4.4.11 Will OSI standards eventually cover all aspects of network and computer security?
Unfortunately, the OSI security and management standards as envisaged for the early-to-middle 1990s may not include a number of

very important areas. At present areas of concern that may not be subject to standards development include:

- physical security parameters for both the network and its host computer systems and terminals;
- identification methods for users, e.g. biometric sensors, access control tokens, etc. (see chapter 3);
- security in the particular operating systems of the computers in the network (see chapter 1);
- analysis techniques for audit trails (see chapter 1);
- suppression of radio frequency emissions from computer systems, terminals, network telecommunications components and connections, etc. Such emissions may contain valuable and extractable information (see chapter 3).

In these areas individual managers will need to make specific risk assessments and introduce appropriate levels of security procedures and technology, e.g. encryption subsystems coupled with access control tokens, electromagnetic screening of terminal and computer rooms, etc.

4.4.12 What trends in network security can be expected in the future?
The move by most telecommunications network providers (common carriers) towards the integrated services digital network (ISDN) has already occurred and is likely to accelerate during the 1990s. The overall problem of locating security services in ISDN networks, and associated end-user equipment, may be tackled in the near future. The level of implementation will go further than the end-to-end mode in which security functions are only performed outside the ISDN and within the end-user or terminal equipment.

4.4.13 What is a 'trusted network' and is it significant to business networks?
The publication in 1987 of the US *'Trusted Network Interpretation'*, the 'Red Book', from its National Computer Security Centre (NCSC) in Washington, outlines an approach to network security particularly pertinent to government users, both military and non-military. It is not yet clear if this report is suitable for non-government and commercial users, where differing security requirements to those of government apply (see chapter 1). It should also be understood that the first version of this report (31 July 1987) was intended for use 'for a period of at least one year after date of signature'. This document can be viewed as effectively comprising two parts. The first aims at providing an interpretation of the earlier US Department of Defense Trusted Computer System Evaluation Criteria (publication DOD-5200.28-STD), the 'Orange Book' (named after the colour of

its covers), for 'trusted computer/communications network systems... ranging from isolated local area networks to wide-area internetwork systems'. The second section sets out additional security services that arise from the nature of data networks, including the problems of network integrity, denial of service, transmission security, etc.

The Trusted Network report is significant in that it has, as one of its main purposes, the aim 'to provide a standard to manufacturers as to what security features and assurance levels to build into their new and planned, commercial network products in order to provide widely available systems that satisfy trust requirements for sensitive applications'. In this aim the overall concept of a trusted network has significance to most corporate networks that involve the distribution of a wide variety of information at various levels of sensitivity, from absolutely open promotional material, for example, to sensitive board-level minutes of meetings, financial statements, and projections. A fundamental concept from the report that may be used in any corporate network design evaluation is one of a 'coherent Network Security Architecture and Design'. This architecture must address the topics of security-relevant policies, objectives and protocols. Management in any enterprise must be sure that such a broad statement of network security objectives exists for an organization before the network is commissioned, even if the various individual network security tools must be put into place on an application-by-application basis.

References

Giuliano, *Scientific American*, September 1982

Information Processing Systems – Open Systems Interconnections – Basic Reference Model, ISO 7498

McClellan, S. T., *The Coming Computer Industry Shakeout: Winners, Losers and Survivors* (New York: John Wiley and Sons, 1984)

Security Architecture, ISO 7498 Part 2, ISO/TC97/SC21/N1528 (31 Oct 1986)

Trusted Network Interpretation of the Trusted Computer System Evaluation Criteria, NCSC-TG-005, version 1 (US National Computer Security Center, US Government Printing Office: 1987-516-224/62674, 31 July 1987).

5 Financial and Banking Networks

W. Caelli

5.1 Overview

Security issues in the finance and banking sectors are now of interest to management in other organizations for two reasons:

- The methods developed to protect financial networks, and the experience gained from the operation of such methods, are apposite in other sectors.
- There is an increasing trend to develop local networks for internal electronics funds transfer and to interconnect such networks into banking systems.

In the 1960s the banking and finance industries introduced computer systems and data communications networks for various aspects of their business, including the delivery of wholesale and retail banking services. This trend accelerated in the 1970s with the increasing power and decreasing cost of on-line computer technology and workstations. Further developments in the 1980s led to the use of on-line computer systems for branch banking activities, including back office and front desk operations, automatic teller services, automatic teller machines (ATMs), electronic funds transfer systems (EFTS), and services. By the mid-1980s large scale EFT networks had been created to provide for many automatic financial services at both the wholesale and retail banking levels, including:

- electronic funds transfer at point of sale (EFTPOS);
- home banking, often provided using videotex services;
- treasurer workstation services, in which a personal computer system at the office of a bank's corporate customer may have

> direct access to the bank's computer systems for a variety of banking services;
> - international bond dealing and related interbank and wholesale services.

The use of data networks, for all forms of electronic funds transfer and related financial activities, has now spread beyond the banking and finance industry to encompass similar activities carried out by a public or private enterprise. The information systems managers of many organizations must now deal with the problems involved in the incorporation of automated transaction-oriented financial services into the overall management information system used by the organization. The new internal financial systems, moreover, may no longer be isolated within an individual enterprise; they may interact directly with other financial transaction networks under the control of both public and private organizations. In particular, the company network could well interact with the financial networks of the banking and finance industry itself.

These developments have led to government regulations and legislation covering the operation of EFT systems and networks. In order to comply with these regulations, EFT systems may be connected directly to government systems for reporting and transaction purposes. This trend is exemplified by the US government's Department of the Treasury Order of October 1986, *Electronic Funds and Securities Transfer Policy: Message Authentication and Enhanced Security*.

By virtue of the authority vested in me as Secretary of the Treasury, the following policy is hereby mandated in order to prevent the undetected, deliberate, or inadvertent unauthorized manipulation, modification, or loss of Electronics Funds Transfer (EFT) data.

1. It is Treasury policy that EFT transactions be properly authenticated. Authentication measures must conform to American National Standards Institute (ANSI) Standard X9.9, American National Standard for Financial Institution Message Authentication or equivalent authentication technique.

2. This policy shall be applied to Federal systems which originate, transmit, relay, receive, or process Federal Government EFT transactions.

3. ...

4. ...

James Baker III
Secretary of the Treasury

Thus the privacy, security, and integrity requirements of banking and financial networks have spread to related information and transaction oriented systems within other organizations. Also the nature of an EFT network may be changing, as other forms of transactions may be recognized as having a financial component of interest to an attacker of that network, e.g. a delivery note for goods or services has a financial value, and thus its security and integrity is equally important as a direct financial transaction.

In an EFT system, authentic messages may be regarded as money, whether they be direct financial transactions or related negotiable transactions as indicated above. Today the management of any organization should be aware of the security requirements and standards for transaction-oriented and related computer networks, where messages generated, transmitted, and stored within the network may be deemed to have a monetary value.

Undetected attacks on these networks, through the introduction of bogus messages, tampering with legitimate messages, prevention of delivery of legitimate transactions, etc. may cause financial loss, or even bankruptcy, for the organization. This chapter deals with the security requirements and standards that apply to the creation and operation of financial data networks, be they developed by the banking and finance industry itself, any other private or public enterprise for its own use, or for interconnection with the networks of the finance industry.

The major security concerns for financial data networks are:

- identification and authentication of the user (see sections 5.2.1 and 5.3.1);
- privacy, integrity, and authenticity of banking/financial messages (see section 5.4.1);
- the physical security of the terminal equipment and connecting telecommunications networks (see section 5.5.1);
- authenticity of attached terminal equipment and workstations (see section 5.5.6);
- control and management of the security and authenticity systems required to protect the network, associated databases, and software systems.

Vital to the security of such networks and terminals is the use of cryptography, usually in the form of the Data Encryption Standard (DES), although more recently public key cryptography schemes such as the RSA system have come into prominence in banking networks (see chapter 1). However, the use of encryption services is only as reliable as the protection offered to the cryptographic keys themselves. For this reason there has been much interest in the

227

1980s in the development and standardization of secure cryptographic key management systems (e.g. ANSI X9.17, Standards Australia 2805.6). Overall these systems must allow for the secure generation, distribution, and storage of cryptographic keys in the network and in the many hosts and switching nodes that are attached to the network (see section 5.5.1).

5.2 Identity and Authentication of the User: Plastic Cards

5.2.1 What are the common forms of user identification?
The access control mechanisms in financial networks have been largely dominated by the requirements of the consumer market. The access techniques must involve low-cost devices that can be conveniently handled by customers with no formal training. The professional users of international banking networks, however, demand a much higher level of security, commensurate with the substantial financial value of their transactions. The current trend is towards more sophisticated access control tokens, both for the financial network user, and to provide greater functionality and security in the consumer market (see chapter 3).

The traditional plastic card and associated PIN combine the 'something the user has' and 'something the user knows' forms of access control. This level of security is, however, inadequate for the professional user of international financial networks; such users not only demand access to the network facilities, they also require some means of electronically signing their transactions. Various forms of see-through security devices are proposed and adopted for such networks, and there is increasing interest in the use of biometric sensors which rely on individual attributes such as fingerprints (see chapter 3).

The plastic card is being overtaken by the more flexible and secure smart card (see section 5.2.10) in some consumer application areas; the next development in this direction is likely to be the supersmart card (see section 5.2.12), which will provide the sophisticated consumer with a powerful personal device for financial and information technology transactions.

5.2.2 What is the form and purpose of the plastic card?
The basic plastic card is now a familiar object to almost every person with a bank account; indeed the proliferation of such cards this has led to the 'pocket-full-of-plastic' problem. The plastic card is cheap and convenient, it is the subject of national and international standards, but it does not guarantee a high level of security.

The card essentially comprises a small sheet of flexible plastic; a magnetic stripe is normally affixed along its length, and customer identification data is embossed upon it. The constituent plastic material may also contain trace elements to provide a means of unique identification as a precaution against the mass production of forged cards. The authenticity of a card can be tested by chemical analysis.

The cards bear printed and sometimes pictorial information to identify the card to the user, and some even carry advertisements. The card may also have a photograph of the owner printed on its surface for additional security and identification, enabling the card to be used for employee identification as well as financial purposes. The printed information may also provide enhanced security against counterfeiting. Two common techniques for this purpose are microprinting and holographic images.

Microprinted material is not visible to the naked eye or even by examination under a small magnifying glass. Similarly, holographic images that are extremely difficult to counterfeit may be employed; such images can also be used to store large amounts of data, which can be read by specially equipped card readers (see section 5.2.7).

The magnetic stripe, when present, consists of a thin strip of magnetic recording material for storage of user information. This identifying data is recorded on one or more of three defined tracks on the stripe.

The card is provided by the card issuer, which may be a bank or some similar organization. Ownership of the card may, however, be retained by the issuer: such is the case with most of the cards used for banking purposes.

The term 'identification card' is defined in the International Standard ISO 7810-1985 (Australian Standard SAA 3521-1988) as: 'A card identifying its bearer and issuer which may carry data required as input for the intended use of the card and for transactions based thereon'. This standard only defines the nature and dimensions of the plastic card, and not the magnetic stripe which may or may not be present on the card, nor does it define the techniques and specifications for any embossing of lettering onto the surface of the card. The international standard covers:

- physical size of the card (width, height, thickness), with three permissible sizes outlined, ID-1, ID-2, and ID-3;
- materials used in the manufacture of the card: flammability, toxicity, temperature, and humidity stability, and deformation properties.

Usage of the card is not limited to any particular application. Indeed such cards have long been used:

- by the banking and finance industry as credit and debit cards;

229

- by physical security companies for use as identity cards for opening doors and other entry and exit systems;
- for computer terminal security in general, when the card must be inserted into the terminal to activate it.

5.2.3 What are the standards governing card embossing?
The term 'embossing' is defined in the pertinent International Standard ISO 7811/1-1985 (Australian Standard SAA 3522.1-1088) as: 'to raise characters in relief from the front surface of a card'.

The information embossed onto the card may be read for visual inspection, transfer of the information to paper via use of an imprinter, or machine reading of the characters. The standard defines the character sets and type founts that are to be used for this embossing. In the case of bank cards this embossing may contain the primary account number, usually 16 digits, against which the card is issued, as well as the identity of the issuer.

The information embossed on the card is not secure and can be read by anybody or by any appropriate machine. A further standard, ISO 7811/3-1985, defines the embossing location on the most popular card, ID-1. Another standard ISO, 7812-1987, goes further and defines the numbering system and registration procedure for the issuer identifiers that may form part of the embossed number.

It is possible fraudulently to emboss a blank card, or to change the embossed characters on a card by heating it evenly, pressing out any current embossing, and then embossing new data.

5.2.4 What standards govern the magnetic stripe?
A plastic card can carry data on a small magnetic stripe attached along its length. The International Standard, ISO 7811/2-1985, defines the placement and physical characteristics of this stripe. The stripe may be used to record either two or three tracks of information, using a magnetic recording technique termed 'self-clocking'. This technique enables a card reader correctly to input the recorded information from a track, even with considerable variations in the speed at which the card is passed through the read/write heads. This technique is essential for reliable reading of cards by manual card readers, where the card is wiped through the reader by hand.

ISO 7811/2-1985 also defines the coding techniques to be used to record information on the tracks. (Tracks 1 and 2 are normally regarded as read-only tracks, while track 3 is read/write). The recorded data conforms to:

track 1:
- recording density 8.3 bits/mm (210 bits/inch)
- coded alphanumeric character set (8 bits/character with odd parity)

230

- maximum 79 characters/track

track 2:

- recording density 3 bits/mm (75 bits/inch)
- coded numeric character set (4-bit binary-coded decimal code with odd parity)
- maximum 40 characters/track

track 3:

- recording density 8.3 bits/mm (210 bits/inch)
- coded numeric character set (4-bit binary-coded decimal code with odd parity)
- maximum 107 characters/track

Various check and sentinel characters are used in each track for integrity purposes. The positions of the recording tracks on the magnetic stripe are defined in two further International Standards, ISO 7811/4-1985 and ISO 7811/5-1985.

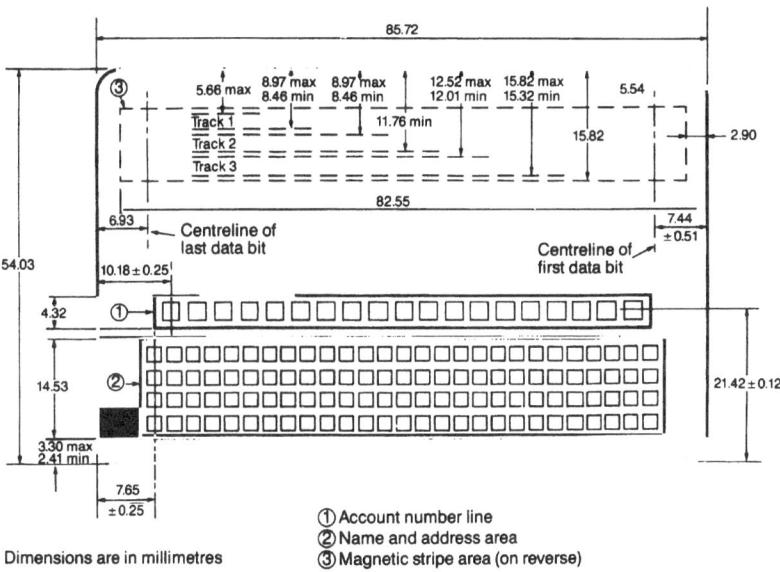

Fig. 5-1 Overall dimensions of a Magnetic Stripe Card

5.2.5 What plastic card standards apply specifically to cards used for financial transactions?
ISO 7813-1987 defines the physical nature of the financial transac-

tions card, its magnetic stripe, embossing, data fields and their format as they are recorded onto the tracks on the magnetic stripe. For example, the data structure for information recorded on track 2 is as follows (BCD = binary-coded decimal):

STX start sentinel: BCD 11
PAN identification number: up to 19 BCD digits
FS   separator: BCD 13
CC   country code: 3 BCD digits
ED   expiration date: 4 BCD digits or BCD 13
ID   interchange designator: 1 BCD digit
SC   service code: 2 BCD digits or BCD 13
DD   discretionary data: balance of available digits
ETX end sentinel: BCD 15
LRC longitudinal redundancy check: 1 BCD digit

maximum record length 40 BCD digits

5.2.6 What are the security problems associated with plastic cards?
Plastic cards are commonly employed in access control systems, particularly in the banking field, because they are cheap, user-friendly, and can be handled by a wide variety of relatively unsophisticated reading devices. The existence of international standards guarantees that an individual plastic card may be used in a multitude of retail and banking outlets on a world wide basis. However, this versatility of the card also makes it an extremely attractive target for the criminal. The plastic card is therefore associated with secondary identification techniques, usually a handwritten signature on a white stripe along the length of the card, and a personal identification number (PIN).

Fraudulent cards may be created by:

- manufacture of illicit cards and recording of false information, using full card-making and recording equipment;
- modification of a genuine card by re-embossing;
- modification of a genuine card by re-encoding of information on the magnetic storage tracks;
- creation of a fake plastic, or even cardboard, card and the addition of a magnetic stripe created from recording tape, etc.;
- purchase of white cards, i.e. cards with blank magnetic stripes without any embossing, and recording of fraudulent data on the tracks, with the optional embossing and overprinting of the card.

Information may be recorded onto the magnetic stripe, in accordance with international standards (see section 5.2.5), using simple magnetic stripe reader/writers connected to the serial port of a personal computer. The production of such fraudulent cards is facilitated by the fact that card reading devices often only read one track, usually track 2. Embossed data, the contents of other tracks, and handwritten signatures are thus not used in many transactions, e.g. PIN dependent ATM transactions.

5.2.7 What are the potential protection mechanisms for plastic cards?
The plastic card is such a cheap and universally accepted identification mechanism that various methods have been proposed, and adopted, to minimize illicit usage, or fraudulent creation of cards. These techniques, often employed in combination, include:

- holographic images and data storage,
- microprinting,
- magnetic stripe watermark,
- encryption of magnetic stripe data.

A holographic image may be attached to the surface of the card. This image is difficult to reproduce, and stocks of it may be rigorously controlled by the card issuer. This technique raises the cost of both legitimate and illicit large-scale reproduction of the card. It does not, however, eliminate the problem of small-scale usage of legitimate cards for illegitimate purposes, e.g. re-recording of data on magnetic stripes, re-embossing, etc. The image may be visually checked by a sales assistant at a point of sale, but cannot normally be sensed by devices such as automatic teller machines. Nevertheless, this technique may be sufficient to prove to a court of law that a particular card is a fake.

Security against large-scale reproduction is enhanced if the image contains data known only to the issuer, or detailed information on the owner of the card. The information in the holograph may be encrypted using a cipher and/or key that is known only to the issuer. In these circumstances, a forger would be compelled to produce identical copies of the one card; a practice that would facilitate the detection of such fake cards.

Microprinting techniques enable information to be hidden on the surface of the card; a particular series of micro characters may be printed onto the card within other characters or in close proximity to them. These characters require microscopic examination to determine their location and value. The security benefits and limitations of this technique are similar to those for the holographic images described above.

The magnetic stripe on the card may contain a magnetic watermark, i.e. a specially encoded magnetic area on the stripe. The watermark provides a permanent record on the stripe which may be sensed by a duly equipped card reader. Such a watermark, which may also be combined with the magnetic stripe contents, inhibits the illicit production of cards and/or the alteration of magnetic stripe data. The watermark may be associated with particular issuers, who administer the stock of appropriate magnetic material for application to their cards. Unfortunately most low-cost point-of-sale terminals and card readers are not equipped to detect such watermarks.

The data stored on magnetic tracks 1, 2, and 3 of the card may also be protected by encryption. The data fields themselves may be scrambled using a standard (DES) or proprietary cipher process with a secret cryptographic key; an authentication code may be added to the card data fields (see chapter 1). This does not prevent the illicit copying of a card but it may compel the illicit copier to make multiple copies of the same card; and such forged cards are more readily detected, just as with multiple copies of a banknote having the same number. Thus this technique prevents the most serious form of attack, i.e. mass production of forged cards each with unique data on the magnetic stripe. Such an attack has national security significance similar to the mass production of forged paper money and coins. At present, however, this technique does not appear to be used for standard bank cards, except for the encryption of the PIN on some cards (see section 5.3.8).

5.2.8 What is the legal position on misuse of credit cards?

In 1984 the US Congress passed the Credit Card Fraud Act (Section 102, of Title 18, US Code). This Act extended the definition of credit and debit cards to the concept of access device. It also deemed the following activities a felony:

- to produce, use, or traffic in counterfeit access devices;
- to possess fifteen or more counterfeit or unauthorized access devices;
- to produce illicitly, traffic in, have control of or custody of, or to possess access device making equipment (Ramsay 1988).

The Act also gave authority to the US Secret Service to investigate any activity that affects interstate or foreign commerce in regard to such fraudulent access devices. In addition, it encompassed the use of legitimate account numbers on illicit cards.

However, it is generally accepted (Anderson 1988) that: 'Legislation, both in Australia and overseas, generally has failed to keep pace with modern technology and trends in this type of crime. It is a worldwide problem for governments and law enforcement agencies'.

Essentially, credit and debit card fraud has to be regarded as similar to the counterfeiting of bank notes or money. The economic effect of such activity may be significant, and legislative action, where it has not already occurred, can be expected in the future.

5.2.9 What will be the plastic card of the future?

In the near future the magnetically encoded and embossed plastic card may be replaced by far more secure identification products such as the smart card (see section 5.2.10), and the supersmart card (see section 5.2.12). These cards are more sophisticated than the plastic card described above; each card contains a microchip that may store and process information related to both the issuer and owner, in such a way that the information may not be illicitly modified. The cards themselves are inherently much more difficult to reproduce without access to stocks of the embedded microchip. By late 1987 over 17 million of CP/8 type smart cards had been manufactured and delivered to users.

5.2.10 What is a smart card?

The smart card employs microelectronics, data processing and computing, cryptography, and physical mounting techniques to produce a personal token that has both a high level of functionality and security.

The smart card is similar in general form to a conventional plastic card, but it has an embedded microchip and exposed contacts or other connecting mechanisms so that it may be plugged into a terminal. The microchip on early smart cards contained only memory cells, used as secure data stores. Modern smart cards now incorporate both memory and a processor providing facilities to:

- process data, e.g. data used to authenticate the card in a terminal;
- identify the card holder;
- encrypt and decrypt messages;
- generate electronic signatures for transactions originated by the card holder.

Standards are currently being developed, or have been developed (e.g. ISO 7816) specifying the physical size and shape of the card, assignment and location of the microchip contacts, electrical signal parameters, and the various communications protocols covering the transfer of messages to and from the card. Recently a contactless smart card has emerged; data transfer between the card and a terminal is achieved by inductive coupling, thus eliminating the requirement for the exposed metal contacts. Such cards are inherently more reliable in operation as there are no electrical contacts which can become dirty or damaged.

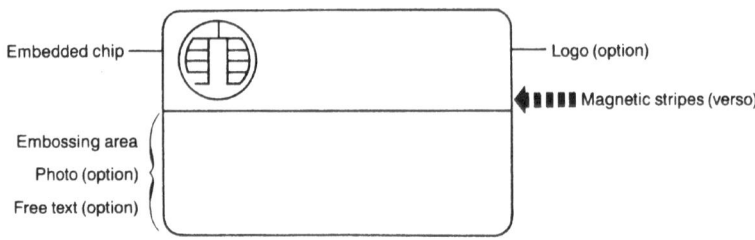

Fig. 5-2 Layout of the Bull smart card

The smart card effectively comprises a complete portable computer on a plastic card, which may contain its own operating system, security mechanism, access control system, cryptographic procedures, and message exchange protocols, together with the electronic sub-systems of a microcomputer.

There is progress on the standardization of smart cards, from a physical dimension viewpoint, but the situation regarding format and type of message exchange is less clear.

One of the first smart cards in common usage, the French CP/8 (accounting for over 80 per cent of cards issued by late 1987) was primarily deployed in the telecommunications, finance, and banking industry. However, other postulated application areas include: portable file for medical, personal and educational data, access control to secure areas, prepaid telephone cards, etc.

The microchips in use have a wide variety of computing power (8-bit and 16-bit word sizes), memory capacities, and technologies. Security features incorporated into smart cards include:

- embedding of a chip manufacturer's code (to protect the cards when being shipped between the factory and the issuer/ customer);
- incorporation of an issuer code into the card after it is personalized;
- a set of independent security parameters that may be used to protect stored data on the card;
- incorporation of cryptographic procedures into the card (e.g. DES, RSA).

The smart card can now be used for EFT transactions services with the additional facilities:

- user PIN checked by the smart card itself;
- coin purse applications (see section 5.2.11).

5.2.11 What is coin purse operation?

Electronic payments with conventional plastic cards usually resemble a cheque process. The users issue an order through a terminal (ATM or EFTPOS) to their banks to debit an account with a stated amount, and to transfer that sum to another account or to initiate a cash dispenser action. The smart card now renders it possible to simulate the direct payment of cash. There is no direct connection between the terminal and the bank; the transaction is between the customer with a smart card and the merchant.

In the coin purse operation the cardholder effectively fills the card with money by authorizing a transfer from the cardholder's bank account. The card is thereafter inserted into a bank authorized terminal to initiate a transaction. The card issues a 'certificate' of payment and the stored sum within the card is correspondingly reduced. This is a convenient system when paying for small transactions such as telephone calls.

5.2.12 What is a supersmart card?

The supersmart card is a more complex version of the smart card. In addition to the microcomputer functions of the smart card, it contains:

- an integrated display, usually a one- or two-line alphanumeric, liquid crystal display (LCD);
- a small keypad.

The supersmart card thus resembles a pocket calculator of the size of a small credit card. It may in fact combine calculator facilities in addition to its use as a bank card. At present the cards may have both 8-bit CPUs and 64K-bit memories on board, and so provide the facilities of a complete personal terminal unit.

The keyboard and display may be used to authorize transactions on a bank account and to perform calculations on account data. Transactions details may be stored and processed on the card. The card may also provide added personal services such as a notebook, address, and telephone directory, clock/calendar, calculator, and reminder service (e.g. notification of payments due).

The card is supplied with a keypad and display because the user may provide authorizations to a third party by connecting the card into the third party's terminal. The cardholder will be provided with a display of the authorized transaction, and will then confirm or deny the authorization by inputting data at the terminal. If the cardholder were to rely on the display and keypad attached to the terminal, there would exist the danger that the third party might have modified the display so that the displayed transaction differed from that authorized. Similarly the terminal keyboard might be untrustworthy, so that a cardholder's denial of authorization might produce the effect of an approval. A integrated keypad/display on the supersmart card obviates such attacks.

The current supersmart cards may be not well suited to everyday use at present since they do not bend, and may be damaged when residing in users' pockets.

5.2.13 Can an individual smart card be used for more than one application?

The on-board computer of the smart card enables it to be used for multiple applications. This implies that the smart card could replace the multitude of cards carried by many bank/credit card customers, thus increasing the range of applications that individual consumers may be prepared to undertake. A multi-function/multi-application smart card could be used for banking and credit card transactions, access to secure areas and networks, storage of personal data, local computation, etc. This means that the smart card of the future may:

- handle applications with widely varying security requirements;
- handle applications from different service providers;
- be capable of upgrade as new applications areas arise;
- be able to remove discontinued applications.

Thus the card must be able to serve the data requirements of each application separately, where this may include security information itself, such as passwords, cryptographic keys, parameters, etc. Current card designs with processors and cryptographic firmware appear to be compatible with securing such multifunctional requirements, and in future the 'company' card may be used more as a wallet/personal token/calculator/*aide-mémoire*.

5.3 Identity and Authentication of the User: PINs

5.3.1 What is a PIN?

PIN is an acronym for personal identification number; a closely associated term is personal identification code (PIC). The PIN is a number, usually 4–8 digits with which customers of automated banking services authenticate themselves when making a transaction. The combined use of a plastic card and an associated PIN strengthens the access control to banking systems (e.g. ATMs) because it combines something the user knows with something the user possesses as joint

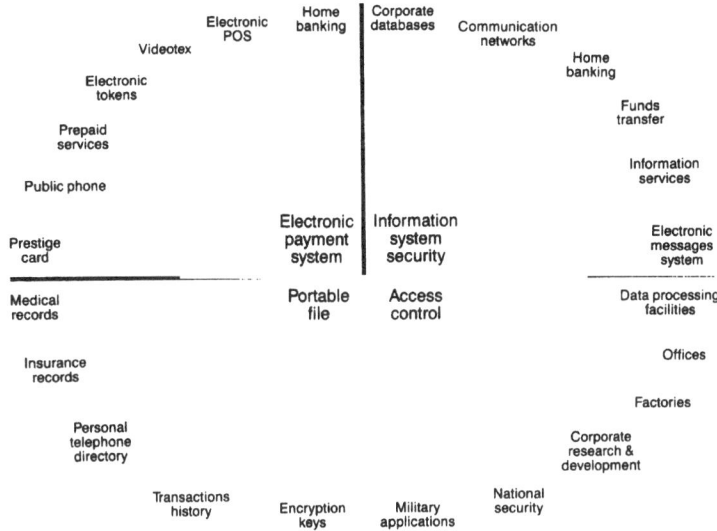

Fig. 5-3 Applications of and opportunities for the smart card

access requirements (see chapter 3). The simple plastic credit or debit card is in itself insecure since the card may be lost or stolen, or information recorded on its magnetic stripe may be read and reproduced onto other, fraudulent, cards (see section 5.2.6). Some banks have moved to the alphanumeric PIC, since customers often find it easier to remember a group of alphabetic characters than a random number; with an easily remembered PIC there is less temptation for the user to write it down. Banks are clearly concerned that many customers record their PINs on pieces of paper carried in purse or wallet, or even on the card itself, since such practices mean that theft of the card also implies theft of the PIN.

5.3.2 How are PINs protected?

The secret PIN forms the basic security method in the normal retail banking EFT service. Thus its security must be guaranteed whenever it is entered by the user into a banking terminal, transmitted on a network, or stored in a banking computer system. The appropriate standards for the management and security of PINs include ANSI X9.8-1982 and SAA 2805.3-1985.

The PIN must be regarded as having a long life-cycle; the average bank user is reluctant to undertake the chore of committing to memory new PIN values. Users will, however, expect to be given the opportunity to change their PIN values if they suspect that the

PIN may have been divulged to some unauthorized person. The appropriate standards are thus designed to protect the PIN for its total life-cycle, from generation through normal usage to eventual deletion.

The security standards for PINs cover the following broad topics that must be carefully considered by any manager creating or maintaining a secure EFT network system. These topics relate to the security of:

- PIN generation and assignment (see section 5.3.3),
- PIN issuance and delivery (see section 5.3.7),
- PIN storage (see section 5.3.8),
- PIN entry techniques (see section 5.3.9),
- PIN verification (see section 5.3.10),
- PIN transmission within a network (see section 5.3.11),
- PIN destruction or deactivation (see section 5.3.12).

The standards also include some further aspects of PIN security in addition to those mentioned above, e.g. associated auditing and verification procedures that must be followed by the issuer of a card. For example, PINs should never be entered into a network via a simple telephone handset; all PIN functions should be handled by specially dedicated and secure equipment associated with a computer system, and not by the general purpose computer system itself. The responsibility for PIN protection lies primarily with the user up to the moment that it is entered into the network; from then on, the network operators must ensure a secure environment.

5.3.3 How are PINs generated?
There are basically three types of PIN generation techniques in common use in the banking industry:

- derived PINs (see section 5.3.4),
- random PINs (see section 5.3.5),
- user-selected PINs (see section 5.3.6).

5.3.4 How are derived PINs developed and used?
In the derived PIN scheme a user's PIN is created as a mathematical or cryptographic function of some data pertinent to that person, e.g. his or her bank primary account number, coupled with, say, his or her date of birth. This data comprises a number which is mathematically manipulated and encrypted to produce the four or six PIN digits. The mathematical manipulation and encryption will be performed as a one-way function, so that it is computationally infeasible to derive the user information from the PIN. If a four-digit PIN

is used, the probability of two users having the same PIN is 1 in 10,000; the odds rise to 1 in a million if a 6 digit PIN is used.

The derived PIN method involves the use of a cryptographic key, known only by the issuer of the card and PIN; the cryptographic key will usually be stored in a secure encryption module attached to a central computer. Knowledge of the key value may be split between two or more bank officials so that no single person can compromise the system security.

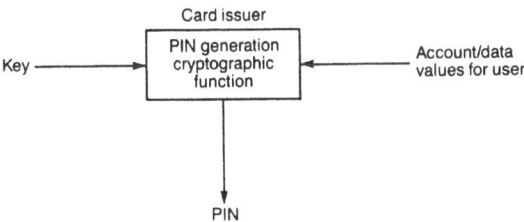

Fig. 5-4   Derived PIN technique

The derived PIN may be related to the information stored on the magnetic stripe of a plastic card. In this case the derived PIN can be computed in an ATM, provided that the ATM is supplied with the cryptographic key. The ATM can compare the computed version of the derived PIN with the value entered by the user via the ATM keypad. Thus the ATM does not need to communicate with the central computer to perform PIN checks, and can continue to dispense cash even when off-line from the central computer.

There are, however, some problems with the derived PIN technique. One such problem occurs if the cryptographic key used (i.e. the PIN derivation key) is illicitly divulged. In this case the attacker could determine the PIN number associated with every user plastic card employing the same cryptographic key. The card issuer would then be compelled to change the cryptographic key and re-issue new PINs to all legitimate users. It is also important that the bank should have the facility to change the cryptographic key for its own security purposes without having to re-issue all the customer PINs. A modification of the derived PIN technique uses a displacement, or offset, value to provide card issuers with more flexibility in relation to cryptographic keys. The displacement value is stored on the magnetic stripe of the plastic card together with the card data. If a cryptographic key change occurs, then a new displacement value is written back onto the associated card by the banking terminal. This displacement value may simply represent the difference between the current value of the derived PIN (i.e. that value computed by the

ATM) and the fixed PIN value entered by the user. Although the displacement value can be read from the plastic card, it will not assist the attacker to compute the PIN.

5.3.5 How is the random PIN developed and used?

A random PIN is generated via some random or pseudorandom number generation technique, and the resulting value is securely stored with the corresponding user account details in the bank's central computer, and in that computer only. The PIN should be encrypted on the account record to prevent compromise of the PIN. When users enter their PIN values on a remote banking terminal, the keyed PIN is compared with the PIN value for that user account stored on the main computer system. Unlike the derived PIN scheme, this requires that a bank terminal, such as an ATM, must be on-line to the central computer system holding the user's account and PIN details. This procedure, moreover, requires secure transmission to the central computer of the PIN input by the user at the ATM, secure storage of the reference PIN on the central computer, and secure comparison of the two values. Banks normally employ a special security control module (SCM), attached to the central computer system, for PIN verification functions.

Secure administrative procedures must also be employed when customers are informed of their PIN values, so that no bank official or external person (e.g. postman) can associate a PIN value with a customer account number.

With the random PIN technique there is no computable relationship between the stored data on the plastic card and the corresponding PIN number.

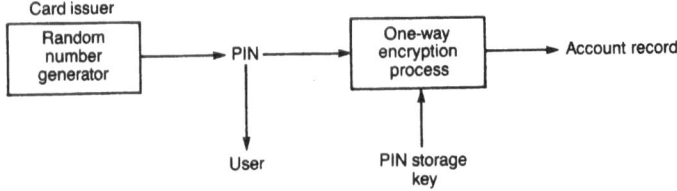

Fig. 5-5 Generation of a random PIN

5.3.6 How are user-selected PINs developed and used?

User-selected PINs are, as the name implies, chosen by the user, and are usually conveyed to the bank where they are stored with the corresponding account numbers. Thereafter use of the PIN is virtually identical with that described for the random PIN (see section 5.3.5).

242

The most significant difference between the administration of user-selected and random PINs lies in the issuing procedures. The account user chooses a PIN value, of say 4–8 digits, and this PIN is associated with the appropriate account or accounts. The PIN is never divulged to anyone, not even to bank officials. It is encrypted the moment the user enters it into a secure terminal on the bank's premises, and it is thereafter stored by the bank in encrypted form. The PIN is not merely encrypted for storage, it is irreversibly encrypted; the bank itself thus cannot determine the plaintext version of the PIN even though it has access to the cryptographic key used. The verification of the PIN, keyed in by a user at (say) an ATM, is performed by subjecting the entered PIN to the same irreversible encryption procedure and comparing the result with the stored value.

This scheme can be used for a number of different styles of EFT operation. For example, the encrypted PIN can be stored with the details of the associated account or accounts in the issuer's system, as for the random PIN case above.

It is, however, possible to arrange for off-line verification of user-selected PINs using a similar technique to that of derived PINs; some function of user data is irreversibly encrypted and the difference, or offset, between that encrypted value and the PIN, is stored on the card. Such offset values enable ATMs to verify PINs locally, given that the ATM is provided with the cryptographic key used in the irreversible encryption process.

The main objection voiced in regard to this scheme is that users may choose easily remembered PIN values closely related to their personal data, e.g. the PIN may be formed from a date of birth, telephone number, car registration number, birthday of some loved one, etc. A user-selected PIC may overcome this problem since the user can select a more easily remembered, but essentially random, set of letters and numbers.

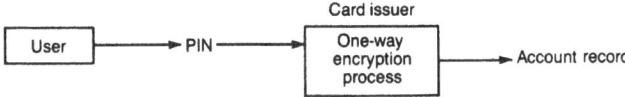

Fig. 5-6 Chosen or user-selected PIN

5.3.7 What principles govern the issuance and delivery of PINs?
The principles governing secure issuance and delivery of PINs are:

- The PIN shall never be printed on any form or list such that it is associated with its corresponding account details.
- The PIN shall only be printed on a secure PIN mailer (or its equivalent) for delivery to the customer.
- The PIN mailer and its associated plastic card or cards are to be mailed to the customer in separate envelopes.

5.3.8 How are PINs protected during storage?

Whenever a PIN is stored, whether in a computer system or on a plastic card, it must be encrypted. The international standards allow this encryption to be either reversible or irreversible. In the case of reversible encryption the PIN can be recovered by a decryption process; with irreversible encryption it is not possible to recover the original plaintext version; comparison of stored and entered PINs is performed by irreversibly encrypting the entered PIN and comparing the two ciphertext versions.

If reversible encryption of the PIN is used, then both the associated PIN cryptographic key value and the decryption process itself must be secure and rigorously controlled. Reversible encryption has the benefit that it enables all PIN values to be re-encrypted under a new PIN encryption key, should the key in current use be compromised.

Irreversibly encrypted PINs cannot be decrypted to plaintext and re-encrypted under a new key. However, it is possible to reversibly encrypt the set of irreversibly encrypted PIN values. This procedure provides a safeguard against situations in which an attacker may be able to match plaintext and ciphertext versions of keys. If such an attack is a matter of concern then the doubly encrypted keys can be partially decrypted and reversibly re-encrypted under a new key.

In particular, if the PIN is stored on the magnetic stripe of a card then it must clearly be protected from compromise if the card is lost or stolen. The PIN must be encrypted with a key that can only be obtained at the point of verification of the PIN.

5.3.9 What security techniques are applied for PIN entry?

The card acceptor is responsible for the security of the PIN in all activities outside the banking system; the operators of the banking network are responsible for PIN security after the PIN has been entered into it. At the point of PIN entry (e.g. at an ATM keypad) both parties share a degree of responsibility for security. This means that the PIN must be entered by the customer in a secure environment; the user must take care to ensure that no one is observing the PIN entry, i.e. that there is no shoulder surfing. The environment and PIN entry equipment must minimize the possibility of the PIN being observed or recorded by other equipment attached to the PIN entry terminal.

The PIN, having been entered, must now be securely processed at the terminal and/or transmitted to the appropriate card acquirer or issuer. This normally means that a secure unit, known as the PIN pad, designed for the safe entry of PINs is a part of the EFT terminal. The layout of the keys on the PIN pad keyboard has become the subject of standardization activity. The requirements for the physical security of the pad are stringent: the PIN pad may be separate from, but connected by cable to, the EFT terminal, or it may be an integral part of the terminal. Strict tamper-resistance standards apply to the PIN pad and its connection to the terminal, in the first case, or to the whole terminal itself, in the second.

5.3.10 How are PINs securely verified?

PIN verification may be performed by direct comparison between an entered and corresponding stored value, or it may involve some degree of computation (see section 5.3.4). The verification may be undertaken by the issuer of the card and PIN or by an agent of the issuer.

If the checking of PINs were performed on a general purpose computer security problems would arise; the cryptographic keys would be available to local software, and there exists the danger that the verification software itself might be vulnerable to attack. It is, therefore, essential that the process of verification be protected; it is usually performed within a security control module (SCM) attached to the issuer's, or acquirer's, computer system, or to the EFT transaction switching system.

5.3.11 What security procedures are adopted for PIN transmission?

The PIN must be cryptographically protected during any transmission, because it is not normally possible to guarantee the physical security transmission medium in an EFT network. Such networks normally involve the telecommunications networks of a country, and are thus deemed to be vulnerable to eavesdropping and other illicit activity.

The current banking standards specify that the PIN be encrypted for transmission using the DEA in its electronic codebook (ECB) mode. With this technique the PIN consists of 4–12 digits, and it is entered by the customer with the most significant digit first, i.e. the leftmost digit. The PIN is then used to create a primary PIN block of 64 binary bits for use in the encryption process (see figure 5-7).

The PIN block is combined with an account number block based on the customer's account number, entered manually into the terminal, or read from the magnetic stripe on the associated plastic card. The account number block is then formed into a 64-bit block

bit 1	5	9	1 3	1 7	2 1	2 5	2 9
C	N	P	P	P	P	P/F	P/F

bit 3 3	3 7	4 1	4 5	4 9	5 3	5 7	6 1
P/F	P/F	P/F	P/F	P/F	P/F	F	F

Bits are numbered 1 to 64 from left to right.

C = Control Field
   Usually four zero bits 0000.

N = PIN Length Entered Field
   Four bits in range 0100 (4) to 1100 (12).

P = PIN Digit
   Four bits in the range 0000 (0) to 1001 (9).

F = Fill Digit
   Four bits with the value 1111 (15).

PF = PIN Digit or Fill Digit depending on length of PIN

Fig. 5-7 Primary PIN block construction

(see figure 5-8), which uses the 12 rightmost numbers of the primary account number (PAN) associated with the card and PIN, excluding the account number check digit. If the PAN is less than 12 digits in length, excluding the check digit, then the digits are right-justified and padded to the left with zeros.

bit 1	5	9	1 3	1 7	2 1	2 5	2 9
0000	0000	0000	0000	A1	A2	A3	A4

bit 3 3	3 7	4 1	4 5	4 9	5 3	5 7	6 1
A5	A6	A7	A8	A9	A10	A11	A12

A = Account number digit.

Fig. 5-8 Account number block construction

The two blocks are combined to form the final Formatted Clear Text PIN Block, which is then encrypted for secure transmission, to the appropriate card issuer or acquirer. The blocks are combined by a simple modulo 2 addition (also known as 'exclusive or') on a bit-by-bit basis; the final 64-bit block is then encrypted using the designated PIN encrypting cryptographic key (see figure 5-9). The receiver of the reversibly encrypted PIN enters the block into a secure decrypting unit to recover the original PIN block, again using the DEA algorithm in electronic codebook mode and the same PIN cryptographic key used for the encryption process.

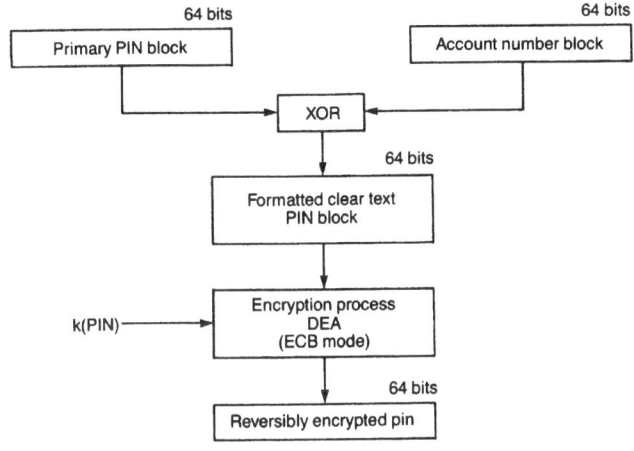

Fig. 5-9 Creation of a reversibly encrypted PIN

5.3.12 When are PINs destroyed or deactivated?

A PIN needs to be destroyed in the case of its exposure, and deactivated when an account is closed. After exposure and PIN destruction a new PIN must be produced for the customer. With account closure both the PIN and the account are deactivated.

With random PINs (see section 5.3.5), the old stored, encrypted value of the PIN, held against customer account information in the bank computer, is overwritten with the encrypted value of the new PIN. For derived PINs, and user-selected PINs, the displacement, or offset, values are changed (see sections 5.3.4 and 5.3.6).

5.4 Privacy, Integrity, and Authenticity of Financial Messages

5.4.1 How are financial messages protected?

Users of financial networks must be protected from both deliberate and accidental alteration, deletion, or duplication of genuine messages, and the injection of fake messages. In some extreme cases even the existence of the message may need to be hidden. The scheme used to guarantee message integrity must be straightforward and readily implementable in both a single banking network and also between networks. The requirement for international standards has been met by, for example, American Standard ANSI X9.9,

Australian Standard SAA 2805.4, etc. The technique to protect such messages is message authentication (see chapter 1); this method involves the addition of a message authentication code (MAC) (see section 5.4.2) to the message. According to these standards the MAC must:

- be used for the validation of the authority of the sender (customer or correspondent);
- be used for the verification that selected contents of the message have not been altered in transit;
- be used by both large and small organizations;
- be implemented in automated systems (SAA 2805.4).

Such standardization will facilitate the migration of these authentication techniques into the non-banking sector, a trend that is likely to grow in the near future. On the other hand such widespread availability of the standards has the implication that potential attackers will be well versed in the security procedures. The protection afforded by such techniques is therefore heavily dependent upon the security and integrity of cryptographic keys used in the computation of the MAC.

The message security system involves the generation by the sender of the MAC, its transmission with its associated financial message, and the verification of the message by the receiver. The generation process is often referred to as 'MACGEN' (i.e. MAC GENeration); similarly verification is 'MACVER'. On receipt of the message the receiver must perform the same algorithm, as the sender, on the message text and thus recompute the MAC. This receiver's version of the MAC is then compared with that transmitted with the message; the receiver will accept the message if the comparison checks out. The sender and receiver alone share the cryptographic key used in the computation of the MAC.

The MAC may be a function of the whole message, or of selected parts of it, as agreed by the sender and the receiver, and in accordance with the appropriate standards. The security of the message authentication is ensured even though an attacker may have the facility to modify the text of a message, since he would be unable to compute the new MAC corresponding to the modified message. Similarly no attacker could compute the MAC for a message that he had produced, but purported to originate from some other source. However, this technique does not, in itself, eliminate the problem of illicit duplication of the financial message. A duplicate copy of a message, together with its MAC, would pass the authentication test and could therefore result in (say) two transfers from a bank account. Date/time stamps, or message sequence numbers, need to be included within the text of authenticated messages to obviate such replay attacks.

The use of message authentication techniques must only be considered to be part of an overall message security scheme. The validity of such schemes must be separately assessed by the participating organizations; such considerations also apply to the evaluation of the necessary auditing and control procedures.

5.4.2 What is involved in the computation of the MAC?

The MAC generation technique involves the use of the data encryption algorithm (DEA) in its cipher block chaining (CBC) mode (see chapter 1). This cryptographic mode of operation produces a ciphertext block that is dependent upon the whole of the message, and upon the sequence of the constituent parts of the message. Thus any attempt to change an individual part of the message, or the sequence of blocks within the message, has an impact upon the subsequent MAC.

The development of the MAC is illustrated in figure 5-10. The initial contents of the shift register (the initialization vector or IV) are set to zero. The message to be authenticated is then split into blocks of 64 bits and fed sequentially into the authenticator. If the last block does comprise 64 bits, then the message bits are left-justified in a 64-bit block and the remaining bits of the block to the right are set to zero.

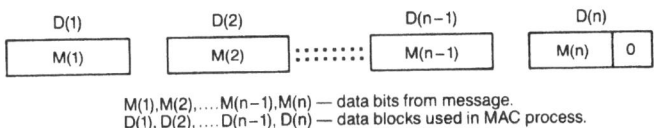

M(1),M(2),....M(n−1),M(n) — data bits from message.
D(1), D(2),....D(n−1), D(n) — data blocks used in MAC process.

Fig. 5-10 Formation of data blocks from the financial message

The blocks D(1) to D(n) all participate in the cryptographic processing using the secret MAC key K(MAC). Each block of data D(m), is first combined with the initialization vector by modulo 2 addition. The resulting sum is fed into the encryptor and the ciphertext output is fed back to the shift register. The 32-bit MAC is derived from the last ciphertext block, all intervening ciphertext blocks are merely used to update the shift register. The procedure can now be summarized as set out in the Australian Standard SAA 2805.4.

This whole process produces a 64-bit final block termed the message authentication block (MAB). The high-order (i.e. leftmost)

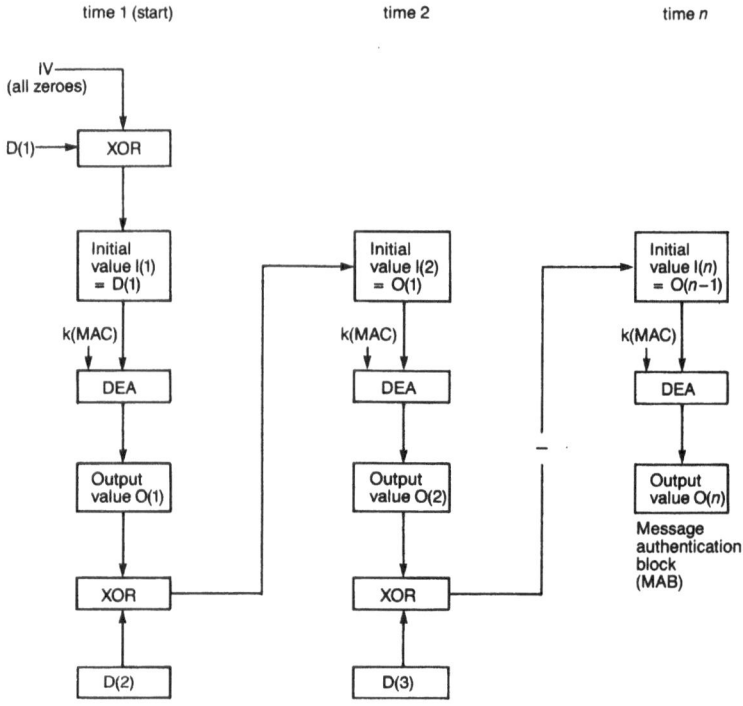

XOR = Exclusive or Operation
K(MAC) = MAC Generation and Checking Key Value (Secret)
IV = Initialization Vector for MAC Process
= 64 Zero Bits

Fig. 5-11 MAC generation process

32 bits of the MAB are selected as the MAC. The MAC is now placed in the message at the choice of locations specified in the standard in the last field of the message, or as a field appended to the message where another MAC field is not defined.

If the field used to contain the MAC is larger in size than 32 bits then the MAC occupies the most significant (leftmost) bits of the field. The MAC of one message may be incorporated in the calculation of the MAC for a subsequent message, so that the messages are effectively chained together for authentication purposes. As the message exchange takes place between the sender and the receiver, the MAC in a message is included in any following calculations of

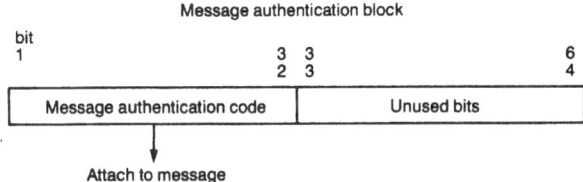

Fig. 5-12   Derivation of the MAC

MACs so that the messages are chained together from an authentication viewpoint.

5.5 Financial Network Security.

5.5.1 Introduction
Financial networks provide for a wide range of network users. At one extreme, individual bank customers will interact with ATMs; in the middleground the EFTPOS network allows retailers to conduct financial transactions relating to the provision of goods and services; while at the other end of the spectrum finance professionals will authorize the transfer of vast sums via terminals in a bank office. Such networks may also be integrated with standard data transmission systems.

It is clear that the security environment of the network terminal can range from a petrol pump EFTPOS terminal in a country garage, completely open to the general public 24 hours a day, through the EFTPOS terminal located in a large departmental store, to a financial trader's dedicated terminal located in a relatively secure office. The terminal users will range from the general public and shop assistants through to highly trained bank officials.

The financial or EFT network may need to be protected to:

- meet national and international standards for EFTS;
- meet inter-bank legal and/or contractual requirements;
- meet national laws related to privacy and EFT services;
- enable the connection and operation of terminal devices, e.g. ATMs, EFTPOS terminals.

In his book *The Wired Society*, James Martin summarized the need for banking network security and the methods of achieving it:

The EFT networks themselves offer new opportunities for ingenious computer crime, and tight security controls need to be built into the systems. The only way to make transmissions safe from wire-

251

tapping is to use cryptography, just as intelligence agencies send coded messages that cannot be deciphered. The technology does exist for making EFT networks sufficiently secure, although on some systems it may not be used adequately....A cause of concern with electronic funds transfer, as in other advanced uses of teleprocessing, is that individual privacy may be eroded. An individual's financial history might be laid bare to government authorities...

The security of financial networks cannot be guaranteed by physical security alone, and cryptography is employed to protect the privacy and integrity of network traffic (see section 5.4.1), on an end-to-end basis. The use of cryptography implies the storage of cryptographic keys at the sender's and receiver's end points, at intermediate nodes within the network, and the transmission of keys through the network. The physical and data security systems in the network must guarantee that such keys are protected from attackers at any point in the network. This implies that the keys must be protected when they are stored within terminals which can be subjected to physical attack, when they are transmitted through the network, stored in host computers or nodes, and when used in cryptographic processing at terminals, switching nodes and host computers. This protection of keys is undertaken by appropriate, and often complex, key management schemes (see chapter 1).

5.5.2 What protection is applied at the terminal end?

The cryptographic processes typically performed in an EFT or EFTPOS terminal include:

- message authentication, and MAC generation and verification (see section 5.4.2);
- PIN protection;
- message privacy.

It would be unsafe to use just one cryptographic key for all three processes since an attacker could well manipulate the cryptographic functions provided to reveal the keys. Thus there are as many as three distinct keys employed for message authentication, PIN protection, and message confidentiality. In addition to these keys it will be necessary to employ key encrypting keys to transmit updated values of the individual cryptographic keys through the network.

Cryptographic key values are normally maintained in the PIN pad that forms part of the EFT terminal. The PIN pad may be fully integrated into the terminal, e.g. in an EFTPOS petrol pump or ATM. In many cases, however, the PIN pad is connected via a cable to the terminal. The small, pocket calculator-style PIN pad may also

hold the magnetic stripe reader for the input of plastic credit/debit
car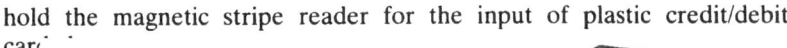

Fig. 5-13 Racal Transcom's EFT terminal

The PIN pad must be designed to be tamper-resistant, since it
houses cryptographic keys; any attempt to force entry to the pad
must result in the erasure of all cryptographic key values. The
cryptographic keys are downloaded to the terminal/PIN pad from the
controlling EFT host system, usually the acquirer, after terminal initialization. The cryptographic keys used to protect the EFT data
(i.e. the data encrypting keys) are themselves encrypted by key encrypting keys (KEKs) during the aforementioned transmission to the
terminal. Such key encrypting keys are called terminal keys, or base
keys, and are initially installed in the terminal by a manual operation
performed according to strict security rules.

5.5.3 What protection is applied at intermediate network nodes?
The network terminals are normally connected to acquirer nodes
operated by the card issuer or the network switching organization.
The network node is usually responsible for checking the authenticity of messages, redirecting them to the host computer, and in
some cases it may give direct approval for some low-value money

transactions.

The processing performed at the network node will necessarily involve some cryptographic operations, and hence access to cryptographic keys. Checking message authentication calls for computation of the MAC (see section 5.4.2) and access to the MAC key. In some cases parts of the message will be decrypted under a terminal-node key, and re-encrypted under a node-host computer key, prior to onward transmission.

These operations cannot be performed securely in the node computer, and are normally undertaken in a secure control module (SCM) linked to, and under the control of, the node computer software. The SCM will comprise a small computer housed in a tamper-resistant unit that securely stores cryptographic keys and performs the aforementioned cryptographic processing.

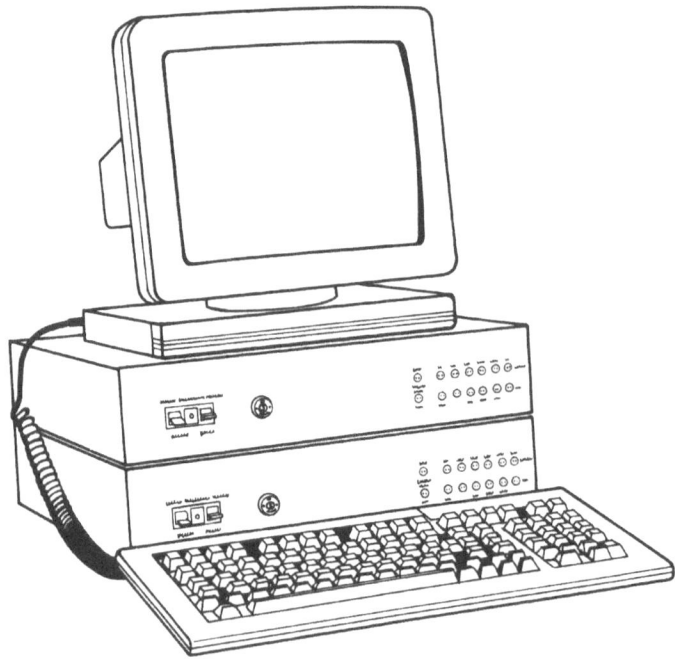

Fig. 5-14 ERACOM's Security control module

5.5.4 What protection is applied at the host computer?

The host computer system, operated by the card issuer, is normally responsible for the ultimate receipt of transaction messages, checking their authenticity, ensuring that the PIN is valid for the customer account, checking that the customer balance is adequate for the transaction, arranging for transfer of funds between accounts, formation of the consequent approval/rejection message, and transmission of that message to the network node. As with the network node (see section 5.5.3), most of the actions will involve some cryptographic processing and access to cryptographic keys. Some host nodes (issuers), and even network switch nodes (acquirers), perform the cryptographic functions with software routines, operating on the computer system under control of the main operating system. Low-cost implementation of the DES algorithm in software is used in these cases. The main concern, however, is that cryptographic keys may be exposed in the main computer system; such implementations do not meet the original US standard, FIPS Publication 46. This is increasingly an unacceptable risk for most EFT networks, particularly if standard operating systems, such as Unix, come into use in financial networks. In the majority of cases an SCM (see section 5.5.3) is used for the secure operation of cryptographic processes and the storage of cryptographic keys. Depending upon performance requirements, the SCM may be connected to the host computer via low speed telecommunications lines or via higher performance connections such as direct channel attachment (e.g. via the block multiplexor channel of an IBM mainframe system) or local area network connection, e.g. an Ethernet link.

5.5.5 Does the protection system have an impact on the performance of the network?

The cryptographic processing will have an impact upon network performance at terminal, the acquirer nodes, and the card issuer host computer (see sections 5.5.2–4). Delays introduced at switching nodes are likely to be the most important factor, since such nodes will have a higher transaction throughput than either the individual terminals or the bank host computers.

DES operations can be performed at a rate of 14 million bits per second, i.e. a 64-bit block can be encrypted or decrypted in 4.5 microseconds, using special purpose microchips. This is a negligible period for most transaction systems, and indeed is insignificant in relation to transmission delay between computer and SCM. The situation is somewhat different with software implementations of DES, where the processing time may affect overall performance. In this case the software decryptions and encryptions undertaken at network nodes may cause intolerable delays on the message switching functions.

PIN encryption and the formation of MAC codes are normally performed in terminals, using ROM-implemented DES algorithms under the operation of the terminal microprocessor. The manual in-put of transaction data, PINs etc. will be the limiting factor in the throughput, and thus delays introduced by such cryptographic processing will be negligible.

The performance of the overall network must be assessed when security options are being examined. Lower-cost solutions may be available at the individual terminal level, but full hardware crypto-graphic devices and high-speed interfaces will probably be required at network node and host levels.

5.5.6 How are network units authenticated?

A serious form of attack can arise if an attacker can masquerade as a terminal to a node, as a node to a host computer, as a host computer to a node, or as a node to a terminal. Most of the authentication is based upon secret knowledge stored in the terminals, nodes, and host computers, e.g. the cryptographic keys used for development of MACs (see section 5.4.2). It is important that each network component checks the authenticity of messages and that the cryptographic keys used are transmitted or developed in a secure manner (see section 5.5.7). It is also essential that secure manual procedures be employed at the initialization of terminals (e.g. loading of cryptographic keys, etc.); all subsequent checks will be based upon the assumption of such initialization.

5.5.7 Are there any standards for EFT network key management?

Standards for the management of cryptographic keys in EFT net-works are emerging on a national and international (ISO) basis. These standards are being developed around three major models for key management and storage:

- master-session keys, whereby keys themselves are encrypted by higher-order key-encrypting keys for transmission through the network. Such keys are changed frequently but on a random basis.
- transaction keys, which are derived from the data of the transac-tion messages, and some secret stored data, by a secure process. Such keys may be individually computed at the terminal, net-work nodes and host computer and therefore are not transmitted through the network.
- public keys, whereby keys for the single-key DES procedure for data protection are transmitted around the network under the control and security of public key cryptography schemes, e.g. RSA (see chapter 1).

By the early 1990s it may be expected that international standards

(ISO) will be in place to ensure secure transport of cryptographic key material between financial enterprises, on an international basis.

References
Electronic Funds and Securities Transfer Policy: Message Authentication and Enhanced Security, order no. 106-09 (US Department of Treasury, October 1986)
Electronic Funds Transfer: Requirements for Interfaces (Standards Association of Australia, Standards House, 80 Arthur St., North Sydney, NSW, Australia)
Financial Institutions, Encryption of Wholesale Financial Messages, ANSI X9.23 (1987)
Financial Services, Retail Key Management: Draft American Standard, ANSI X9.24 (April 1988)
Key Management (Wholesale): American National Standard, ANSI X9.17 (1985)
Meyer C. H. and S. M. Matyas, *Cryptography: A New Dimension in Computer Data Security* (New York: John Wiley and Sons, 1982).

6 Office Automation Security

W. Caelli

6.1 Overview

6.1.1 Office automation
The concept of office automation has grown markedly over the last ten years; it now encompasses far more than photocopiers, word processing, and local accounting functions. A modern automated office may comprise a wide range of user workstations, linked via a local area network (LAN) to file servers and gateways to main computer systems. The range of software systems on the workstations have expanded to include desktop publishing, electronic mail, secretarial services such as schedule and diary planners, project planning, costing systems, financial planning, etc. In many cases the data is downloaded from corporate databases held on mainframe computers.

The office automation network may be only one of a number of LANs in use within an enterprise. Increasingly manufacturing areas, warehousing, and storage groups, marketing and sales offices, etc. each maintain their own workstations and local area networks with separate or combined links to a corporate data centre. The networks may also be interlinked with shared servers and connected to external sources of information via gateways. This is exemplified by the place of an office automation system in an integrated manufacturing organization. Individual departmental responsibilities may result in different functions being performed by different groups but information flows may be fully integrated.

The office automation systems are now the subject of standards developments and they are gradually being integrated into open systems environments.

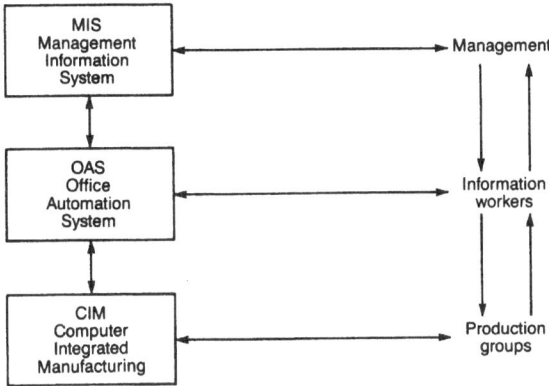

Fig. 6-1 Functional separation in integrated systems

6.1.2 Security

Office automation has created an entirely new security environment which is distinct both from that of the old manual office and that of the modern computer centre.

Much of the security in manual offices derived from the continual supervision of co-workers and established patterns of privileges. A large report could be taken from a desk and copied on a photo-copier, but anyone using the office photocopier for an extended period would be observed. Files might be removed from filing cabinets, but an office hierarchy would establish that certain staff owned drawers in specific cabinets, and their use by others was likely to draw comment. These intrinsic safeguards tend to disappear with the advent of office automation. Workstations tend to become private facilities for individual workers, and the nature of their actions is not apparent to a casual observer. A few keystrokes can send a confidential marketing plan to a competitor.

The information security problem is recognized in well-managed computer centres, but the nature of safeguards established for that environment are not necessarily appropriate to the electronic office. There are significant differences between the security environment of the computer centre and the automated office. For example, the computer centre will simultaneously handle a mass of disparate transactions, whereas office automation systems will tend to process a single file, or document (e.g. cash flow projection) through to completion. Staff in the office may have global access rights to all in-formation in the office, and the use of all the processing/

259

communication equipment, photocopiers, word processors, telephones, facsimile, etc. The information handled will range from routine to highly confidential. In the office environment, there is simply none of the isolation of information that may be inherent in the suites of application program packages operating on the organization's data processing systems. Moreover, an office environment is characterized by a high rate of change in the type of work and in the way it is performed; whereas the applications systems in computer centres may have a lifetime of many years. Managers in offices spend most of their time coping with the exception to the rules.

Information security policies and plans must exist, however, regardless of whether information is stored and processed on a corporate mainframe system or on small office-based systems. In fact the information in the small systems may be of more value to an adversary than the raw, unprocessed data on a corporate database, where numerous detailed records may hide overall company plans and activities. At the office system level the data is contained in descriptive memoranda, letters, reports, charts, diagrams, spreadsheets, etc., making the overall information package far more interesting, and valuable, to a competitor (see chapter 3).

While the information security problem is no less severe in the office than in the computer centre, and the consequences of poor security may be even greater, it can be much more difficult to change working routines. The problem may be one of user perception of the risks and responsibilities associated with the office system. Users may consider that mainframe countermeasures are inappropriate in an office, even though their workstations may be directly connected to the computer centre. As a first step an office manager needs to determine the level of security services and systems available on the small computers and local networks employed in the office automation system, together with their shortcomings. For example, a minicomputer-based LAN server may have good password systems but no on-line monitoring facilities.

Security of the office system may be considered to be a departmental rather than organizational concern. Certainly the security measures must be fully supported by office managers, but they need to reflect the organization's security stance, and the sensitivity and vulnerability of the information processed in the office. The starting point for this concern may well be an internal or external audit, and classification of data. The manager must then take into account the possibility that procedures and safeguards which have prevented security incidents for the last decade may have been completely negated by the implementation of office automation systems installed in the previous few months.

6.2 Communications and Logical Security

6.2.1 Introduction
Office automation systems will provide an entry point to aa host of external communications systems. At present the security standards of such systems are still under active discussion. It is, however, important for office managers to be aware of the security implications of such systems and their potential impact upon office security. These communications systems are also likely to interconnect directly with local processing systems. Hence office managers must consider the potential security loopholes at interfaces, and the means available for ensuring end-to-end security. The communications systems that play a part in the office are:

- personal computer to mainframe links (see section 6.2.2),
- telex and facsimile (see section 6.2.3),
- electronic mail (see section 6.2.4),
- voice mail (see section 6.2.5),
- electronic data interchange (see section 6.2.7).

The security considerations at interfaces and for end-to-end security include:

- document authentication (see section 6.2.7),
- control of printer output (see section 6.2.8),
- audit trails (see section 6.2.9).

6.2.2 What are the security problems associated with links between office personal computers and mainframes?
The problems can be divided into those of security of the personal computer software and those directly associated with the communication link and mainframe system. If the software in the personal computer is readily available to unauthorized users, then there exists the danger that it may be illegally modified. Trojan Horses embedded in the software may capture sensitive data, and either store it for future access by the attacker or pass it directly over the communication link to the attacker's workstation.

The security problems associated with the link itself depend upon the manner in which it is implemented. It may be:

- a direct-dial link using the normal telecommunications network, through the office PABX or a separate line with an appropriate modem;
- a link via a LAN and gateway to the mainframe, usually via a dedicated line between the gateway and the mainframe shared by many workstations, and even many LANs in different areas;

- a private dedicated telephone line, usually operating at high speed, enabling the office workstation to appear as a mainframe terminal, e.g. an IBM 3278/3276 or equivalent device;
- an ISDN 64 kilobit per second link through the office's ISDN-compatible PABX unit.

Each of these links presents a set of unique security problems, together with a number of technical and managerial security solutions. For example, in the simplest case of a direct-dial phone line to the mainframe, call-back modems may be used. Such modems may also incorporate encryption facilities, and require the user to enter a password before connection to the mainframe is granted. There is also a trend to access control systems that demand individual identification of both the user and the terminal to the mainframe system.

6.2.3 What are the security implications of telex and facsimile systems?
In recent years there has been a switch from the use of telex to facsimile for text communication between organizations. Increasingly these services are integrated into office workstations; together with electronic mail, they tend to remove the centralized control hitherto exercised on such text communication services.

This trend will continue with moves towards electronic data interchange (EDI) and the overall integration provided by ISDN. A particular area of concern is the legal status of documents (e.g. sales orders) received over these various services.

Telex is a common form of communication for sensitive information in the organization. It is a format accepted worldwide, and in various countries telex messages have a legal status. Increasingly, however, the telex network is being interlinked with data communications and even voice-grade networks worldwide. Telex messages may be created on a personal computer workstation and then sent via the telex network to a telex machine in a foreign country. Similarly, a telex interface on an office workstation may receive these messages while still being used for office work, the telex function operating in the background. Telex messages may need to be managed by an appropriate officer of the enterprise; this officer should be involved in the setting up of the procedures for the receipt of incoming messages, the filing of paper copies, and for the distribution of those messages. In addition the manager will be concerned with systems for the integration of Telex traffic with data networks. Telex messages should be subject to internal authorization; it has also long been a practice in the banking and finance industry for important telex messages (e.g. those involved in actual money transfers) to be authenticated by the addition of an authentication code to the message. In the past, this code was produced with the aid of a code book, but today a small, pocket calculator-type encryption/authentication device may be used to create and display such authentication codes. These authentication devices may be held by the telex or security manager, or incorporated into the workstation. Telex lines may also be encrypted for added protection of the telex message traffic.

Facsimile has spread rapidly throughout offices. Travelling executives now equip themselves with portable facsimile terminals. The cost of these devices has fallen and their specifications are subject to international standardization, e.g. CCITT Group 2/3/4.

For the last couple of years the security implications of fax has been given increasing attention. New generation fax machines can provide the following facilities:

- storage of incoming messages: an access authorization code must be entered before the message is printed out, (i.e. personal mailbox facility);
- message-logging with details of number of pages sent, addresses and time of transmission;
- time/date stamp plus address of sending and receiving machines incorporated in messages.

Users may employ a message cover sheet in a standardized format that incorporates the enterprise logo, a non-trivial message sequence number, etc. when messages/documents are to be sent. The recipient can then check the source of the document with a simple telephone call. Such precautions are necessary to obviate the danger of fraudulent documents transmitted by facsimile, e.g. fake invoices for non-existent services.

Fax cards are now available as expansion boards for personal computers, thus a word processor or desktop publishing workstation may now be used to create and transmit fax documents.

There is a distinct difference between fax and telex transmissions from a security viewpoint: telex transmissions require a designated telecommunications address, whereas fax transmission can originate and arrive at, any telephone receiver point.

The coding scheme for facsimile transmission is a published standard. It is therefore possible to wiretap fax messages, illicitly receiving confidential information, or even injecting false transmissions. Such attacks may be countered with encryption devices added to fax units, and there is a US standard for such devices (FIPS Publication Number 1028). Such encryption does not overcome the problem of illegal access to printed fax messages, and it may be necessary to keep office fax machines in a secure area. Fax documents are normally printed on receipt, cut into pages, and ejected into a paper tray. From here other office staff may easily read confidential documents and take photocopies, returning the fax original to the paper tray. A locked box, with a receiving slot, for received facsimile messages is a simple but effective precaution against this type of attack.

6.2.4 What concerns exist with the security of electronic mail services?
Electronic mail (E-mail) services employ special-purpose software packages in workstations and host computer systems, together with similar packages, usually from the telephone switching computers of the PTT, to provide for the exchange of messages between users of disparate systems. Normally a user registers with an appropriate service offered by a common carrier, and then sends and receives text messages in standardized formats. The user is usually given a mailbox that is used to receive messages, and which is protected with a user password. The mailboxes essentially comprise data files stored within the computer-based store and forward communications switching system supplied by the common carrier.

Unfortunately a number of different E-mail systems exist worldwide, with widely varying security features. In the near future, however, all these systems will probably interconnect with systems conforming to ISO X.400 electronic data interchange or EDI standards and the associated X.500 directory services standards (i.e. the 'telephone directory' of EDI). This set of international standards details the techniques and formats to be used for the interconnection of message systems worldwide. Other E-mail services include those based on videotex systems such as Prestel. In addition, companies and other enterprises may set up their own proprietary E-mail services that in turn interface with those provided by the common carrier for a particular country.

From a management viewpoint it would be wise to create a checklist of security concerns to discuss with the providers of a network service. This checklist may involve addressing the questions:

- Are there any coding restrictions that could have an impact upon the use of cryptography to protect messages? Some E-mail systems only accept the printable ASCII characters; an encryption system, such as the DES, when used in cipher feedback mode (see chapter 1), as recommended for this class of data, produces all values of a 7- or 8-bit field.
- What access control facilities exist for mailboxes? E.g. type, issue, and changing of passwords, user-definable techniques (e.g. use of hand-held token in addition to passwords) (see chapter 2).

- Integrity and control subsystems within the E-mail service, including maintenance of message integrity from accidental or deliberate alteration, deletion of messages from the mail box, notification to the receiver and sender of access to the messages (i.e. end-to-end delivery assurance).
- Audit trail maintenance for the mail boxes and the system.

Office managers also need to give careful attention to the use of E-mail services in terms of designated authorized users, cost, and type of material sent over the system. They should ensure that they are as knowledgeable on the use of the system as their junior staff. They should also guard against the illicit importation, or development, of software that could automatically transmit workstation files over the network.

6.2.5 What are the security risks of voice mail systems?

Voice mail, or voice messaging, systems operate in a similar fashion to electronic mail, except that the individual messages comprise digitized audio data, which are transmitted to user mailboxes, retrieved, and played to the recipient. They share the security characteristics of E-mail systems, from a confidentiality viewpoint, but they have the advantage that the voice characteristics of the speaker are retained in the message. An attacker may therefore have rather more difficulty in modifying messages or injecting false messages.

6.2.6 How can office data and software be protected against malicious modification?

Personal computers do not normally have operating systems that provide the degree of protection afforded by mainframe computers. A user with access to a computer can modify data and programs stored on a diskette or hard disk, and the only evidence of the change will be the time/date stamp on the file, and even this safeguard can be bypassed.

A degree of protection against intentional, malicious modification is provided by encryption of data on diskette or hard disk (see chapter 3), the corresponding plaintext can only be accessed by an authorized user of the workstation holding the appropriate cryptographic key. Access to such workstations is protected by password control. Note that this protection only prevents an attacker from making meaningful changes to the data. It is still possible for the data to be destroyed or vandalized, but the owner will at least be aware of the changes made since the corresponding plaintext will be badly garbled.

Encryption also provides good protection against the introduction of external data or software. For example, an attacker could not substitute a diskette containing modified data for an office diskette, because it would not be possible to produce the corresponding encrypted version. Similarly viruses (see chapter 3) could not be loaded, wittingly or unwittingly, if the workstation decrypted all incoming data and software. All data and programs loaded onto a workstation in this case would have to originate from a designated office systems manager, who would supply correctly encrypted diskettes to be read by the workstation. It would be possible in principle for a virus to be implanted on the disk before it was encrypted by the supervisor for later distribution but, it is to be hoped, the office systems manager and information security officer would check new software and data of this sort for such malicious systems as viruses.

6.2.7 *Is it possible to protect electronically processed and transmitted documents against modification?*

It is possible to adapt the message authentication code (MAC) technique (see chapter 5) used in financial messages to protect the authenticity of documents. A document authentication code (DAC) is developed and attached to the document.

The DAC is formed by a cryptographic process operating on the contents of the document to create a form of checksum that cannot be falsified by an attacker. The DAC can be computed as the contents of the document are formed; it is added to the document for storage and transmission. It may be displayed on the printed document, e.g. at the bottom of the last page, as a check of validity, and for identification purposes.

Such DACs provide protection for sender and receiver against third-party attacks. An extension of this approach is to employ a digital signature (see chapter 1), produced by public key cryptography, to protect recipients against senders who later repudiate their messages, and senders against purported recipients who develop false messages.

Such authentication and digital signature techniques employ encryption but do not provide for the confidentiality of the message (see chapter 1). If confidentiality is required then the whole composite electronic document may again be encrypted, using a cryptographic key available to only the nominated security officers for the organization concerned.

Cryptography employed for confidentiality and authenticity can be provided by software packages but such software may seriously degrade the performance of workstations. Moreover, the essential cryptographic keys will not be provided with the apposite degree of security. Hardware systems (e.g. encryptor boards) are available;

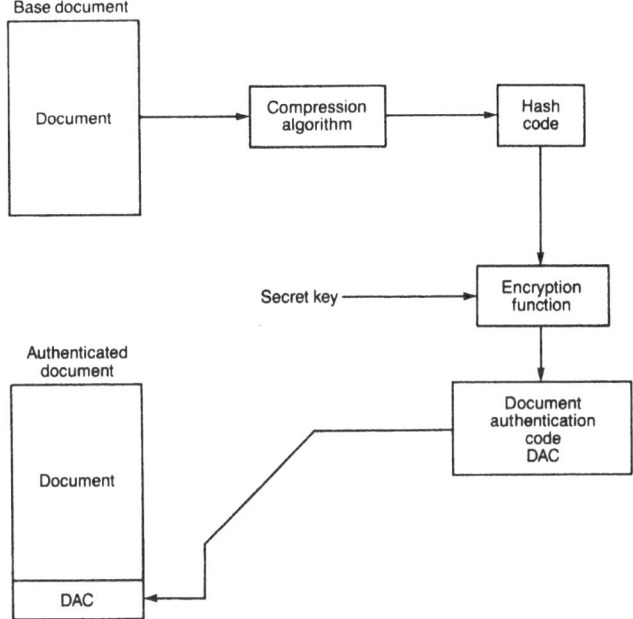

Fig. 6-2 Document authentication code

these overcome the aforementioned difficulties (see chapter 3). The cost of this specialized equipment may be expected to decrease markedly in the next few years as growing demand for better office security leads to manufacturing economies of scale. Such encryption hardware may become standard features of personal computer workstations in particular areas, e.g. banking and finance industries.

6.2.8 What control can be exercised on printer output?
There is little point in encrypting sensitive data during transmission and storage if it eventually appears as hard copy output on an un-supervised printer (see chapter 1). Normally printers attached to office workstations or LANs simply print out the data sent to them by office workstations. A printer access authorization unit may be employed to control such output; with this device all office printing (e.g. production of company proprietary documents) may be closely controlled (see figure 6-3).

Sensitive data is directed to protected printers located in a physic-ally secure area, normally under the control of authorized officers, who control the use of the printers with a special access card, e.g. a smart card, or equivalent token. The token is inserted into the

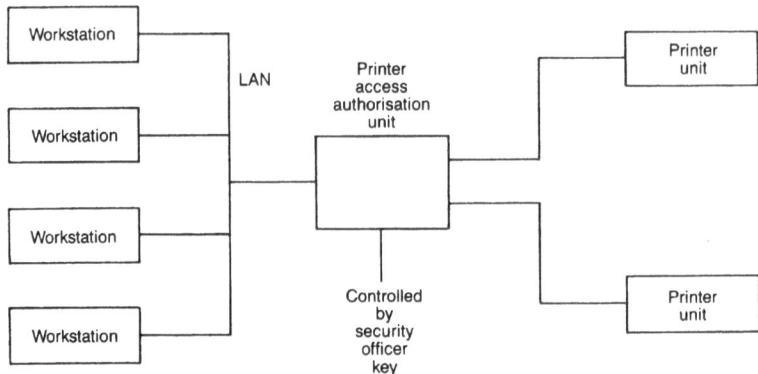

Fig. 6-3 Printer access authorization unit

access control unit and a corresponding PIC is entered on a keypad. The access control unit may provide full audit trail information, recorded back onto the security token in an encrypted form for later analysis. The access control unit may also add appropriate corporate identity codes to the documents, perform reformatting of documents according to office standards, and provide a set of documents with identifying numbers. Such an access control system is a logical development of current printer buffers which receive data from one or more workstations and produce hard copy off-line.

6.2.9 Are audit trails necessary in office automation systems?

All office systems should provide for audit trails to be securely created and maintained. All office transactions, from a change to a document in a word processing system to an entry in the sales order ledger, should be subject to scrutiny from an audit trail. Moreover, the audit trail itself needs to be protected from illicit tampering by workstation users. Each audit trail record should identify:

- the type of transaction and its contents,
- the system user,
- the workstation and network used,
- time/date of transaction and the transaction serial number.

It should also be possible for both internal and external auditors to examine the audit trail records. This facility may entail the creation of appropriate report generation programs for the audit system. Unfortunately, most word processing and desktop publishing packages for personal computers (e.g. under MS-DOS) do not appear to have any audit trail capabilities.

268

6.3 Physical Security of Office Systems

6.3.1 Introduction
Office systems have different physical security aspects to those of computer centres. On the one hand the office system cannot be physically isolated and protected like a computer centre (see chapter 3); it is essential that organizational personnel have free access to the area, and hence to the equipment. On the other hand the nature of the equipment is such that it is unlikely to be a prime target for (say) a terrorist attack. The major physical security considerations that are introduced with the implementation of the electronic office are as follows:

- theft (see section 6.3.2),
- continuity of power supply (see section 6.3.5),
- access control (see section 6.3.6),
- waste disposal (see section 6.3.7),
- fire (see section 6.3.8).

6.3.2 How can office magnetic disks and cassettes be protected against theft?
There are really two aspects to this problem:

- theft of disks or tapes directly;
- unauthorized removal of data contained on the magnetic media (see section 6.3.3).

If the disks or cassettes are stolen for their intrinsic value, then the damage to the organization depends upon whether backup copies exist, and whether sensitive data accidentally falls into the wrong hands. The failure to maintain backup copies of data indicates a serious security failure of line management and should be treated as such (see chapter 3).

Since those suffering the loss of disks or cassettes are unlikely to be apprised of the thief's motives, it must be assumed that sensitive data lost in this manner was taken for its own sake, and the possible deleterious effects upon the information security of the organization considered. If the loss or disclosure of the data will have a significant impact on the organization then this possibility should have been foreseen and contingency plans developed.

The direct theft of disks or cassettes may thus have an impact upon the organization out of all proportion to the retail price of the items. The technology employed against shoplifters could be exploited; a small magnetic detection strip attached to each diskette or tape cartridge is detected by sensors installed at each entrance and exit to the office area. This potential solution has not generally been employed because the sensors would have to be located at manned exits and no other exits should exist. It would, moreover, involve a major cost to guard against the loss of relatively low-cost items, and would provide no protection against theft of data that had been copied on a diskette brought into the office.

In general the best protection against loss of sensitive data arising from incidental pilfering of magnetic media is a good level of office discipline. Staff should be warned of the serious disciplinary consequences of illegal removal of such material, and media containing sensitive data should not be left unattended so that it can be removed by visitors, casual workmen, etc.

6.3.3 How can the deliberate theft of sensitive data be prevented?
An attacker who intends to remove sensitive data stored on diskette or magnetic tape can either steal the items or use an office personal computer to copy the data onto a blank diskette or cassette. The precautions against incidental pilfering (see section 6.3.2) may be insufficient to stop the planned theft by an office worker or authorized visitor. If, on the other hand, the data is copied onto a blank diskette or tape then there will be no evidence of the loss of the data.

One approach is for all organizational media to be colour coded, e.g. all company or departmental diskettes could be green. Diskettes may be manufactured with coloured covers displaying a photograph or other printed material, such as the organization's trade marks and logos, etc. Thus all diskettes in use could be printed with the corporate logo, together with some appropriate message relating to ownership, regulations on handling, etc., both on the diskette itself and on the associated paper envelope. Office regulations should then prohibit the use of unmarked diskettes or tapes, and the presence of any such unmarked media would be immediately apparent to office supervisors. Likewise a corporate diskette or tape cartridge should never appear outside the organization.

A much higher level of security against the deliberate theft of data can be provided by cryptography (see chapter 1). Diskettes and tape cartridges may be encrypted by software and/or hardware subsystems in the office workstations or LAN servers. Such encryption can be transparent to the user; when the diskette is loaded onto the official workstation, which contains the appropriate cryptographic key (see chapter 1), the loaded data is decrypted before being displayed; likewise plaintext data from the screen is encrypted before it is stored on the diskette. If the diskette is stolen or copied then it will be of no value to the attacker because it will be unreadable on any device that lacks access to the requisite cryptographic keys. If the diskette is pilfered then office managers are at least assured that sensitive data could not have been disclosed.

Diskettes and related media must be treated as any other office record, i.e. when not in use, or at the end of a work period, all storage media are securely locked away in office cabinets. The media should not be left in plastic storage boxes on desks or cabinet tops.

6.3.4 How can the office equipment be protected against theft?
The systems that make up a total office automation system may be small, lightweight, and valuable. Besides the normal personal computer-based workstation, portable and laptop systems may be used for remote locations or travelling members of staff. If these systems contain hard disks, then the theft of such a unit may mean the loss of confidential data in addition to a valuable asset. Printers, facsimile units, personal computers, interface cards in workstations, personal photocopiers, laser printer cartridges, and other consumables are also attractive items for a thief.

The theft of personal computer workstations may be rendered more difficult by the use of ergonomically designed desks and work areas. Such furniture is designed to improve productivity, but it also has the advantage of increased security. Personal computers may be incorporated into such desks, and their cabinets firmly locked to prevent illicit removal of components or addition of bugging devices. In any event all personal computer cabinets should be lockable to prevent removal or insertion of cards. Cables may be screwed and locked into position, e.g. the cable connection between a personal computer keyboard and the main processing unit. In a more sensitive area these physical locks may incorporate tamper-resistance, detection, and alarm features.

6.3.5 What action needs to be taken in respect of power supplies?
A loss or interruption of power supplies to an individual workstation can cause severe problems for office staff and possible loss of data integrity. Loss of power to the office can bring it to a complete standstill.

Some systems have automatic power restart. This can cause problems for office staff. The restoration of power after an interruption will not cause the system to be in the same state as that immediately before the loss of power; this can be disconcerting to office staff and may lead to problems of data integrity. It is important that office procedures be established for recovery from such interruptions.

Loss or interruption of power to a workstation can arise from:

- accidental removal of power cable,
- power supply failure,
- transients on power line.

Cable must not be allowed to trail over floors where they can cause accidents and consequential loss of power to workstations. Office staff should not have to plug in and unplug individual items of equipment because there are insufficient power sockets. It is not uncommon for unattended workstation backup routines to be rendered useless by office cleaners removing plugs from power points in order to connect up vacuum cleaners.

Access flooring, which provides a space below the office false floor for cables etc., is becoming a feature of modern offices. However such flooring can introduce a data security hazard if data communication cables are accessible but hidden; illegal taps or bugs attached to underfloor cables may go unobserved.

The power supply on personal computers is not as rugged as those of minicomputers and mainframes. They will therefore be more susceptible to interruptions on mains power supply lines. This problem may be overcome with the installation of an uninterruptible power supply (UPS). The system may be used to protect a cluster of important office systems, e.g.:

- PABX unit,
- one or two workstations and peripheral devices,
- telex and/or facsimile units.

Power supplies may also suffer from spikes or other disturbances arising from the presence of heavy electrical equipment. Such transients can affect personal computers and workstations, and they may be removed with line conditioners. These items are relatively inexpensive and are connected between the workstation and the power supply.

6.3.6 What is the role of access control in office automation security?
The implementation of office automation systems will tend to render offices more attractive to the thief and the attacker. It may well, therefore, be necessary to upgrade physical access control.

In the first instance security staff should be brought into the planning of office automation systems; they can warn of potential security problems associated with siting equipment in offices which present difficulties from a controlled access viewpoint.

It is also important to keep security staff fully briefed on staff changes. For example, ex-employees must be recognized as such, and not afforded access privileges by security guards.

Access control systems (see chapter 3) are increasing in sophistication and can ensure good security without undue inconvenience to the user; they can also provide monitoring of access activities for enhanced control, and post mortem analysis of security incidents. The obverse side of access control (i.e. safe evacuation in case of fire, etc.) also requires careful attention.

In any considerations of access control one must never forget the office cleaner. They have excellent opportunities to access workstations for long periods without supervision. They can also accidentally switch equipment on or off, examine the contents of papers on desks, look in unlocked filing cabinets, etc.

6.3.7 What precautions need to be observed in waste disposal?

Information is routinely discarded and sensitive papers are normally gathered for shredding. The electronic office tends to increase the volume of paper throughput. The manager therefore needs to give careful consideration to the question of waste disposal. The areas of concern are:

- aging of trash,
- secure disposal of paper,
- secure disposal of magnetic media.

There is a good case for storing all waste paper, magnetic media, etc. for a specified period (e.g. one week) before destruction (see chapter 1). Such a routine can provide a form of backup, and guard against unforeseen catastrophes, e.g. total loss of electronically stored transaction data. The trash should be stored securely and labelled (e.g. in bins with day of week and department name).

Most office paper (e.g. from laser printers) is of high quality and is likely to be recycled. Sensitive documents must be shredded; the degree of shredding should be sufficient to ensure that no information can be gleaned from it. Like backup, shredding is a time-consuming chore that may be easily neglected. Office managers must ensure that this is not the case. If a substantial amount of paper is to be shredded then automatic feed machines should be purchased.

Diskettes are commonly thrown into wastepaper-baskets. However, it must be remembered that competent programmers can easily resurrect quantities of data from 'erased' or damaged diskettes, even if they appear to be unreadable to the user (see chapter 3). Shredders exist for shredding the cardboard and light plastic of floppy diskettes, usually of the 8 inch or 5.25 inch variety. The rigid outer case of the microfloppy diskettes cannot be readily destroyed, but the inner oxide coated material may be easily removed and shredded.

Undamaged magnetic media are reusable, but they may also con-

273

tain sensitive data. A service should be provided in which users return unwanted diskettes to the security or stores officer. This officer may then use a full erase program on a workstation to remove completely any stored files by overwriting them with a known bit pattern, and then reformat the medium for reuse. At the same time a media test program could check for the reliability of the medium, e.g. any damaged or marginal sectors or tracks on a diskette, etc.

6.3.8 Are there any additional fire risks in the automated office?
Most offices already contain potential fire hazards such as photocopiers, coffee-making equipment, etc. However, with the use of full colour displays and laser printers the number of sources of fire has increased. Colour displays in particular contain higher-voltage tubes while laser printer units, like photocopiers, contain high-temperature ink fusers. Thus every room area should have clearly marked carbon dioxide or Halon fire extinguishers as recommended by the organizations's insurance company and local fire authorities (see chapter 3).

6.4 Procedural and Personnel Security

6.4.1 What procedures should be created for the introduction of office automation and workstations?
An early consideration of security factors will enhance the effectiveness of systems and procedures introduced to minimize the likelihood of security incidents, and reduce the damage resulting from accidental or malicious acts. The attitudes of the potential users in the office organization must be taken into consideration and acknowledged. Existing policies for office procedures and directives will need to be assessed and modified as necessary in collaboration with office supervisors and representatives. The areas that require consideration are:

- personnel responsibilities (see section 6.4.2);
- training (see section 6.4.5);
- acquisition, implementation, and maintenance (see section 6.4.8);
- backup (see section 6.4.9);
- support team (see section 6.4.10);
- insurance (see section 6.4.11);
- legal aspects (see section 6.4.12);
- review of procedures (see section 6.4.13).

6.4.2 How should personnel responsibilities be allocated?
Management must specify those responsible for:

- overall control of the office systems;
- risk assessment and evaluation (see chapter 2);
- contingency planning (see chapter 3);
- backup and recovery services for data and software (see chapter 3);
- definition of the privacy requirements for office information (see section 6.4.3);
- definition of the various areas of activity in the new automated environment;
- training and education related to the office systems;
- system documentation;
- maintenance and insurance;
- liaison with security officer.

6.4.3 Should office workers be granted the right of privacy with regard to their data?

Many employees will store personal information in desk drawers or filing cabinets, on the basis that they need access to it during office hours, but they would consider that such information should not be disclosed to organizational officials. For example, an executive may maintain a private diary with details of domestic commitments, doctors' appointments, holidays, etc. so as to ensure there was no clash with business appointments. Full details of personal expenditure may be kept because some items may relate to business trips. It is likely that such data will migrate to executive workstations and reside on software diaries, stored telephone numbers, spreadsheets.

The presence of electronically stored private data is a potential source of conflict with the information security requirements of an office. On the one hand such data may be held to be the sole concern of the worker. However, a situation could arise in which personal data relating to other individuals were stored among such private data, causing a conflict with the organization's responsibilities under data protection legislation (see chapter 7).

The potential problems need to be recognized at the outset. The security officer needs to specify the extent to which such private data may be stored, if at all, and the degree of confidentiality that workers can expect in regard to such data. This implies some classification of office data:

- organizational ownership,
- departmental ownership,
- user or personal ownership.

Such a classification needs to exist at an awareness level even though it will be impossible to police it. If private data are permitted on the system then the rules under which this is permitted need to be specified. For example, the data should not contravene the organization's data protection policy, it should be made available to specified management undertaking investigations into computer abuse, etc. (see chapter 7).

6.4.4 What are the security problems associated with the private use of office equipment?

There are two aspects of this problem:

- use of office systems for private use;
- use of private systems for official use.

Unofficial use of office systems is regarded as a traditional 'perk' of the office worker. Photocopiers have been used to produce copies of notices for social functions, favourite recipes, etc. The question here is to what extent does private use of systems represent a security hazard in the new environment of an electronic office. There are probably four major areas of concern:

- introduction of unofficial software,
- misuse of communications systems,
- uncontrolled movement of information,
- uncontrolled flow of privileges.

If personal computers are used for playing games, study assignments, etc. then there exists the danger that software will be brought into the office and such software may contain malicious code, computer viruses, etc. (see chapter 3) and lead to corruption of corporate data and software. Alternatively such software may be pirated and cause legal problems or bad publicity for the organization concerned.

Private use of telephones is uncommon; however, private use of communications networks may have more serious implications for an office manager. Such misuse can produce horrendous telecommunications charges and also lead to serious legal situations, e.g. in the case of transmission of obscene messages, illegal communication or personal data, etc. Careful monitoring of communication traffic, and strict rules on use of such facilities, should be established at the outset to obviate problems arising from potential misuse.

If employees develop the habit of using office personal computers etc. for private use then they are likely to transport private floppy diskettes in and out of the office. It is then all too easy for company data to be carried out accidentally, or for diskettes to be 'borrowed' for private use.

Office workers with authorized access to workstations may well be asked to share that access with other office workers, who want to produce a private letter on the word processor, or play a game on a personal computer. If this habit develops then an attacker can easily breach security without raising suspicion by asking for a password 'as a favour'.

The above examples indicate that the major danger of unauthorized use of office automation systems is that it leads to the habit of breaking security rules. In the first instance no harm is intended or occasioned. However, the common breach of such security rules may well lead eventually to serious accidental or malicious damage in terms of information security.

The private purchase of personal computers for domestic or personal 'professional' use has increased dramatically in the last five years. This trend leads to two potential problem areas:

- incompatibility between office and private software;
- uncontrolled movement of office information and software.

All computer users tend to favour the versions of software packages with which they are familiar. Requests may then be made for an office worker to bring in his or her own software, at no cost to the company, rather than force the trouble and expense of retraining onto the office system. It would be better to suffer the cost of purchasing the software than to allow the worker to import their personal packages. As indicated above, there are dangers in the unofficial importation of software.

If private computers are to be used to process office information then the flow of sensitive data will be uncontrolled. This may be an acceptable risk in the case of responsible executives working at home, on business trips, etc. However, a wise precaution would be to supply encryptor boards (see chapter 3) for all such privately owned personal computers. If diskettes are then lost or stolen outside the office the manager can be assured that they contain only encrypted data, and will therefore be useless to an attacker.

6.4.5 How can security awareness be enhanced among office staff?
There are strong arguments for security awareness training programs for office staff at all levels. For example, the PABX switchboard operator should be fully familiar with emergency procedures: fire, flood, bomb threats, etc. The effectiveness of such training will, however, depend upon both the expertise and dedication of the security officers, and the level of overt support from senior and line management (see chapter 1).

The main aim of security awareness training will be to create an appreciation of the need and benefits of security in the organization. This can be achieved by:

- short training workshops with half-day sessions totalling up to two days;
- organization of discussion groups for particular sections;
- security briefing for new employees;
- regular newsletters and notices emphasizing particular security topics;
- films, videotapes, and other audio/visual aids;
- dissemination of the organization's security policy in standing orders and manuals of procedures;
- security reminders on log-on screens for computer terminals and personal computer software.

6.4.6 What topics should be covered in a security awareness training package?

A typical office security training session may incorporate a number of topics:

purpose of the security policy and awareness program:
- office background and examples of problems that have occurred;
- information processing undertaken in the office and its role in the organization;
- balance between the requirements for security, cost, impact on working efficiency, etc.

security aspects of office operations:
- managerial and supervisory responsibilities for information processing and security;
- information processing systems employed in the office, security mechanisms (or lack of them) of the systems;
- information processing procedures in the office, associated security procedures, details of particular areas of security sensitivity, e.g. personal data, confidential information, financial transactions;
- induction of new staff;

role of the office in the: information processing organizations:
- organizational information for which the office is responsible;
- secure collection, storage, processing, and onward transmission of information; which section supplies information to the office; which section receives office processed information;
- responsibilities and authority of staff in other sections, in respect of information handled in the office;
- checks of integrity of information, data entry controls, what

to do if checks fail, recovery from errors, backup procedures, care of magnetic media, password security, contingency plans; response to abnormal circumstances (see chapter 3):

- evacuation procedures in case of fire, etc.;
- dealing with strangers in the office;
- reporting unusual events;
- responsibilities for the security of information in emergency situations;
- disaster recovery.

6.4.7 How should office security awareness programs be developed?

Procedures must be established for the design, implementation, and review of awareness programs. Such programs should be developed by a small team and checked by the security officer for compliance with the organizational security policy (see chapter 1). The guidelines for the program should be published in standing orders, manual of procedures, etc.

The training material should be aimed at the level of technical competence of the staff, with extensive use of visual aids, cartoon diagrams, and minimal use of jargon. Easy access to security procedures may be provided via a menu and 'help' file, accessible from office workstations.

6.4.8 What are the security implications involved in acquiring and implementing new office automation systems?

A clear policy on the acquisition of new hardware and software systems, and their introduction into the office system, is essential from a security viewpoint. New communications facilities may open the door to hackers; untested software may contain bugs or viruses (see chapter 3), or may breach software licensing agreements (see chapter 7). Overall responsibility for the operation of such new equipment and its associated data must be specified. Training on the operation of the equipment and the associated security measures is an essential feature of such acquisitions. The impact of the equipment on existing workloads and responsibilities must also be taken into account; the new acquisition may well imply that junior office staff now have direct access to sensitive data.

The maintenance arrangements for office automation systems should conform to specified policies. Inadequate routine maintenance can result in loss of processing facilities at critical times, but it is also important to consider the security loopholes that can arise from the absence of clear maintenance guidelines. Maintenance staff should be required to identify themselves to senior staff when they enter the office, procedures for the removal of equipment must be established, and maintenance staff should not normally have access to sensitive data. The maintenance of hard disk systems raises particular security difficulties (see chapter 3), and contractual agreements with maintenance organizations need to address this issue.

The impact of the new equipment on contingency plans, insurance, etc. (see chapter 3) must also be considered.

6.4.9 Who should have responsibility for backup of office data?
The housekeeping routines associated with effective backup represent a chore that can all too easily be neglected when staff are working under pressure, and it is precisely on those occasions that accidents arise leading to the need for the backup material (see chapter 3).

The provision of a backup and other services from the computer centre may prove to be more effective than exhortations from the security officer. The centre may operate a service to:

- allow users to backup data files via workstation-to-mainframe links onto centre disk packs (this obviates the requirement to load, label, and store backup diskettes);
- retain a full set of backup copies for software packages installed on the office workstations;
- provide indexed directories of software packages to workstation users, together with the latest update information;
- provide more advanced services for users such as high-speed printing services, statistical analyses, etc.

With the provision of such services the security officer could reasonably lay down the requirement that the centre hold a copy of all workstation software, organizational and departmental files, etc.

6.4.10 What is the role of a support team?
In larger organizations there may well be a case for the establishment of an office systems support team. This team may be part of an information centre set up in the main computer and data processing centre itself. The team should have members with expertise in:

- data communications subsystems on personal computers,
- office automation software packages,
- printer devices and associated desktop publishing software,
- local area networks,
- electronic mail,
- business software systems.

In addition to their expertise these team members should be able to establish good relations with non-technical staff, office workers, managers, etc. In this way the team can ensure that security procedures are understood and not bypassed.

6.4.11 What actions need to be taken in relation to insurance?
A record of all serial numbers of equipment and software packages in use must be maintained and made available to the company's insurance company or agents (see chapter 3). At the same time this record could also maintain a register of the locations and users of equipment and software.

6.4.12 Are there any legal problems in relation to office systems security?
The legal implications of office automation equipment may be serious since office staff may have an insufficient understanding of the technical nature of the equipment, and the legal complexities surrounding information processing equipment have escalated in recent years (see chapter 7). The major areas of concern are:

- data protection,
- copyright,
- legality of electronic documentation.

It is important that all staff are familiar with the organizations responsibilities in regard to the UK *Data Protection Act* (see chapter 7). They should not undertake unofficial collection and electronic storage of personal data, nor should they disclose official personal data to unauthorized people, particularly in response to telephone calls. On the other hand they must be aware of, and conform to, the organization's policy of granting individuals access to their own personal data.

Copyright may be easily breached when using copying equipment or personal computers. It is most important that unauthorized software should not be introduced into the office, and authorized software must not be copied or used beyond the terms of the software licence.

The trend towards electronic communication of documentation, e.g. electronic mail, electronic data interchange, facsimile, etc. also requires attention from the security and the legal viewpoints. In particular, electronic mail documentation will lack a handwritten signature and therefore not have the requisite legal status.

6.4.13 What reviews should be conducted when new office automation systems are introduced?
An electronic office presents an entirely new situation from a security viewpoint, and many established procedures, working

arrangements, safeguards, fallback systems, responsibilities, etc. will need to be reviewed. For example:

- access to sensitive information may now be available to junior staff;
- safeguards against fraud, etc. may have inherently relied upon redundancy in the previously manual system (e.g. senior staff may no longer routinely overview all documentation);
- previous contingency plans may no longer be valid;
- staff may not be able to perform the same range of office duties and therefore there is less staff backup;
- junior staff may have access to expensive processing and communications facilities.

Reference
Finch, 'Security of Office Systems', in *Office Systems*, ed. A. A. Verrijn-Stuart and R. A. Hirschhelm (Elsevier Science Publishers, B.V. (North Holland), 1986).

7 Security and the Law

D. Longley

7.1 Overview

The law has areas of white, black, and grey. Most of us ensure that we remain in the white areas, and assume that any one who does us grievous harm will be considered to reside in a black area. In this way we believe that we are behaving reasonably to our fellow man, and that if anyone harms us then we will get redress from the law. Unfortunately it sometimes transpires that we find ourselves, possibly with some adversary, in a grey area. In this case we seek the advice of a trained legal mind. This approach to the legal system, of course, assumes that we know the location of the white–grey, and the black–grey boundaries with a sufficient degree of approximation to position ourselves. These boundaries are, however, time- and space-dependent. Laws are changed by parliament, hopefully with sufficient publicity and at a slow enough pace for us to be aware of the changes. They also differ from place to place, as some luckless tourists have discovered.

At present managers find that the legislation concerning information technology renders it difficult for them to adopt the approaches described above. The technology has produced revolutions in the manner in which organizations conduct themselves, and in the very nature of their business. Information is now an asset that must be guarded, and at the same time collected, processed, stored, and communicated, with a minimum of manual intervention, possibly on a worldwide basis. The suppliers, processors, subjects, recipients, and those directly affected by the data may never meet, and may well have unfriendly feelings towards one other. The knowledge held by individual employees may be crucial to the success of an organization, but employee attitudes and mobility may cause that knowledge to move to a competitor. Managers may find that legal liabilities have arisen owing to the actions, inadvertent or malicious, of employees, or simply because new technologies have produced entirely new situations.

Not only has the technology produced new situations but also the apposite legislation is changing both in terms of space and time. The position of the grey areas is frankly open to speculation in some fields, particularly those associated with software copyright. In these circumstances an unwary manager may well find that he has blundered into a grey or even a black area, or, more likely, that an adversary who has done great harm is safe from criminal or civil proceedings. This chapter will not dwell on the debates within the grey areas but will rather seek to indicate the location of the boundaries at the time of writing between the white, grey, and black areas, at least for the UK manager.

The following sections deal with three areas of prime concern from the legal viewpoint:

- data protection,
- computer crime,
- copyright.

Data protection concerns the legal responsibilities that UK organizations have when they store and process personal data on a computer. Unless the data so stored and processed is subject to exemption, the organization must formally register with the Data Protection Registrar, and ensure that personal data is thereafter treated in accordance with the provisions of the Act. Storing personal data that is not included in the registration details, storing incorrect personal data, disclosing such data to unauthorized recipients, refusing to allow data subjects reasonable access to their own data, transmitting the data to overseas destinations not included in the registration, failing to gain approval for changes in the handling of personal data, etc. can result in civil action, or even criminal charges against the company. In extreme cases the organization may be forbidden to store or process electronically the personal data. A company may find itself in some difficulty simply because employees were unaware of the provisions of the Act. There may also be a substantial workload produced by the registration procedures. The *Data Protection Act* may well have an impact upon senior management and the role of the security officer.

Whereas with data protection an organization is in danger of finding itself the defendant in a civil or even criminal proceedings, with computer crime the reverse is true: the greatest danger is probably that of its being the actual, or potential, victim. The problem is that the role of information as an asset which can be stolen, and that of a computer which can be misused, is not currently well established in law.

The problem of actual computer fraud, on the other hand, lies not so much in determining that it is in fact illegal, as in investigating and proving the case. Computer transactions are transitory and may leave inadequate traces of intermediary operations; the detailed knowledge of the information processing system may lie only with the perpetrators of the fraud. The attitudes, lifestyles, intelligence, skill, and mobility of computer personnel is rather different from that of the bookkeepers of yesteryear.

The protection of information assets could well place the manager as either the defendant or the plaintiff in a court action. Copyright is a new battlefield for computing companies and it is becoming increasingly difficult to remain clear of the grey areas. The whole question of copyright of software, and electronically stored and processed information is likely to keep the legal profession wealthy for some time. The use of new technologies can change the nature of organizations and so cause them to drift into those difficult grey areas. A manager of an engineering manufacturing business may exploit desktop publishing to overcome the problems of production of technical manuals; such a manager can well become a publisher unwittingly without appreciating the legal implications of these actions. Some organizations have sought to increase their competitiveness by providing information services with their product. In other cases information received from organizations may be used in novel ways, e.g. it may be fed directly into systems in which an error in the information could have a major financial impact, or even cause the loss of life. Thus organizations may have created situations in which they might unwittingly become liable to heavy consequential damages owing to some fault in their information processing systems, or actions of their personnel.

The message that comes from these sections is that which has arisen elsewhere in this book: good management is the only guaranteed safeguard. It is essential that management demonstrates that it has initiated, implemented, monitored, and reviewed procedures to ensure compliance with civil and criminal law. This approach is extremely important when organizations may find themselves in the grey or black areas owing to the actions of employees, or as the result of unforeseen system errors.

It is also important to recognize that the law may not be able to provide redress in cases where one might reasonably feel that it should. The whole question of the legality of hacking is currently unresolved. However, managers are, not unreasonably, incensed when their computer systems are invaded, valuable staff time is spent in investigating incidents, or they are subjected to unfavourable publicity as the consequence of such actions. There may also be difficulties encountered in seeking police help to investigate computer fraud if the evidence that such fraud has been committed is nebulous, but nevertheless of distinct concern to management. In these circumstances internal defences and investigation teams may prove to be the best solution.

The checklist for management in terms of security and the law is:

- Ensure that management is fully aware of the current state of legislation.
- Draft contracts of employment, and contractual arrangements with independent contractors, with due regard to the legal aspects of data security (see section 7.5.5).
- Formally state the organization's policy on data protection, computer crime, and protection of information assets.
- Ensure that all staff are trained and kept aware of their responsibilities in regard to data protection, computer crime, and protection of information assets.
- Ensure that all information assets handled by the company are as carefully audited as if they were money.
- Ensure that managers implement personnel policies consistent with maximum protection for the organization, both in terms of security of information assets and defence against external liabilities arising from misuse of information.
- Ensure that the procedures to be employed in the handling of information assets are designed to be consistent with legal requirements, recorded, widely known throughout the organization, monitored, and reviewed.
- Ensure that individuals or teams are appointed and trained to deal with internal investigations of suspected computer/information asset abuse.
- Take out appropriate insurance cover against losses resulting from computer crime and legal liabilities arising from information technology misuse (see chapter 3).

It is clearly important that management, and in particular information processing managers and security officers, are aware of changes of legislation that may have an impact upon their organization. To achieve this, however, it must be recognized that changes in overseas, as well as domestic, legislation can directly affect the company. When Sweden introduced its data protection legislation, a British company lost a contract to produce embossed cards simply because the new laws prohibited the export of the personal data that was to be printed on the cards. It must also be recognized that the legal advisors to the organization need to be conversant with operations within it if they are to appraise the potential impact of new legislation, or even recent civil cases. This is particularly so if information technology has produced changes in the nature of the company. For example, a legal adviser may not be aware that an engineering company has developed a powerful and potentially profitable piece of computer-aided design software, or that a distributor has increased its competitiveness by the provision of a powerful information service to its customers. In the former case the company may be failing to protect its copyright, and in the latter it could be drifting towards dangerous liabilities owing to a failure to ensure the accuracy of its data. It is therefore important that lines of communication be established between legal advisors, security officers, and information processing managers to gauge the impact of changes in the law relevant to data security.

Contractual arrangements with employees, or independent contractors, must be made in the light of the problems that can arise from the transfer of knowledge and expertise between organizations. It may be difficult to differentiate between an information asset and the knowledge and skills acquired by an employee, or contractor, particularly in the information technology field. Such knowledge can be transferred to a competitor when an employee leaves or a contractor undertakes the next project. On the other hand it is possible that liabilities can arise if a new employee exploits trade secrets belonging to a previous employer. Legal expertise is essential in drawing up contracts (see section 7.5.5).

The organization must take a clear stance on areas such as data protection, computer crime, and copyright. Given the complexity of large-scale information processing and communications systems, the size and mobility of a workforce, the enormous mass of information contained in modern systems, the volume of transactions, the wide variety of sources and sinks of data, etc., there is a significant probability that liabilities will arise from an unforeseen eventuality. An important starting point, in any defence, will be a clear statement by senior management that all reasonable precautions are to be taken to avoid such a situation. The clarity of the management view will also ensure that middle management are encouraged to refine such a policy, with detailed directives to their staff on the proper actions to be taken in handling data.

Having stated their policy, management must then ensure that employees and contractors are fully aware of their responsibilities and the proper actions to be taken. Induction training of employees, awareness programs, screen messages upon log-on, reminding staff that certain data must be handled according to instructions (e.g. warning that subsequent screens will display personal data that must not be revealed to unauthorized persons), etc. will serve to remind staff of proper routines. Such programs will also provide a form of defence if the organization is accused of negligently disclosing personal data (see section 7.2.19.8).

Organizations are becoming increasingly liable for information that they hold or provide. Inaccurate data can cause serious accidents, loss of life or serious financial loss. An American company was sued for $12 million when it was held that inaccurate graphs produced for use by airline pilots were responsible for an airline crash. Information supplied can arise from a wide variety of sources and be subjected to extensive processing. If data is in error then a post hoc investigation may well be unable to trace the source of such error, and hence it may prove impossible to guarantee the error will not recur. An effective system of audit trails (see chapter 1) ensures that all such errors are traced to source. If a company is accused of negligently providing inaccurate data then an audit trail that traced the error to data supplied from an external source (which the organization had every reason to believe to be reliable) would at least exonerate all internal data handling and processing procedures.

Without doubt the most serious source of accidental or malicious damage to data will arise from people's actions. It may be extremely difficult to give an absolute guarantee that a piece of software will always perform to specification, but it is a great deal easier than to give such guarantees about a large, mobile workforce. People make mistakes, perform the same tasks with different degrees of skill and aptitude at different times, change loyalties, seek out security loopholes, ignore instructions, cut corners, forget training, etc. It is necessary, but not sufficient, for management to specify proper procedures. Management – particularly middle management – must ensure that they continuously monitor and react to personnel under their control (see chapter 1). Middle management must also provide the example of required behaviour. There is little point in notices warning against illegal copying of personal computer software, if middle management is seen to seek economies in departmental budgets by acquiring pirated copies.

Management should not expect all staff, particularly junior staff, to be fully aware of the intricacies of the *Data Protection Act*, copyright legislation, etc. Clear and detailed instructions on the handling of data must be developed, distributed, monitored, and reviewed. An updated record of such instructions should also be kept. The existence of such instructions, and actions taken to ensure adherence to them, would again prove to be a useful defence against a legal charge of negligently handling data.

An investigation of actual or suspected computer crime will demand a high level of skill, possibly across a variety of disciplines, and a detailed knowledge of an organization's information processing systems and procedures. It is unlikely that any one person in the organization could conduct such an investigation; it would also be extremely unwise to assume that such an individual would be incapable of committing a crime. Any degree of incompetence in an investigating team would almost certainly destroy vital evidence, enable wrongdoers to cover up their misdeeds, provide ample ammunition for a defence lawyer, and probably create industrial unrest. When a sufficient degree of suspicion has developed to justify calling the police it will still be necessary to provide internal expertise to assist them in their enquiries.

It is therefore suggested that a cross-disciplinary team be formed and trained to conduct internal investigations into suspected computer crime. The nature and training of such a team will naturally depend upon the size and functions of the organization. In a commercial organization one could envisage that it would contain, *inter alia*, an accountant/auditor, a data processing manager, a personnel officer, and a security officer. The team would need to raise their skills, in all of these areas, to some common base level, so as to ensure good intercommunication in the investigation phase. After this basic training a series of case studies of increasing complexity should be undertaken to develop the level of skill consistent with their function.

Finally, recognizing that no single precaution or set of precautions will ever cover all eventualities, get the best insurance cover available against losses arising from computer crime and legal liabilities (see chapter 3).

The following sections deal in more detail with the areas of data protection, computer crime, and copyright. The intention is, as stated above, to indicate where the current state of UK legislation places the manager concerned with data security. No attempt is made to navigate through the hazards that can arise in the grey areas of the legislation; such is a task for a well-briefed legal expert. The purpose of these sections is to indicate some of the precautions that should be taken to keep, as far as possible, on the right side of the law and to protect one's organization from the wrongdoer and from unnecessary litigation.

7.2 Data Protection

7.2.1 What legislation covers data protection in the UK?
There are two Acts that are designed to allow individuals to check personal data held by organizations: the *Consumer Credit Act, 1974* and the *Data Protection Act, 1984*.

The *Consumer Credit Act* (see section 7.2.2) is directed to credit reference agencies. The *Data Protection Act, 1984* is much broader in its area of concern and covers all organizations that maintain personal data in a form that is processed or intended to be processed on behalf of the data user (see section 7.2.4).

7.2.2 What type of organization is subject to the Consumer Credit Act 1974?

The *Consumer Credit Act, 1974* concerns credit reference agencies, which are defined in the Act as persons 'carrying on a business comprising the furnishing of persons with information relevant to the financial standing of individuals, being information collected by the agency for that purpose'. There are two important factors on the range of data covered by the Act:

- the data is concerned with individuals, not companies (i.e. an agency that restricted its activities to the creditworthiness of companies is not subject to the Act);
- unlike the *Data Protection Act, 1984*, the Act covers data held in manual files as well as computer data.

Companies that are not credit reference agencies have no requirement, under the terms of this Act, to supply details of personal data, nor can they demand information from an agency holding details of the credit worthiness of their company.

However, if the company is a creditor, owner, or any negotiator that has been negotiating an agreement with a debtor or a hirer, it has a legal obligation under the Act. If the hirer or debtor requests, in writing, to know if a credit reference agency has been consulted, and the name and address of the agency, then there is a legal obligation to respond to that request. The request must, however, be made not later that 28 days after the agreement was made, or other negotiations ceased; the request must then be answered within seven working days. Failure to answer under these circumstances is a criminal offence.

7.2.3 How are credit reference agencies affected by the Consumer Credit Act, 1974?

Credit reference agencies must respond to consumer requests about stored data concerning the consumer's financial standing. An agency comes under the terms of this Act if it supplies any information about the financial standing of the individual; the Act is not restricted to individuals seeking credit within the financial limits of the Act. Moreover there is no restriction on the form in which the data is held.

Under the terms of this Act credit reference agencies must respond to requests from consumers who seek:

- to determine whether or not the agency holds information on their creditworthiness,
- details of that information,
- to amend or delete incorrect information.

Failure to respond, under the conditions of the Act, is a criminal offence, and could lead to deregistration of the agency under the Act.

7.2.4 *What organizations are affected by the* Data Protection Act, 1984?

The *Data Protection Act, 1984* covers any organization holding personal data which has been, or is in a form in which it may be, processed by a computer. The Act actually specifies 'in a form that can be processed by equipment operating automatically in response to instructions for that purpose'. There are some exemptions to the Act, but it is the responsibility of data users to ensure that they conform to the Act.

The Act also covers computer bureaux which process personal data for someone else.

7.2.5 *What are the principles of the* Data Protection Act, 1984?

The *Data Protection Act* was formulated to be consistent with the principles of a Council of Europe convention:

- The information to be contained in personal data shall be obtained, and personal data shall be processed, fairly and lawfully.
- Personal data shall be held only for one or more specified and lawful purpose or purposes.
- Personal data held for any purpose or purposes shall not be used or disclosed in any manner incompatible with that purpose or those purposes.
- Personal data held for any purpose or purposes shall be adequate, relevant, and not excessive in relation to that purpose or those purposes.
- Personal data shall be accurate and, where necessary, kept up to date.
- Personal data held for any purpose or purposes shall not be kept for longer than is necessary for that purpose or those purposes.
- An individual shall be entitled:
    at reasonable intervals and without delay or expense: to be

informed by any data user whether he holds personal data of which that individual is the subject; and to access to any such data held by a data user; and where appropriate, to have such data corrected or erased.

- Appropriate security measures shall be taken against unauthorized access to, or alteration, disclosure or destruction of, personal data and against accidental loss or destruction of personal data (see Appendix E for an international survey of data protection laws).

7.2.6 How can a manager tell if the data that an organization holds is subject to the Data Protection Act, 1984?
An organization is a data user if it 'holds' data. To hold such data three criteria must be met:

- The data must form part of a collection of data processed or intended to be processed by the user, or on his behalf.
- The user must be the person who controls the contents and the use of the data.
- The data must be in the form in which they are processed or are going to be processed.

The first point is that the data need not be exclusively personal data: it need only contain some personal data for the Act to apply. An engineering organization which designs ergonomic furniture, and has a design database, could well include in that database the physical details of individuals: such data might well come within the definition of personal data (see below). Note that it is not necessary to own or operate a computer to be a data user; if an organization employs a computer bureau to do the processing then it is still a data user since it 'controls the content and use of the data'. The second important point is that the data should be processed, or intended to be processed. This means that manual files are not included. However, the advent of optical scanners may have some impact on the definition of data intended to be processed: if the data is stored in printed form, and input into a computer with an optical scanner, then it is in a form intended to be processed. If your organization is not a data user as defined above then it may come within the definition of a computer bureau and still be subject to the Act. A computer bureau processes data for somebody else, either by carrying out the processing on the bureau's computer, or by allowing the other person to use the bureau's computing facilities.

Having determined whether or not the definitions of data user or computer bureau apply then it is necessary to consider whether the data in question is personal data. The information covered by the

Act is data that is 'in a form that can be processed by equipment operating automatically in response to instructions given for that purpose' and is 'personal data'.

The definition of personal data is 'data consisting of information which relates to a living individual who can be identified from the information (or that and any other information in the possession of the data user), including any expression of opinion about the individual but not any indication of the intentions of the data user in respect of that individual'. Some categories of personal data are however exempt from the Act (see section 7.2.7).

There are a number of points which may be expanded at this stage. First, the data only concerns living human beings; data on deceased people is not included. An organization with historical or research data on dead people is thus not subject to the Act. Second, it is not possible to avoid the Act by simply removing the names and addresses of individuals from the file containing other personal details. If an identifying number (e.g. works number) is used to identify the personal data, and a separate file relates that identifier to names and addresses, then the living individual can be identified from that and other information in the possession of the organization. Individuals need not even be identified by their names and addresses; if the information is sufficient (e.g. a unique set of qualifications) to identify the individual then it would be considered to be personal data.

A possible source of confusion can arise from the criteria 'including any expression of opinion about the individual but not any indications of the data user in respect of that individual'. This means that the statement 'Smith is not managerial material', which is a statement of opinion, would be included, but 'there are no plans to promote Smith to managerial level', which is a statement of intention, would be excluded from the definition. In all aspects of the operation of the Act it is, however, necessary to recall the principles upon which it is based (see section 7.2.5). Any attempt to evade the principles by deliberately restating opinions as intentions would be frowned upon by the Registrar.

7.2.7 What personal data is exempt from the Act?

Data may be exempt from the Act in terms of registration (see section 7.2.15), access provisions (see section 7.2.8), from non-disclosure provisions (see section 7.2.12), or from some combination of all three. The classes of exempt data are:

- payroll, pension, and accounting data (see section 7.2.7.1);
- membership details of unincorporated clubs (see section 7.2.7.2);

- simple name and address files and word processing data (see section 7.2.7.3);
- data held for statistical or research purposes (see section 7.2.7.4);
- data relating to the prevention or detection of crime or the collection of tax (see section 7.2.7.5);
- purely domestic data (see section 7.2.7.6);
- data declared to be of national security importance (see section 7.2.7.7);
- certain classes of legal data (see section 7.2.7.8);
- certain classes of health and social work data (see section 7.2.7.9);
- backup data (see section 7.2.7.10);

7.2.7.1 What exemptions apply to payroll, pension, and accounting data?

It was recognized during the drafting of the Act that payroll, accounting, and pension data is widely processed, and the data contained therein is unlikely to be of major concern to individuals from a privacy viewpoint. Such data was therefore declared to be exempt from registration (see section 7.2.15) and access rights (see section 7.2.8). Moreover much of this data can be disclosed for activities such as auditing or actuarial advice.

However, this exemption is closely restricted. The personal data must not include details beyond those strictly required for the declared purposes, nor must the data be used for any other purposes. Moreover, the data must not be disclosed, except for the restricted range of auditing and actuarial advice, and data users must take reasonable care to avoid disclosure (see section 7.2.12). Failure to conform with these restrictions can lead to loss of exemption.

7.2.7.2 What exemptions apply to membership details of unincorporated clubs?

If an unincorporated club only holds membership details necessary for its own purposes, and the members have given their consent to the data being held, then it is exempt from registration (see section 7.2.15) and access provisions (see section 7.2.8). Such exemption, however, does not automatically apply if the club seeks to use the information for other purposes. For example, a sports club would need to seek the consent of individual members before it disclosed its membership details to (say) a supplier of sporting equipment.

7.2.7.3 What exemptions apply to simple name and address files and word processing data?

Simple name and address files are exempt from registration (see section 7.2.15) and access provisions (see section 7.2.8), provided that they are used solely for the purpose of distributing articles or information, and the data subjects have given their consent to the data being held. It is a condition of exemption that the data user did not disclose the information, and also took reasonable care to prevent the disclosure (see section 7.2.12).

Personal details contained within word processing systems are exempt provided that the system is only employed to manipulate text and not to process the personal data held. Thus a letter held on a word processor, containing confidential opinion on an employee would be exempt. However a mailing list which contained (say) details of sexual characteristics would not be exempt, nor would a list file of personal data if the word processor contained additional facilities which permitted the file to be processed beyond merely rearranging the text.

7.2.7.4 What exemptions apply to data held for statistical or research purposes?

Data held for statistical or research purposes are not exempt from registration (see section 7.2.15) but they are exempt from access provisions (see section 7.2.8), provided that the data is not used or disclosed for any other purpose. Moreover, within the stated purpose the data must not be made available in a form that identifies the individual. The latter restriction may be more demanding than it first appears; clearly all identifying information must be removed from the data.

7.2.7.5 What exemptions apply to data relating to prevention or detection of crime, or collection of tax?

Data held for the purposes of prevention or detection of crime, or collection of tax are exempt from access provisions (see section 7.2.8) if such access would prejudice those purposes. This applies not only to police and taxation authorities, but may also be used by an employer to deny access to a file in which details of a suspected fraud were held.

The exemption also extends to any person to whom the data is passed and who discharges statutory duties. Thus such data passed to an ombudsman would still be exempt even though the ombudsman was not strictly holding the data for the same purpose.

In some circumstances the non-disclosure provisions on data may be exempted if that data is required for one of these three purposes. Thus an employer may pass personal data normally subject to a non-disclosure provision (see section 7.2.12) if such data were required by the police in an investigation.

Note that such exemptions must be justified by the data user if called upon to do so by the Registrar or the courts, and the data user would be required to indicate that the data was held for:

- the prevention or detection of crime,
- the apprehension or prosecution of offenders,
- the assessment or collection of taxes.

7.2.7.6 What exemptions apply to purely domestic data?

A home computer user who stores personal data is exempt from registration (see section 7.2.15), access (see section 7.2.8), and non-disclosure provisions (see section 7.2.12), provided that such data is held purely for domestic or recreational purposes. Thus details of the family, a file on the activities of a rock star held by a teenage fan solely for recreational purposes, etc. would be completely exempt. The exemption would not apply, however, if the data were held for business purposes; small businessmen using a home computer are subject to the Act if their computer files contain personal data on clients, customers, etc.

7.2.7.7 What exemptions apply to data declared to be of national security importance?

As one might expect, HM Government allows a Secretary of State or Minister of the Crown to exempt data from registration (see section 7.2.15) or access (see section 7.2.8) or non-disclosure provisions (see section 7.2.12) on the grounds of national security. The Minister can also certify that such data may be exempt from just the access or non-disclosure provision.

7.2.7.8 What exemptions apply to certain classes of legal data?

Data relating to information received from a third party and held as information relevant to a judicial appointment, and data which could be subject to a claim of legal professional privilege in legal proceeding is exempt from access provisions (see section 7.2.8).

7.2.7.9 What exemptions apply to certain classes of data related to health or social work?

The Secretary of State has the authority to exempt data which is:

- personal data relating to the physical or mental health of the data subject;
- personal data relating to social work, if it is considered that access to such data is likely to prejudice the conduct of such social work;
- subject to an existing enactment that prohibits or restricts the disclosure of personal data.

In each case the exemption may cover registration (see section 7.2.15), access (see section 7.2.8), or non-disclosure provisions (see section 7.2.12), or some combination of these.

7.2.7.10 What exemptions apply to backup data?
Backup data is normally exempt from access provisions (see section 7.2.8) of the Act. This exemption is granted in respect of the data held on backup media because such data might well differ from the original data; backup data necessarily refers to the stored data at backup time and the original data is likely to have been updated. Revealing two different sets of personal data might therefore cause some confusion. In addition, requests for access to backup data could be extremely disruptive to the organization. Such backup data might well be held in a secure store some distance from the computer. Transporting and loading such data on the computer could be expensive in terms of interruptions to processing, and deleterious to the security arrangements of the organization. The Registrar must, however, be convinced of the argument for exemption; the claim of backup data exemption must not be used deliberately to hide personal data from the data subject.

7.2.8 What are the access provisions of the Act?
One of the principles of the Act (see section 7.2.5) is that data subjects are entitled to know if personal data concerning them is stored, to examine such data, and to have a right to correct or delete any incorrect items. A data user therefore has an obligation to meet such access requirements, unless the data is exempted from the access provision (see section 7.2.7). In meeting the access provision the data user must also ensure that non-disclosure provisions (see section 7.2.12) are not violated, i.e. access is not granted to someone without the right of access, and that data so revealed does not also refer to some other data subject. Thus a data user must comply with a request for access if:

- the data is not exempt from the access provision;
- the data user is satisfied that the enquirer and the subject of the requested personal data are the same person;
- the request is in writing;
- the requested information can be revealed without disclosing personal data of a third party;
- the request is accompanied by a fee fixed by the data user, such a fee not exceeding the statutory maximum as determined by the Act.

A request to know if a file is kept must be treated as a request for the appropriate personal data in that file.

In providing the requisite personal data, the data user must ensure that such data is meaningful; if codes are used in connection with the data for efficiency of storage or processing then the meanings of such codes must be supplied to the data subject with the data.

The data user must reply to a request for access within 40 days; there are special provisions, however, for examination marks. If the data user refuses to comply with the request then the data subject may apply to the Registrar, a High Court or a County Court. The Registrar has the power to compel compliance with the request. However, an organization has some defence against data subjects who are clearly misusing the right by making excessive, repeated requests; in such cases a court may support the data user's refusal to respond to the request.

7.2.9 Do data subjects have a right to correct their personal data held by a data user?

The right to correct or delete incorrect personal data is contained within the eight principles underlying the Act (see section 7.2.5). Having obtained access to the personal data (see section 7.2.8), a data subject can apply to a court or the Registrar to have any incorrect data amended or deleted. If the data originates from a third party, and the data subject considers such information to be inaccurate or misleading, then the data subject can ask for the inclusion of a statement to that effect with the stored data.

7.2.10 Can personal data be changed between the time a request for access is received and the data revealed to the data subject?

There are two conflicting requirements here:

- It would be disruptive to the data user if personal data had to be frozen (i.e. excluded from normal updating operations) for the period between initial receipt of request for access, and the handover of the information to the requestor.
- There exists the danger that the data user might deliberately sanitize personal data before opening it for access.

A data user is thus permitted to continue normal updating of data after a request for access has been received. However, the Registrar will need to be satisfied that any subsequent changes of data only relate to normal updating, which would have occurred whether or not the request had been received.

7.2.11 Does a data subject have a right of compensation if stored personal data is found to be incorrect?

A court may award compensation for loss, damage, or distress suffered by the data subject that resulted from incorrect data held by the data user (see section 7.2.9). A data subject may also make a complaint and a request for help from the Registrar in such circumstances. The data user can put forward a defence that:

- the damage was suffered before 11 May 1986;
or
- all reasonable care was taken to ensure the accuracy of the data;
or
- the data was supplied by a third party and that fact was recorded with the data, and a correction notice was included when requested by the data subject.

Note that the Act creates certain cases of compensation, but a data subject may also be able to pursue a civil claim for compensation under circumstances not covered by the Act.

7.2.12 What are the non-disclosure provisions of the Act?
Under the principles underlying the Act a data user has a responsibility to ensure the privacy of personal data. The responsibility extends beyond merely guaranteeing not purposely to disclose that data to an unauthorized third party. The data user must specify at registration (see section 7.2.15) all people who may receive the data, and then take all reasonable precautions to protect access from anybody not so specified, including hackers.

A data user must therefore ensure that data is neither deliberately nor accidentally disclosed to anyone other than persons specifically recorded in registration documents as receivers of the information (see section 7.2.15) unless:

- The data is exempt from non-disclosure provisions (see section 7.2.7).
- The disclosure is to the data subject or a person operating on behalf of the data subject.
- The data subject has consented to the disclosure.
- The disclosure is made by a data user or computer bureau to an employee or agent in order to allow them to perform their contractual obligations.
- The person making the disclosure had reasonable grounds for assuming that the abovementioned circumstances prevailed.
- The disclosure is required by a rule of law or ordered by a court.
- The disclosure is made for the purpose of obtaining legal advice.
- The disclosure is made in the course of legal proceedings in which the data user is a party or witness.

7.2.13 Does a data subject have a right to compensation for loss or unauthorized disclosure of personal data?
A data subject may claim compensation in the courts for any loss suffered as a result of:

- a loss of personal data;
- destruction of personal data without the authority of the data user or computer bureau;
- disclosure to a third party, or access gained by a third party, if such access is without the authority of the data user or computer bureau.

Such compensation cannot be claimed for damage suffered before 12 September 1984. Note also that authorized disclosure is not liable to compensation. If a data user deliberately discloses information, within the terms of the registration, then no offence has been committed. If the disclosure is outside the terms of the registration (e.g. to a person not specified within the registration) then the Registrar may take action against the data user, but the Act provides no grounds for compensation. The data subject may, nevertheless, be able to take civil action for (say) defamation.

The data user or computer bureau is not subject to damages if the destruction or disclosure of data was deliberate; in other circumstances they may claim that all reasonable precautions were taken to prevent such loss or disclosure.

If a court awards damages for unauthorized access, and there exists a substantial risk of further unauthorized disclosure, then the court may order that the data be erased.

7.2.14 If an organization is a data user or a computer bureau, what action should it take to conform to the Act?
The organization should take the following steps:

- nominate a senior member of management to be responsible for the organization's compliance with the Act (the security officer (see chapter 1) would appear to be the most appropriate person);
- determine whether the organization holds personal data that is not exempt from registration (see section 7.2.7);
- register the organization with the Data Protection Registrar if required to do so under the terms of the Act (see section 7.2.15);
- ensure that all proposed changes in the holding of personal data are notified to the manager as designated above.

If registration is required then the organization should:

- set up a system to ensure that all employees comply with the Act;
- set up a system to deal with requests for access to personal data (see section 7.2.19);
- ensure that all reasonable precautions are taken to avoid loss or unauthorized disclosure of personal data (see section 7.2.19);
- update registration according to proposed changes in processing or holding of personal data (see section 7.2.19);
- renew registration as required under the Act (see section 7.2.17).

7.2.15 How does an organization register under the terms of the Act?
The total process of registration can be very demanding for a large organization, because it will involve a complete survey of all personal data held or processed under the terms of the Act. This survey will require the personal data holdings to be identified, together with the sources of such data, the persons to whom such data is revealed, and the names of any countries to which the data may be transmitted. This survey could well lead to a consideration of the policy on holding and processing personal data (see section 7.2.19). The current policy should be reviewed in the light of the eight principles underlying the Act (see section 7.2.5). The Registrar may refuse registration if the proposed system of personal data holding and processing is considered to be contrary to those principles.

The formal process of registration involves the completion of application forms available from the Registrar. The forms comprise Part A, which must be completed by both data users and computer bureaux, and Part B, which is completed by data users.

Part A only requires basic information concerning the data user or computer bureau. Part B is much more demanding in terms of the information required:

- description of personal data to be held;
- description of the purposes for which the data is to be held;
- description of the intended sources of the information;
- description of the persons to whom the information on personal data may be conveyed;
- the names or description of any country, outside the UK, to which the data may be transferred;
- an address for requests for access (see section 7.2.19.5).

Completion of Part B can be on an omnibus basis, or a separate Part A and Part B may be completed for each major storage/processing system in the organization. The advantage of separate registrations for systems arises from the access provisions of the Act.

A request for access only refers to the systems described in Part B of the form. If an omnibus Part B is employed then, for each access request, the data user must examine every data store for the requisite personal data. If a separate Part B is employed, then the data user is only required to respond in terms of the information held on the system described in the particular registration form selected by the data subject. Of course data subjects can make multiple requests against each Part B registered by the user, but each such request will require an individual access fee. Multiple registrations will be accepted by the Registrar if the size and nature of the stored data clearly warrants such compartmentalization. However, the Registrar will query such registrations if they are seen to be a deliberate attempt to thwart legitimate requests for access from data subjects.

Part B is extremely complicated; the Registrar has categorized much of the required information, for example there are 70 standard purposes for which the data can be held. Applicants are permitted to use free text descriptions but are strongly advised to use the standard categories whenever possible. Use of free text descriptions is likely to come under much closer inspection by the Registrar and lead to delay, or worse.

7.2.16 What are the consequences of non-registration?

It is a criminal offence to hold non-exempt (see section 7.2.7) personal data, if the data user or computer bureau is not registered. The non-registration can result from a failure to register, a refusal of registration by the Registrar or a de-registration by the Registrar. A failure to register, or a failure to amend a registration (see section 7.2.17), when details of a current registration are no longer accurate due to changes of personal data holding or processing, is a very serious matter. Once an application for registration is made, the organization may deal with personal data as described in the application. Even if the Registrar subsequently seeks to refuse registration (see section 7.2.17), or to de-register (see section 7.2.17) the organization, there is a period during which processing and storage of the personal data may continue.

7.2.17 What formal action is required after registration?

If the registration is accepted by the Registrar then the organization may continue to operate in the manner described by the registration until:

- a renewal of registration is required;
- changes in the holding or processing of personal data, or other relevant organizational details (e.g. address, registered personal,

etc.) such that the details of the registration are no longer accurate;

- the Registrar indicates some concern with the activities of the organization by informal approaches, an enforcement notice, or a de-registration notice.

Normally registration is for a period of three years. A reminder for re-registration will be sent by the Registrar; at renewal of registration all proposed changes in the registration details must be reported. One of the principles of the Act is that data concerning individuals should be maintained no longer than is necessary for their stated purposes; renewal of registration presents a good opportunity to review data holdings and delete unnecessary personal data.

It is an offence to fail to keep the registration up-to-date. Changes may be proposed in the details of data holdings, sources of data, intended destinations of data, etc. Also changes in the organization, relevant to the registration (e.g. names of partners) should be reported in the form of an amendment to registration.

The Registrar can take action if an organization is in breach of the rules. In addition to informal contacts, which attempt to rectify problems, the Registrar has the power to issue enforcement, de-registration, and transfer prohibition notices. The organization will have specified times to respond to such formal notices, and also an opportunity to appeal against the Registrar's rulings. Nevertheless failure to act in accordance with the Registrar's advice or notices could lead to enforced changes in the registration, or in an extreme case to the withdrawal of registration. Any such de-registration could have a serious, even catastrophic, impact upon the organization's activities, since the holding and processing of personal data would have to cease upon the enforcement of the de-registration notice.

7.2.18 What are the managerial implications of the Act?
The Act creates a situation in which an organization can be subjected to criminal charges, heavy claims for compensation, and a withdrawal of the right to hold and process data essential for the operation of the organization. Moreover these penalties relate to activities which, in the past, were not subject to legislation.

Compliance with the Act clearly requires more than the completion of a bureaucratic form. Management must set up infrastructures and procedures to ensure that all employees are aware of, and conform to, the Act. Management must also make available the resources necessary to ensure that such infrastructures and procedures are initiated and operated continually and effectively. The necessary managerial actions are as follows:

- appoint a senior member of management to have full responsibility for all aspects concerned with the Act: the security officer would appear to be appropriate nominee in many cases (see chapter 1);
- review the organization's policy in regard to personal data (see section 7.2.19);
- develop the organization's policy with respect to the implementation of the Act (see section 7.2.19);
- review the organization's data security stance (see chapter 1);
- review personnel procedures (see section 7.5.1);
- set up a review and reporting mechanism to ensure continuous and continual compliance with the Act.

7.2.19 What review should be conducted on the policy concerning personal data?

Clearly one of the effects of the Act is to change the status of personal data from an asset to a liability. There is a common human tendency to collect and maintain information, because it might at some future time be useful. This attitude is quite contrary to the principles underlying the Act (see section 7.2.5). The data collected and held should be only that which is required for specified purposes, and such data should be held for no longer than is strictly necessary for its stated purposes. Great care should be taken with the collection of data, so that all data sources are identified, and the data is labelled as originating from that source. Care must be taken that errors do not occur when data is input into storage or processed. The data must be stored so that it is safe from unauthorized disclosure, but readily available when a request for access is received. Management may therefore decide to review its policy on personal data. Such a policy might include statements on:

- the personal data that is to be held by the organization (see section 7.2.19.1);
- handling of personal data (see section 7.2.19.2);
- level of management who are authorized to initiate new collections of personal data (see section 7.2.19.3);
- the use of personal computers to store and process personal data (see section 7.2.19.4);
- arrangements for dealing with requests for access to personal data from appropriate data subjects (see section 7.2.19.5);
- disclosure of personal data;
- forwarding personal data to other countries;
- data protection awareness programs (see section 7.5.2);
- security of personal data (see section 7.2.19.8);
- personnel policies (see section 7.5.1);

- contact with the Registrar (see section 7.2.19.9);
- review and reporting (see section 7.2.19.10).

Management may also decide that such a policy should be a formal statement of the organization and widely distributed. The existence of such a policy document would assist the organization to prove that it had taken reasonable precautions against contravention of the Act, in cases of complaint to the Registrar or court actions.

7.2.19.1 What should be included in the policy statement on the personal data held and processed by the organization?
It is clearly important that holdings of personal data should not exceed that required for the functioning of the organization, nor should such data be held longer than necessary for its purposes. To act otherwise both conflicts with the principles underlying the Act (see section 7.2.5) and could be an unnecessary liability to the organization. For example, if data may be exempt if it is pruned down to the level necessary for payroll or mailing lists (see section 7.2.7.1).

If an excessive amount of data is held then it will incur an overhead in terms of ensuring its accuracy, checking on the sources of such data, ensuring the security of the data, and providing access to it, while guarding against unauthorized disclosure, etc.

A policy statement on the personal data that may be held by the organization, including the amount of detail associated with such data, can thus ensure that the overheads are kept to a minimum. The policy statement could also indicate under which circumstances personal data should be held only on manual files. Although a large-scale conversion, from computer to manual files, is probably an over-reaction to the Act there may well be a case for ruling that a limited amount of highly sensitive data is stored only on manual files.

7.2.19.2 What policy statements are appropriate to the handling of personal data?
Management is required to ensure that personal data is:

- only obtained from registered sources;
- labelled with the name of any originating third party;
- not contaminated with errors introduced during internal handling or processing;
- provided to appropriate data subjects in a form that is readily intelligible;
- kept secure from unauthorized disclosure;
- not expanded with additional details inconsistent with the registration form;

- not supplied to overseas countries other than those included in the registration.

Guidance should therefore be given to line management on all these topics. Although computer staff will be primarily concerned, it must be recognized that the handling of waste computer printouts, responding to telephone enquiries by terminal operators, setting up personal computer files, etc. are activities that can have a major impact on the handling of personal data.

7.2.19.3 What policy statements are appropriate to the level of management authorized to initiate new collections of personal data?

Management must be in a position to prove that any employee who develops a computer file of personal data in contravention of the Act has disobeyed a clear directive of management. If new personal data files are essential then they must have management approval, and cause the initiation of an amendment to registration. A policy statement is therefore required on the level of management which may initiate a request for an amendment to holdings of personal data, changes of sources, persons to whom disclosure may be made, etc. The statement should also make clear that no such changes to personal data may be implemented until explicit approval has been obtained from the appropriate member of senior management.

7.2.19.4 What statements on personal computers should be included in the policy statement?

Personal computers are likely to be senior management's Achilles Heel in terms of the Act. If an ambitious salesman buys a personal computer and develops a detailed computer file on customers then it is likely that serious breaches of the Act will eventuate. Line management have generally been keen to switch their computer files from the computer centre to personal computers. If the personal computer is on-line to corporate data, then personal data files may be downloaded onto personal computers, expanded with additional details, disclosed through lax security, etc.

The safest policy would be to state that personal computers may normally only be used to view personal data. Personal data should not be downloaded to floppy diskettes, printed on local printers, etc. Given a good access control system (see chapter 3) and a log-on screen reminding users of the restrictions on use of personal data, then the organization would be seen to be taking all reasonable precautions in this regard.

A particular concern with personal computers is that these devices are often used as standalone word processors, and as such come within a grey area of exemption (see section 7.2.7.3). Management could arrange for such word processing packages to be enhanced with a program that provides guidance on the restrictions of use of word processors in relation to personal data.

7.2.19.5 What statements on access provisions should be included in the policy statement?

Management may take any position between a very free approach to access provisions and one that seeks only to provide the minimum degree of access consistent with the legislative requirements of the Act (see section 7.2.8).

The free access approach could well be a policy that all personal data held by the organization would be printed and forwarded to the appropriate data subjects automatically and at appropriate intervals; the frequency of such distribution would be related to the volatility of the data. Thus data held by personnel departments might be sent to employees every twelve months, with a request that the personnel department be informed of any inaccuracies within the data.

At the other extreme, management may decide not to encourage access and charge the highest fee permitted. The access requests would be subject to a stringent examination of the user's identity and delayed up to the 40-day maximum. The data might be supplied in a legally intelligible, but not user-friendly, format.

Whichever approach is adopted it is important that the policy statement defines:

- which members of staff are authorized to respond to access requests;
- the actions to be taken by any other member of staff if they receive a request for access;
- identity checks to be employed before access to data is provided;
- checks to be performed to determine if data is exempt from access provisions (see section 7.2.7);
- fee to be charged for access;
- maximum time interval for responding to a request;
- checks to be performed to ensure that no data referring to a third party is revealed;
- format of data supplied, meanings assigned to codes, etc.;
- actions to be taken when the data subject requests that purported incorrect data be rectified;
- response to requests from persons other than the data subject (see section 7.2.12);
- action to be taken when it apears that access requests are deliberately vexatious (e.g. specification of frequency of requests

which is considered by management to be excessive, upward reporting of such requests, etc.).

In general the demand for access to personal data is growing but it is not currently believed to be a major problem for organizations. It is possible, however, that this situation will change after 1992 because data protection is taken far more seriously in Europe. In 1988 the Registrar reported that complaints received from the public had risen, and were running at a rate in excess of 1000 per year.

7.2.19.6 What matters concerning disclosure of data should be included in the policy statement?

Management must ensure that employees do not disclose personal data to persons other than those listed in the registration as permitted receivers of particular items of personal data. The policy of restricting the number of staff authorized to deal with access requests (see section 7.2.8) will also serve to discourage unauthorized disclosure. The policy statements apposite to disclosure should include:

- which members of staff are authorized to make such disclosures;
- checks to be performed to ensure that requests are consistent with registration details: it may be possible to provide computer assistance for this purpose (e.g. some means of accessing details of authorized receivers of particular data files);
- records to be kept of all such disclosures (see section 7.2.12);
- reporting of instances where disclosure was refused;
- actions to be taken when a request emanates from overseas (see section 7.2.19.7);
- seeking permission from data subjects to reveal their stored personal data for specified purposes (e.g. release of curriculum vitae of consulting staff to clients).

7.2.19.7 What policy statements are required in terms of export of personal data overseas?

Management must ensure that requests for details of personal data emanating from overseas receive careful handling, even if such requests originate from persons normally authorized to receive the data. Moreover the inclusion of personal data in printed form, as part of (say) a marketing exercise providing curriculum vitae of consulting staff, could well be in breach of the Act if the printed data were derived from a computer file. Policy statements in this instance should deal with:

- inclusion of personal data in printed material routinely sent overseas;

- names of staff authorized to send personal data overseas;
- checks to be performed to ensure that personal data sent overseas is consistent with registration details (see section 7.2.15);
- records to be kept of all such disclosures.

7.2.19.8 What should management specify in terms of security of personal data?

It is not sufficient to guard against only the deliberate disclosure of personal data; management also has a responsibility to guard against accidental disclosures, and attempts by hackers to break into the computer system. The general data security policy of the organization (see chapter 1) may also contain a section on the procedures to safeguard any personal data files that are particularly sensitive, e.g. encryption of computer files relating to patient diagnoses. The use of security logs and audit trails (see chapter 1) may prove to be of particular benefit in relation to personal data transactions. If the organization can provide an automatic record of all transactions, accesses, etc. relating to a data item, then it will be in a strong position if faced with accusations of unauthorized disclosures, etc.

In formulating the policy on security for personal data, it must be recognized that the precautions taken need to do more than satisfy top management. A situation may arise in a court of law in which a case for compensation in respect of unauthorized disclosure will hinge on the resources expended in securing the data. The precautions taken may be judged against the best that can be achieved with modern technology, not merely with those commonly employed in other organizations.

7.2.19.9 What policy statements are appropriate in relation to the contact with the Registrar?

It would be wise to ensure that all correspondence and other contacts with the Registrar are conducted by an appointed member of management, who is fully conversant with the Act, the organization's registration details, and the handling of personal data. This approach will ensure that senior management is immediately and fully informed of any concerns expressed by the Registrar in relation to the organization's compliance with the Act. Moreover it will ensure that the information provided to the Registrar is accurate, timely, and sufficient for his purposes.

7.2.19.10 What should management specify in terms of review and reporting procedures?

This aspect of policy should include statements on:

- recording of all transactions, accesses, and disclosures of personal data (see sections 7.2.8 and 7.2.12);
- reporting on all proposed changes in the handling and storage of personal data (see section 7.2.15);
- recording and reporting of requests and correspondence with data subjects;
- reporting on all contacts with the Registrar;
- reporting on all significant security events relating to personal data (e.g. hacking attempts);
- regular reviews of personal data holding and processing to ensure accurate information for registration renewals.

7.3 Legal Protection of Information Assets

7.3.1 Is there any legal protection against loss of information assets?
The phrase 'loss of information assets' needs to be more closely defined before this question can be answered; it could imply:

- confidential information that is copied and shown to an unauthorized person (see section 7.3.2);
- information that is maliciously erased (see section 7.3.4);
- information that is maliciously altered (see section 7.3.4);
- information representing a considerable level of effort or expertise that is exploited by someone else (see sections 7.3.5 and 7.3.6);
- information that is of commercial value to an organization which is known to an employee or ex-employee and used by that employee for his or her own benefit, or the benefit of his or her new employer (see section 7.5.5).

7.3.2 Is there a legal right to confidentiality?
No, there is no legal right to confidentiality. If a firm makes a decision to change its marketing plans, and a visitor to the firm spots that information on a VDU, and reports it to a rival company, then no crime has been committed. The firm has no legal redress unless the visitor has broken some contractual agreement with the firm not to reveal such information.

Information cannot be stolen because theft implies an intention to deprive the owner permanently of the asset; in the case of information the owner retains the original information. In a classic case a student copied a set of examination papers, leaving the original copy in place: it was ruled that no theft had been committed. In some instances, however, it is possible that the process of removing the information may itself involve a criminal act. (see section 7.3.3). The act of copying information may, however, be a breach of copyright.

7.3.3 Is there any illegality in gaining unauthorized information?

The act of removing information may involve illegality only in some associated sense. If the information is contained on storage material (e.g. paper or magnetic disk) then there is an act of theft of that material. If some electrical device is used (e.g. a computer or a photocopier) then a theft of electricity may be involved. If the act of removing the information, or inserting some eavesdropping device, involves unauthorized entry into premises then it can be dealt with as trespass or even burglary. Also the use of such an eavesdropping device may contravene the UK *Wireless Telegraph Acts*, or involve illegal interference with telephone lines.

Although trespass into premises is recognized, under current legislation there appears to be no illegal act involved in an unauthorized person accessing a computer; there has been discussion of the question of whether the act of entering someone else's password can be construed as forgery – this would appear not to be the case. Some future specific computer-related legislation may clarify this issue.

Any attempt to gain information by inducing an employee to reveal it may lead to legal action, since an inducement to breach of contract is involved; if payment were made to the employee then an act of bribery could be claimed.

If more than one person were involved in such illegal acts, as described above, then it could result in a charge of conspiracy.

7.3.4 Is it illegal to erase or alter data?

The malicious erasure of data could have extremely serious consequences for an organization; such acts may involve little more than the entry of a few commands at a computer terminal, or wiping a powerful magnet across backup tapes or disks. Legal redress may be obtained under common law since such acts involve wrongful interference with goods.

If a program is maliciously altered (e.g. to write rude messages) then again the wrongful interference with goods may be invoked. If the purpose of the additional information is for more serious criminal purposes (e.g. to alter a financial transaction in favour of the offender) then the offender may be charged with theft or obtaining property by deception.

A charge of criminal damage may also be brought in the case of malicious damage to data. If more than one person were involved in such illegal acts as described above then it could result in a charge of conspiracy.

7.3.5 Is it possible to protect information with patents?

A patent is used to protect an invention, which must be entirely

311

novel. Such patents must be registered under the *Patents Act*; the application will be subject to examination on its claim of originality and can be challenged. Although computer hardware is frequently the subject of patent it is, in general, not possible to register a patent for 'a program for a computer' or 'the presentation of information'. Clearly some information (e.g. the design of a hardware system) can be protected by a patent inasmuch as the patent represents a monopoly to exploit the invention. In general, however, the mass of information held by an organization could not be protected with a patent. In some cases, however, copyright protection may be available (see section 7.3.6).

7.3.6 Can information be given legal protection with copyright?

In the UK there is one Act covering copyright, the *Copyright, Designs and Patents Act, 1988* (the CDPA). Copyright protection differs from that offered by patent (see section 7.3.5) in two important respects. First, eligibility for copyright does not demand the criterion of invention, and second, there is no requirement to register copyright. Provided that the information is in one of the forms recognized for copyright (see section 7.3.7) then the person claiming copyright need only prove that it is his or her own work and that it represented a sufficient degree of labour, skill, or judgement. Computer software is now protected by copyright (see section 7.3.7), and a wide range of material that may be regarded as the information asset of an organization may be protected by copyright.

The protection afforded does not, of course, relate to all malicious acts that can have an impact upon data; the erasure of a computer file containing copyright material would not be covered. Copyright only endows the owner of the copyright with legal redress against specified infringements of copyright (see section 7.3.12).

7.3.7 What information assets can be copyrighted?

The categories of material covered by the CDPA are:

- literary works,
- dramatic works,
- musical works,
- artistic works,
- sound recordings, cinematograph films (including video films), and radio and sound broadcasts.

The CDPA rules that computer programs are literary works, and are protected since they are recorded in writing or otherwise. Writing includes any form of notation or code, no matter what medium it is recorded on. This includes magnetic media.

The term 'literary works' covers virtually any material that is written in words or figures, or recorded in some tangible form that can be translated into words or figures. It does not imply any criterion of literary merit. The material can be copyrighted if it is an independent creation of an author, and not merely copied, with or without minor modifications, from some other source. List of names beginning with the same initial pair of letters, copied from a telephone directory could not be copyrighted. On the other hand a market researcher who, as a result of a survey conducted or commissioned by the researcher, produces a list of names of householders with given hobbies could claim copyright for the list since it was an independent creation that required a sufficient degree of labour, skill, or judgement.

'Artistic works' covers plans, drawings, photographs, etc. As with literary works, the term does not imply a criterion of artistic merit. The detailed flowchart produced by a systems analyst could be protected by copyright, as could screen displays.

It is clear that computer programs, internal reports, marketing plans, mailing lists, databases, etc. can be protected by copyright, whether in printed form or stored on the computer. The material must, however, be the independent creation of the person claiming copyright, or an independent creation commissioned by that person (see section 7.3.10). If the material has been obtained from other sources, including printed material, then, unless specific approval for copying has been obtained from the owner of the copyright, an infringement of copyright has been perpetrated (see section 7.3.12).

7.3.8 *What action is necessary to claim copyright?*
Unlike patents (see section 7.3.5), no specific action is required to register copyright. The right to copyright exists as soon as the author has produced the work. If some other person later infringes the copyright then the author normally has some legal redress (see section 7.3.12). Claims that the infringer was ignorant of the existence of the copyright would not, in themselves, be regarded as an effective defence.

However, it may be extremely difficult for a plaintiff in a copyright infringement action to prove the copyright, unless care is taken to preserve all records and to publicize the existence of the copyright. It is important to make a formal notification of copyright by appending the copyright sign ©, the proprietary of the copyright and the date of publication (e.g. © B. Pascal 1988). This is particularly important if protection of copyright is sought abroad under the reciprocal arrangements that exist with certain other countries under the Berne Convention and the Universal Copyright Convention (UCC). In the case of printed material this notice of copyright should be printed on the first page of a publication or on the back of a title page.

The recording of copyright on software, or material in machine-readable form is somewhat more complex (see section 7.3.9).

7.3.9 What precautions need to be taken in claiming copyright for software or other machine readable data?

The question of copyright for computer software is now one of some complexity (see section 7.3.7), and considerable care needs to be taken to inform others of the existence of the claim to copyright. The US Copyright Office has issued guidelines for possible locations of copyright notice:

- a copyright notice (© name date) embodied within the material so that it is printed, near the title or at the end of the work, on all printouts;
- a copyright notice that is displayed at the user's terminal upon log-on;
- a copyright notice that is continually displayed at the user's terminal during usage of the material;
- a copyright notice printed on a label and permanently affixed to the container of the material (e.g. box, cartridge, cassette, disk, etc.).

In addition the owner of the copyright should retain all documentation produced in the development of software which could help to prove that the owner had indeed undertaken the development process and not merely copied the software. It is also suggested that the owner may include fingerprints in the code. Such fingerprints provably serve no useful purpose, (e.g. sections of code that are never accessed) but their existence in an alleged infringer's software would serve to indicate that the software had been copied and not developed independently.

7.3.10 Who owns copyright?

Copyright normally resides with the author of the material unless it was produced under the terms of employment. An employee will not therefore hold copyright of material developed in the normal course of duty to an employer, unless the contract of employment specifically states the contrary. If the work is commissioned then the ownership of the copyright is decided according to the contractual terms of the commission. Companies employing software houses or contract programmers should ensure that the contract specifically assigns to the company the copyright of any programs produced, and that the programmer has the right to assign the code; i.e. the copyright does not belong to a third party (see section 7.3.17). In the case of software in which an author co-operates with a skilled programmer, the copyright may either be shared or assigned to the author alone; the circumstances would depend on the contractual arrangements between the programmer and the author and, if no such contractual arrangements existed, on the contribution of the programmer. If the programmer merely coded the program according to direct instructions then it is likely that it could be claimed that the programmer did not contribute a sufficient degree of independent creation to justify a share of authorship. Where software is 'computer-generated' (i.e. produced by another program, so that there is no obvious human author), copyright is owned by the person who made the arrangements for the software to be produced.

Copyright may also be assigned to another party by a contractual arrangement.

7.3.11 How long is the copyright restriction valid?

Copyright lasts for 50 years from the date of first publication, or other disclosure of the work, or 50 years from the death of the author (last surviving author if there were more than one), whichever is the later. The last date of protection is 31 December of the appropriate year. This would appear to be an adequate period for most computer-based data. If the work is computer-generated, copyright lasts until the end of the 50th year after it is created.

7.3.12 What degree of protection is provided by copyright?

A copyright owner has legal redress against anyone who undertakes one of the following actions without the licence of the copyright owner:

- reproduction of the work in any form;
- publication of the work;
- performing the work in public;
- broadcasting the work;
- transmission of the work to subscribers of a cable program;
- adaptation of the work;
- in relation to an adaptation of the work, any of the acts specified above.

In the particular case of computer material, infringement would comprise:

- making unauthorized copies of the work (this includes copying it from a disk into RAM for the purpose of running the program; purchasers of software will be licensed to do this, but someone

315

who borrows the software will not be unless the licence says so);
- adapting the material;
- reproducing or otherwise using all or part of the material;
- publishing or broadcasting the material (e.g. transmitting by teletext or viewdata systems as telesoftware);
- selling or letting the material for hire, or offering to do so;
- importation of infringing material without authorization.

There are some exceptions to these rules of infringement (see section 7.3.13).

The term 'adaptation' includes translation, which is defined to include 'in relation to a computer program, a version of the program in which it is converted into or out of a computer language or code, or into a different computer language or code'. Thus if a source code program is compiled into a machine code version then an act of adaption has taken place, and hence an infringement of copyright. This does not apply if the translation occurs only incidentally in the course of running the program (e.g. an interpreter translating source code at run-time).

If an adaptation is made to copyright material with the permission of the copyright owner, and a sufficient degree of input from the adaptor is put into the process, then a new copyright for the adapted material could be claimed by the adaptor. Thus an upgrade of a program to include new facilities could justify a new copyright; but merely converting it from one language to another, or re-arranging a few lines of code, would not.

The question of the degree to which it is claimed that new software is adapted from previous copyrighted software is a subject of active debate in the legal field. At the time of writing there is considerable confusion in the software market (see section 7.3.18).

7.3.13 What defence may be offered against a charge of infringement of copyright?

It may be possible to claim that some infringements of copyright are justified on the basis that they are necessary for public good. In the case of printed material and software such arguments may apply in the case of:

- use of the material in bona fide research or private study;
- use in the course of reporting for the press, television, etc.;
- use for bona fide criticism or review;
- use in legal proceedings or the reporting of such proceedings.

Ignorance of the existence of the claim to copyright is not a defence, even though there is no register that the defendant could access to determine the claim for copyright. However, damages will not be awarded if the defendant did not know, and had no reason to believe, that the work was copyright, though other remedies are still available.

In general a defendant against whom an action is taken may leave it to the plaintiff to prove the claim for copyright. This may be difficult for a plaintiff who took insufficient care in making the claim public knowledge, and failed to maintain sufficient records of the development of the material.

7.3.14 What is the position of a purchaser of software in terms of copyright infringement?
A purchaser of software does not normally obtain copyright ownership of the software, except in the case that the software was specifically commissioned, and the copyright assigned by the authors to the other party (see section 7.3.10). Purchase of the software normally involves a licence for the buyer to use the software under conditions specified by the vendor. Such a licence may allow the purchaser the rights to operate the software on one or more machines, make copies for backup purposes, make adaptations to the software provided that the use of such adaptations do not extend beyond the customer's needs, etc.

7.3.15 What are the penalties for infringement of copyright?
Infringement of software is a criminal offence if such infringement is knowingly committed by the infringer. The copyright owner is likely to pursue civil action, however, if the outcome has a reasonable chance of being profitable.

The civil action can be very expensive for the defendant if infringement is proved. The copyright owner can claim the full market value for every pirated copy sold, less the cost of producing such copies, that would have been incurred by the copyright owner. Thus a defendant who sold a substantial number of pirated software packages at a very low price could be faced with a claim for damages based on the same number of packages at the much higher price normally charged by the copyright owner.

7.3.16 Does copyright protection extend overseas and vice versa?
There are two international conventions that extend copyright protection overseas and vice versa – the Berne Convention and the Universal Copyright Convention. Under these conventions copyright protection is extended to all territories that are signatories to them. The protection provided within each country depends upon the copyright laws of that country, and the conventions establish that the

nationals of member states have reciprocal rights to those of the nationals of the particular country.

7.3.17 How can an organization ensure that it is not infringing the copyright of others?
It is probably more difficult to guard against infringement of other copyrights than it is to safeguard one's own copyright. The main sources of danger are:

- infringement of software copyright;
- employees who bring with them material from a previous employment;
- independent contractors who use material developed for a previous employer, and to whom copyright was assigned.

Infringement of software copyright can arise from the importation of pirated software, taking copies of software and executing it on machines beyond the licence agreement, and illegal adaptations of software.

In the case of machines operated by the computer centre, it is important to undertake regular audits of software, and maintain records of all licence agreements, even after the software is removed from the machines. The audits and cross-checks with licence agreements can ensure that no infringements occur, or at least go unchecked. If it is found that licence agreements have been unwittingly broken, then the software supplier should be contacted and agreement on some form of recompense discussed.

The problem is, of course, much more difficult in the case of personal computer software, where pirated diskettes may lie around in employees' desks. The organization should ensure that all employees are aware of the necessity to conform to licence agreements, and of not purchasing pirated software. This information could be included in contracts of employment, displayed on notice boards, etc. In addition, some form of check on all personal computer software purchases should be implemented. There should be a requirement for internal requests for purchase to be accompanied with a statement that the requester agrees to abide with software licence agreements, and that the software in question is from a bona fide supplier.

The use of copyright material in relation to contractors may be particularly difficult to control. Contracts of employment or for services should deal with this matter, explicitly warning that copyright is not to be infringed. In addition, the authors of material to which the organization intends to claim copyright should sign a statement to the effect that it is their independent creation, and to the best of their knowledge does not infringe the copyright of others or,

318

if it was produced by a third party, that the authors have been granted the right to exploit the software.

7.3.18 Is there any difference between the copyright for works on paper and computer software?

The most significant difference between the copyright of works on paper and of computer software arises from the interpretation of 'adaptation', which appears to have a more restricted meaning when applied to works on paper than it has to computer programs.

The 'look and feel' criterion has been invoked in computer software copyright cases in the USA. If the gap between the protection afforded to works on paper and computer programs widens then it will give rise to another area of controversy. At what stage in development does a computer program cease to be an ordinary literary work, and become a computer program? In the initial stages a program exists only as a specification which could not be executed on a machine. It then goes through a succession of design stages until the final working program emerges. At what point in this metamorphosis does the work become a computer program, and enjoy enhanced copyright protection?

7.3.19 Does an author have 'moral' rights in law?

The *Copyright, Designs and Patents Act, 1988* introduced the concept of an author's moral rights into English law. These rights are:

- the right to be identified as the author;
- the right to object to derogatory treatment of the work;
- the right not to have a work falsely attributed to him or her as author.

The first two of these rights do not apply to computer programs, but all three apply to other works such as manuals. Unlike copyright, moral rights cannot be assigned to another person. The first two of these rights last as long as the copyright; the third ends 20 years after the author's death.

7.3.20 When may software be resold?

If the buyer of a piece of software has the right to make a copy or make adaptations of it, he is entitled to pass on those rights to any other person with the software. This right comes either from the licence contract with the copyright owner, or through some rule of law. This right is often restricted by the terms of the software licence. If the owner retains a copy of the software, that copy becomes an infringing copy.

7.3.21 Can software be rented?

The *Copyright, Designs and Patents Act, 1988* has changed the law on software rental. Rental of computer programs is now a breach of copyright. However, regulations may be made under the Act for the compulsory licensing of all or certain classes of software unless the copyright owners have already set up a licensing scheme.

7.3.22 What is the position of articles designed to break copy protection?

Any person who makes, imports, sells, hires, or offers for sale or hire an article that is designed to circumvent a method of copy protection infringes the copyright in any work that employs that method of copy protection. The article must be specifically designed or adapted to circumvent that protection, and the defendant must know or have reason to believe that it will be used for that purpose. The same applies to publishing information that will help break a copy protection method.

7.4 Computer Crime

7.4.1 What constitutes computer crime?

This is an area of some confusion, some actions such as hacking which are clearly unethical and undesirable do not as yet constitute a crime. Donn B. Parker has defined:

- computer crime: illegal computer abuse implying the direct involvement of computers in a crime (also see below);
- computer-related crime: a broader term covering any illegal act for which knowledge of computer technology is essential for successful perpetration;
- computer abuse: any intentional act involving a computer and one or more perpetrators which made, or could have made, gain, and one or more victims suffered, or could have suffered, loss.

The UK Audit Commission defined:

- computer fraud: any fraudulent behaviour connected with computerization by which someone intends to gain dishonest advantage.

A report to the US Department of Justice defined:

- computer crime: any crime where the perpetrator has to have a technical knowledge of computers to engage in crime.

7.4.2 Is there any evidence that computer crime has reached serious proportions?
If one includes credit card frauds with computer crime, on the basis that computers are extensively used in the administration of such systems, then it is not difficult to get figures rising to hundreds of million of pounds sterling as annual losses. Using the definitions of computer crime given above, however, the figures become less astronomical. Statistics published in relation to computer crime must be treated with extreme care. They may be analysed and manipulated to provide answers to specific questions, such as 'What is the average loss due to computer crime?', etc., but in general the quantity and quality of available statistics may be insufficient for this purpose.

It must be noted that computer crime statistics cover only reported, detected incidents. It is likely that there is a considerable bias in such statistics; organizations may well be more prepared to report one type of crime than another, some incidents may be more readily detectable than others, and there are no statistics on undetected or unreported crimes. Some of the conclusions that have been drawn from such statistics may not, therefore, be a good basis for management security policy. For example, many reports tend towards the view that 'few of these frauds required sophisticated manipulation of computer procedures but rather took advantage of weaknesses in fairly basic control procedures' (*The Computer Law and Security Report*, vol. 2, no. 6 (March–April 1987), p. 12). Indeed, it would appear that the majority of computer crimes involve no more than the fraudulent manipulations of source documents before their input into a computer system. However, while it is certainly true that the majority of recorded, detected cases involves employees exploiting control loopholes, it must be recognized that middle management has some experience, developed over many years, of clerical-level employees committing conventional frauds by using loopholes in accounting control procedures. If sophisticated computer manipulation is employed for fraudulent purposes, then the perpetrators are likely to have considerably more skill in concealing their frauds; computer transaction data is fundamentally transitory, and management will have virtually no experience in detecting such crimes.

Similarly there is likely to be a high degree of bias in reporting computer crime. Hackers have gained overkill publicity for their exploits: it is therefore not unreasonable for management to tend to play down fears on computer crime. In these circumstances one might well expect that management would be more prepared to report those computer crimes that were similar to pre-computer era frauds. On the other hand there could be a marked reluctance to report crimes which could have an impact upon the public confidence in an organization. Banks would not be keen to give publicity to computer frauds which might reflect badly on their ability to safeguard customers' funds, government agencies would be sensitive to publicity of hacker exploits into national defence computers, etc.

In general one would have to admit that hard evidence gleaned from statistics does not point to a major computer crime wave, particularly of the ultra-sophisticated category. However, it is suggested that the statistical evidence available does not permit a high degree of extrapolation for future actions, and it may not form a good basis for management decision-making.

7.4.3 Does computer crime have potentially serious consequences for management?

There is no doubt that computer crime, in one form or another, could potentially have catastrophic consequences for some organizations. The term 'societal vulnerability' has been coined to cover the possibility of loss, injury, or the denial of human rights to a significant segment of the population, as well as potential weakening of social stability or risk to national sovereignty, as a result of dependence on computer-based technology.

A highly organized, well-trained terrorist group, could wreak havoc in a society where aircraft, chemical plants, nuclear power stations, missiles, etc. were subject to computer control, and inadequate attention were paid to computer security. Attack on computer systems by terrorist groups (e.g. CLODO) have been reported in France and Italy.

In the financial sector money flows through electronic funds transfer systems, and stock-markets are linked by massive communication networks and operated on a 24-hour basis. False information, or even significant disruption of processing/communication systems, could cause major problems and possibly stock-market fluctuations. Such actions could also bring rich rewards to organized crime, which would have the finance, organization, and expertise to undertake such coups.

The well-publicized activities of the Chaos Club, whose members penetrate computer networks internationally, have indicated the problems that management have to face when they are under attack by highly skilled hackers.

7.4.4 How does management assess its dangers from computer crime?

This is a classic risk analysis exercise (see chapter 2). The threats from criminals will tend to vary from organization to organization, but included are:

- massive one-off frauds in banking networks;

- persistent salami-type frauds in social security offices;
- manipulation of inventory figures in distributor's computers;
- terrorist attack on government computers or readily identified 'establishment' organizations, including the activities of some fringe groups such as the Animal Liberation Front (see chapter 3);
- stealing confidential information from large commercial organizations (e.g. oil companies);
- holding the system to ransom by threatening to destroy data of organizations which depend upon customer confidence (e.g. threats on customer data in banks);
- ransom threats that software has been corrupted by the introduction of time bombs in life-dependent computer systems (e.g. air traffic control, radiotherapy control systems);
- ransom threats to publicize the information that viruses have been injected in the products of software houses;
- threats to disrupt communication systems at critical times (e.g. on-line gambling systems, stock market systems).

Having estimated the threats, then the vulnerabilities of the system must be considered, security systems postulated, costed, and their effectiveness estimated, etc.

7.4.5 Are there any side effects of computer crime?

The side effects of computer crime may prove to be more damaging than the crime itself. The direct costs will be staff time spent in investigations, police reporting, and court appearances. If civil proceedings are contemplated, the legal costs, travel expenses for witnesses, etc. are likely to be daunting, particularly if the case involves the use of an international communications network. If the crime reveals a serious weakness in security procedures, then the cost of additional security measures, software modifications, etc. may well cause budgetary problems. The indirect costs will arise from an impact on staff morale produced by internal or police investigations.

With the current state of the law, an organization operating a computer system may appear to be in a uniquely unenviable position. If a hacker gains access to the organization's computer system it may prove to be impossible to obtain any legal redress in the criminal or civil court (see section 7.4.6). However, the organization may, as a direct result of the attack, find itself as defendant in a civil action. For example, if the hacker gains access to a file of personal data, the UK *Data Protection Act* allows the appropriate data subject to sue the organization for unauthorized disclosure of personal data (see section 7.2.12).

7.4.6 Does the law offer protection against computer crime?
The law offers protection against conventional wrongdoers. Some, but by no means all, computer crimes and computer abuse may involve transgression of criminal codes, or could be dealt with by civil action (see section 7.3.3). The UK *Data Protection Act* (see section 7.2.4) renders misuse of computer-stored or processed personal data a criminal offence, while the *Copyright (Computer Software) Amendment Act* (see section 7.3.7) extends the protection of copyright from literary works to computer software.

The contentious area of hacking has been subjected to considerable debate, and attempts have been made to prosecute hackers with existing laws. However, it would appear that at present there is no certainty that hacking or non-malicious misuse of computers (e.g. to play games) is a criminal offence.

A threat allied to hacking is electronic eavesdropping. It has been demonstrated that relatively unsophisticated electronic equipment can pick up and display the data appearing on VDUs in nearby buildings (see chapter 3). Such eavesdropping would not appear to be an offence under existing legislation.

Some computer frauds may escape prosecution because the current English fraud laws would seem to require a human mind to be deceived, if the fraud is based upon deception. Recently it was held that deception in a legal sense had not occurred when a false Value Added Tax return was made directly to the tax office using a tele-communication system to the revenue computer.

It would appear that organizations should use internal discipline regulations (e.g. for employees, students, etc.) or where possible contractual arrangements (e.g. for independent contractors, clients with access to computer systems, etc.) to provide for some redress against offending, identifiable hackers or misusers of computer facilities. This situation may well change in the immediate future; there is active debate throughout the world on legislation to cover computer crime. Unfortunately when, and if, legislation is passed it is likely to be different for each country, and in some cases for different states within a country. Moreover, future developments in information technology may well create new situations that could render some proposed legislation as archaic as licensing hours.

7.4.7 How may computer crimes and frauds be categorized?
It may be useful to categorize some computer frauds and computer crimes:
   • fraud or embezzlement in which the computer system is a component of the transaction but in which there is no interference with, or misuse of, the computer's normal operation by legitimate users;

- fraud or embezzlement which takes advantage of some aspect of the normal computer operation (e.g. a gap in the controls exercised by the computer);
- fraud or embezzlement in which the computer system is deliberately misused (i.e. system penetration);
- theft of hardware, software, or data (see section 7.4.10);
- ransom of computer system facilities or data (see section 7.4.11).

In each case the term 'computer system' is used to cover any data communications network associated with the computer. The significance of these categories lies in the controls necessary to prevent, inhibit, or detect such crimes. If a computer merely replaced a formal manual system, then any fraud that could be perpetrated on the original system can be equally well performed on the updated one. In this case the organization simply failed to perform according to well-established commercial or administrative practices.

Computer systems may be more vulnerable to fraud than the previously manual systems if unwritten, informal safeguards of the original system are not replaced with formal controls, or if the volume of transactions grows to a level that renders traditional controls ineffective.

Sometimes the computerization of the system introduced new facets of operation which left control gaps for fraudulent activities. A common problem arose with the automation of document input; certain inherent safeguards of the original manual system were lost, or due consideration was not given to the exceptional cases which inevitably arise in practice (see section 7.4.13).

The system penetration cases involve manipulation of computer systems so as to bypass completely the controls built into the total administrative and computer system. In effect the computer system enables a fraud to be conducted that could not be undertaken on a manual system. For example, a hacker might access a financial database via a telephone link, but could not have had access to a set of ledgers held in a safe (see chapter 3).

The processing or communications facilities computer system itself may be misused for trivial game playing, for the development of complex software packages to be sold by the perpetrator, or simply to run the accounts of an employee's business venture. The employee will probably be authorized to access the system, and thus controls on the type and amount of usage need to be applied to detect and discourage this type of misuse (see chapter 3).

Vandalism of computer hardware or data could well become more common. Cases have already arisen in which well-planned raids were made on company data held on magnetic tapes, and threats were made to destroy the only available copies of that data unless substantial ransom were paid (see section 7.4.11).

7.4.8 What is the most important internal safeguard against computer fraud?

The first and most effective safeguard against computer fraud is good management. One of the commonest failings is to assume that the technical wizardry of hardware and people has created an entirely new environment in which the conventional wisdoms no longer apply. Everybody in an organization is accountable to top management in a manner determined by top management, and in the final analysis top management itself is accountable to the shareholders. The concept that computer departments cannot operate without total flexibility and autonomy is one that may be favoured by a certain class of computer professionals, but it can lead to substantial problems.

Management must build a macro-controlled environment, which includes the computer system, so that they have feedback on the operational state of the organization, irrespective of the operations occurring in the computer system. They will also need to be assured that the computer system itself is subjected to good management procedures at all levels – personnel, hardware, and software.

When the computer system is introduced into a company for the first time (and a myriad of small firms have bought personal computers in recent years) management must re-examine their traditional controls and ask two fundamental questions:

- Were there unwritten, informal controls that have been removed by computerization?
- Will the volume of transaction processing overwhelm the conventional controls?

If the security of the manual system relied in part on the physical security of ledgers in an office safe, or the detection of unusual handwriting in the account books, then the easy access to a personal computer, or the anonymity of stored data will present new control problems which must be tackled. Particular attention must be paid to the development and archiving of audit trails when conventional internal documentation is replaced by computer processing (see chapter 1).

A more insidious problem arises when the volume of transactions builds up with the advent of the computer system. Informal controls such as observations by clerks on unusual orders, excessive payments, etc. may disappear. Management may find, too late, that it is impossible to conduct a post hoc investigation because the manual effort of checking is excessive, and at worst they may discover that the whole system is completely out of control. Some of the really horrendous computer frauds were perpetrated when management were overwhelmed by the sheer volume of transactions, and had succeeded in convincing themselves that everything was probably all right, or at least would not be investigated.

7.4.9 Are there any well-known weak links of security in computer systems?

It must be recognized that the internal controls within a computer system rely absolutely on certain assumptions about the input and outputs from the computer. If a valid password is entered at a terminal then the computer will assume that the commands are originating from a user specified to hold that password. Data entered into the system can be checked only for internal consistency; the computer has no way of knowing if it originates from a printed company invoice, or from an imaginative terminal operator. An invoice may be printed by the computer on the company's forms or on those of another company, or on waste blank paper that will be discarded. Indeed, with the advent of desktop publishing it is possible for employees to design and print fake company stationary for the purpose of fraudulent transactions.

Particular attention must therefore be directed to controls of interfaces so that it is guaranteed that all the authorized data, and only the authorized data, is passed from one section to the next. Particular problems can arise with the automation of document handling; a computer may reject documents that would have been accepted by clerks. If the system does not have a well-controlled exception handling system, then a fraud may be perpetrated. Cases have been reported in which bank employees deliberately defaced the magnetic characters on cheques so that they would be rejected by the computer and could then be conveniently 'lost', thus assuring that payment was made but the employees' bank accounts were not debited. Other cases have arisen in which deposit slips with magnetically encoded account numbers belonging to the fraudsters were left at bank branches so that unsuspecting depositors used the slips, and funds were then credited to the accounts selected by the fraudsters.

Data entry must be carefully controlled (see chapter 1) and all data entry operators must be fully trained and well supervised. Some aggregate of data entered into the computer must be subject to independent checks so that both accidental and malicious miskeying will be detected. It is particularly important that the computer should perform internal consistency checks on its data, and thus inhibit the passage of obviously incorrect data (e.g. an alphabetic character entered into a numeral field, or unreasonable data). The problem is well understood in established data processing centres, but can be overlooked when a tax consultant purchases a personal computer.

Computer systems are most vulnerable when a software crash occurs and the internal checks are not working, thus allowing an attacker to penetrate the system. An inadequately tested program can crash for a variety of reasons. For example, how many programs take into account the fact that, in the year 2000, February will be a normal leap year, unlike, 1900, when February had 28 days. What will be the security consequences of a program failing to recognize this?

The control of output documents or media is also important. Such documents may authorize payments, grant privileges, contain confidential data, etc. There is little point in applying sophisticated technical controls on data within the computer if documents can be lost or copied in transit from the computer centre. Computer printouts are voluminous and often have only a short useful life. Proper precautions for the disposal of printouts must be applied when such printouts contain privileged data; in one reported case confidential company data was found on a printout that had been given to a primary school painting class (see chapter 6).

7.4.10 What precautions need to be taken against computer theft?
There are three forms of theft in computer/communication systems:

- theft of hardware and storage media,
- theft of data,
- theft of facilities.

Hardware and storage media thefts fall within the realm of conventional security within an organization (see chapter 3); however, it must be recognized that some computer thefts present new problems from a security viewpoint. The personal computer introduced a valuable asset into offices which hitherto probably contained few assets of interest to an opportunistic wrongdoer. Theft of internal printed circuit boards, detachable keyboards, etc. is becoming more prevalent. Most of these items can be hidden in a briefcase, and their loss may go unnoticed for some time. It must also be recognized that the theft of storage media also implies loss of the associated data. One of the authors of this book had the whole contents of a book in draft form stolen because some felonious student needed a few floppy diskettes (see chapter 6).

The theft of data in its own right becomes an increasing hazard as employees have access to mailing lists, draft tender documents, marketing plans, etc., which have a value in excess of several years' salary of junior employees. In many cases (e.g. mailing lists) the data has most commercial value if it is stolen in machine-readable form. Control on the supply of magnetic tapes from computer centres is relatively straightforward, but many distributed systems now allow staff to download files onto word processor or personal computer floppy diskettes. Strict access controls (see chapter 3) and security logs (see chapter 1) of file printouts are therefore essential to protect data with high commercial value.

The theft of facilities arises when employees use computing power for their private purposes or send personal messages over communication links. Programmers have been known to develop substantial software packages for subsequent sale, or to process accounts of small family businesses on company mainframe computers. It is also not unknown for computers to be used to host a variety of games. These activities have serious consequences if they deprive the organization of the use of such facilities for legitimate purposes, e.g. if they cause a downturn in response time or a delay due to congestion on communication lines. In extreme cases they can cause companies to embark upon expensive enhancements to their computer/communication systems. Security logs of computer usage (see chapter 1), particularly outside normal working hours, user files, etc. should highlight any major infringements, and checks on communications traffic will serve a similar purpose. Similar precautions can be taken against misuse of personal computers (see chapter 3).

7.4.11 How can ransom attacks be thwarted?

Ransom can take the form a threatened physical attack against a processing system, stored data in situ, or stolen stored data; it may also relate to a threat to inject computer viruses (see section 7.4.12). The realistic ransom level clearly depends upon the estimated cost to management of the outcome of the successful attack. If management have designed security systems guaranteed to minimize the chances of success of malicious attacks, or if the computer/communications system is distributed so that an attack at any one point can be covered by spare capacity elsewhere, then the realistic value of the ransom will be substantially reduced. In other words, the vulnerability to this form of ransom is substantially reduced by the sensible implementation of good physical security methods, access control, and so forth.

A variation of the ransom threat lies in the theft of backup tapes, and in associated threats to wipe out master files, etc. Such threats can originate most realistically from employed staff with legitimate access to backup material and the opportunity to install time bombs in the computer software. Duplication of backup tapes, which in itself is a sensible protective measure (see chapter 1), and strict control on the issue of such tapes by a duly authorized custodian can minimize the risk of this form of attack. It is also important that backup media cannot be maliciously or accidentally corrupted during transit or storage (see chapter 1).

7.4.12 Are viruses a serious threat?
Like all computer crime and terrorism, the potential threat of viruses to large information-processing systems, varies from the significant to the catastrophic (see chapter 3). The most significant danger, however, probably arises in installations that have a large population of professional computer users and where security does not have a high priority, e.g. college campuses.

If individual users are allowed to import software from outside sources, particularly bulletin boards, electronic mail networks, etc. then there is a significant danger than viruses could be introduced into the organization. If the virus is imported on personal computer floppy diskettes, then it can be spread from one personal computer to another. If one user employs a diskette with a virus and the same computer is subsequently used by another, without the computer being switched off between users, then the virus may spread to the second user's diskette. The virus spread will be much faster if personal computer software is uploaded into a host computer and subsequently downloaded into other personal computers.

Mainframe computers will be less susceptible to viruses inasmuch as more control is normally exercised upon the importation of large packages to be run on the mainframe, as compared to personal computer packages that may be stored but not normally run on the mainframe.

Precautions can be taken against viruses; a common technique is to ensure that the software has not changed between successive runs. Authentication of software, by means of cryptographic techniques similar to those used for the authentication of messages, can ensure both that any modification to software will be highlighted by an authentication check and that no attacker can undetectably interfere with the authentication check.

The impact of a virus attack will depend upon the general level of data and computer security employed. If a virus destroys files then the original can be restored by backup techniques. It is of course essential that duplicate backup systems are available at all times. It is also essential to ensure that all viruses are eliminated from the system before such backup data is loaded. If real-time systems are affected then standby systems must be ready for instant action, and the standby system must have been suitably isolated so that it was not itself susceptible to the same virus. If a network is used, it is also important to check that no viruses are lodged in the network communications processors, otherwise they could conceivably re-infect the mainframe, if that were the intention of the attacker who planted it.

7.4.13 Is there a checklist for management of the actions to be taken to prevent computer fraud?

The measures of effective control against computer fraud include:

- an incentive scheme for staff to seek out and report security loopholes;
- good commercial and administrative practices (see chapter 1);
- prevention or reduction of attack;
- separation of duties (see chapter 1);
- control of input and output (see chapter 1);
- control of amendments;
- structured walk-through;
- good documentation (see chapter 1);
- job rotation (see chapter 1);
- split knowledge or dual control (see chapter 1);
- increasing the difficulty of concealment/realization;
- good personnel procedures (see chapter 1);
- fidelity guarantee and computer crime insurance (see chapter 3);
- early detection;
- monitoring of access violations (see chapter 1);
- reviewing unusual circumstances;
- audit trails (see chapter 1);
- fraud detection models;
- employer response;
- public prosecution (see section 7.5.10).

7.5 Law and Personnel

7.5.1 How does the Data Protection Act impinge upon personnel policies?

Management has a responsibility to personnel inasmuch as they must be made aware that certain actions which relate to personal data can now be criminal offenses or make the employee liable for damages in a civil action. Management also needs to defend itself against irresponsible actions of employees in regard to misuse of personal data. If management can demonstrate that they have taken care to inform all employees of the procedures to be adopted in handling personal data then it will assist in a defence that all reasonable precautions were taken against (say) an unauthorized disclosure of personal data (see section 7.2.12).

7.5.2 What specific actions need to be taken in order to inform staff of the provisions of the UK Data Protection Act?
Management need to inform staff of their responsibilities under the *Data Protection Act* by:

- a statement in the conditions of employment that they are required to observe the Act in general, and the organization's procedures in particular;
- distribution of guidelines on actions to be taken in specific instances when dealing with personal data (all staff whose duties require them to handle personal data should be given written instructions relating to their particular responsibilities, e.g. staff handling external telephone enquiries must be told not to provide personal data over the telephone);
- training on the Act given during induction courses for new staff;
- reminders on specific precautions to be given whenever personal data is accessed (e.g. messages on VDU screens, computer printouts, etc.);
- appropriate line management informed of the organization's registration details and any amendments, renewals, etc.

7.5.3 What action should be taken in regard to personnel records kept by an organization?
Clearly personnel records will be the subject of any audit and review of personal data required by the registration procedures (see section 7.2.15). However, for many organizations the personnel records may represent the whole of their holdings of personal data, and some general guidelines may therefore be given.

- If personnel records are mainly held on the computer for payroll and accounting purposes, then the amount of detail held should be reviewed. If more information is held than is strictly necessary for accounting purposes then the organization may decide to delete it, or transfer that additional information to manual files, so that exemption for the stored or processed personal data can be claimed (see section 7.2.7.1).
- Data held on computer files in regard to ex-employees should be reviewed. In general, management should specify the maximum period that such data is required, and thereafter delete it (see section 7.2.5).
- All personnel data should be checked for accuracy, preferably by sending it to the employee and requesting corrections.
- Sources of external data should be included with the personnel data. If references were obtained from external sources, under an agreement of non-disclosure, then such references should only

be held in manual files.

- Seek agreement with appropriate trade unions or professional bodies on the handling of personnel data.
- Ensure that all codes used in the records should have explanatory notes when such records are provided in response to an access request.
- Ensure that the records are organized such that the record of one employee does not contain personal details of another.
- Determine the policy on responding to requests for access from employees (see section 7.2.19.5).

7.5.4 What actions are required in relation to external staff and the UK Data Protection Act?

In many cases computer and communications equipment will be subject to maintenance contracts, and management cannot be expected to ensure that all maintenance personnel employed by external contractors are fully trained and briefed on the workings of the Data Protection Act. On the other hand such maintenance engineers are likely to have special privileges, from the viewpoint of computer or communication system operations, in order to diagnose faults, etc. This is a problem for all aspects of computer and data security (see chapter 3). Formal agreements between an organization and an external contractor should include statements specifying that:

- The contractor will only allow authorized personnel to access equipment and data. All such personnel need to be aware of the provisions of the *Data Protection Act* and that their conditions of employment should require them to maintain the security of personal data.
- Personal data held by the contractor will be maintained in a secure environment.
- The transportation or communication of personal data undertaken by the contractor will be performed in a secure manner.
- Personal data will either be returned to the organization after repair or will be completely erased from all storage media, or disposed of by secure means if in hard-copy form.
- The contractor will impose similar conditions to those specified above, upon any subcontractor.

7.5.5 Is it possible to protect information assets from actions by employees, contractors, and ex-employees?

Since all employees, ex-employees, and contractors are known to an organization, and have entered into some contractual arrangement with it, then it is easier to gain legal redress for their actions than from some outside person, e.g. a hacker. On the other hand it must be recognized that such personnel will carry in their heads information that may have a considerable impact upon the well-being of the organization. It could be extremely difficult to differentiate between a piece of intelligence which 'belongs' to an organization, and is known by an ex-employee, and an enhanced knowledge which an experienced employee would expect to have after working in a particular field for the duration of employment.

Organizations are wise to ensure that their contractual arrangements provide them with maximum protection against loss of information assets, both during and after the period of employment or contract. It is, however, not sufficient to rely solely upon such contracts; indeed, attempts to impose excessive restrictions by contractual means can well backfire, and actually provide a lower degree of protection than less restrictive conditions. Thus, in addition to contractual clauses, certain precautions need to be taken in relation to employees and contractors as part of normal working routines, for example:

- ensuring that employees are made aware of the confidentiality of certain material;
- maintaining a record of work produced by employees and contractors;
- ensuring that ownership of copyright of relevant material is recorded and publicized.

An organization has a right to protect its information assets; equally employees or contractors have a right to exercise their skill, knowledge, and expertise; and the public has a right to ensure that monopolies of knowledge and skill do not act against the public interest. An organization should ensure that its actions in protecting its information assets will be considered to be reasonable in the circumstances of their implementation.

7.5.6 How does the status of staff affect protection of information assets?

It is extremely important that the status of personnel be clear to both parties, and be consistent with the law. Personnel may be employees, and have either a contract of fixed duration or a full contract of employment, or they may be independent contractors, and be employed under contract for services. In the computing field it is quite common for programmers, analysts, etc. to be employed as independent contractors, but remain with an organization for lengths of service comparable with other computing employees. Their status should be unambiguous and agreed by both staff and employers. It is not sufficient, however, merely for both parties to agree upon the label, i.e. employee or contractor. If the nature of the relationship is clearly consistent with an employer–employee role then a merely mutual agreement that the relationship be considered as a contract for services may not stand up in a court of law.

The distinctions between employee and contractor may be quite significant in terms of ownership of copyright (see section 7.3.10). Moreover, an employee has an implied duty to give faithful and loyal service to the employer; misuse of information assets would clearly conflict with this duty. A contract of employment can also deal specifically with the protection of confidential information both during and after employment. Such clauses need to be drafted with considerable care, however, since excessive conditions may not be legally binding (see section 7.5.8). If the person concerned is not an employee but a contractor with a contract for services, then more specific clauses are required in the contract, dealing with copyright ownership, disclosure of confidential information, etc.

7.5.7 To what extent does a contract of employment provide implicit protection against misuse of information assets?
An employee is bound by a contract of employment to give faithful and loyal service to the employer. This means that the employee should undertake no actions that could have a deleterious effect upon the employer, unless the actions were designed to bring to the attention of the proper authorities breaches of the law perpetrated by the employer.

The employee in particular should not work during his or her leisure time for another company, if such work were for a competitor and so created a conflict of interest. The employee should take all reasonable precautions to safeguard the employer's confidential information during employment. The employee should not use the employer's time or facilities to develop products for the benefit of the employee or some other company, e.g. use computer facilities to develop computer programs for personal use or gain.

On the other hand the employer should take care to ensure that the employee is aware that certain information is confidential, and that its release to others might cause harm to the employer. It may be extremely difficult for an employee to differentiate between that knowledge and expertise which is acquired in the course of employment and becomes an integral part of the employee's own skills and expertise, and that which is, in effect, a trade secret which should not be revealed.

7.5.8 Is an employer protected against loss of confidential information after employment?
When employment has ceased, the employee is no longer bound to

provide loyal and faithful service, but is bound not to reveal confidential information, e.g trade secrets. During employment the employee is bound by the legal and faithful service requirements not to undertake the collection of confidential information to be used in later employment. Thus an employee may reasonably remember information during the course of employment. Such information becomes part of the employee's own knowledge and skills, and the employee cannot be prevented from later using that knowledge, unless it is of the nature of a trade secret. The employee may not, however, deliberately seek to collect printed or other recorded forms of information for later use, even if such information is less confidential than trade secrets, e.g. lists of customers.

The employer will be concerned to ensure that confidential information is not passed to a subsequent employer, and also to ensure that the employee does not use knowledge and skill gained during employment to set up in competition.

The implied terms of a contract of employment may be considered inadequate by some employers, particularly in the information technology business where workers are commonly poached by competitors. In these cases the employer should:

- make sure that employees are explicitly informed which information is confidential;
- draft contracts of employment which explicitly state that declared confidential information is not to be disclosed after employment;
- warn employees against the deliberate collection and recording of confidential information, for use after the period of their employment.

The employer may also seek to include terms which inhibit the employee from setting up in competition for some period, and within some location, after employment. In doing so the following points need to be considered:

- An employee will have gained knowledge, skills and expertise during employment with the organization; it would be unreasonable to restrict the employee from exercising those attributes in subsequent employment.
- The clauses should not be so restrictive as to be an attempt to stifle reasonable trade competition.
- The employer may be able to use the springboard doctrine to prevent an ex-employee from continuing to develop a product that was initially developed during employment.

The drafting of the contract clauses must be undertaken with considerable skill. If they are restrictive to the extent that they are considered unreasonable then they may be overturned in a court of law. In this case they will have no effect, and it would be as if no restrictive clauses at all were drafted, whereas less restrictive clauses might have been accepted.

7.5.9 To what extent do the copyright laws safeguard an employer against loss of information assets?

Copyright can be used to protect information assets (see section 7.3.6). The copyright of works produced by an employee or apprentice in the course of their employment is owned by the employer. No such implied contract exists for independent contractors unless the work in question is specifically commissioned. The following points are therefore relevant to copyright protection:

- All contracts for services should specifically assign ownership copyright to the organization for any material developed by the contractor in the course of the contract.
- Records should be kept of material developed by employees in the course of their employment to ensure that the employees do not claim that the material was developed in their spare time, etc.
- Organizations may wish to extend their contracts so that copyright ownership of all material produced by an employee during the course of employment is assigned to the organization.

The last point needs some careful consideration. It could be that the rule should only apply to material which could reasonably be produced during the course of employment. Thus a computer programmer would assign ownership of all computer programs and documentation, but not of a musical composition. However, if no such precautions are taken, then a situation might arise that the organization failed to claim ownership of copyright for some work of the employee. The employee could then claim that this implied that the employer had assigned to the employee the right to ownership of copyright for material developed during employment. The contracts of staff should also contain clauses requiring them to ensure that they do not knowingly infringe the copyright of others (see section 7.3.17).

7.5.10 How does computer crime have an impact upon personnel policies?

Although many aspects of computer abuse, computer crime, and even some computer fraud are not completely covered by legislation, an organization can use internal discipline and contractual procedures

337

to safeguard itself against the actions of employees and independent contractors. Contracts of employment and contracts for services should deal with misuse of computer/communication facilities and organizational data, e.g. attempts to bypass access controls, electronic eavesdropping, use of computing/communication facilities for private purposes, etc.

Reference
Edwards, C. and Savage N., *Information Technology and the Law* (London: Macmillan, 1986).

Acknowledgement is given to Mr Chris Reed of Queen Mary College, London for his advice on the *Copyright, Designs and Patents Act*, 1988.

Appendix A Security Models

A.1 Bell–La Padula Model

Bell–La Padula is a security model originally formulated for military systems. The subjects of the model represent processes, and the objects represent containers of information (e.g. files). The security system comprises sensitivity levels (e.g. confidential, secret, and top secret); information may also have compartment designations where the compartments may, for example, indicate areas of activity. A security level comprises therefore both a sensitivity level and a set of compartments. The access types comprise: Read, Append, and Write. Append allows alteration to a file without observation, while Write permits both observation and alteration.

The system is considered to move from one state to another with

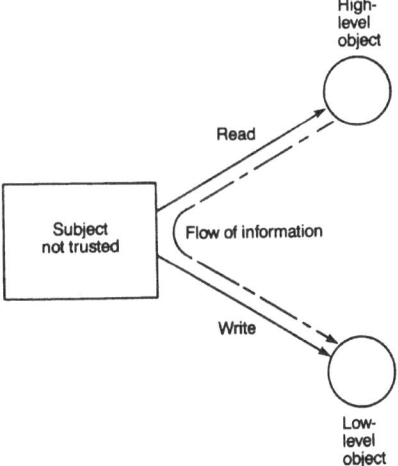

Fig. A-1 Bell-La Padula model. Information flow showing the need for the star property in order to prevent a malicious subject from extracting information from a top-secret object and putting it into a confidential object. (*source*: IBM)

each request for access. The state of the system is characterized by:

- the current access set, where each access has a subject, object, and access type;
- an access matrix;
- the security levels of all subjects and objects.

The system's response to a request is determined by a rule: if it can be proved that each rule applied to an appropriate request results in a secure state then the system is said to be secure.

A secure state is defined by the 'simple security property' and the 'star property'. The term 'dominates' used in these properties is defined by the condition that one security level (A) dominates another security level (B) if (1) A's sensitivity level is greater. than or equal to that of B and (2) A's sets of compartments contain those of B's.

A simple security property is one in which, for a read access type, the level of the subject dominates that of the object. This level does not prevent, however, a subject with a given sensitivity level writing information at that level into an object with a lower sensitivity level.

The star property does not permit such writing to a lower sensitivity level and is defined by:

- the subject's level dominates that of the object for Read access types;
- the object's level dominates for Append access types; and
- the levels are equal for Write access types.

Discretionary security, a third property of the model, requires that the access matrix explicitly authorizes every access.

A.2 Orange Book

The Orange Book represents a set of criteria, designed by the US Department of Defense, for security in a single computer system with several users. The criteria are divided into divisions and classes. A division represents a major improvement in the overall confidence that can be placed in the computer to protect sensitive information; the divisions are divided into classes of increasing desirability from a computer security viewpoint.

Division D deals with minimal protection and contains only one class, i.e. those systems that have been evaluated but fail to comply with the requirements for a higher evaluation class. Division C deals with discretionary protection and classes, in this division, and provides need-to-know protection and accountability of subjects for the actions they initiate. Class C1, within Division C, deals with Discretionary Security Protection. The Trusted Computer Base (TCB) of systems of this class provides separation of users and data to satisfy the requirements of discretionary security. The TCB incorporates controls which can restrict user access on an individual basis; it thus enables users to protect data from accidental reading or writing by other users. The C1 environment is one in which computing users access data of the same level of security. The second class in this division, C2, is concerned with controlled access protection, and enforces a more finely grained discretionary access control than Class C1. Users are made individually accountable for their actions by log-on procedures, resource isolation, and auditing of events related to security.

Division B is concerned with mandatory protection. This division requires that the TCBs preserve the integrity of sensitivity labels and employ them to enforce a set of mandatory access control rules. This division has three classes related to labelled security protection, structured protection, and security domains.

In addition to all the features of Class C2 described above, Class B1 demands an informal statement of the security policy model, data labelling, and mandatory access control over named subjects and objects. The next level up, Class B2, is concerned with structured protection. In this case the TCB is based upon a clearly defined, documented security policy requiring that the discretionary and mandatory access control of Class B1 systems be extended to all subjects and objects in the data processing system; in addition covert channels are addressed. Finally, Class B3, dealing with security domains, specifies that TCBs satisfy reference monitor requirements that mediate all access of subjects to objects, are tamper-resistant, and are sufficiently small to be subjected to analysis and test.

The topmost Division A is concerned with verified protection; it is characterized by the formal security verification of the mandatory and discretionary controls used to protect sensitive information processed and stored by the computer. The two classes of this division are Class A1, verified design, and Class A2, verified implementation.

The feature that essentially distinguishes systems in this class from those of Class B3 is the analysis, derived from formal design specification and verification techniques, which provides a high degree of assurance that the TCB is correctly designed. Class A2 systems are a logical extension of Class A1 in which the systems require a formal verification of implementation as well as design; such systems are beyond the current state of the art for most practical applications.

A.3 RACF

Resource Access Control Facility is an IBM software security product which assists in the control of user access to application data sets, volumes, transactions, and terminals.

The main functions performed by RACF are user identification and verification, authorization checking, logging, and administration. If a user is not identified to RACF then that user will be unable to access the resources it protects unless those resources have a universal access. Authorized users are required to enter a password which has only a limited life. In addition to checking the user ID and password, RACF may also check the user's authority to access the system via the specific terminal employed. Moreover, the system access for a particular user may be limited to specific time periods on specified days. Authorization-checking controls the resources that may be accessed by a given user and the manner of such accesses, e.g. reading or updating. Having checked the user and controlled the access to the resource, RACF records user–resource interactions and can alert management to variances from expected use of the system. The administration of an installation's security can be managed by RACF in a variety of ways, e.g. flexible control of access to protected resources, protection of installation defined resources, transparency to end-users, etc.

Appendix B Cryptography

B.1 Data Encryption Standard

The Data Encryption Standard specifies an algorithm to be implemented in electronic hardware devices and used for the crypto-graphic protection of computer data. The algorithm is a product cipher employing 64-bit data blocks and a 64-bit key. The standard was published by the National Bureau of Standards in January 1977 as FIPS Publication 46. It became mandatory for US federal agencies in June 1977.

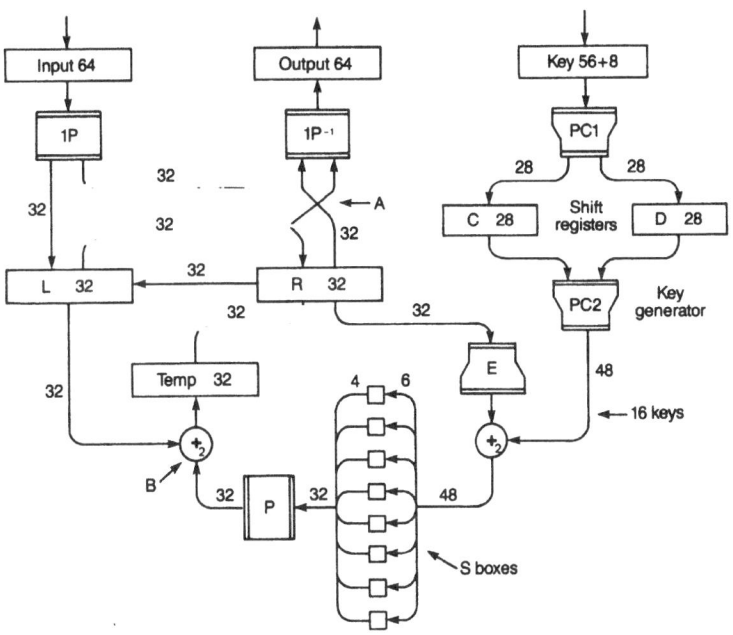

Fig. B-1 Data encryption standard: data flow

343

DES is based upon an earlier product cipher named Lucifer and developed by IBM. It uses 64-bit data blocks and a 64-bit key. The cryptographic key, however, employs 8 parity bits and thus from a cryptographic viewpoint it is only a 56-bit key. The flow of data in the DES algorithm is illustrated in figure B-1.

The data is subjected to transpositions and substitutions in P boxes (IP, IP⁻¹, E, and P) and S boxes respectively. The key is also subjected to transpositions in permutation boxes PC1, PC2, and shift registers C and D. There are 16 rounds of operation for the data and each round involves operations with a different 48-bit key developed from the original 64-bit cryptographic key.

The operations on the data are illustrated in the ladder diagram of figure B-2.

The input data block is first subjected to a straight permutation, IP. In this case the bits are simply rearranged as shown in table B-1.

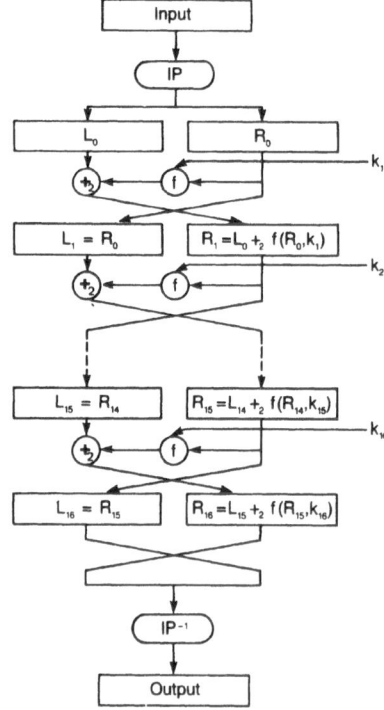

Fig. B-2 Data encryption standard: operations on data

Thus the first octet of the input appears in bit positions 40, 8, 48, 16, 56, 24, 64, and 32 of the output respectively. Neither this permutation nor the input to it is affected by the key; it has been included for convenience of implementation but it has no cryptographic function. The output of this stage is split into two 32-bit blocks, the left-hand block is passed to 32-bit register L32, and the right-hand to R32.

The 32 bits of R32 are then subjected to the expanded permutation E, shown in table B-2. In this case some of the inputs appear in two output positions, e.g. bit 4 occurs in output positions 5 and 7. In this way the 32-bit input block is both transposed and expanded into a 48-bit output block.

Table B-1

58	50	42	34	26	18	10	2
60	52	44	36	28	20	12	4
62	54	46	38	30	22	14	6
64	56	48	40	32	24	16	8
57	49	41	33	25	17	9	1
59	51	43	35	27	19	11	3
61	53	45	37	29	21	13	5
63	55	47	39	31	23	15	7

Table B-2

32	1	2	3	4	5
4	5	6	7	8	9
8	9	10	11	12	13
12	13	14	15	16	17
16	17	18	19	20	21
20	21	22	23	24	25
24	25	26	27	28	29
28	29	30	31	32	1

The output of the E block is added modulo 2 to the first-stage output of the key generator; the result is subjected to a substitution cipher in eight S boxes. These S boxes operate in parallel, each

Table B-3   S Boxes

		0	1	2	3	4	5	6	7	8	9	10	11	12	13	14	15
	0	14	4	13	1	2	15	11	8	3	10	6	12	5	9	0	7
S1	1	0	15	7	4	14	2	13	1	10	6	2	11	9	5	3	8
	2	4	1	14	8	13	6	2	11	15	12	9	7	3	10	5	0
	3	15	12	8	2	4	9	1	7	5	11	3	14	10	0	6	13
	0	15	1	8	14	6	11	3	4	9	7	2	13	12	0	5	10
S2	1	3	13	4	7	15	2	8	14	12	0	1	10	6	9	11	5
	2	0	14	7	11	10	4	13	1	5	8	12	6	9	3	2	15
	3	13	8	10	1	3	15	4	2	11	6	7	12	0	5	14	9
	0	10	0	9	14	6	3	15	5	1	13	12	7	11	4	2	8
S3	1	13	7	0	9	3	4	6	10	2	8	5	14	12	11	15	1
	2	13	6	4	9	8	15	3	0	11	1	2	12	5	10	14	7
	3	1	10	13	0	6	9	8	7	4	15	14	3	11	5	2	12
	0	7	13	14	3	0	6	9	10	1	2	8	5	11	12	4	15
S4	1	13	8	11	5	6	15	0	3	4	7	2	12	1	10	14	9
	2	10	6	9	0	12	11	7	13	15	1	3	14	5	2	8	4
	3	3	15	0	6	10	1	13	8	9	4	5	11	12	7	2	12
	0	2	12	4	1	7	10	11	6	8	5	3	15	13	0	14	9
S5	1	14	11	2	12	4	7	13	1	5	0	15	0	3	9	8	6
	2	4	2	1	11	10	13	7	8	15	9	12	5	6	3	0	14
	3	11	8	12	7	1	14	2	13	6	15	0	9	10	4	5	3
	0	12	1	10	15	9	2	6	8	0	13	3	4	14	7	5	11
S6	1	10	15	4	2	7	12	9	5	6	1	13	14	0	11	3	8
	2	9	14	15	5	2	8	12	3	7	0	4	10	1	13	11	6
	3	4	3	2	12	9	5	15	10	11	14	1	7	6	0	8	13
	0	4	11	2	14	15	0	8	13	3	12	9	7	5	10	6	1
S7	1	13	0	11	7	4	9	1	10	14	3	5	12	2	15	8	6
	2	1	4	11	13	12	3	7	14	10	15	6	8	0	5	9	2
	3	6	11	13	8	1	4	10	7	9	5	0	15	14	2	3	12
	0	13	2	8	4	6	15	11	1	10	9	3	14	5	0	12	7
S8	1	1	15	13	8	10	3	7	4	12	5	6	11	0	14	9	2
	2	7	11	4	1	9	12	14	2	0	6	10	13	15	3	5	8
	3	2	1	14	7	4	10	8	13	15	12	9	0	3	5	6	11

accepting 6-bit inputs and generating 4-bit outputs (see table B-3). The 48-bit input is divided into eight 6-bit blocks, each of which enters one of the S boxes. Each S box may be considered as a ROM containing data organized in four rows and 16 columns; thus each position in the matrix for the S box corresponds to one of the 64 possible inputs. The matrix element is determined by the row selected by bits 1 and 6 of the input, e.g. 1xxxx0 selects row 2. Bits 2 to 5 of the input determine the column of the matrix element, e.g. if the first 6-bit block of the input is 110000 then row 2 column 8 of the first S box is selected giving output 1111 (decimal 15).

The 4-bit outputs of the eight S boxes are collected to form a 32-bit output block which is then subjected to straight permutation P (see table B-4). This permutation simply transposes the 32-bit input, giving a 32-bit output, e.g. bit 1 of the input is transposed to bit 9 of the output. The 32-bit output of P is 'exclusive or-ed' to the contents of the L32 register, and the result is placed in a temporary 32-bit store.

Table B-4

16	17	20	21
29	12	28	17
1	15	23	26
5	18	31	10
2	8	24	14
32	27	3	9
19	13	30	6
22	11	4	25

The contents of the register R32 are transferred to the L32 register and R32 is then updated with the contents of the temporary 32-bit register. This completes the first of the 16 rounds; the key generator then produces a new 48-bit key and the process is repeated with the new contents of L32 and R32. After 16 such iterations the contents of the L and R registers are cross-fed into the right- and left-hand 32-bit input blocks of IP^{-1} permutation box, which produces the inverse permutation of IP and the output of the encryption routine.

The DES key has 64 bits, but only 56 bits may be independently selected; the remaining 8 bits are parity bits and therefore have no cryptographic function. The key generator accepts a 64-bit key input into the permutation box PC1 where every eighth bit is discarded and the remaining bits are permuted according to the data in table B-5 (i.e. bit 57 appears as output bit 1, bit 8 is discarded, and bit 9 is transposed to bit 7). The leftmost 28 bits of the output are transferred to shift register C and the rightmost to shift register D. The data in these registers is shifted to the left 1 or 2 bits, before each of the 16 rounds (see table B-6). The contents of these registers are then fed into selected permutation box PC2 (see table B-7) providing a 48-bit key output which is 'exclusive or-ed' with the output of the E permutation.

Table B-5

	57	49	41	33	25	17	9
	1	58	50	42	34	26	18
C	10	2	59	51	43	35	27
	19	11	3	60	52	44	36
	63	55	47	39	31	23	15
	7	62	54	46	38	30	22
D	14	6	61	53	45	37	29
	21	13	5	28	20	12	4

The process of decipherment is surprisingly straightforward and effectively repeats the encipherment action with the order of keys k_1, k_2, ... k_{16} reversed.

The decipherment process can best be described in terms of the algebraic representation of the transformations. Let R_j, L_j, k_j represent the contents of registers L32, R32, and the 48-bit key (figure B-1) in the jth round. During encipherment:

$$L_j = R_{j-1} \tag{1}$$
$$R_j = L_{j-1} \oplus_2 f(R_{j-1}, k_j) \tag{2}$$

where $f(R_{j-1}, k_j)$ is the output of the P box in the jth round and $\oplus_2$ represents exclusive or operation. These equations may be rewritten:

$$R_{j-1} = L_j$$
$$R_j \oplus_2 f(R_{j-1}, k_j) = L_{j-1} \oplus_2 f(R_{j-1}, k_j) \oplus_2 f(R_{j-1}, k_j)$$

Now $$A \oplus_2 A = 0$$

Hence
$$R_{j-1} = L_j \tag{3}$$
$$L_{j-1} = R_j \oplus_2 f(R_{j-1}, k_j) \tag{4}$$

These equations indicate that decipherment is performed by effectively performing the encipherment process with the order of the 16

Table B-6 Key shifts for encipherment

Key	Number of shifts to the left
k_1	1
k_2	1
k_3	2
k_4	2
k_5	2
k_6	2
k_7	2
k_8	2
k_9	1
k_{10}	2
k_{11}	2
k_{12}	2
k_{13}	2
k_{14}	2
k_{15}	2
k_{16}	1

Table B-7

14	17	11	24	1	5
3	28	15	6	21	10
23	19	12	4	26	8
16	7	27	20	13	2
41	52	31	37	47	55
30	40	51	45	33	48
44	49	39	56	34	53
46	42	50	36	29	32

keys, k_1, k_2, ... k_{16}, reversed. To illustrate this point consider the contents of L32 and R32 (figure B-1) after the 15th round of encipherment. If these data blocks are L_{15}, R_{15} respectively then after one more round of encipherment:

$$L_{16} = R_{15} \qquad\qquad (5)$$
$$R_{16} = L_{15} \oplus_2 f(R_{15}, k_{16}) \qquad\qquad (6)$$

The ciphertext is produced by cross-feeding these quantities to IP^{-1}. With decipherment the ciphertext is fed into IP, reversing the effect of IP^{-1}, and then into registers L32 and R32. Thus if the data in these registers in the first round of decipherment is L_{D1} and R_{D1} then $L_{D1} = R_{16}$ and $R_{D1} = L_{16}$. Moreover, the first key employed in the decipherment round is k_{16}. Hence after one round of decipherment:

from equation (1) $\qquad\qquad L_{D2} = R_{D1}$

from equation (2) $\qquad\qquad R_{D2} = L_{D1} \oplus_2 f(R_{D1}, k_{16})$

hence from equations (3) and (4) $\qquad R_{D2} = R_{16} \oplus_2 f(L_{16}, k_{16}) = L_{15}$

and from equations (1) and (5) $\qquad L_{D2} = R_{D1} = L_{16} = R_{15}$

Hence the first round of decipherment has reversed the last round of encipherment with the contents of L32 and R32 exchanged. This process is continued for the successive rounds of decipherment and after 16 rounds the contents of L32 and R32 are cross-fed into IP^{-1}. This effectively eliminates the reversal of the contents of L32 and R32. The final stage of decipherment, permutation IP^{-1}, reverses the initial stage of encipherment, IP, giving the original plaintext.

The production of the keys in reverse order for decipherment is undertaken by the key generator. During encipherment the contents of the 28-bit shift registers C and D are moved to the right a total of 28 times. Thus the first key for decipherment k_{D1} corresponds to k_{16}. The subsequent set of shifts for C and D during decipherment are given in table B-8.

The processes of encipherment and decipherment depend upon the sequence of keys produced by the key generator. If, for a particular key, $k_1 = k_{16}$, $k_2 = k_{15}$, ... then the same sequence is generated in the encipherment and decipherment processes; in this case double encryption will produce the original plaintext message. Such keys are termed 'weak keys'. A similar situation arises in the case of pairs of keys A, B with the property $A_1 = B_{16}$, $A_2 = B_{15}$, ... In this case

Table B-8 Key shifts for decipherment

Key	Number of shifts to the right
k_{D1}	0
k_{D2}	1
k_{D3}	2
k_{D4}	2
k_{D5}	2
k_{D6}	2
k_{D7}	2
k_{D8}	2
k_{D9}	1
k_{D10}	2
k_{D11}	2
k_{D12}	2
k_{D13}	2
k_{D14}	2
k_{D15}	2
k_{D16}	1

encryption by one key followed by encryption with the second again produces the original plaintext; such key pairs are termed 'semiweak keys'.

The security of DES has been the subject of considerable debate and a US Senate investigation. The debate centred on the length of the DES key and upon the possibility that secret trapdoor functions were designed into the S boxes (no documentation on the design and reasons for the structure of the S boxes has ever been released). The effective length of the DES key is 56 bits, and the possibility of a special purpose DES machine, with multiple parallel processors, that could search through all possible keys has been debated, but the conclusion of the Senate Select Committee was that the security of DES was adequate for its proposed field of use within its planned time-span. The effective length of DES keys can be increased by multiple encipherment; this technique is employed for key encrypting key encipherments in some key management schemes.

DES effectively transforms a 64-bit plaintext block into a 64-bit ciphertext block using a 56-bit key. It has the advantage of no message expansion and a comparatively short key. In effect, for a given key, DES may be considered as a codebook with 2^{64} entries. Thus the conventional DES mode is actually termed 'electronic codebook'. It has a cryptographic weakness if highly formatted messages are enciphered with the same key. An attacker can detect the presence of commonly occurring ciphertext blocks and probably deduce plaintext–ciphertext pairs, or at least gain some information on the nature of the traffic. Other modes of DES operation (i.e. cipher block chaining, cipher feedback and output feedback) can overcome these deficiencies of electronic codebook operation.

DES may be implemented in software or hardware. LSI implementations can provide computation times of the order of microseconds, thus providing high data rates for secure communication channels.

Following NSDD-145 the US government has ruled that, with the advent of the Commercial COMSEC Endorsement Program in 1988, the NSA will no longer endorse new DES-based products for government use, although previously endorsed DES-based products may continue to be used by the US government for an indefinite period.

B.2 DES Modes of Operation: Cipher Block Chaining

Cipher block chaining is a mode of operation which overcomes the cryptographic weakness of the electronic codebook mode. The ciphertext output is dependent upon the key and all previous plaintext blocks of the message. Thus highly formatted messages will not suffer from the repetition of ciphertext blocks experienced with electronic codebook. The operation is illustrated in figure B-3. A 64-bit shift register is loaded with a data block, termed the 'initialization vector'. The first 64-bit plaintext block is 'exclusive or-ed' with the contents of the shift register and the resulting 64-bit block is encrypted using key k. The 64-bit ciphertext output is both fed into the shift register and sent to the receiver. The first cipher output C_1 depends upon P_1 and the initialization vector IV; the second depends upon P_2 and C_1 (i.e. upon P_2, P_1, and IV).

At the receiving end the shift register is loaded with the same initialization vector, IV. The first received block of ciphertext, C_1, is decrypted and the output of the decryption block is 'exclusive or-ed' with the contents of the shift register IV to reproduce the first plaintext block, P_1. The ciphertext block, C_1, is also fed to the shift register ready for the receipt of the second cipher text block C_2. The operation of cipher block chaining may be described mathematically. For encipherment:

$$C_n = ek(P_n \oplus_2 C_{n-1})$$

where $ek(P)$ = ciphertext produced by encryption of P with key k

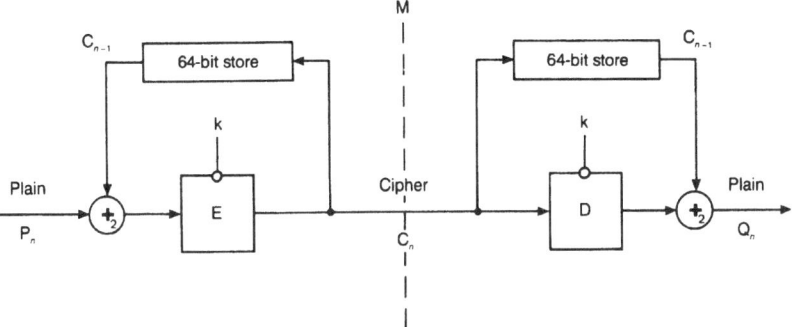

Fig. B-3 Cipher block chaining

and $\oplus$ indicates modulo 2 addition. The output of the decryption unit Q_n is given by

$$Q_n = dk(C_n) \oplus_2 C_{n-1}$$

where $dk(C_n)$ is the data block produced by decryption of ciphertext block C_n with key k.

Hence
$$Q_n = dk(ek(P_n \oplus_2 C_{n-1})) \oplus_2 C_{n-1}$$
$$= P_n \oplus_2 C_{n-1} \oplus_2 C_{n-1} = P_n$$

Both the receiver and the sender must share the common value of the initializing variable, IV, which is transmitted from the sender to receiver, normally under encipherment with a secret key. It is not strictly necessary to keep IV secret in order to protect the secrecy of the plaintext, but an attacker must be prevented from modifying the received value of IV. If an attacker can alter IV then the first output block of the received plaintext message can be changed at will by the attacker, but the subsequent plaintext blocks will be unaffected. It is for this reason that IVs are normally encrypted for transmission.

CBC requires that messages comprise a multiple number of 64-bit blocks. The last block of the message may be padded with zeros, but this will provide an analyst with useful information. Random characters may also be employed in the place of zeros, but the receiver needs to know both that such padding is included, and the number of padding characters at the end of the message. A padding indicator may be inserted as the last character transmitted and this indicator informs the receiver of the number of padding characters. If it is important that the length of the ciphertext should be equal to that of the plaintext (e.g. if an encrypted file is to occupy the storage space previously allocated to the plaintext file) then padding is not acceptable and alternative solutions must be employed.

A 1-bit error in a input plaintext message will affect every succeeding transmitted ciphertext block, but will only affect the corresponding bit in the received plaintext. A loss of a bit, or the addition of a spurious bit, in the ciphertext will cause a lack of synchronism between the transmitted and received streams, and will completely garble the received plaintext. If a 1-bit error occurs in the ciphertext then the data blocks of received plaintext will be affected. The first corrupted block will arise as a result of decryption of the changed ciphertext block; the plaintext block will be garbled, and the second plaintext block will be affected by the 'exclusive or-ing' of the corrupted ciphertext block with the output of the decipherment unit. In this case only the bit of plaintext block correspondg to the corrupted bit of the ciphertext block will be affected.

B.3 DES Modes of Operation: Cipher Feedback

Cipher feedback is a stream cipher mode of operation suitable for applications where the data cannot be formed into 64-bit blocks before encryption. In some applications the data is treated as individual bits, bytes, or frames, etc. For example, a character terminal will transmit individual 8-bit characters; these characters must be transmitted as they are generated, thus they cannot be collected into 64-bit blocks for encryption.

In cipher feedback a pseudorandom stream of bits is 'exclusive or-ed' with the plaintext stream to form the ciphertext stream. At the receiving end the same pseudorandom sequence is 'exclusive or-ed' with the ciphertext stream to reproduce the plaintext. The pseudorandom sequence is generated from the ciphertext stream itself. 64-bit shift registers are initialized with an initialization vector, IV, at the transmitting and receiving ends. The contents of these registers are then input to DES encryptor units, using the same secret key at the transmitter and receiver. A segment of the DES unit 64-bit output, of the same length as the plaintext block to be enciphered, is then selected and 'exclusive or-ed' with the data stream. Thus if the data to be enciphered is in the form of 8-bit blocks then the leftmost octet of the DES 64-bit output is selected as the segment for the pseudorandom stream. The ciphertext block (e.g. 8-bit character) is fed to the transmitter's shift register and transmitted to the receiver. At the receiving end it is fed into the receiver's shift register, and also 'exclusive or-ed' with the receiver's pseudorandom stream to

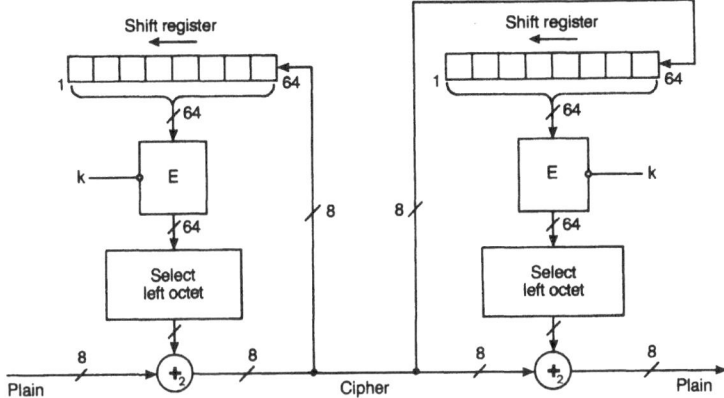

Fig. B-4 Cipher feedback

produce the plaintext output.

The DES encryption effort is greater with the cipher feedback than with the CBC mode since each input block demands encryption of a 64-bit block; thus if the input is divided into bytes then encryption of eight successive bytes requires eight DES operations in cipher feedback and only one DES operation in CBC.

The initialization vector, IV, can be simply transmitted as a random 64-bit preamble to a message. If this preamble represents too large an overhead then the shift registers may be initialized with an agreed value (e.g. all zeros), and a shorter preamble transmitted; the use of a short preamble may, however, be ill-advised if the messages are highly formatted.

Cipher feedback displays error extension; a 1-bit error in the transmitted ciphertext will produce a corresponding 1-bit error in the plaintext followed by a number of garbled output blocks as the error works its way through the shift register. If the input is a byte stream then eight garbled bytes in the output will follow the byte with the 1-bit error.

B.4 DES Modes of Implementation: Output Feedback

Output feedback is a stream cipher DES mode of operation. In the output feedback mode a cryptographic bit stream is 'exclusive or-ed' with the plaintext to produce the ciphertext at the transmitter; an identical system at the receiver equipped with the same cryptographic key produces the same cryptographic bit stream, which is 'exclusive or-ed' with the ciphertext to reveal the original plaintext. The crypto-graphic bit stream may produce 1-bit, 1-byte blocks, etc. to be 'exclusive or-ed' with the corresponding blocks in the plaintext. The cryptographic bit stream block is also fed back to the shift register to form the input to the DES encryption unit, where it is encrypted to provide a 64-bit output, the leftmost segment of which is selected for the next cryptographic bit stream block. The shift registers must be initialized with the same initialization vector, IV. This IV is transmitted in plaintext from the transmitter to the receiver as the preamble of the message. It is not necessary to transmit a full 64-bit block for this purpose; it may be arranged that both shift registers be initially set to zero and (say) eight bits transmitted to set the IV. Short preambles may, however, be ill advised if highly formatted messages are transmitted.

The major advantage of output feedback, as compared with cipher feedback, lies in its lack of error extension. A 1-bit error in the ciphertext will only produce a corresponding 1-bit error in the plaintext at the receiving end. This lack of error extension is advantageous in applications such as voice scrambling where the plaintext is highly redundant; a 1-bit error can be tolerated, whereas a number of garbled blocks will produce an irritating output dis-turbance. On the other hand an absence of error extension allows an attacker to introduce planned and undetectable changes in the re-ceived plaintext. A loss or spurious addition of a block in the ciphertext stream will cause a loss of synchronism between the transmitting and receiving data streams; the received plaintext will thereafter be garbled.

B.5 Public Key Cryptography

Public key cryptography is an asymmetric cryptosystem, i.e. one in which the enciphering and deciphering keys are different, and in which it is computationally infeasible to calculate one from the other, given the enciphering algorithm.

In public key cryptography the enciphering key is made public but the deciphering key is kept secret; it has advantages over symmetric ciphers, such as DES, in the areas of:

- security of messages, from a variety of sources, directed to an individual organization;
- key management;
- digital signatures.

If a number of individuals wish to send secure information to a

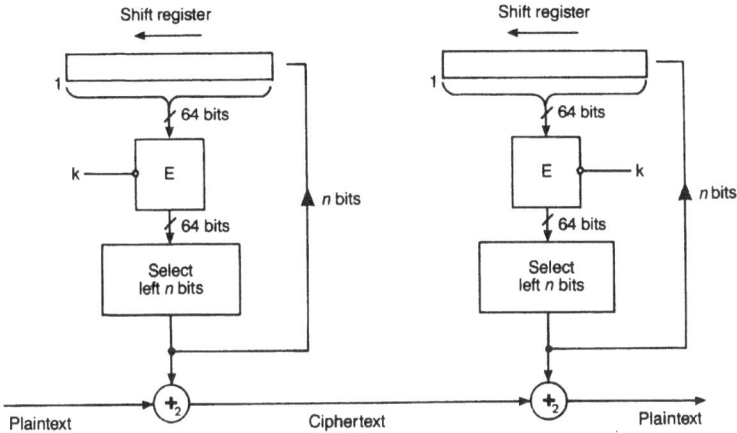

Fig. B-5 Output Feedback

central organization then symmetric ciphers require that initial arrangements be made for the individual and the organization to share a unique secret key. Public key cryptography on the other hand enables the organization to publish a single enciphering key, possibly in a public directory, and potential senders of the messages need only access this directory, encipher their message using the public key and agreed algorithm, and transmit it to the organization. Such senders will be unable to decipher messages sent by other individuals using the same key because the deciphering key is secret and held only by the organization in question. The secrecy of the public key is not required but it is essential that the integrity of the key in the public directory be guaranteed. If an attacker could replace an organization's public key, with an enciphering key produced by the attacker himself, who would also hold the corresponding deciphering key, then secret information destined for the organization would be available to the attacker. It is also important that users do not use highly formatted messages, because an attacker has a completely free choice in chosen plaintext attacks. Thus an attacker could take an intelligent guess at the meaning of certain repeated blocks in ciphertext messages encrypted with a given public key, and then check out those guesses by enciphering them with the public key and comparing the results with the ciphertext blocks.

Key management is another area in which public key cryptography is likely to make significant inroads. Since it is no longer necessary to exchange a secret key before establishing secure communications, then public key cryptography may be used for the transmission of

357

key encrypting keys and data keys. This technique has advantages over the use of public key cryptography for the message encipherment itself, inasmuch as symmetric ciphers, such as DES, are less computationally demanding than current public key cryptography methods.

Some public key cryptography algorithms provide elegant digital signature techniques. If the deciphering key can be used for encipherment, and vice versa, then the receiver can decipher a message using the public key, and be sure that the received message could only have been enciphered by the holder of the secret 'deciphering' key.

Diffie and Hellman were the first to publish a paper introducing the concepts of public key cryptography; their work *New Directions in Cryptography* appeared in 1976. The idea of a nonsecret enciphering key was a major advance in cryptography; it implies that there is no requirement at all for a secure channel between the sender and receiver of messages. In the absence of cryptography a secure channel is essential to maintain the whole message secret from the enemy; with conventional cryptography the requirement for a secure channel is reduced to that for the transmission of the cryptographic key. Public key cryptography enables a sender to access an enciphering key (e.g. from a public directory), encipher a message, and send it to the recipient, who must hold the private deciphering key; at no stage is a secure channel required.

Cryptography may thus be considered to have developed in three phases. Originally the encryption algorithm and any associated keys were kept secret. In the second phase the encryption algorithms were made publicly available but the encryption and decryption keys, which might or might not be identical, were not revealed. With public key cryptography both the method of encryption and the enciphering keys are made public; the secrecy of the cipher depends upon the security of the private deciphering key.

These three stages of development represent increasing demands upon the cryptographic algorithm, which can be represented by $C = f(M,E)$, where C is the ciphertext, M is the plaintext, E is the enciphering key and f is the encryption routine.

If both the encryption algorithm, f and the encryption key, E, are secret the cryptanalyst is provided with no information except that the ciphertext represents a meaningful message in a given natural language. The cryptographic routine can in these circumstances be a relatively simple operation.

When the encrypting algorithm, f, is public knowledge and the encrypting key, E, is secret then the demands upon the cryptographic routine depend upon the length of the key. If the key is random, and of the same length as the message, then the routine can again be relatively simple because the cryptanalyst has insufficient information to recover the plaintext message. If, however, the key is relatively short compared with the message, then the techniques of information theory indicate that the redundancy of natural languages provides the cryptanalyst with sufficient information to decipher the ciphertext. In mathematical terms, the cryptanalyst must attempt to compute an inverse function $E = h(M,C)$. The complexity of the encryption routine must be such that this process is computationally infeasible.

With public key cryptography the cryptanalyst is, in theory, provided with sufficient information to decipher the message without any recourse to a study of the redundancy of the plaintext language. Since both the encryption algorithm and the encryption key are publicly available, a mathematical analysis will indicate the relationship between the unknown deciphering key and the known enciphering key and algorithm. Thus the cryptographic algorithm must be such that it is computationally infeasible for a cryptanalyst to perform the inverse function $M = p(C,E)$. In mathematical terms this implies that the enciphering algorithm, f, must be a one-way function. The public key cryptographer has, however, a much more demanding task than that of merely producing an efficient one-way function; while the cryptanalyst must be prevented from computing $M = p(C,E)$, it is clearly important that the legitimate recipient be able to obtain the plaintext message with reasonable computational efficiency. Thus the additional restriction on $f(M,E)$ is that it be a trapdoor one-way function, i.e. the legitimate user, armed with a private deciphering key, D, can easily compute the function $M = g(C,D)$.

B.6 Public Key Cryptography RSA

In public key cryptography, Rivest–Shamir–Adleman, an algorithm named after its designers, is of extreme importance in public key cryptography. It uses a trapdoor one-way function based upon the computational difficulty of factoring the product of large prime numbers (i.e. integers with several hundred decimal digits). Thus the computation involved in multiplying two large prime numbers p and q is minimal but it is computationally infeasible to derive the factors p and q from a product n consisting of several hundred decimal digits. A large computer would take about a billion years for a 200-digit number.

The process of developing the keys and encrypting/decrypting the messages are described below.

- Two large prime numbers (p and q) are randomly selected and

359

their product n is determined. This value of n is made public.
- The Euler totient function of n (i.e. the number of integers in the range $1 \ldots n-1$ that are coprime with n) is determined. Since p and q are primes this is given by $\phi(n) = (p-1)(q-1)$, provided that $p \neq q$. This value is kept secret.
- Select an integer E in the range of $2 \ldots \phi(n)-1$. This is the public encrypting key.
- Calculate the private deciphering key D from $E.D = 1$ mod $(\phi(n))$. E must be selected so as to be coprime with $\phi(n)$ to ensure that D exists; the restriction on E can be checked with the computation of D. If the algorithm provides no solution for D then another value of E must be selected.

D is the deciphering key and is kept secret. The values of E and n are made public, but the calculation of D demands a knowledge of $\phi(n)$ and computation of this function by an attacker involves the computationally infeasible factoring of n into p and q.

- The public encrypting key E, and n, are made publicly available (e.g. in a directory).
- For encryption the data is broken into blocks M_1, M_2, $\ldots$ with block lengths chosen so that the individual message blocks have a numerical value less than n. The blocks are then raised to the power E modulo n, i.e. the ciphertext blocks C_1 etc. are calculated by:

$$C_1 \equiv M_1{}^E \pmod{n}$$
$$C_2 \equiv M_2{}^E \pmod{n}$$

- Decryption of the ciphertext message is performed by a similar operation to that described above, except that the ciphertext blocks are raised to the power D modulo n, i.e.:

$$D_i \equiv C_i{}^D \pmod{n} \equiv M_i{}^{E.D} \pmod{n}$$

- The original message is recovered by the deciphering process because $C^D \pmod{n} = M^{E.D} \pmod{n}$, and under the rules of modulo arithmetic the exponent may be reduced modulo $\phi(n)$. The exponent of C is $E.D$, and by the definition $E.D = 1$ (mod $\phi(n)$). Hence:

$$M_i \equiv M_i{}^{E.D} \pmod{n}$$

This process can be illustrated by a simple example.

- Select $p = 101$, $q = 103$. Hence $n = 101 \times 103 = 10403$.
- $\phi(n) = (p-1)(q-1) = 10200$.
- Select E to be coprime with 10200 and in the range 2 .. 10119. Let $E = 97$.
- Compute D using Euler's Generalization:
  $97.D = 1 \pmod{10200}$.
  Compute $\phi(\phi(n))$, i.e. the number of integers in the range 1.. 10199 that are coprime with 10200, $\phi(\phi(10403)) = 2560$.

$$D \equiv E^{\phi(\phi(n))-1)} \pmod{\phi(n)}$$
$$\equiv 97^{2559} \pmod{10200} = 8833$$

  Note that $97 \times 8833 = 856801 \pmod{10200} = 1 \pmod{10200}$.
- E and n are published in a public directory as 97 and 10403 respectively.
- Sender wishes to send message $M = 33$. This is encrypted as $C = 33^{97} \pmod{10403} = 4933$.
- The receiver decrypts this message using the secret key D:

$$D = 4933^{8833} \pmod{10403} = 33$$

It would appear that an attacker could decrypt the message by repeated encryption thus raising the ciphertext message by successive powers of E modulo n until plaintext was recovered. In practice, however, with encryption and decryption keys using 100 or more decimal digits the number of iterations would be excessive, and this form of attack would be computationally infeasible.

There have been a number of studies on potential attacks on RSA. These have indicated that the integers p and q need to be selected with some care and that both $p-1$ and $q-1$ should have one large factor each.

RSA is a major step forward in public key cryptography. It provides an elegant method of digital signature. The encryption/decryption processes are more computationally demanding than those of DES and knapsack ciphers, and may therefore have an impact upon the maximum data rates for network encryption systems. The size of keys for RSA are also considerably greater than those for DES but are less than that required for knapsack ciphers. In key management, RSA could be employed to encipher the DES keys in a network, thus removing the requirement of complex techniques to transmit key-encrypting keys; the traffic in key-encrypting keys is much lower than that of network data and the additional computational load of RSA encryption/decryption would not significantly affect the throughput.

B.7 Stream Cipher

Stream cipher is a method of encryption with the capability of providing perfect secrecy. The plaintext is encoded into numbers (usually binary), and a key stream of random numbers is combined with the plaintext to form the ciphertext. The receiving end is supplied with an identical key stream of random numbers; the mathematical inverse combination of ciphertext and key stream reveals the plaintext. If the key stream of binary numbers is added modulo 2 to the plaintext then the operation of encipherment and decipherment are identical. This technique does not require that the plaintext be formed into blocks with a blocksize determined by the cryptographic algorithm designer; the plaintext may be enciphered in segments of any desired length, even down to bit-by-bit encipherment. It is therefore valuable in transmission systems where the messages may need to be encrypted character by character or even bit-by-bit.

The major practical disadvantage of this technique lies in the requirement of the secure transmission between sender and receiver of key streams of the same length as the messages. In practice a shorter secret key is used to generate pseudorandom bit streams at the transmitter and receiver.

B.8 Message Authentication

In authentication, the processes are undertaken to ensure that:

- the message originated with the purported sender;
- the message contents have not been accidentally or intentionally altered or rearranged;
- the message has been received in the sequence that it was sent by the originator; and
- the message was received by the intended recipient.

Message authentication is therefore concerned with the identities of the sender and receiver, modifications to message contents, and the problem of replay. It is assumed that undesirable changes may be wrought by accident (e.g. noisy communication lines) or a malicious third party. The problem of disputes where the sender accuses the receiver of message alteration or attempts to revoke the message lies within the realm of digital signatures.

The authentication of message origin requires that the sender and receiver share secret information unavailable to an attacker. If Parties A and B share two cryptographic keys, k_A and k_B, then only Party A can send messages encrypted with k_A to Party B and vice versa; each party is then assured of the message originator. Alternatively, if appropriate public key cryptography is employed (i.e. one not involving message expansion) then each party can encrypt messages with their private deciphering key. In this case Party B can decrypt a message using Party A's public enciphering key. The message from Party A could not have originated with an attacker, but on the other hand any attacker can now decipher the message with the public enciphering key.

If the two parties share a cryptographic key for both outgoing and incoming messages then they can still be sure that messages were not originated by an attacker. However, the danger of replay now exists, because each party uses the same cryptographic key for both encipherment and decipherment. An attacker can now redirect a message from Party A back to Party A, or record it and replay it later to Party A, who would accept it as a message from Party B. This form of attack can be obviated by the use of a field within the encrypted message, indicating the direction of message flow.

If it is undesirable or impractical to use cryptographic keys as the basis of originator authentication then the two parties can share secret passwords, e.g. PW_A and PW_B. It is not sufficient, however, simply to include these passwords within encrypted messages, since an attacker could insert ciphertext blocks containing the passwords into bogus messages or use a replay attack. If passwords are employed they must be protected against modification by authentication procedures used to guarantee the message contents, i.e. the passwords must form an integral part of the authenticated message.

The accidental alteration of messages can arise from operator error in transcribing data, or from noisy communication channels. Operator errors can cause one character or digit to be replaced by another, or digits or characters to be transposed during keyboarding operations. Check fields are commonly employed in data entry operations, particularly when financial transactions are involved. The message is subjected to an algorithm and a short check field is produced. Since the message is considerably longer than the check field the transformation will necessarily be many-to-one, i.e. a significant number of original messages will produce the same check field. The function of a good check field algorithm is to ensure that each member of the set of messages producing a given check field is sufficiently dissimilar from all other messages in the same set, that the probability of miskeying one message to produce another is extremely low.

Errors in messages due to noisy communication lines, etc. are the responsibility of the provider of the communication facility, and will be handled by error-detecting codes employed in the communication system.

Authentication techniques employed against accidental message modification provide no defence against an intelligent malicious attack. A message can be altered, the new authenticator computed, and the new message plus modified authenticator forwarded to its intended recipient. Effective safeguards against an attacker demand that:

- the attacker is unable to modify the message and make corresponding alterations to the authenticator;
- the attacker is unable to assign a valid authenticator field to a bogus message;
- the attacker is unable to transform the message to another that has the same authenticator; and
- the attacker is unable to replay an authenticated message.

Defence against malicious modification of a message demands at least a degree of message redundancy and a secret key denied to an attacker. Encryption provides only partial defence against message modification and does not guarantee that changes in ciphertext will be detected by the recipient of the plaintext. In block ciphers a 1-bit change in the ciphertext block will produce a completely garbled plaintext block, but interchange of ciphertext blocks may well produce an altered but apparently meaningful message. In some stream ciphers an attacker can change any individual bit in the plaintext message without any side effects.

If a cipher has a property of error propagation then any change in the ciphertext will affect the whole of the successive plaintext. If the last block of the plaintext is redundant information already known to the receiver (e.g. the last block is simply a repeat of the first block) then an alteration to the ciphertext will be detected by changes in the last plaintext block.

Most common modes of encryption exhibit some degree of error extension but do not provide error propagation. In this case the message authenticator must be some function of the whole plaintext message, or at least its sensitive parts, as in the case of check fields to guard against keyboarding errors. If the message and authenticator are encrypted then the attacker is prevented from altering or re-arranging the ciphertext and making corresponding changes to the authenticator. Moreover, with a well-designed authentication routine, the attacker is unable to assign an authenticator to a bogus message or change the plaintext message for another with the same authenticator value. The danger of replay, however, remains.

The process of authentication with encryption involves:

- operation upon the plaintext blocks $(M_1, M_2, M_3, \ldots M_n)$ with

the authentication algorithm to provide the authenticator ($A(M)$), where ($M = M_1, M_2, M_3, \ldots M_n$);
- encryption of the augmented message ($M_1, M_2, M_3, \ldots M_n, A(M)$);
- decryption of the total message at the receiver;
- recomputation of the authenticator by the receiver on the basis of the received blocks ($M_1, M_2, M_3, \ldots M_n$); and
- comparison of receiver-computed authenticator with that contained in the message.

The length of the authenticator and the design of the authentication algorithm must be selected to provide a high degree of confidence in the authentication procedure. If the authenticator is n bits long then the probability that a randomly selected message will give rise to a particular authenticator is 2^{-n}, e.g. with a 3-bit authenticator there is a 1 in 8 chance of making an undetected alteration to the message. In practice 32 bits is considered an adequate length for an authenticator field.

Authentication routines using modulo 2 addition of successive plaintext blocks are demonstrably insecure since an attacker can often insert selected ciphertext blocks without affecting the plaintext authenticator. A common authentication method, employed in the ANSI X9.9 standard, involves the use of CBC, or cipher feedback, on the message content; a portion of the last ciphertext block, which is a function of the whole plaintext message, is selected as the authenticator.

In some cases it is desirable that the message contents be transmitted in plaintext and defence against attack is provided by encrypting only the authenticator itself. An attacker is thus prevented from modifying the message and simultaneously making compensating changes to the authenticator; similarly, an attacker is prevented from developing an authenticator to append to a bogus message. It is possible, however, for an attacker to compute the plaintext version of the authenticator for any plaintext message. Thus there exists the possibility that an attacker might develop a bogus message, which produced the same authenticator as a previously transmitted message, and append the encrypted authenticator to the bogus message. Use of CBC, or cipher feedback, for the computation of the authenticator can thwart such an attack, but the problem of replay remains.

B.9 Key Notarization

In key management, key notarization is employed in conjunction with cryptographic facilities, termed 'key notarization facilities', at each node in a network. Interchange keys are associated with each node and node pair in the network. Interchange key IK_{ii} forms the basis of a key encrypting key used for the encipherment of local data encrypting keys, while IK_{ij} is designated for the encipherment of data keys used in communications from node i to node j. The actual key encrypting keys, used for local and communication data encipherment, is a function of the appropriate interchange key and the identifiers of the user or users.

If DES encryption is used then a 64-bit interchange key IK_{ij} is allocated for communication from node i to node j; users X and Y, at nodes i and j respectively, are allocated 28-bit identifiers x and y. The 64-bit key encrypting key for the encryption of data keys used in communications from X to Y are produced by a mathematical manipulation of IK_{ij} and identifiers x and y:

- the first 7 bits of the 28-bit identifier x are 'exclusive or-ed' with the first 7 bits of the interchange key IK_{ij};
- the 8th bit of the key IK_{ijxy} is produced as a parity bit of the 7 bits thus produced;
- the next 7 bits of the identifier x are 'exclusive or-ed' with the bits 9 to 15 of IK_{ij};
- bit 16 of IK_{ijxy} is developed as parity bit of the 7 bits thus produced; and
- the process is repeated for the remaining 14 bits of identifier x and the 28 bits of identifier y. The result of these operations is 64-bit parity-checked DES notarized key IK_{ijxy}.

A user Y at node j receives ciphertext from user X at node i, encrypted under data encrypting key k_d. User Y also receives data encrypting key k_d encrypted by notarized key IK_{ijxy}. In order to recover the plaintext message, user Y identifies himself, to the key notarization facility, with password PW_y and enters the identity of the transmitter X, the ciphertext, encrypted data encrypting key and a decryption command. Interchange key IK_{ij} is stored in the key notarization facility and notarized key IK_{ijxy} is then formed from the identifiers x and y by the mathematical algorithm described above. The data key k_d is recovered from $eIK_{ijxy}(k_d)$ by decryption with IK_{ijxy} within the tamper-resistant key notarization facility; this key is then used to decipher the ciphertext.

Key notarization restricts the use of keys to specific users at specific nodes for specific purposes. Thus user Y can use the data key k_d, received under encryption with IK_{ijxy}, to decipher messages from X at node i; the key can be used for no other purposes. This restriction on the use of DES keys can be employed in digital signature schemes.

Each user X at node i identifies himself with an identity number ID_x and secret password PW_x. The password is held in secondary storage encrypted under the notarized key IK_{iixx}. The password input by the user is thus similarly encrypted and compared with the stored value. Upon user authentication the facility is placed into an active state for the user and can thereafter perform encryption, decryption, authentication, decryption/re-encryption functions, etc. Data keys and initialization vectors, etc. are generated within the facility according to the requests of users. The facility also contains interchange keys for communicating nodes; these keys are, however, required at both sending and receiving nodes and must therefore be loaded into the facility by authorized personnel under secure conditions.

Appendix C Access Control

C.1 Password

A password is a popular form of knowledge test for access control; it comprises a string of alphanumeric data or a phrase that must be entered into a system to gain access to a physical area or a resource. Normally the password is associated with a user identification, the user inputs the user ID, and then responds to the request for the password. The user ID is usually transmitted in clear to the host computer, but the password may be protected in transmission. The use and misuse of passwords is now common; management must adopt sensible measures to ensure that they provide an appropriate degree of security. In particular the password robustness must be matched to the level of security required. The factors affecting password management are listed below.

- Users must be trained and motivated to ensure the effectiveness of the password access control. In particular they must be fully aware of the repercussions of failure to protect their passwords, and ensure that measures are taken to detect a lack of password security (e.g. by auditing accesses).
- Passwords should be easy to remember so that users need not make written records of them.
- Passwords should be changed regularly.
- System records of passwords should be protected (e.g. by encryption).
- The system must combat attempts to derive a password by successive log-on attempts.
- Passwords must not be displayed during log-on at a terminal, etc.

The design of passwords to facilitate their use without recourse to written records can take one of several forms. In general the length of a password should be consistent with the level of security required; access to top secret information may reasonably demand a lengthy password, but systems designed to reduce the incidence of

368

computer game playing should not burden legitimate users with memorizing 20-digit numbers. Some systems allow the users to select their own passwords; this enables users to select some easily remembered string of characters or digits, but it has also led to passwords that are too short, or easily derived from a knowledge of the names of the user's spouse or daughter. Phrases are more easily remembered but they also substantially increase both the time taken to enter them at a keyboard and the probability that a legitimate user will make a significant number of typing errors, and hence be mistaken for an attacker. Phonetic passwords can be both short and easily remembered, e.g 'joglin' is easier to remember than 'zxdswv'. Phonetic password generators can generate such random passwords.

The management of passwords must be designed to ensure that:

- They are disabled as soon they are known to have been compromised, or as soon as an employee resigns, retires, is transferred, and – most particularly – if the owner's loyalty to the organization is known to have changed (e.g. an employee under notice of dismissal).
- Passwords must be changed periodically: such changes minimize the danger of compromise and also ensure the regular notification of changes in users.
- Users must be encouraged to change passwords if they believe them to have been compromised or if they find them difficult to remember.

C.2 PIN Management and Security

In banking and data security, PIN management and security emcompasses the set of processes involved in the generation, assignment, delivery, issuance, storage, entry, verification, transmission, deactivation, and destruction of PINs.

PINs may be employed in two types of environment:

- an organization where selected employees or members use PINs to gain access to the organization's facilities (e.g. computer systems, databases);
- an EFT or EFTPOS network serving one or more financial institutions and an extremely large, diffuse customer base. The general principles of PIN management and security are common to both application areas, but the number of users, the relationship between the user and the system, and the potential damage resulting from inadequate PIN management and security are quite different in the two cases. Since the magnitude of the task and the complexity of the environment is greater in the case of

EFT and EFTPOS systems, PIN management and security will be considered from that viewpoint.

An EFT or EFTPOS system must guarantee the security of the customer's identification and the integrity of the customer's unique transaction from customer to card issuer to customer, irrespective of the location of the terminal used by the customer. Such terminals will usually be unsupervised, and, in the case of EFTPOS systems, they may be vulnerable to modification and misuse by dishonest retailers or retailers' employees.

The risks attendant upon the discovery of PINs by unauthorized persons can arise from:

- misuse of lost or stolen cards;
- mass fraud arising from the production and misuse of counterfeit cards.

The potential loss arising from the misuse of lost or stolen cards is limited by the time period between the loss and its reporting to the card issuer, and the maximum permitted value of daily transactions. Moreover, many illegal acquirers of such cards will lack the ability to determine their PINs.

The mass fraud that could, however, be perpetrated if counterfeit cards were produced, and the corresponding PINs derived or obtained, is a major source of concern. The misuse of a card would not be reported to a card issuer until the customer had checked a monthly (say) statement and reported the fraudulent transaction. The card issuer would then be faced with the following problems:

- the major administrative costs of rectifying the effects of individual fraudulent transactions;
- the problem of customers reporting legitimate transactions as fraudulent because they had forgotten the transaction or were fraudulently exploiting the situation;
- the loss of customer confidence.

It is therefore important that the processes involved in the generation, assignment, delivery, issuance, storage, entry, verification, transmission, deactivation, and destruction of PINs should obviate the possibility of PIN disclosure.

PINs may be employed in a transaction interchange system where customers enter their identification and authentication details when initiating transactions at terminals connected to the acquirer's network. The message details are transmitted to the card issuer who has the responsibility to authenticate the customer and authorize the transaction. PINs may also be employed in a private network where the authentication of customers and authorization of transactions are performed entirely within the network.

PINs may be generated as derived PINs, randomly generated PINs, or customer-selected PINs. A derived PIN is a function of the customer's account number or some other non-secret identifying information; the derived PIN may therefore be verified by applying the same algorithm to the customer-identifying information used to derive the PIN, and comparing the result with the PIN value input by the customer at the terminal. Clearly, the ability to calculate the PIN must be restricted to the card issuer, e.g. DES encryption may be employed and the secrecy of the key maintained. The PIN may be verified at a terminal that has access to the key used in the derivation algorithm, without storing the PIN on the card. The PIN generation technique should be fully automated and the results printed on a PIN mailer to avoid employees gaining access to customers' PINs. Such derived PINs must be encrypted before storage.

A randomly assigned PIN is produced by a random process such that a knowledge of any sequence of generated PINs will not enable the determination of any other PIN. The generated PINs must lie within the range of permissible PINs, in terms of character set and PIN length. Randomly assigned PINs may be difficult to remember and hence increase the danger that customers will make written records that could be lost or stolen with the card. Methods of generating sequences of characters that are easier to remember are available, but this technique considerably reduces the range of assigned PINs for a given PIN length, and hence requires rather longer PINs. The generation of such PINs demands strict security precautions to prevent card issuer employees gaining unauthorized access to PIN information, combined with customer identification.

Customer-selected PINs are likely to be such that they are easily remembered, but there exists the strong possibility that such PINs will bear a deducible relationship to the customer's personal details: names of children, birthdate, car registration numbers, etc. Since customers will tend to reject a large number of possibilities within the PIN range, the minimum PIN length must be sufficient to provide a wide range of PINs in use.

The delivery mechanism for a PIN must be such that it does not appear in clear form where it can be linked to customer identification. PINs must not be mailed in the same envelope as the corresponding credit or bank cards, and the return address on the envelope must be different from that used with the card. The PIN shall be printed in such a manner that it is only visible to the customer. If a customer has more than one card it is important that the information accompanying the PIN be sufficient for the customer to correlate the PIN with the appropriate card, but insufficient to compromise the PIN if it is intercepted. Card issuers must provide adequate security to protect the PINs in the handling of PIN documents, returned envelopes, waste material, etc.

The reporting by a customer of a customer-selected PIN should not involve the revealing of that PIN to a card issuer's employee; if an employee is authorized to initiate the entry of a PIN by a customer then that employee's identity should be incorporated in the transaction record. Customers may inform the card issuer of their PINs in person, by mail, or by telephone. Input of a PIN by the customer in person requires that:

- the card issuer employee authorized to initiate the input must check the customer's identification;
- the employee's identity must be checked and authenticated by the system; and
- the PIN entry process must be initiated by the employee and disabled immediately upon the PIN entry.

With mail or telephone entry of customer selected PINs the procedures adopted must ensure that any person intercepting the customer's mail, or eavesdropping on the telephone call, would be unable to relate the PIN to the customer's account information. In mailing, the customer needs to be informed that the returned form holding the PIN number and the associated envelope must not contain the customer's name, address, or account-identifying information. The form needs to contain a control number to enable the card issuer to correlate the PIN with the customer account number; this control number may, for example, be an encrypted form of the account number. Telephone inputs must be to an audio response or recording system to avoid the possibility that the customer will accidentally, or in responding to an invitation to do so, reveal a name or address.

Once issued, PINs may need to be changed or customers may need to be informed of forgotten PINs. The security arrangements in this case must be no less stringent than those for the issuance and delivery of new PINs. Customers must be informed by mail that their PINs have been changed. This correspondence should not contain the PIN and it should contain instructions to inform the card issuer immediately if the change had not been requested by the customer. If the change is initiated by the customer at an unattended terminal, then the old PIN must be entered; some additional form of identification (e.g. a one-shot PIN change authorization card) may also be required. Replacement of an exposed PIN may require special security arrangements, depending upon whether the PIN is derived, randomly assigned, or customer-selected. For example, if a derived PIN is exposed then some data element employed in generating the PIN (e.g. the offset) must also be changed.

PINs must always be encrypted before storage, and such encryption may be either reversible or irreversible. Reversible encryption allows the original PINs to be recovered and re-encrypted with a new key. If the encryption key is compromised, however, it must be considered that all PINs encrypted under that key have been compromised and protection by re-encryption under a new key will be too late. Irreversible encryption ensures that the original PINs cannot be revealed, but PINs of limited length may be determined by an exhaustive search, i.e. every PIN in the limited range is subjected to the irreversible encryption algorithm and compared with the stored encrypted values. Irreversible keys cannot be decrypted and re-encrypted under new keys; however, this facility may be achieved by the reversible encryption of irreversibly encrypted PINs for storage. All PINs should be combined with information related to the customer account number, before encryption, to obviate the danger that stored PIN values are modified by an attacker. PINs written on the magnetic stripe of a customer card must be encrypted, reversibly, or irreversibly. Again some account-identifying information must be combined with the PIN before encryption, in case an attacker has the facilities to erase and rewrite the contents of the stripe.

Customers and users are responsible for the secrecy of their PINs; after entry into the system, however, the card acceptor is responsible for PINs in transit, storage, or processing. At the point of entry there is an overlap of customer and card acceptor responsibility. The customer should ensure that onlookers are unable to observe the sequence of key entry, and the design of the terminal must preclude the visual display or printing of entered PINs.

The verification of PINs is the responsibility of the card issuer or delegated agent. PINs may be verified by comparison of received data and a PIN retrieved from storage that corresponds to the customer account number. The verification may involve an algorithm performed on an entered PIN and comparison with an encrypted value of the PIN stored on the card, or an algorithm performed on account data and compared with the entered PIN. Such algorithmic verification can be undertaken at a remote location, on- or off-line, provided that the requisite encryption keys are available at that location. A check digit may be included in a PIN to check the reasonableness of the entered PIN; this facilitates an early detection of a miskeyed PIN, but such check digits do not authenticate the PIN data. PINs are encrypted both during transmission and in storage; different cryptographic keys are used for these processes. Encryption for transmission is reversible, but stored values may be reversibly or irreversibly encrypted. With reversible encryption employed both for transmission and storage the comparison may be performed by decryption of both the transmitted and stored keys and by comparison of clear text values. Such decryption comparisons must, of course, be performed in a secure environment. Alternatively, one PIN may be decrypted and then re-encrypted with the second key for comparison of encrypted values. For reversible-transmission, irreversible-storage systems the transmitted PIN must be decrypted and then subjected to the irreversible encryption process for comparison with the stored value.

The protection of PINs in transmission may be achieved by physical security of the transmission medium or by encryption. Physical security of the transmission medium involves monitoring against unauthorized connections and possibly physical protection (e.g. a continuous metal conduit, pressure sensors in a pressurized conduit, etc.). Such physical protection, which may also involve shielding electromagnetic radiation, tends to be both complex and expensive. Encryption techniques demand secure modules for the storage of master cryptographic keys and encryption/decryption processes.

PINs are deactivated when a customer account is closed, a user ceases to have access privileges, or a PIN is compromised. Such intentional deactivation should involve the physical destruction of written records, erasure of electronic storage media, etc. Precautions must be taken against the accidental or deliberate destruction of stored PIN data, and backup copies held in a secure location must be subjected to the same level of encryption security applied to the original data.

Appendix D Communications Security

D.1 Electronic Listening Device

Electronic listening devices may be secreted in a room or connected to telephone equipment to collect and transmit information to an eavesdropper. The bug is used to listen into a conversation in a room, and comprises a miniature microphone, amplifier, transmitter, and power source. It will transmit the conversation in the form of a radio frequency signal that can be received as far as 10 kilometres away, depending upon the radio frequency used, the power of the transmitter, and the density of the buildings in the transmission path.

Such devices can be as small as a low-denomination coin and are easily inserted into pens, ashtrays, staplers, clocks, light fittings, etc. The presence of bugs can be detected by a wide-frequency-range radio receiver connected to an audio device or oscilloscope.

Telephone taps are similar to bugs except that they do not contain a microphone or power source, and are connected in series or parallel with a telephone line. Since they require no power source they can remain in operation indefinitely and need not be inserted into a secure area such as an office. The telephone tap can be connected to the appropriate telephone line at various points, e.g. at distribution frames located on the same floor, in the basement, or outside the office building. Such taps may be used to eavesdrop on conversations, facsimile, telex, or computer data. The presence of telephone taps may be detected by inserting a signal on the line and checking for echoes from interception points, checking variations in line voltage or resistance from the normal value, or by physical inspection.

Protection against room bugs includes the use of a modulated ultrasonic sound transmission which will blanket the audio signals in the receiver. Protection against telephone bugs includes voice-scrambling devices and transmitted masking tones, but such

375

techniques require equipment at both the receiving and transmitting ends, i.e. an unscrambler, or filter to remove the masking tone is required at the receiver.

D.2 Telephone Intrusion

Intrusion into a computer system by dial-up access is a common form of attack by hackers. Such attacks have increased in recent years due to:

- the facilities of dial-up networks,
- the availability of penetration equipment,
- intruder expertise,
- bulletin boards.

Increases in telephone network facilities in recent years have allowed intruders to dial directly into computer systems from many parts of the world, permitting, for example, intruders in the Middle East and Europe to dial up computers in the USA. The decreasing cost and increasing power of personal computers and modems allows even teenagers to acquire sophisticated intrusion equipment. Hackers sometimes display an extremely high level of technical expertise; pirate bulletin boards allow such hackers to disseminate their knowledge, acquired passwords, intrusion software, etc.

Defence against dial-up attacks includes special software, administrative practices, and add-on hardware. The operating security facilities should be fully exploited, and vendor-supplied passwords, which often convey a high level of privilege, should be deleted. Administrative routines include disconnecting modems in periods when legitimate users do not require access, enforcement of good password practices, logging attack events, limiting the number of log-on attempts, and concealing information about the computer system until password controls have been satisfied. It is suggested that no entry be permitted on a call after one unsuccessful log-on attempt, but the system should invite retry attempts so as to collect information on the intruder.

Add-on security devices may be categorized as one-end and two-end systems. One-end systems are installed either at the host computer or, less commonly, on the legitimate user's terminal. Port protection devices are connected at the host computer; security modems for user terminals incorporate security features integrated into the modem. Two-end devices provide enhanced security with the presence of security hardware at both ends of the legitimate telephone connection; such devices communicate with each other to perform security functions.

D.3 Port Protection Device

A port protection device is connected to the communications port of a host computer and has the function of authorizing user access to the port. The PPD may operate between host and modem, or between the modem and telephone set. The PPDs may have up to four typical features:

- password tables,
- call-back to originator,
- camouflage,
- attack signalling and logging.

All PPDs require that users enter passwords in order to access the dial-up port. These passwords are in addition to those required for log-on to the computer itself, PPDs limit the number of password attempts per telephone connection. With the callback-to-originator feature the user is required to enter the password, a PPD table is searched to locate the user's telephone number corresponding to the entered password, the call is disconnected, and the PPD calls back the user. This facility can, however, be subject to attack: if the intruder can trick the PPD into falsely sensing a line disconnect then the call-back is thwarted. Moreover, if the PPD reserves a set of lines exclusively for call-back then an intruder can camp on one of them with a ringing signal and intercept a call-back attempt to a valid user.

If the PPD is connected between the telephone set and modem then it can camouflage the computer by responding to calls with a synthesized human voice. For a PPD connected between the modem and computer the camouflage is produced by means of a screen display which is quite different from that of the computer display. Attack signalling and logging facilities provide warning signals and records of dial-up attack attempts.

D.4 X.400

X.400 is an CCITT standard for message-handling systems which includes specifications for the network architecture, protocol structure, implementation detail, message transfer elements, and content protocols. X.400 is a fully developed application layer of the open systems interconnection model and it introduces the concept of sub-layers termed 'user agents' (UA) and 'message transfer agents' (MTA).

The user agent is analogous to the user of a postal system who addresses and posts a letter. The message transfer agents are effectively the sorting offices which provide for the distribution and final

377

delivery of the message (see figure D-1). The MTAs as a group are termed the 'message transfer system' (MTS).

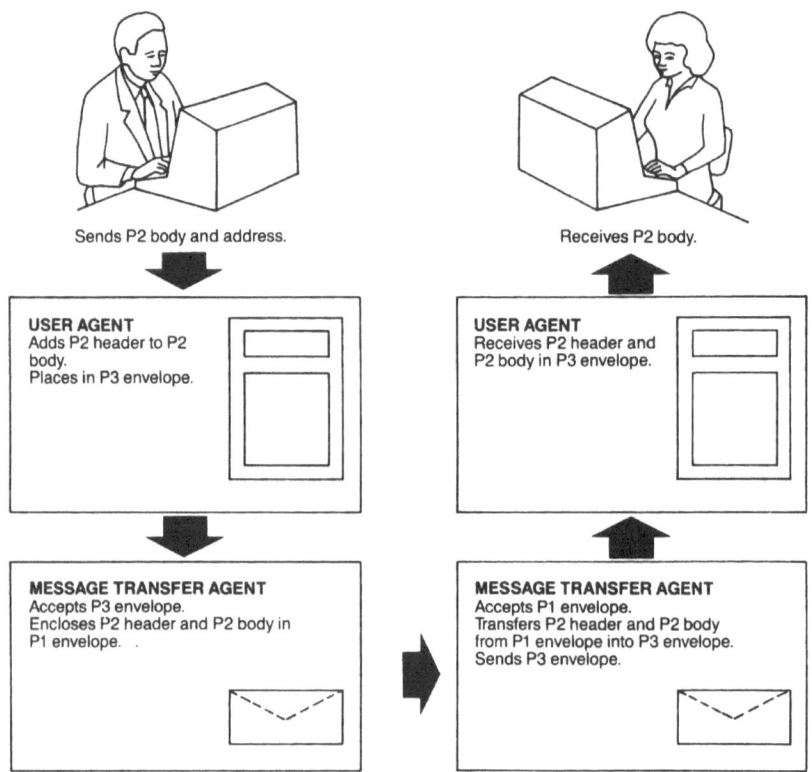

Sends P2 body and address.

Receives P2 body.

USER AGENT
Adds P2 header to P2 body.
Places in P3 envelope.

USER AGENT
Receives P2 header and P2 body in P3 envelope.

MESSAGE TRANSFER AGENT
Accepts P3 envelope.
Encloses P2 header and P2 body in P1 envelope. .

MESSAGE TRANSFER AGENT
Accepts P1 envelope.
Transfers P2 header and P2 body from P1 envelope into P3 envelope.
Sends P3 envelope.

Fig. D-1 X.400

The three major protocols within X.400 are the relay protocol, P1, the message header and body protocol, P2, and the submission protocol, P3. The user interface is not defined, thus allowing considerable flexibility in the manner in which the message is written, displayed, stored, and retrieved.

A typical message has an envelope and a message content which comprises the message header and body. The P2 protocol refers to the message header, including elements such as: originator, recipient, subject, copy recipients, reply-to indication, reply-by indication, priority, sensitivity, expiry date, blind copy, specification of delivery time, delivery notification address, cross references to other messages, obsolete message references, and reply-to message reference. P2 also defines the various body parts of the message including, telex, voice, fax, teletex, videotex.

The P3 protocol covers the envelope standard for the transmissions between the user agent and the message transfer agent. Thus the user sends the message body and address to the user agent who adds the P2 header to the P2 body, and places it in a P3 envelope (see figure D.4.1).

The P1 protocol refers to the envelope standard when the message is being routed from one message transfer agent to another. The MTA accepts the message in the P3 envelope from the UA, and encloses the P2 header and body in a P1 envelope for transfer to the next MTA. At the receiving end the MTA accepts the P1 envelope, and transfers the P2 header and body into a P3 envelope for submission to the receiving UA. The latter accepts the P3 envelope and passes the P2 body to the receiver.

It is anticipated that the main application area of X.400 will be in office systems using connections between personal computers and networks.

The specific advantages of X.400 to OEMs and their customers are:

- reduced development costs resulting from the use of clearly defined specifications;
- purchase of off-the-shelf software, reducing development times;
- OEM development staff need less specialist knowledge of proprietary communications systems;
- users will not be locked into individual manufacturers;
- elimination of wasteful conversion between different services;
- modular expansion;
- reduction in telephone usage;
- reduction in paper usage.

Appendix E Data Protection

Data Protection Laws at a Glance

Country	Legislation	Passed	In force	Physical Persons
Austria	Data Protection Act	18 Oct 1978	1 Jan 1982	Yes
Canada	Privacy Act	17 July 1982	1 July 1983	Yes *1
Denmark	Private Registers Act	8 Jun 1978	1 Jan 1979	Yes
Finland	Data Protection Act	4 Feb 1987	1 Jan 1988	Yes
France	Data Processing, Data Files & Individual Liberties Act	6 Jan 1978	1 Jan 1980	Yes
Germany	Data Protection Act	27 Jan 1977	1 Jan 1979	Yes
Guernsey	Data Protection Act	30 Jul 1986	11 Nov 1987	Yes
Iceland	Systematic Recording of Personal Data Act	5 Jun 1981	1 Jan 1982	Yes
Isle of Man	Data Protection Act	16 Jul 1986	Not available	Yes
Israel	Protection of Privacy Act	23 Feb 1981	11 Sep 1981	Yes
Jersey	Data Protection Act	30 Apr 1987	11 Nov 1987	Yes
Luxembourg	The use of Name-Linked Data in Computer Processing Act	31 Mar 1979	1 Oct 1979	Yes
New Zealand	Wanganui Computer Centre Act		1976	Yes
Norway	Personal Data Registers Act	9 Jun 1978	1 Jan 1980	Yes
Sweden	Data Act	13 May 1973	1 Jul 1974	Yes
UK	Data Protection Act	12 Jul 1984	11 Nov 1987	Yes
USA	Freedom of Information Act		1966	Yes *4

Legal Persons	Automated Data	Manual Records	Export Licence [all] [some]	DPA may restrict exports
Yes	Yes		Yes	
	Yes	Yes		
Yes	Yes	Yes	Yes	
	Yes	Yes		Yes
Yes *2	Yes	Yes		Yes
	Yes	Yes	DPC decides.	For imports see *3
	Yes˙			Yes
Yes	Yes	Yes	Yes	
	Yes			Yes
	Yes			Yes
	Yes			Yes
Yes	Yes		Yes [Licence also needed for import of name-linked data]	
	Yes			
Yes	Yes	Yes		Yes
	Yes		Yes	
	Yes			Yes
	Yes	Yes		

Notes

*1 Canada's Access to Information Act and Privacy Act covers only the federal government and federal agencies.

*2 France's data protection law was extended to legal persons on July 3rd 1984 by an administrative decision of CNIL, the data protection authority.

*3 Two alternative arrangements are possible for name-linked data to be imported into Germany:

(i) the importer takes responsibility for the data on behalf of the party making the transfer. Data subjects have full data protection rights.

(ii) the party making the transfer takes responsibility. The German party is merely a service provider and data subjects have no right to access or prior notification.

*4 The USA's *Freedom of Information Act* was passed in 1966, came into force in 1967 and was amended in 1974 and 1976.

- All European data protection laws cover the public and private sectors, and give data subjects a right of access to records on themselves, together with a right of correction or a right to file a note of disagreement. In addition, they all contain provisions for imposing penalties on those who breach the law. Several of these have been amended.

- DPA means Data Protection Authority. DPC means Data Protection Controller (within an organisation)

- Belgium, Greece, Ireland, Italy, Netherlands, Portugal, Spain and Switzerland have introduced data protection legislation. The Australian Federal Government has pledged to introduce privacy legislation.

- Several states also have their own open government laws. *The Privacy Act* was passed in 1974 and covers the federal government only. Each agency has to publish in the Federal Register at least annually a notice of the existence and character of its system of records. There is also sectoral Federal data protection legislation for example, the *Federal Fair Credit Reporting Act* and the *Family Educational Rights and Privacy Act* of 1974. In May 1987, the US Senate passed the *Computer Matching and Privacy Protection Bill* which will be considered by the House of Representatives. The bill covers federal agencies and requires them to follow certain standards when carrying out computer matching to ensure that individuals are not harmed by unauthorised use of name-linked information or refused government benefits because of inaccurate data.

- The following table was compiled from information provided by the newsletter *Privacy Laws and Business*, whose permission to publish these findings is gratefully acknowledged.

- Further information from 3 Central Avenue, Pinner, Middlesex, HA5 5BT, United Kingdom. Phone: 01-866 8641

Appendix F List of Questions

Chapter 1 Data Security

1.1 Overview

1.2 Security Policy and Organizational Structure

1.3 Personnel and Responsibilities

1.4 Data Ownership and Data Handling Responsibilities

1.5 Access Control and Cryptographic Controls

List of Questions

1.6 Information Flow Control

1.7 Security of Stored Data

1.8 Monitoring and Audit Trails

1.9 Military and Commercial Security

Chapter 2 Computer Security Risk Analysis and Management

2.1 Overview

2.2 Risk Analysis and Management

2.3 Conventional Computer Security Risk Analysis and Management

2.4 Courtney Technique of Risk Analysis

2.5 CRAMM Risk Analysis

2.6 Conclusions

Chapter 3 Countermeasures

3.1 Overview

3.2 Physical Security

List of Questions

3.3 Access Control

3.4 Personal Computer Security

3.5 Contingency Planning

3.6 Insurance

Chapter 4 Communications Security

4.1 Overview

4.2 Network Security

4.3 Security on IBM Systems

4.4 OSI Security

Chapter 5 Financial and Banking Networks

5.1 Overview

5.2 Identity and Authentication of the User: Plastic Cards

5.3 Identity and Authentication of the User: PINs

5.4 Privacy, Integrity and Authenticity of Financial Messages

5.5 Financial Network Security

Chapter 6 Office Automation Security

6.1 Overview

6.2 Communications and Logical Security

6.3 Physical Security of Office Systems

6.4 Procedural and Personnel Security

Chapter 7 Security and the Law

7.1 Overview

7.2 Data Protection

List of Questions

7.3 Legal Protection of Information Assets

7.4 Computer Crime

7.5 Law and Personnel

Glossary

Abbreviations

AFIPS   American Federation of Information Processing
            Societies
AFR   US Air Force Regulation
ANSI   American National Standards Institute
AR   US Army Regulation
DOD   US Department of Defense
FIPS   US Federal Information Processing Standards
OPNAVINST   US Office of Naval Operations Research
SAA   Standards Association of Australia

access control In computer security, procedures designed to limit entry to a physical area, or to limit use of a computer/communication system, or computer stored data, to authorized personnel.

access control matrix In access control, a matrix that relates subjects, objects and access types. A subject is an active entity capable of accessing objects, e.g. a program in execution, a user in a time-sharing system. An object is an entity to which access is controlled, e.g. a file, memory segment, program. An access type is a kind of access to an object, e.g. an access type to a program may be: execute, read source listing; to a file it may be: read, write, append. The access control matrix is a two dimensional array with objects listed horizontally, subjects listed vertically and each cell contains the access type that the given subject has for the corresponding object. *See* append, execute, object, read, subject, write. *See* **Fig. G-1**

acquirer In banking, an institution within a transaction interchange network that receives identification and authentication information from a terminal. The acquirer is responsible for obtaining payment for the card acceptor from the card issuer. (SAA) *See* card acceptor, card issuer.

	Program 1	Segment A	Segment B
Process 1	Read Execute	Read Write	
Process 2			Read

Fig. G-1 Access control matrix

active wiretapping (1) In computer security, the attaching of an un-authorized device, such as a computer terminal, to a communications circuit for the purpose of obtaining access to data through the generation of false messages or control signals, or by altering the communications of legitimate users. (FIPS)
(2) In communications security, wiretapping for the purposes of obtaining access to data by the generation of false messages or control signals, alteration of communications of legitimate users or the denial of services to legitimate users.

ADP Automatic Data Processing.

ALE *See* Annual Loss Expectancy.

alphanumeric Pertaining to a character set that contains letters, digits and usually other characters, e.g. punctuation marks.

ambush code In computer security, a special code for an access control system, or digital keypad entry, which provides a warning, to a remote control point, that the user is under duress.

American National Standards Institute A body which organizes committees formed of computer users, manufacturers, etc., to develop and publish industry standards, e.g. ANSI FORTRAN, ANSI Standard Code for Periodical Identification. ANSI X3 is concerned with computer and data processing standards, ANSI X9 with banking standards.

Annual Loss Expectancy In risk management, a measure of the potential annual cost of a threat to system security. *See* threat.

ANSI *See* American National Standards Institute.

ANSI X3.T1 The ANSI Technical Committee in Encryption.

ANSI X3.105-1983 An ANSI standard for Data Link Encryption.

ANSI X3.106 An ANSI standard for Modes of operation of Data Encryption Algorithm.

ANSI X3.92-1981 An ANSI standard for the Data Encryption Algorithm. *See* DEA.

ANSI X4.13-1973 An ANSI standard for the specifications for credit cards.

ANSI X4.16-1976 An ANSI standard for magnetic stripe encoding for credit cards.

ANSI X9.1 An ANSI standard for Magnetic Stripe Data Contents for track 3.

ANSI X9.2-1980 An ANSI standard for interchange message specification for debit and credit card message exchange among financial institutions.

ANSI X9.3 An ANSI standard for specifications for check endorsements.

ANSI X9.4 An ANSI standard for OCR scannable bill line. *See* OCR.

ANSI X9.5 An ANSI standard for Financial Institution Numbering System. (FINS)

ANSI X9.7 An ANSI standard for bank cheque background and convenience amount field.

ANSI X9.8 An ANSI standard For PIN Management and Security.

ANSI X9.9 An ANSI standard to authenticate financial messages, including fund transfers, letters of credit, security transfers, loan agreements, and foreign exchange control. The standard defines the minimum set of message elements to be included in the authentication process.

ANSI X9.12 An ANSI standard for specification for fully registered municipal securities.

ANSI X9.13 An ANSI standard for specifications for placement and location of MICR printing. *See* MICR.

ANSI X9.14 An ANSI standard for specification for securities transactions interchange forms.

ANSI X9.16 An ANSI standard for securities for standard formats for message types.

ANSI X9.17 An ANSI standard for key management in the wholesale banking EFTS developed by the ANSI X9 Financial Services Working Party. The scope of the standard is:

- control during the life of the keying material to prevent unauthorized disclosure, modification, or substitution;
- distribution of keying material to permit interoperability between cryptographic key equipment or facilities using the DEA algorithm;
- ensuring the integrity of keying material during all phases of its life, including the generation, distribution, storage, entry, use, and destruction;
- recovery in the event of failure of the key management process or when the integrity of the keying material is questioned. *See* DEA.

ANSI X9.18 An ANSI standard for paper specification for cheques.

ANSI X9.19 An ANSI standard for Financial Institution Retail

Message Authentication.

ANSI X9.20 An ANSI standard for Securities for Institutional Delivery System.

ANSI X9.21 An ANSI standard vocabulary and data elements for funds transfers and related advices.

ANSI X9.22 An ANSI standard for specifications for standard telex formats for wholesale financial services messages.

append In access control, a privilege that enables a user to add data to the end of a file but not to read it nor modify any existing data. *Compare* execute, read, write.

application program In programming, a program, usually written in-house, for a specific user application, e.g. payroll.

ASCII American Standard Code for Information Interchange, pronounced 'askee'. A standard data transmission code that was introduced to achieve compatibility between data devices. It consists of 7 information bits and 1 parity bit for error-checking purposes, thus allowing 128 code combinations. Of these 32 are used for upper case characters and a few punctuation marks, another group of 32 characters is used for numbers, spacing, and additional punctuation symbols; the third group of 32 characters is assigned to lower case characters and some rarely used punctuation symbols. The last set of 32 characters is allocated to machine and control commands, e.g. line feed, carriage return.

asymmetric cipher In cryptography, a cipher in which it is computationally infeasible to deduce the enciphering key from the deciphering key or vice versa. *Compare* symmetric cipher. *See* public key cryptography.

asynchronous In data communications, pertaining to a form of data transmission in which there can be variable time intervals between characters but the bits within a character are sent with fixed time intervals. Start and stop elements are used to indicate the beginning and end of characters. *Compare* synchronous.

ATM *See* automated teller machine.

attacker In computer and data security, the person who attempts to overcome the computer or data security measures.

audit trail (1) A set of records that collectively provides documentary evidence of processing used to aid in tracing from original transactions forward to related records and reports, and/or backwards from records and reports to their component source transactions. (DOD)

(2) In computer security, a chronological record of system activities which is sufficient to enable the reconstruction, review, and examination of the sequence of environments and activities surrounding or leading to each event in the path of a transaction from its inception to output of final results. (FIPS)

(3) In programming, a clerical or automated method for tracing the transactions affecting the contents of a record.

(4) In banking, the ability to view what the system has completed in the past.

authentication In computer security, the act of identifying or verifying the eligibility of a station, originator, or individual to access specific categories of information. (FIPS) *See* message authentication, peer entity authentication.

authentication code In data security, a set of characters which are derived from the text of a message, or parts thereof, and which may be subsequently used to check if any changes have made to the message. *See* message authentication code.

automated teller machine A device that provides for cash withdrawals, payment of bills, account balance enquiries, deposits, and transfers of funds between accounts.

background In computing, pertaining to a job of relatively low priority in a multitasking environment; computer resources are only allocated to it when they are not required for higher priority foreground tasks.

backing storage In computing, an intermediate storage medium (e.g. magnetic tape, magnetic disk, etc.) onto which data is entered for later processing by the central computer.

backup The actions involved in transferring data from magnetic disk to tape or to disk for off-line storage.

Bell–La Padula model In computer security, a formal transition model of computer security policy that describes a set of access control rules. In this formal model, the entities in a computer system are divided into abstract sets of subjects and objects. The notion of a secure state is defined and it is proven that each state transition preserves security by moving from secure state to secure state; thus, inductively proving that the system is secure. A system state is defined to be 'secure' if the only permitted access modes of subjects to objects are in accordance with a specific security policy. In order to determine whether a specific access mode is allowed, the clearance of a subject is compared to the classification of the object, and a determination is made as to whether the subject is authorized for the specific access mode. The clearance/classification scheme is expressed in terms of a lattice. (DOD) *See* mandatory access control, object, subject. *See also* Appendix A.1.

binary code A coding system employing groups of the binary digits, 0 and 1, to represent a letter, digit or other character in a computer, e.g. the decimal number 6 is represented by binary 110, i.e. $(1\times4)+(1\times2)+(0\times1)$.

binary coded decimal A method of representing decimal numbers where each digit of the number is represented by four bits. These bits can represent numbers in the range 0–15 but only the representations for 0–9 are employed. This coding allows very long decimal numbers to be precisely represented, and is therefore often employed in applications in the financial transaction areas.

binary number In mathematics, a number expressed in binary notation, e.g. 101 is the binary number representing 5.

biometric sensor In access control, a device for positive personal identification. The techniques include recognition of eye blood vessel patterns, hand geometry, palm prints, and signature analysis.

block cipher In cryptography, a cipher in which the plaintext must be assembled into blocks with a blocksize determined by the cryptographic algorithm designer; the corresponding ciphertext block depends only upon the cryptographic key, the algorithm, and the plaintext block. Thus for any given cryptographic key the cipher effectively provides a massive codebook with entries for every possible plaintext block and corresponding ciphertext block. *Compare* stream cipher.

bug (1) In communications security. *Synonymous with* electronic listening device.

(2) In programming and hardware, an error in a program or system. The term is reputed to have originated in the days of an electromechanical computer using relays. An inexplicable error was traced to the wings of an insect lodged between the contacts of a relay.

bulletin board A remote public access system for personal computer users. A bulletin board provides a variety of services geared to the requirements of the user population. The user requires a communications software package and a modem to establish dial-up connection to the system.

call-back In computer security, a procedure established for positively identifying a terminal dialling into a computer system by disconnecting the calling terminal and re-establishing the connection by the computer system's dialling the telephone number of the calling terminal. (FIPS) *See* port protection device, telephone intrusion.

capability list *Synonymous with* access control matrix.

card acceptor In banking, the party accepting a credit card and presenting transaction data to an acquirer. (SAA) *Compare* acquirer, card issuer.

card issuer In banking, the institution (or its agent) that provided the card holder with the card being used in the current transaction. The institution is also responsible for paying the acquirer for goods or services on behalf of the card holder. (SAA) *Compare* acquirer, card acceptor.

CDPA The *Copyright, Designs and Patents Act, 1988.*

central processing unit In computing, the unit containing the circuits that control and perform the execution of instructions. It generally contains the arithmetic logic unit, a number of special registers, and control circuits. The CPU handles the decoding and execution of instructions, performs arithmetic and logic functions, provides timing signals, etc.

Chaos Club In computer security, a West German club of experienced hackers who have claimed success in attacking computer systems in Europe. It was alleged that Chaos members broke into the NASA computer system.

checksum In cryptography, a fixed length block that is produced as a function of every bit in the message.

cipher block chaining In cryptography, a mode of operation that overcomes the cryptographic weakness of the electronic codebook mode. The ciphertext output is dependent upon the key and all previous plaintext blocks of the message. Thus highly formatted messages will not suffer from the repetition of ciphertext blocks experienced with electronic codebook. *Compare* cipher feedback, electronic codebook, output feedback. *See also* Appendix B.2.

cipher feedback In cryptography, a stream cipher mode of operation suitable for applications where the data cannot be formed into 64-bit blocks before encryption. *Compare* cipher block chaining, electronic codebook, output feedback. *See also* Appendix B.3.

ciphertext In cryptography, unintelligible text or signals produced through the use of cipher systems. (FIPS) *Compare* plaintext.

CLODO In computer security, a French underground organization, the committee to liquidate or neutralize computers.

coin purse In banking, a mode of smart card operation in which the user charges up the card with credit and the corresponding amount is deducted from the user's bank account. The smart card may then be used to pay for goods or services; at each transaction the amount on the smart card is correspondingly reduced. *See* smart card.

common carrier In communications, a company whose business is to supply communication facilities to the public. The term is derived from the interstate commerce concept of carrying goods. In the US a communication common carrier comes under the jurisdiction of relevant state organizations, and if it operates interstate facilities it will be subject to FCC regulations. Common carriers can carry telemetry, facsimile, television, and data messages.

communication protocol In data communications, a formally specified set of conventions governing the format and control of inputs and outputs between two communicating systems.

communications security The protection that ensures the authenticity of telecommunications and that results from the application of measures taken to deny unauthorized persons information of value which might be derived from the acquisition of telecommunications. (FIPS)

compiler In programming, a program designed to translate a high-level language source program into a corresponding machine code program.

computationally infeasible In cryptanalysis, pertaining to a computation that is theoretically achievable but which is infeasible in terms of the time taken to perform it with the current or predicted power of computers.

computer abuse Any intentional act involving a computer and one or more perpetrators which made, or could have made, gain and one or more victims suffered, or could have suffered, loss. *See* computer crime, computer fraud, computer related crime.

computer bureau In legislation, as defined by the UK *Data Protection Act, 1984*, a person carries on a computer bureau if he provides other persons with services in respect of data, and a person provides such services if: (a) as agent for other persons he causes them to be processed; or (b) he allows other persons to use equipment in his possession for the processing.

computer crime (1) Illegal computer abuse implying the direct involvement of computers in a crime.
(2) Any crime where the perpetrator has to have a technical knowledge of computers to engage in crime. *See* computer abuse, computer fraud, computer related crime.

computer fraud Any fraudulent behaviour connected with computerization by which someone intends to gain dishonest advantage. *See* computer abuse, computer crime, computer related crime.

computer related crime A broader term covering any illegal act for which knowledge of computer technology is essential for successful perpetration. *See* computer abuse, computer crime, computer fraud.

computing resource A blanket term covering the collection of people, procedures, operations, programs, hardware devices, files, input data, output results, networks, or databases that supports the computerized part of an organization.

COMSEC *See* communications security.

contamination In data security, the introduction of data of one sensitivity and need to know with data of a lower sensitivity or different need to know. This can result in the contaminating data not receiving the required level of protection. (AFR)

contingency planning In computer security, the action of formulating plans by an organization to respond to the conceivable range of incidents, accidents, and disasters that could occur: mistakes by operating staff, loss of personnel due to sickness, death or strikes, hacker activity, theft, fraud, vandalism, alteration or destruction of software or data, fire, flood, power failure, excessive weather conditions, electrical disturbances, failure of environmental protection (air-conditioning, fumes, dust), terrorist attack, aircraft, vehicle, meteorite or satellite impact, chemical spillage, building construction failure, nuclear reactor incidents or other radiation effects, earthquakes, volcanos, avalanches, etc.

copyright In software and publishing, the right to prevent copying. The copyright owner has the right to prevent copying of the form in which an idea is expressed, but not the idea itself. Computer programs are protected under the same laws that cover literary works in those countries that have copyright legislation. However the use of an idea, or an algorithm, obtained by studying source code of a copyrighted program is not, in itself, an infringement of copyright.

covert channel In computer security, a communication channel that allows a process to transfer information in a manner that violates the system's security policy. (DOD)

CPU *See* central processing unit.

credit reference agency In legislation, persons carrying on a business comprising the furnishing of persons with information relevant to the financial standing of individuals, being information collected by the agency for that purpose.

cryptanalysis The steps and operations performed in converting encrypted messages into plaintext without initial knowledge of the key employed in the encryption algorithm. (FIPS)

cryptographic control In data security, the use of cryptographic techniques to protect information when transmitted over a link or when stored in a computer.

cryptographic key In cryptography, a parameter (e.g., a secret 64-bit number for DES) used by a cryptographic process that makes the process completely defined and usable only by those having that key. (FIPS)

cryptography The art or science which treats of the principles, means, and methods for rendering plaintext unintelligible and for converting encrypted messages into intelligible form. (FIPS)

cryptosystem In cryptography, the documents, devices, equipment, and associated techniques that are used as a unit to provide a single means of encryption (enciphering or encoding). (FIPS)

CSRAM Computer Security Risk Analysis and Management. *See* risk analysis, risk management.

database management system In programming, a set of programs that facilitates the creation and maintenance of a database and the execution of programs using the database.

data circuit terminating equipment In data communications, a piece of equipment located at either end of a data circuit which provides all the functions needed to establish, maintain, and terminate a connection. It also carries out the signal conversion and coding between the data terminal equipment and the telephone line. *Compare* data terminal equipment.

data encrypting key In cryptography, a cryptographic key used for encrypting (and decrypting) data. (FIPS) *Compare* key encrypting key.

data encryption algorithm In cryptography, an encryption standard, ANSI X3.92-1981, identical to the cryptographic function that forms part of the Data Encryption Standard, FIPS Pub 46. *See* data encryption standard.

data encryption equipment In cryptography, hardware used for encryption and decryption operations and storage of cryptographic keys. *See* security control module.

data encryption standard In cryptography, the Data Encryption Standard specifies an algorithm to be implemented in electronic hardware devices and used for the cryptographic protection of computer data. The algorithm is a product cipher employing 64-bit data blocks and a 64-bit key. The standard was published by the National Bureau of Standards in January 1977, as FIPS Publication 46. It became mandatory for US federal agencies in June 1977. *See also* Appendix B.1.

data subject In legislation, as defined by the UK *Data Protection Act, 1984*, an individual who is the subject of personal data. *See* personal data.

data terminal equipment In data communications, any piece of equipment at which a communication path begins or ends, e.g. a VDU. *Compare* data circuit terminating equipment.

data user In legislation, as defined by the UK *Data Protection Act, 1984*, a person who holds data. A person holds data if:

- the data form part of a collection of data processed or intended to be processed by, or on behalf of, that person;
- that person (either alone or jointly or in common with other persons) controls the contents and use of the data comprised in the collection; and
- the data are in the form in which they have been, or are intended to be, processed as mentioned above or (though not for the time being in that form) in a form into which they have been converted after being so processed and with a view to being further so processed on a subsequent occasion.

DBMS *See* database management system.

DCE *See* data circuit terminating equipment.

DEA *See* data encryption algorithm.

DEE *See* data encryption equipment.

defensive depth   In computer security, a principle of design such that attackers should be compelled to overcome a series of safeguards to achieve their objectives, e.g. access to a highly sensitive area should require passage through the maximum number of controlled areas, and violation of one control point should initiate an alerting and reinforcing of all adjacent control points.

derived PIN   In banking, a PIN that is generated from some information related to the customer's account number or identity. The PIN is derived by an algorithm involving a secret key. Such PINs may be verified at any location, with access to the secret key used in the algorithm, without requiring storage of the PIN on the customer's card. *Compare* random PIN, user-selected PIN. *See* PIN.

DES   *See* data encryption standard.

dial-up   In data communications, pertaining to systems that can be accessed over a telephone network.

digital signature   In cryptography, a data block appended to a message, or a complete encrypted message, such that the recipient can authenticate the message contents and/or prove that it could only have originated with the purported sender. The digital signature is a function of: (a) the message, transaction or document, to be signed, (b) secret information known only to the sender, and (c) public information employed in the validation process.

directory   In computing, a file that stores relationships between records in other files. The directory contains an overview of the data held.

disaster recovery plan   In computer security, the planned sequence of events that allows for the recovery of a computer facility and/or the applications processed there.

discretionary access control   In access control, a means of restricting access to objects based on the identity of subjects and/or groups to which they belong. The controls are discretionary in the sense that a subject with a certain access permission is capable of passing that permission (perhaps indirectly) on to any other subject. (DOD) *Compare* mandatory access control.

displacement   *See* offset.

driver   In programming, a software routine which performs low-level input/output functions for an input/output device.

DTE   *See* data terminal equipment.

dumpster diving   In data security, a method of obtaining confidential information by examining the contents of legitimate users' waste paper baskets, trash cans, etc.

dynamic password   In access control, a method based on the use of random numbers and effective against replay attacks. A user is given a device, rather like a pocket calculator, but having a protected DES key. This key is also stored in protected form in a computer system. After log-on at a terminal the user is challenged by a random number. This number is entered into the device to produce a response number which in turn is keyed into the terminal by the user. The response is the DES output of the challenge, encrypted under the secret key. The computer checks the response by performing the same calculation on the random number using the secret key corresponding to the user ID. Since the key is unique to the user, the user's identity can be confirmed; the security is further enhanced through the use of a PIN in conjunction with the cryptographic device. In some systems the device is placed over the designated area on the VDU screen and a photosensor in the device detects the random number produced by the terminal. The required user's response is then displayed on a liquid crystal display of the device. *See* DES.

EDI *See* electronic data interchange.

EFTPOS *See* electronic funds transfer point of sale.

EFTS Electronic Funds Transfer System. *See* electronic funds transfer.

electronic codebook In cryptography, a DES mode of operation in which one or more 64-bit input blocks produce corresponding 64-bit ciphertext blocks by successively presenting the input blocks for encipherment. For a given key DES effectively provides an electronic codebook with 2^{64} entries of plaintext–ciphertext pairs. If messages are highly formatted then certain ciphertext blocks are likely to recur and be of value to an attacker. *Compare* cipher block chaining, cipher feedback, output feedback. *See* data encryption standard.

electronic data interchange In computing and communications, the transmission of documents from one computer to another over a network. Consider the case of a vehicle manufacturer with many different component suppliers. If all parties have computer systems in which a standard has been agreed for electronic data interchange, such as X.400, then everyone benefits. Much paperwork is eliminated, suppliers can respond more rapidly to production requirements and the manufacturer does not have to re-key supplier invoice details. This eliminates transcription errors and reduces handling costs, particularly if the participants are multinational organizations using a global network.

electronic eavesdropping In data security, the interception of wireless transmissions, e.g. radio or microwave transmissions, or information-bearing electromagnetic energy emanating from electronic devices.

electronic funds transfer In banking, an automated system for transferring funds from one bank account to another using electronic equipment and data communications rather than paper media such as cheques and the postal system.

electronic funds transfer point of sale In banking, pertaining to a point of sale terminal that is connected by communication line to a financial institution's computer. The terminal will normally read and transmit the information recorded on the magnetic stripe of a credit card and provide for the input of transaction details via a keyboard.

electronic listening device In communications security, a device used to collect transmit information to an eavesdropper. Such devices may be secreted in a room or connected to telephone equipment. *See also* Appendix D.1.

electronic mail In data communications, a facility enabling users to exchange information addressed to a particular individual, or a group, using computer communication facilities.

electronic signature *Synonymous with* digital signature.

enciphering algorithm In cryptography, a set of mathematically expressed rules for rendering information unintelligible by effecting a series of transformations through the use of variable elements controlled by the application of a key to the normal representation of the information.

encryption In cryptography, the process of transforming data in to an unintelligible form in such a way that the original data either cannot be obtained (one-way encryption) or cannot be obtained without using the inverse decryption process (two-way encryption). (FIPS)

encryptor board In computing, a hardware device that encrypts data before storage on magnetic disk and decrypts the data after retrieval from the disk.

end-to-end encryption In communications security, encryption of information at the origin within a communications network and postponing decryption to the final destination point. (FIPS) *Compare* link encryption, node encryption.

error-correcting code A code designed to detect an error in a word or character, identify the incorrect bit or bits, and replace them with the correct ones. The number of incorrect bits that can be corrected depends upon the number of redundant bits used in the code. *Compare* error detecting code.

error-detecting code In codes, a code designed to detect, but not correct, an error in a word or character. The number of incorrect bits that can be detected depends upon the number of redundant bits in the code. *Compare* error correcting code.

error extension In cryptography, an effect that arises when noisy communication channels produce errors, or an attacker introduces changes, in transmitted ciphertext, and such errors result in even lengthier errors in the subsequent received plaintext. For example, in cipher block chaining a single bit error in the ciphertext will produce a garbled 64-bit plaintext block and a single 1-bit error in the succeeding plaintext block. *See* cipher block chaining,

exclusive-or *See* modulo 2 addition.

execute In access control, a privilege which enables a user to execute a specific program or perform transactions using that program. *Compare* append, read, write.

expansion card In computing, a card added to the system in order to mount additional chips or circuits so as to extend the system capability.

facsimile In communications, pertaining to the transmission of images over communication links which have a lower bandwidth than that necessary for video signals. The image is scanned by a light beam and a signal representing the brightness of the section of the image under the scanning beam is transmitted over the link in the form of a modulated analogue or digital signal. At the receiving station the signal drives an energy source to reproduce the image by photographic, thermal, or xerographic techniques.

fiat shamir In cryptography, a technique similar to RSA in which users can prove their identity to a verifier by an exchange of information. The exchange of information continues until the verifier has a high probability of correctly authenticating the user. The important advantages of this technique are that a wiretapper cannot derive sufficient information to masquerade as the user on some future occasion, the verifier cannot masquerade as the user, and the user may remain anonymous. *See* RSA, zero knowledge proof.

field In computing, an element of a record. *See* record.

file server In computing, a sophisticated form of disk server that maintains a complete logical file system. Networked microcomputer users can access information in the same directory areas and the file server mechanisms will deal with the problems of unauthorized access, concurrent accesses etc. A heterogeneous mix of microcomputers can also be accommodated by software, which resides in the microcomputers and converts operating system requests into equivalent file server requests. *See* server.

filter In computing, a security kernel responsible for enforcing the requirements of multilevel security.

floppy diskette In computing, a thin flexible magnetic coated disk contained in a rigid or semirigid protective jacket. The floppy diskette provides microcomputer users with a cheap, high-capacity, direct-access backing store. The floppy diskette is contained within an envelope which is coated in its exterior to provide a cleaning action. The envelope has a number of apertures for the drive spindle, index hole to signal the start of a sector and a write-inhibit notch. *Compare* hard disk.

front-end processor A small computer used to handle communication interfacing, e.g. polling, multiplexing, or detection for another computer.

gateway In data communications, equipment used to interface networks so that a terminal can communicate with a terminal or computer on another network.

hacker (1) In programming, a computing enthusiast. The term is normally applied to people who take a delight in experimenting with system hardware, software, and communication systems.
(2) In data security, an unauthorized user who tries to gain entry to a computer network by defeating the system's access controls.

handshaking In computer security, a procedure to ensure that communication has been established between two genuine nodes in a communications network. Handshaking procedures are designed to ensure that an attacker cannot elicit information from one node by operating a fake node. One method of handshaking relies upon two genuine nodes sharing a secret key. When node A wishes to establish communication with node B then node A generates a random number (RN), encrypts it under the secret key, shared with node B, and transmits the encrypted message to B. At node B the random number is revealed by decryption. This random number is operated upon with a non secret algorithm, the result (f(RN)) is encrypted with the same shared key and transmitted back to node A. At node A the message is decrypted and compared with the value f(RN) produced by subjecting the original random number to the algorithm f.

hard disk In backing storage, a direct-access storage device with a rigid magnetic disk. *Compare* floppy diskette.

home banking In banking, the use of a domestic communications terminal, usually viewdata, to conduct transactions on the user's bank account. *See* viewdata.

inference control In computer security, a control employed to prevent an enquirer from using data in a statistical database to obtain information concerning an individual. For example, if an individual were the only member of a particular ethnic group in a community, and the database contained the sums of welfare payments to all ethnic groups in the community, then an enquiry on the total payments for the whole community, coupled with a second enquiry on the payments to all ethnic groups except that of the individual in question, would reveal details of payments to that individual.

information centre In computing, a service strategy as well as an organization within a data processing department that provides a direct interface to end-user computing and supports services for it.

information flow control (1) In data security, control on the flow of information within a computer system and as it leaves the computer system.

(2) In data security, controls concerned with the right of dissemination of information, irrespective of what object holds the information. While access controls regulate the accessing of objects, information flow control addresses what subjects might do with the information contained in them. *See* object, subject.

initialization vector (1) In cryptography, a number used as a starting point for encryption of a data sequence to increase security by introducing additional cryptographic variance and to synchronize cryptographic equipment. (ANSI)

(2) In cryptography, the content of the shift register in stream ciphers, or block ciphers with chaining, immediately before the encryption or decryption of the input stream. *See* cipher block chaining, stream cipher.

integrated services digital network In communications, an integrated digital network in which the same digital switches and digital paths are used to establish different services, e.g. telephony and data. The ISDN concept represents a logical development in the provision of public communication services, recognizing the economies made possible by the advent of digital technologies, the increasing demands for a wide range of communication services and the need to provide the customer with a single interface to which can be connected a wide variety of user communication devices: voice, facsimile, data, videotex, alarm sensors, etc.

integrity locking *Synonymous with* spray paint.

intruder In data security, a person who seeks to make illegal use of a data communication system. The intruder may listen in and attempt to decipher a ciphertext message or seek to interfere actively with the messages.

irreversible encryption In cryptography, a cryptographic transformation of plaintext such that there is no corresponding decryption operation. This technique can be employed, for example, to store passwords in a secure manner. The password, subsequently entered by a user, is subject to the same encryption process and the result compared with the stored encrypted password. *Compare* reversible encryption.

ISDN *See* integrated services digital network.

issuer *See* card issuer.

IV *See* initialization vector.

key distribution and control In cryptography, the processes involved in the distribution and control of keys include: (a) appointment of cryptographic personnel, (b) responsibilities of cryptographic personnel, (c) shipment and receipt of keying material, (d) storage of keying material and encryption/authentication device physical keys, (e) use of keying material, (f) destruction of keying material, (g) archiving of keys.

key encrypting key In cryptography, a cryptographic key used for encrypting (and decrypting) data encrypting keys or other key encrypting keys. (FIPS)

key exhaustion In cryptanalysis, an exhaustive attack technique in which the attacker possesses a fragment of the plaintext, the correspondi .g ciphertext, and has knowledge of the cryptographic algorithm. A trial key is selected, the plaintext is encrypted with this key, and the result compared with the known ciphertext. Alternatively if only ciphertext is available then it is decrypted with the trial key and the resulting plaintext is then inspected to see if it corresponds to a meaningful message. *Compare* message exhaustion.

keying material In cryptography, the data (e.g. keys and initialization vectors) necessary to establish and maintain cryptographic keying relationships. (ANSI) *See* cryptographic key, initialization vector.

key management In cryptography, the processes concerned with the generation, distribution, storage, and destruction of cryptographic keys and related information, e.g. initialization vectors. Encipherment effectively transfers the problem of ensuring the secrecy of a mass of data to that of protecting the secrecy of a cryptographic key. The problems associated with the various aspects of key management depend upon the range of the cryptographic techniques, the environment, and applications in which the cryptographic keys are employed. *See* cryptographic key.

key notarization In cryptography, a method of applying additional security to a key utilizing the identities of the originator and the ultimate recipient. (ANSI) *See also* Appendix B.9.

key registry In cryptography, a secure store for cryptographic keys. In public key cryptography the registry will hold public keys; such public keys may be accessed freely but it is important that no attacker can modify, or inject, public keys in the registry. *See* public key.

LAN *See* local area network.

LCD *See* liquid crystal display.

link-by-link *See* link encryption.

link encryption In communications security, the application of on-line crypto-operations to a link of a communications system so that all information passing over the link is encrypted in its entirety. (FIPS) *Compare* end-to-end encryption, node encryption.

liquid crystal display In electronics, a display device made of two glass plates sandwiched together with a special fluid. The liquid darkens when a voltage is applied.

local area network In data communications, a high-bandwidth bi-directional communications network that operates over a limited geographic area, typically an office building or a college campus. *Compare* municipal area network, wide area network.

logical access control In access control, the use of procedures related to information and knowledge, e.g. passwords, rather than physical security. *Compare* physical access control.

logic bomb In data security, a part of a program that is triggered by a combination of events in the system and activates a fraud. *Compare* time bomb, Trojan Horse.

look and feel In legislation, a principle that has been invoked in copyright cases; if two products are so similar that one 'looks and feels' like the other then it may be considered that an infringement of copyright has been committed.

MAB *See* message authentication block.

MAC *See* message authentication code.

MACGEN In authentication, MAC generation: the process undertaken by the sender to generate the message authentication code. *See* message authentication code.

MACVER In authentication, MAC verification: the process undertaken by the recipient to verify the message authentication code. *See* message authentication code.

magnetic ink character recognition The identification of characters printed with ink that contain particles of a magnetic material. MICR is used in the banking industry to record transmitted codes and account numbers on checks for data processing.

mailbox In communications, an area of storage provided to receive and store electronic mail messages. *See* electronic mail.

malicious code In computer security, a section of program code that is intentionally included in a system for the purpose of causing loss or harm. *See* logic bomb, time bomb, Trojan Horse, virus.

MAN *See* municipal area network.

mandatory access control In access control, a means of restricting access to objects based on the sensitivity (as represented by a label) of the information contained in the objects and the formal authorization (i.e. clearance) of subjects to access information of such sensitivity. (DOD) *Compare* discretionary access control. *See* object, subject.

masquerading In data security, an attempt to gain access to a system by posing as an authorized user. (AR) *Compare* spoofing.

master cryptographic key In cryptography, a long-life key to a cryptographic function, used to encrypt long-term data or other cryptographic keys.

master-session key In cryptography, a system in which each communication session has a distinct data encrypting key, termed the session key. These session keys are communicated through the network, encrypted under a key-encrypting key termed the 'master key'. *Compare* transaction key. *See* data encrypting key, key encrypting key.

message authentication (1) In banking, the technique used between the sender and receiver to validate the source and part or all of the text of a message. (ANSI)

(2) In authentication, the processes undertaken to ensure that: (a) the message originated with the purported sender, (b) the message contents have not been accidentally or intentionally altered or rearranged, (c) the message has been received in the sequence that it was sent by the originator, and (d) the message was received by the intended recipient. *See also* Appendix B.8.

message authentication block In banking, a block that is a cryptographic function of all data in a message or extended message generated under control of a transaction key. The MAB is split to form the Message Authentication Code (MAC) and the message authentication code residue (MAC residue). (SAA) *See* message authentication code.

message authentication code (1) In authentication, a number that is the result of passing a message through the authentication algorithm using a specific key.

(2) In banking, a code in a message between the sender and receiver used to validate the source and part or all of the text of the message. The code is the result of an agreed calculation. (ANSI)

(3) In banking, a group of characters included with a message for the purpose of verifying that the message has not been fraudulently changed. The code is a cryptographic function of all data in the message generated under control of a transaction key, and is therefore statistically unique to that message. The MAC is part of the message authentication block (MAB). (SAA) *See* message authentication block.

message exhaustion In cryptanalysis, a form of attack in which all possible plaintext combinations are encrypted and the corresponding ciphertext stored for future reference. In public key cryptography, the encrypting key is known by the cryptanalyst and thus the received ciphertext can be checked against the stored plaintext–ciphertext pairs. If the encryption key is not known then the process is conducted for all possible keys, if subsequently a fragment of plaintext and corresponding ciphertext is available then the stored plaintext–ciphertext pairs can be searched and the

411

corresponding key determined. *Compare* key exhaustion.

MICR *See* magnetic ink character recognition.

microchip In computing, a microprocessor, i.e. a CPU and RAM on a chip. *See* CPU, RAM.

midnight attack In cryptography, an attack in which a complex communication session, between a host and a terminal, including the transmission of the session key, encrypted under the terminal key, is wiretapped and recorded. Later (figuratively at midnight) the attacker gains access to the unattended terminal and inputs to it the recorded host–terminal traffic, thus masquerading as the host to the terminal. The terminal deciphers the recorded ciphertext using the recorded encrypted session key. This attack can be thwarted by handshaking. *See* handshaking, masquerading,

modulo 2 addition A method of combining two binary numbers. Each pair of digits is combined such that

$$0+0 = 0$$
$$0+1 = 1$$
$$1+1 = 0$$

municipal area network In data communications, a proposed form of communications network lying between the LAN and the conventional telecommunications network. It will provide for the connection of information units over, say, a 20 kilometre radius (e.g. within a city area) and at very high speed (generally, in the order of 100 to 200 million bits per second). The MAN may then connect to a nationwide and international WAN at lower speeds, say 64 kilobits per second to 2 million bits per second respectively. *Compare* local area network, wide area network.

need to know (1) The necessity for access to, knowledge of, or possession of certain information required to carry out official duties. Responsibility for determining whether a person's duties require that possession of, or access to, such information and whether the individual is authorized to receive it rests upon the individual having current possession, knowledge, or control of the information involved and not upon the prospective recipient. (OPNAVINST)
(2) In data security, a policy that restricts access to classified information to personnel whose duties necessitate such access.

node-by-node *See* node encryption.

node encryption In communications security, a method of encryption of network data in which the data is decrypted within an intermediate node, and re-encrypted under a different key for onward transmission. The decryption and re-encryption is performed in secure modules, and thus plaintext is not transmitted through the node. *Compare* end-to-end encryption, link encryption.

object In computer security, a passive entity that contains or receives information. Access to an object potentially implies access to the information it contains. Examples of objects are: records, blocks, pages, segments, files, directories, directory trees, and programs, as well as bits, bytes, words, fields, processors, video displays, keyboards, clocks, printers, network nodes, etc. (DOD) *Compare* subject.

object code In programming, the code of a user's program after it has been translated. *Compare* source code.

OCR Optical character recognition.

off-line In computing, pertaining to processing equipment that is not connected to a computer or network, or the operations performed on such equipment. *Compare* on-line.

offset In banking, a number that mathematically relates a calculated identification code to a customer selected, or random PIN.

one-way function In cryptography, a function $f(x)$ such that it is easy to compute $f(x)$ given x, for any x in its domain, but that the inverse is computationally infeasible. *See* computationally infeasible.

on-line In computing, pertaining to data processing and communication equipment that is connected to a computer or communication channel. *Compare* off-line.

open systems interconnection In data communications, pertaining to an ISO reference model intended to co-ordinate the development of standards at all levels of communication. The objective is to allow purchasers of communication equipment much greater freedom in mixing and matching equipment as well as a greater degree of protection against obsolescence. The model has seven layers: physical, data link, network, transport, session, presentation and application. The concept of the layers provides for a considerable degree of independence between the multifarious and complicated operations involved in data communications. At each level the process believes that it is communicating with its corresponding layer in the receiving host; it does this by accepting messages from the layer vertically above it, adding control information to it, and passing it on to the layer immediately below it. At the receiving end the process is reversed, messages are received from the layer below it, control information is stripped off, and the message passed up to the next level.

operating system In computing, a program or group of programs which provides the user with a range of general purpose facilities for normal usage of the computer.

Orange Book In computer security, a set of criteria for security in a single computer system with several users, designed by the US Department of Defense. The criteria are divided into divisions and classes. A division represents a major improvement in the overall confidence that can be placed in the computer to protect sensitive information; the divisions are divided into classes of increasing desirability from a computer security viewpoint. *Compare* Red Book. *See also* Appendix A.2.

OSI *See* open systems interconnection.

output feedback In cryptography, a stream cipher mode of DES implementation. *Compare* cipher block chaining, cipher feedback, electronic codebook. *See* DES. *See also* Appendix B.4.

ownership In data security, the right of users to dispense and revoke privileges for objects they own, e.g. access on programs and data. *See* object.

PAN *See* primary account number.

parity check In codes, a form of redundancy check. The convention of odd or even parity is selected, the number of bits in a grouping is counted, and a parity bit is added, if necessary, to produce parity with the selected convention. Upon receipt of the grouping the number of bits is checked and an error reported if the selected parity is not found. Parity checking detects the loss or unwanted inclusion of an odd number of bits.

passphrase In access control, a sequence of characters, longer than the acceptable length of a password, that is transformed by a password system into a virtual password of acceptable length. (FIPS) *See* password.

password In access control, a popular form of knowledge test for access control. A password is a string of alphanumeric data or a phrase that must be entered into a system to gain access to a physical area or a resource. Normally the password is associated with a user identification, the user inputs the user ID, and then responds to the request for the password. *See also* Appendix C.1.

patch In programming, a section of code added to object code and thus not affecting the source code. Such patches may therefore bypass normal control procedures and could be used for illegal program modification.

peer entity authentication In communications security, pertaining to the action of communicating parties seeking to verify each others identities. *See* authentication, masquerading.

perfect secrecy In cryptography, a condition defined by the situation in which the conditional probability that the plaintext message P was sent, if ciphertext message C was received, is equal to the probability that plaintext message P was transmitted. Thus receipt of the ciphertext message provides no additional information to an attacker on the nature of the plaintext message.

personal data In legislation, as defined by the UK *Data Protection Act, 1984*, data consisting of information which relates to a living individual who can be identified from that information (or from that and other information in the possession of the data user), including any expression of opinion about the individual but not any indication of the intentions of the data user in respect of that individual.

personal identification code In access control, a unique alphanumeric code used to identify an individual, usually in combination with a physical token, such as a magnetic stripe card. The token is entered into an appropriate computer/communication terminal to effect a transaction. *Compare* personal identification number.

personal identification number (1) In access control, a unique number entered by a user before a remote terminal or point of sale terminal can be used to transfer information or complete a transaction.

(2) In banking, the 4- to 12-position alphanumeric code or password the customer possesses for authentication. (ANSI) *See also* Appendix C.2.

physical access control In access control, measures designed to control access to a physical area or device, e.g. computer room or terminal. *Compare* logical access control.

physical security (1) In computer security, the use of locks, guards, badges, and similar administrative measures to control access to the computer and related equipment. (FIPS)

(2) In computer security, the measures required for the protection of the structures housing the computer, related equipment and their contents from damage by accident, fire, and environmental hazards. (FIPS)

PIC *See* personal identification code.

PIN *See* personal identification number.

PIN mailer In banking, a document containing a PIN in clear form. The document must be printed under conditions of high security that ensure that an employee cannot open, read, or closely examine the document. The mailer is often produced as a multipart sealed form so that the PIN can only be read by unsealing the form.

PIN offset *See* offset.

PIN pad A keypad used to enter a PIN. *See* PIN.

plaintext In computer security, intelligible text or signals that have meaning and that can be read or acted upon without the application of any decryption. (FIPS) *Compare* ciphertext.

port protection device In computer security, a device connected to the communications port of a host computer which has the function of authorizing user access to the port. *See also* Appendix D.3.

primary account number In banking, the PAN consists of the issuer identification number, and it identifies the issuer to which the transaction is to be routed. The account number comes next. It identifies to whom the transaction is to be applied. The last element is the check digit. (ANSI)

pseudorandom number In computing, a number generated by a specific algorithm to approximate to a random number. Such algorithms are designed to produce numbers with specified statistical properties.

public key In cryptography, the cryptographic key used to encipher messages in public key cryptography. This key is made generally available by the intended receiver of the ciphertext. *See* public key cryptography.

public key cryptography In cryptography, an asymmetric cryptosystem, i.e. one in which the enciphering and deciphering keys are different and in which it is computationally infeasible to calculate one from the other, given the enciphering algorithm. In public key cryptography the enciphering key is made public but the deciphering key is kept secret; it has advantages over symmetric ciphers such as DES in the areas of (a) security of messages, from a variety of sources, directed to an individual organization, (b) key management, (c) digital signatures. *See* digital signature, DES, key management, RSA. *See also* Appendix B.5.

RACF In computer security, Resource Access Control Facility, an IBM software security product which assists in the control of user access to application data sets, volumes, transactions, and terminals. *See also* Appendix A.3.

RAM *See* random access memory.

random access memory In memory systems, a memory chip used with microprocessors. Information can be both read from, and written into, the memory, but the contents are lost when the power supply is removed.

random PIN In banking, a PIN produced by random number selection. *Compare* derived PIN, user-selected PIN. *See* PIN.

read In access control, a privilege that enables a user to read a file but not to add data to that file or to modify it. *Compare* append, execute, write.

read only memory In memory systems, a storage device whose contents can only be changed by a particular user, by particular operating conditions or by a particular external process. Read only storage can include storage media where the writing action is inhibited by the operating system or by some mechanical device, e.g. a tag on a diskette. The term implies a storage device not designed to be modified by conventional write procedures, and which is used to store permanent information in computers and microcomputers.

record In data structures, a collection of related data treated as a unit, e.g. details of name, address, age, occupation, and department of an employee in a personnel file. *Compare* field.

Red Book In communications security, a US Department of Defense publication to extend the evaluation classes of Trusted Systems Evaluation Criteria to trusted networks. *Compare* Orange Book.

Registrar In legislation, the UK official with responsibility for administering the *Data Protection Act*.

registration In legislation, the process required of a non-exempt data user, or computer bureau, to inform the Registrar of its details of processing and storing personal data, under the terms of the UK *Data Protection Act*. *See* computer bureau, data user, personal data, Registrar.

replay In authentication, a form of attack in which the message sequence is changed or a stored data item is replaced with a previously stored value. This form of attack can succeed even if the message or stored data item is authenticated or encrypted. In its simplest form, an attacker can simply record a message, including its authenticator, and re-insert it into the communication link. Such a message could, for example, cause a financial transaction to be performed twice.

residue In computer security, data left in storage after processing operations, and before degaussing or rewriting has taken place. (FIPS)

reverse engineering A process by which the design of a product is determined by a detailed study of the product itself.

reversible encryption In cryptography, a DEA transformation of plaintext in such a way that the encrypted text can be decrypted back to the original plaintext. *Compare* irreversible encryption. *See* DEA.

risk In computer security, the loss potential that exists as the result of threat–vulnerability pairs. Reducing either the threat or the vulnerability reduces the risk. (AFR) *See* threat, vulnerability.

risk analysis In risk management, the minimizing of risk by effectively applying security measures commensurate with the relative threats, vulnerabilities, and values of the resources to be protected. The value of the resources includes the impact on the organization, the automated system supports, and the impact of the loss or unauthorized modification of data.

risk assessment In risk management, an analysis of system assets and vulnerabilities to establish an expected loss from certain events based on estimated probabilities of the occurrence of those events. The purpose of a risk assessment is to determine if countermeasures are adequate to reduce the probability of loss or the impact of loss to an acceptable level. (OPNAVINST)

risk management A disciplined approach adopted to identify, measure, and control uncertain events in order to minimize loss and optimize the return on the money invested for security purposes. The objective of risk management is to attain the most effective precautions against: (a) destruction of assets, (b) unauthorized modification or manipulation of company data, (c) unauthorized disclosure of company data, (d) access of company assets and data processing services to unauthorized personnel. In the field of computer security, risk management encompasses risk analysis, management decision making, and implementation of security measures and reviews. *See* risk analysis.

ROM *See* read only memory.

RSA In cryptography, Rivest–Shamir–Adleman, an algorithm named after its designers which is of extreme importance in public key cryptography. It uses a trapdoor one-way function based upon the computational difficulty of factoring the product of large prime numbers (i.e. integers with several hundred decimal digits). Thus the computation involved in multiplying two large prime numbers p and q is minimal but it is computationally infeasible to derive the factors p and q from a product n consisting of several hundred decimal digits. A large computer would take about a billion years for a 200-digit number. *See* public key cryptography. *See also* Appendix B.6.

safeguard In computer security, a protective measure to mitigate against the effect of system vulnerability. *See* vulnerability.

salami In data security, pertaining to a method of perpetrating a fraud which is spread over a large number of individual transactions, e.g. a program that does not round off figures but diverts the leftovers to a personal account.

schema In databases, a map of the overall logical structure of a database.

SCM *See* security control module.

security audit In data security, an examination of data security procedures and measures for the purpose of evaluating their adequacy and compliance with established policy. (FIPS)

security control module A tamper-resistant module used to store securely cryptographic keys and process cryptographic algorithms.

security log A log of security significant events, e.g. log-on, accesses to protected files, number of attempts at password entry, etc.

security module *See* security control module.

security officer In this book the term used to refer to the senior member of management responsible for the organization's information security, or a person delegated by that person to undertake specific information security responsibilities.

see-through security In access control, an access control technique in which a user employs a token in the form of a pocket calculator to compute dynamic passwords. *See* dynamic password.

sentinel A marker indicating the beginning or end of a section of data.

separation of duties In computer security, the structuring of system-related jobs so that each has as little security exposure as is feasible for efficient operation. For execution of critical tasks, the intervention of more than one person should be required. In general the opportunity for any one person to subvert or damage the system must be minimized.

server In computer networks, a unit at a node of a network that provides a specific service for network users, e.g. a printer server provides printing facilities, a file server stores user files.

session key In cryptography, a cryptographic key used only for a limited period, e.g. a user session at a terminal, and then discarded. Session keys are the lowest-level keys used in a key hierarchy and are not used as key encrypting keys. *Compare* terminal key. *See* key encrypting key.

shoulder surfing In computer security, a method of obtaining knowledge of user passwords, log-on procedures, etc. by looking over the shoulder of a terminal user.

smart card In banking, a plastic card similar in appearance to a normal credit card but which has an integrated circuit embedded in the plastic. The circuit has two broad functions: intelligence and memory. The card is activated by insertion into a terminal and receives signals from the terminal, performs functions according to those signals and a program stored in the card's internal memory, sends out response signals, and updates its internal memory. *Compare* supersmart card.

societal vulnerability In computer security, the possibility of loss, injury, or the denial of equal rights to a significant segment of the population, as well as potential weakening of social stability, or risk to national sovereignty as a result of dependence on computer-based technology. (AFIPS)

source code In programming, the original code of a user's program before being translated, e.g. compiled, assembled, interpreted. *Compare* object code.

spoofing In computer security, the deliberate inducement of a user or a resource to take an incorrect action. (FIPS) *Compare* masquerading.

spray paint In computer security, a technique employing cryptographic checksums to ensure that the security classification or data of a database record cannot be undetectably altered by an attacker. A MAC is computed for the message comprising the record and its classification, using a secret key. The technique is so named because a record is indelibly 'coloured' with its classification. *See* MAC. *Synonymous with* integrity locking.

springboard doctrine In legislation, 'a person who has obtained information in confidence is not allowed to use it as a springboard for activities detrimental to the person who made the confidential communication, and springboard it remains even when all the features have been published or can be ascertained by actual inspection by any member of the public'.

statistical database In computing, a database containing aggregate information concerning large subsets of entities, e.g. census data. Such data can be misused to reveal information concerning individuals unless some form of inference control is employed. *See* inference control.

store and forward In data communications, a system that stores message packets at intermediate points before further transmission.

stream cipher In cryptography, a method of encryption with the capability of providing perfect secrecy. The plaintext is encoded into numbers, usually binary, and a key stream of random numbers is combined with the plaintext to form the ciphertext. *Compare* block cipher. *See also* Appendix B.7.

structured walkthrough In computing, a manual technique of verifying program code. Each member of a team has a well-defined function. The programmer outlines the operation of the program and a discussion is held to detect any potential problem areas and to identify possible improvements.

subject In computer security, an active entity, generally in the form of a person, process, or device that causes information to flow among objects or changes the system state. (DOD) *Compare* object.

supercomputer An extremely powerful mainframe computer used for complex mathematical calculations demanding high speed and storage, e.g. weather forecasting.

supersmart card In banking, a proposed new form of smart card with a microprocessor and 64 kilobytes of memory, a calculator with touch keys, a display window, a synthesized magnetic stripe, and battery. Such a card will allow off-line verification, identification, and authorization. It will also be possible to use this card with conventional ATMs and terminals; the user can simulate the magnetic stripe of conventional cards by keying instructions with the keyboard. In addition to the functions of conventional smart cards the supersmart card will provide the user with off-line display of customer information, transactions, account balances, credit limits, etc. *Compare* smart card.

symmetric cipher In cryptography, a cipher in which the enciphering and deciphering keys are equal, or can easily be deduced from one another. *Compare* asymmetric cipher.

synchronous In data communications, pertaining to a transmission method in which each bit is transmitted according to a given time sequence. It can provide a higher bit rate than asynchronous transmission but requires that the receiver and transmitter maintain exact synchronization over an extended period. *Compare* asynchronous.

system penetration In computer security, a violation or circumvention of operating system safeguards. *See* operating system.

tailgating (1) In access control, the practice of using one access card for successive use by two or more individuals.

(2) In communications security, a phenomenon in which an unauthorized user may be connected to a computer system, via a network, immediately after an authorized user has vacated the system. The unauthorized user will gain all the privileges of the authorized user.

tamper-resistant module In data security, a device in which sensitive information, such as a master cryptographic key, is stored and cryptographic functions are performed. The device has one or more sensors to detect physical attacks by an adversary trying to gain access to the stored information, in which case the data is immediately destroyed.

tape streamer In computing, a magnetic tape transport designed primarily for reading or writing continuous streams of data, as in backup operations.

telephone intrusion In computer security, the intrusion into a computer system by dial-up access; a common form of attack by hackers. *See also* Appendix D.2.

telesoftware In computing, the transmission of software to an intelligent videotex terminal, or to a microcomputer programmed to emulate a videotex terminal.

teletext A method of transmitting information, stored on a computer, to domestic television sets suitably adapted. In broadcast services the data signals are transmitted in conjunction with normal TV programs. *Compare* viewdata. *See* videotex.

telex In communications, TELetypewriter EXchange service, an automatic dial-up teletypewriter switching service provided by common carriers. *See* common carrier.

Tempest-proofing In communications security, the prevention of undesirable radiation emission from a computer system which might otherwise enable an eavesdropper to record confidential information. Electromagnetic emission can escape by a variety of routes; to eliminate this risk, source suppression and encapsulation are used, together with shielding of all cables.

terminal key In cryptography, a key-encrypting key supplied to the terminal and used for the encryption of session keys. *Compare* session key.

421

threat In computer security, an aspect of the system environment that, if given an opportunity, could cause a harmful event to occur. *Compare* safeguard, vulnerability.

time bomb In computer security, a form of malicious code in which the damaging routine is triggered at a given time/date. *Compare* logic bomb, Trojan Horse. *See* malicious code.

track In access control, one of three horizontal paths on the magnetic stripe of a magnetic stripe card, along which data is recorded.

traffic padding In communications security, a technique used to disguise traffic flows; it includes padding messages out to standard lengths, generating spurious messages, and spurious connections.

transaction key In cryptography, a technique in which the cryptographic key, employed to protect a transaction, is derived at the terminal and host computer, using secret information available at each. Thus the key does not have to be transmitted. *Compare* master session key.

transparent Pertaining to a process or procedure invoked by a user without the latter being aware of its existence.

Trojan Horse In computer security, a computer program with an apparently or actually useful function which contains additional (hidden) functions that surreptitiously exploit the legitimate authorizations of the invoking process to the detriment of security. For example, making a 'blind copy' of a sensitive file for the creator of the Trojan Horse. (DOD) *See* **Fig. G-2**

trusted In data security, pertaining to software and hardware systems that have been designed and verified to avoid compromising, corrupting, or denying sensitive information.

uninterruptible power supply In computing, a device inserted between a power source and a system, to ensure that the system is guaranteed a precise, uninterrupted power supply, irrespective of variations in the power source voltage.

UPS *See* uninterruptible power supply.

user-selected PIN In banking, a PIN chosen by the user and conveyed to the bank where it is stored with the corresponding account numbers. Thereafter use of the PIN is virtually identical with that described for the random PIN. *Compare* derived PIN, random PIN. *See* PIN.

van Eck phenomenon In computer security, a phenomenon pertaining to radiation from a VDU or microcomputer. Van Eck reported that electromagnetic radiation from a VDU is unique to the particular type of device, and is at frequencies in the UHF range. Under optimum conditions this radiation can be received as far as 0.66 to 1.25 miles away, and translated to readable display. The

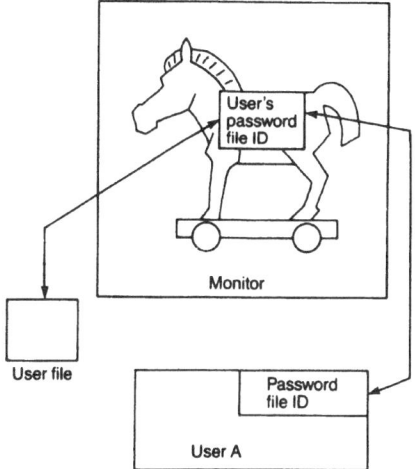

Fig. G-2 Trojan Horse

In this example of a Trojan horse, a software performance monitor evaluates a software program, as well as gathering sensitive data associated with the program. Reproduced with permission of IBM Corp.

radiation can moreover be detected, and the data displayed, with relatively standard electronic components.

VDU Visual display unit, a computer terminal.

videotex The term covers two separate technological developments: viewdata and teletext. In the former case a communication link providing simple two-way communication is established between the user and host computer through a telephone network. With teletext the information flow is simplex and broadcast over TV wavebands in conjunction with normal television programs. *See* teletext, viewdata.

viewdata An interactive information service using a telephone link between the user and a host computer. The user employs a special terminal or an adaptor linked to a domestic TV set. *Compare* teletext. *See* videotex.

virus In computer security, a section of code introduced into a program for malicious purposes, e.g. at some stage the inserted code will trigger a process which will, for example, eliminate files. The virus is present in a program, and when the program is run the virus writes itself into other programs in main memory or backing store. The effects of the virus can therefore extend to many users.

voice mail In communications, a system in which spoken information is digitized and stored either in a network memory or in the appropriate apparatus at the destination for the message. The spoken message is later retrieved by the called party.

vulnerability In computer security, a weakness in automated system security procedures, administrative controls, internal controls, and so forth, that could be exploited by a threat to gain unauthorized access to information or disrupt critical processing. (AFR)

WAN *See* wide area network.

watermark tape In banking, a material used for magnetic stripes which is designed to increase the difficulty of manufacturing counterfeit cards. A permanent magnetic watermark is induced into the material by exposing it to an appropriate varying magnetic field while the magnetic particles are held in a resinous lacquer; the material is then dried, thus fixing the orientation of the magnetic particles. One track of the card is used to check the watermark, and the track is subjected to a constant magnetic field before reading. Thus any attempt to counterfeit the watermark pattern by magnetizing a conventional magnetic stripe is thwarted by the erasing effect of the constant magnetic field.

white card fraud (1) In banking, a form of credit card fraud using a counterfeit credit card. A blank white plastic card, with a magnetic stripe, is manufactured and the stripe is encoded with the details contained in a genuine client's credit card (such information having been obtained illegally from the appropriate financial institution). The cards are then used to obtain money from ATMs. The perpetrator may also emboss the account number or other information on the card.

(2) In banking, a form of fraud in which a stolen credit card is heated, e.g. by boiling in water; the old embossed digits are pressed out and new numbers re-embossed.

wide area network In data communications, a comprehensive multi-mode network connecting large numbers of terminals and computers spread over a wide area. *Compare* local area network.

wiretapping In communications security, the unauthorized interception of messages. The purpose of passive wiretapping is to disclose message contents without detection, while active wiretapping involves the deliberate modification of messages, sometimes for the purpose of injecting false messages, injecting replays of previous messages (e.g. to repeat a credit transaction), or deleting messages. Authentication protects against message modification and injection of false messages by making it infeasible for an opponent to modify or create messages that meet the authentication criteria. *See* active wiretapping.

write In computer security a fundamental operation that results only in the flow of information from a subject to an object. (DOD)

Compare read. *See* object, subject.

X.400 In data communications, a CCITT standard for message handling systems which includes specifications for the network architecture, protocol structure, implementation detail, message transfer elements and content protocols. *See also* Appendix D.4.

zero knowledge proof In access control, a technique for the verification of users such that a wiretapper, or observer, would be unable to gain sufficient information to later masquerade as the user. The user requesting access proves, by means of a dialogue, that the user is in possession of secret information, known only to the user, without revealing that information. In effect the verifier asks a number of random questions; if the user gives a correct answer then the probability that the user is genuine is increased. The dialogue continues until the verifier is satisfied that the possibility of an attacker giving such correct answers is sufficiently low. *See* fiat shamir.